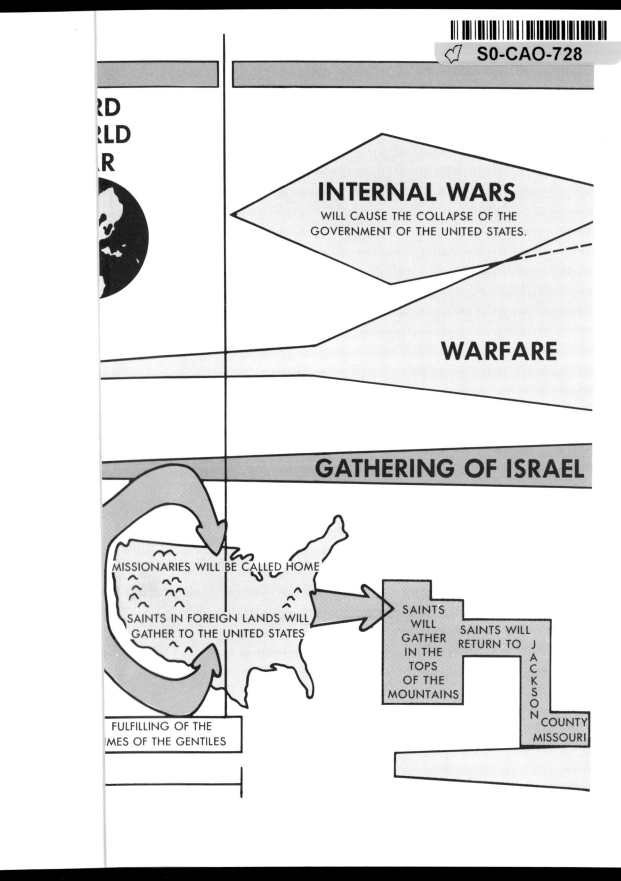

PROPHECY —
Key to the Future

PROPHECY —
Key to the Future

by

Duane S. Crowther

Bookcraft
Salt Lake City, Utah

Lithographed in the United States of America
PUBLISHERS PRESS
Salt Lake City, Utah

DEDICATION

To my wife Jean,
who loves and heeds the words
of the prophets.

INTRODUCTION

Why a Book On The Future?

The purpose of prophecy was stated by an early apostle of the Church, Elder George A. Smith, who said that "all the prophecies have aimed at the gathering of the people, and saving them in the last days."[1] Parley P. Pratt, another early apostle, spoke of the profit and advantage which is gained from understanding how to fulfill the conditional aspects of prophetic promises and told of the comfort and patience that a knowledge of prophecy brings to that reader who reads with understanding.[2]

In the Latter-day Saint view, no seeker for truth can fulfill his goal without understanding in some measure the events of the future, for truth is defined in the scriptures as "knowledge of things as they are, and as they were, and *as they are to come.*"[3] The events of the future are signs of the times—indications of the imminence of the Advent of the Lord. Says the *Doctrine and Covenants,*

> Ye look and behold the figtrees, and ye see them with your eyes, and ye say when they begin to shoot forth, and their leaves are yet tender, that summer is now nigh at hand;
>
> Even so it shall be in that day when they shall see all these things, then shall they know that the hour is nigh.
>
> *And it shall come to pass that he that feareth me shall be looking forth for the great day of the Lord to come, even for the signs of the coming of the Son of Man.*[4]

According to Orson Pratt, another early apostle, those who have the spirit of prophecy within them will be the ones who will know and understand the signs of the times:

> But the Latter-day Saints are not in darkness; they are the children of light, although many of us will actually be asleep.

---

1. *History of the Church,* 6:18.
2. See Parley P. Pratt, *A Voice of Warning and Instruction to All People,* (Salt Lake City: Deseret News Press), pp. 7-8.
3. *Doctrine and Covenants* 93:24.
4. *Doctrine and Covenants* 45:37-39.

We shall have to wake up and trim up our lamps, or we shall not be prepared to enter in; for we shall all slumber and sleep in that day, and some will have gone to sleep from which they will not awake until they awake up in darkness without any oil in their lamps. But, as a general thing, the Saints will understand the signs of the times, if they do lie down and get to sleep. Others have their eyes closed upon the prophecies of the ancient Prophets; and not only that, but they are void of the *spirit of prophecy* themselves. When a man has this, though he may appeal to ancient Prophets to get understanding on some subjects he does not clearly understand, yet, *as he has the spirit of prophecy in himself, he will not be in darkness; he will have a knowledge of the signs of the times; he will have a knowledge of the house of Israel, and of Zion, of the ten tribes, and of many things and purposes and events that are to take place on the earth; and he will see coming events, and can say such an event will take place, and after that another, and then another*; and after that the trumpet shall sound, and after that certain things will take place, and then another trump shall sound, &c., &c.; and he will have his eye fixed on the signs of the times, and that day will not overtake him unawares.[5]

The Lord has placed great importance on the events of the last days, for prophecies and explanations of that period are the most prominent theme of the four standard works! This book is written to assist the reader in studying them carefully and systematically.

---

5. *Journal of Discourses,* 7:189. The reader will note that Orson Pratt is often cited in this work. He was the one among the early Elders of the Church who was singled out by the Lord and given the specific commandment to "lift up your voice and spare not, for the Lord God hath spoken; *therefore prophesy,* and it shall be given by the power of the Holy Ghost." (D & C 34:10) Throughout his lifetime his teachings were characterized by explanations of the events which were to come and by a strong awareness of his prophetic calling. Of all the authorities of the Church, Orson Pratt apparently had the soundest and most comprehensive understanding of the events of the last days. The early leaders of the Church kept close watch on the teachings put forth by the brethren. On one occasion Orson Pratt apologized in a general conference for overstepping the bounds of doctrine in regards to his teachings about the nature of God. He explained that the authorities had called him to task for something he had said. Yet there seems to be a complete acceptance by his contemporaries of his teachings on the last days, which is a strong evidence supporting the acceptability and correctness of his teachings.

The Objectives of This Book

This book has been written to accomplish three goals:

First, the author has attempted to establish the important events of the future in *correct chronological order*. Such an order can be determined with accuracy and certainty for almost all of the prophesied events. Care has been taken to indicate the basis upon which each chronological event and order has been determined. Where the order of coming events cannot definitely be determined, the known facts have been presented but no effort has been made to force an interpretation.

The second objective of this book is to *provide an understandable and well-documented discussion of each of the prophesied events which are to come upon the earth*. Special attention has been given to controversial areas. Each chapter has a summary designed to integrate the important points of the chapter and to clearly set forth the general patterns of future events. Some readers might enjoy reading all the chapter summaries first before reading and studying the entire book.

Third, a great deal of material which previously has been inaccessible to the average Latter-day Saint reader is here compiled. An important contribution is made in the *collection of material* pertaining to internal conflict in the United States, the fulfilling of the times of the Gentiles, the plagues and pestilence which will come upon the earth, the evaluation of controversial areas such as the "White Horse Prophecy," and many other areas of general interest.

Is This Study Authentic and Reliable?

The original draft of this work was entitled "A Study of Eschatological Prophecies Found in the Scriptures and in the Works of General Authorities of the Church of Jesus Christ of Latter-day Saints." It was submitted and accepted as a master's thesis by the Department of Scripture, College of Religious Instruction, Brigham Young University.

The study is limited to scriptural passages and to interpretive comments and prophecies made by General Authorities. Much of the element of chance and error is thus eliminated. The quotations in each case have fallen into patterns which seem to establish the veracity of the whole. The author has been, in some measure, aware of the pitfalls which accompany an undertaking of this kind, and has endeavored to avoid them. In any correlation of prophecy there is danger in forcing scriptural interpretations. Particular effort has been expended in the preparation of this work to see that quoted material is cited in such a manner as will be harmonious with its context and with its author's real intent. An effort has been made to document the items contained herein clearly and fully, although the scope of this work is so far-reaching that of necessity only a portion of the evidence available is here presented. In an effort to show all sides of some areas of controversy, varying viewpoints have been quoted.

There is always a limitation upon the acceptance of prophecies not found in the scriptures. The limitation was set by Joseph Smith himself in 1843. He recorded that on one occasion he "visited with a brother and sister from Michigan, who thought that 'a prophet is always a prophet;' but I told them that *a prophet was a prophet only when he was acting as such.*"[6] The decision as to whether statements by General Authorities are merely private opinions or are inspired interpretations must rest with the reader. Responsibility must also rest with the reader for his personal decision as to whether or not the prophecies recorded herein were given when the Authority was functioning in the prophetic office or whether they merely represent his personal understanding of the future. In short, the reader must test the inspiration of the statements quoted with the power of the Holy Spirit which prompts him. Thus this work is not an effort to state the doctrine of the Church but rather to set forth in an understandable manner the comments and interpretations which various Latter-day Saint Church leaders have made. It should be read and interpreted in this light.

In the final analysis, the true test of prophecy is its fulfillment. As Jeremiah stated, "When the word of the Prophet shall come to pass, then shall the prophet be known, that the Lord hath truly sent him."[7]

Acknowledgments

The author is deeply indebted to the members of his graduate committee, Ellis Rasmussen, Hyrum Andrus and Eldin Ricks, for their assistance and guidance in preparing the book in its

---

6. History of the Church, 5:265.
7. Jeremiah 28:9.

original form as a thesis. Appreciation is also expressed to Katherine Cromwell and Thyrza Berrett who rendered valuable assistance in the typing and revising of the final draft. Certainly my greatest appreciation is for my lovely wife, Jean, who has worked faithfully with me for many months so that this study could be completed. Her love and devotion have borne me up in many moments of discouragement, and she has willingly undertaken any and every task which has needed attention.

—D.S.C.

CONTENTS

CONTENTS—(Continued)

CHAPTER   Page

CONTENTS—(Continued)

CONTENTS—(Continued)

CONTENTS—(Continued)

LIST OF ILLUSTRATIONS, MAPS, AND CHARTS

A KNOWLEDGE OF THE FUTURE

As Revealed By Ancient and Modern Prophets

By
Duane Swofford Crowther

Among the variety of commodities which attract the attention of mankind, there is one thing of more value than all others. Comparatively few have ever possessed it although it was within the reach of many others, but they were either not aware of it, or did not know of its value. Kind reader, this treasure is foreknowledge; a knowledge of things future! Let a book be published entitled A KNOWL-EDGE OF THE FUTURE, and let mankind be really convinced that it did give a certain, definite knowledge of future events, so that its pages unfolded the future history of the nations, and many great events . . . it would be above price.

(Adapted from **A Voice of Warning,** by Parley P. Pratt.)

KEY TO ABBREVIATIONS USED IN THE FOOTNOTES

The following is a list of abbreviations which have been used in the footnotes of this work:

CN	Church News
DN	Deseret News
DEN	Deseret Evening News
HC	History of the Church
IE	The Improvement Era
JD	Journal of Discourses
JI	Juvenile Instructor

The standard abbreviations for the Scriptural books are used. Other books and publications have been footnoted in the usual manner.

Because of the importance of certain portions of many of the statements cited, the author has made extensive use of italics to add emphasis.

CHAPTER ONE

War To Be Poured Out Upon All Nations

The Beginning of War in The Last Days

On December 25, 1832, Joseph Smith uttered a prophecy "concerning the *wars* that will shortly come to pass, beginning at the rebellion of South Carolina."[1] It was twenty-eight years later, on April 12, 1861, that his prophecy began to be fulfilled. On that day Southern troops opened fire on the Union fort at Charleston, South Carolina. This statement, which has come to be known today as the "Prophecy on War," described other details of the War Between the States also. It stated that "the Southern States shall be divided against the Northern States,"[2] and held that the Southern States would "call on other nations, even the nation of Great Britain,"[3] for assistance. American history readily affirms that this war was between the Northern and the Southern States. As early as May, 1861, the Southern Confederacy sent commissioners abroad to Great Britain, France, Holland and Belgium to seek recognition and aid from foreign powers.

The prophecy was even more far-reaching than a prediction of the War Between The States. Its assertion that a time would come when Great Britain would call upon other nations in order to protect itself from still other nations extended the prophecy down to the time of the First and Second World Wars.[4] In these wars England formed alliances with France, Russia, the United

---

1. D & C 87:1.
2. D & C 87:3. For a careful consideration of the fulfillment of the various aspects of this prophecy, see CHC, 1:294-303.
3. D & C 87:3. Eleven years later he stated once again that "the commencement of difficulties which will cause much bloodshed previous to the coming of the Son of Man will be in South Carolina. It may probably arise through the slave question." D & C 130:12-13.
4. This was clearly Charles A. Callis' interpretation of the matter. Said he, during a conference address while telling of a conversation he had with a minister, "Joseph Smith, the Prophet of God, foretold the great Civil War; he likewise predicted by the gift and the power of the Holy Ghost, that the World War would come to vex the nations." CR, April, 1923, p. 22.

States, and other nations in an effort to repel the Nazis or Central Powers.

The Prophecy on War stated that "the time will come that war will be poured out upon all nations, *beginning* at this place (South Carolina)."[5] England's calling for assistance, however, played an important chronological part in this prophetic timetable given to Joseph Smith, for the revelation stated that when England calls on other nations for assistance, "*Then* war shall be poured out upon all nations."[6] Thus it is that wars were to begin in the last days with the rebellion of South Carolina but the sign of their reaching world-wide proportions was to be England's appeal for help in the world wars.

According to the prophecy, wars among the nations are to continue with devastating effect, for "thus, with the sword and by bloodshed the inhabitants of the earth shall mourn,, and shall "be made to feel the wrath, and indignation, and chastening hand of an Almighty God, *until the consumption decreed hath made a full end of all nations.*"[7] The message of Joseph Smith's Prophecy on War, then, is that God has allowed a series of wars to be poured out upon the earth.[8] These wars, beginning with the War Between The States in 1861, were to gain world-wide proportions at a time when England would seek alliances with other nations (World Wars I and II). The wars are to continue until the consumption decreed by God has made a full end of all nations.

We find ourselves today in the midst of this series of wars. We know of many wars which have already served to fulfill

---

5. D & C 87:2.
6. D & C 87:3.
7. D & C 87:6.
8. Bishop Joseph L. Wirthlin, during the General Conference in October, 1958, took for his subject the Prophecy on War. He chronicled the wars which have already taken place in the following manner: "The Prophet Joseph gave us this marvelous revelation in 1832. The Civil War came in 1861; the war between Denmark and Prussia in 1864; Italy and Austria in 1865 and 1866; Austria and Prussia in 1866; Russia and Turkey in 1877; China and Japan in 1894 and 1895; Spanish-American in 1898; Japan and Russia in 1904 and 1905; World War I in 1914-1918; then the next war was a comparatively small one, Ethiopia and Italy, when the people in that land of Ethiopia were taken over and controlled by Italy. I am grateful to the Lord that they now have their freedom. Then, the World War just passed and, of course, the Korean War." CR, October, 1958, p. 33.

Joseph Smith's utterance. Those who accept the prophecy as a revelation from God are committed to the belief that such wars will continue until the present nations of the earth are consumed.

Slaves Are To Rise Up
Against Their Masters

After telling how war will be poured out upon all nations at the time England seeks aid from foreign powers, the Prophecy on War adds another item in its chronology of the future. It says,

> And it shall come to pass, after many days, slaves shall rise up against their masters, who shall be marshaled and disciplined for war.[9]

This prophecy has often been taken as a reference only to the negroes in the United States. Some Latter-day Saints, however, recognize in the prophecy a much broader meaning. Said Bishop Joseph L. Wirthlin while commenting on this phase of it in 1958,

> In many cases I am quite sure we all think this has to do particularly with the slaves in the Southern States, but *I believe, brethren and sisters, that it was intended that this referred to slaves all over the world, and I think of those, particularly in the land of Russia and other countries wherein they have been taken over by that great nation* and where the people are actually the slaves of those individuals who guide and direct the affairs of Russia and China, and where the rights and the privilege to worship God and to come to a knowledge that Jesus Christ is His Son is denied them.[10]

During the past few years, the world has witnessed a continuing series of rebellions, uprisings, and stormy negotiations of people who have sought to throw off what they considered to be oppression and tyrannical rule. France, England, Portugal, and Belgium have seen the deterioration of their colonies and have released many of their subjects to form new and independent governments. Latin America, Africa, the Near East—these areas have seen continual difficulties as their oppressed peoples have fought to throw off their political and economic rulers. Within the United States we also are witnessing a continual struggle for race equality as the negroes and other racial groups strive to rise socially, culturally, and economically. These tensions

---

9. D & C 87:4.
10. Wirthlin, *op cit.*, p. 32.

throughout the world would seem to indicate that we have
entered into the period Joseph Smith prophesied would follow
the first spreading of war to all nations, when "slaves shall rise
up against their masters, who shall be marshaled and disciplined
for war."

The Purpose of Wars Is To Prepare
For The Preaching of The Gospel

Since the Prophecy on War was given, war has, to some
degree, been regarded by some Latter-day Saints as having functioned as an instrument for the overthrow of rulers and governments which would not allow the gospel to be preached by Latter-
day Saint missionaries. This was Orson Pratt's teaching in 1875:

> At the present time there are some nations who will not
> permit any religion to be proclaimed within their borders ex-
> cept that which is established by law. *When God shall cast
> down thrones, which he will soon do; when He shall overturn
> kingdoms and empires, which time is very near at hand, then
> other governments will be formed more favorable to religious
> liberty, and the missionaries of this Church will visit those
> nations. . . .* And so we might enumerate what God is doing
> among these despotic powers, overturning and changing long-
> established usages and institutions, that His servants may go
> by His own command; to deliver the great and last message of
> the Gospel to the inhabitants of the earth, preparatory to the
> coming of His Son.[11]

On another occasion he stated that.

> The day will come when the nations of Europe will have
> warred among themselves sufficiently long, and those despotic
> governments are torn down, and when the hand of oppression
> and tyranny has been eased up, and when the principles of
> religious liberty have become more fully and more widely
> spread, that *the Elders of this Church will traverse all these
> nations*; and then we shall have use for these Seventies that
> have been organizing so long.[12]

Parley P. Pratt also applied the philosophy that the purpose
of war is to prepare the unreceptive nations to receive the gospel.
He carried the application beyond the Gentile nations to the
oriental nation of Japan, and said that "politically speaking,

11. JD, 18:63-4.
12. JD, 7:186.

some barriers yet remain to be removed, and some conquests to be achieved, such as the subjugation of Japan, and the triumph of constitutional liberty among certain nations where mind, and thought, and religion are still prescribed by law."[13] He continued by stating that this subjugation of Japan was to take place before the gathering of the tribes of Israel to Palestine.

Elder Harold B. Lee, in the October, 1954, General Conference of the Church, quoted the above statement and commented:

> Subjugation means conquering by force. I want to say to you that one of the most significant things that I have seen in the Far East is the fulfillment of what Elder Parley P. Pratt testified would be one of the significant developments necessary to the consummation of God's purposes, "The subjugation of Japan and the triumph of constitutional liberty among certain nations where mind and thought and religion are still prescribed by law."[14]

He then elaborated on how World War II had opened up the way for effective missionary work in that nation.

Two Periods of War: Preparatory Wars and Wars of Complete Destruction

According to Joseph Smith's Prophecy on War, wars are to be poured out until a full end to all nations has been made. But it appears that the characteristics of the early era of this warfare differ from the characteristics of the latter era. As was discussed in the preceding section, the purpose of a portion of this warfare is to allow the gospel to enter into areas where it has been prohibited in the past. This apparently is the characteristic of only the *early* period of warfare, or the period of preparatory wars. It appears that a characteristic of this early period of warfare has been and will continue to be that the converts in these newly-proselyted nations will be persecuted by the people of those nations. Orson Pratt taught in 1859 that after the missionaries had penetrated into these nations, they

> . . . have got to *do a great deal of preaching before the times of the Gentiles are fulfilled;* [they] have got to go and build up the Church of the Lamb of God among those nations, and set ministers over them, and go and build up more . . . *that when*

---

13. Parley P. Pratt, *Key to the Science of Theology* (Fifth Edition, Salt Lake City: George Q. Cannon and Sons Co., 1891), p. 76.
14. CR, October, 1954, p. 126.

the multitudes gather to fight against them they may be armed with the power that comes from heaven.[15]

While speaking of future missionary efforts in Europe, Pratt said that after the Church is established in Europe,

> They [the unconverted people who have witnessed the activities of the missionaries] are to gather together in multitudes, like other nations, to fight against it; and so they will in Austria, Spain, Portugal, and in all the modern nations of Europe, as well as those nations that inhabit Asia and Africa.[16]

According to Elder Pratt, it will also be characteristic of the period of preparatory wars that the converts made in foreign countries will be advised to remain in their home areas. They will not, it seems, be called to leave their homes and gather to the American Zion even though they will have to endure hardships and persecution. This is the present policy of the Church, as is evidenced by the building of temples and the formation of stakes on foreign soil during the past decade. Pratt spoke of the "unwise prayers" of American Saints that the European converts would soon be gathered to America and commented:

> When the time comes that the Saints of the Lamb of God are scattered upon all the face of the earth, among all nations and kingdoms of the Gentiles, and the *multitudes gather against them to battles*, we shall not find such unwise prayers answered. *The Saints, instead of being all gathered out, will still be among the nations,* for the power of the Lamb of God to descend upon the Saints of the Most High that are among all the nations and kingdoms of the Gentiles, and not only upon these, but also upon His covenant people, the descendants of Jacob; and *they are to be armed with righteousness and the power of God in great glory.* But gather them all out, and where have you got your Saints? It would completely falsify this saying.[17]

Elder Levi Edgar Young taught that these wars and persecutions will be for the ultimate benefit of the saints:

> This is a day of sore trial for all the inhabitants of the earth. Nations are tottering and governments are in danger of being overthrown. Hardly a day passes but what we hear of some terrible catastrophe or some awful tribulation that has

---

15. JD, 7:187.
16. JD, 7:186.
17. JD, 7:186.

come to the children of men. "Darkness covers the earth, and gross darkness the people." We are being disciplined; and when we come to know the wisdom of this, we will look upon the whole of life as a means of sanctification. . . . I sincerely believe that these days are bringing us closer and closer to God.[18]

But after the missionaries have penetrated into all these nations, and persecution has risen against the converts who are now there, it has been held by Church leaders that the type of warfare which will be waged throughout the earth will eventually change. No longer will war serve the purpose of preparing the nations to hear the gospel, but it will become an instrument of terrible destruction and annihilation. Orson Pratt contrasted these two types of war:

> This war that is now taking place [war between Austria and the allied powers of France and Sardinia] will not result in that dreadful extinction that is foretold in the Book of Mormon, and which will rage among all the nations and kingdoms of the Gentiles, or in other words, among the nations of Christendom. *The one is a war preparatory to the proclamation of the Gospel; the other is a war of terrible destruction, which will not better the condition of those who escape.*[19]

It appears that the line of demarcation between these two periods and types of warfare will be the fulfilling of the times of the Gentiles,[20] when the Spirit of the Lord will entirely withdraw from the Gentile nations, for he said,

> By-and-by, when the Lord has made bare his arm in signs, in great wonders, and in mighty deeds, through the instrumentality of his servants the Seventies, and through the instrumentality of the churches that shall be built up, and *the nations and kingdoms of the earth have been faithfully and fully warned,* and the Lord has fulfilled and accomplished all things that have been written in the Book of Mormon, and in other revelations pertaining to the preaching of the Gospel to the nations of the Gentiles and to the nations of Israel, by-and-by

18. CR, April, 1933, p. 121.
19. JD, 7:186.
20. The next chapter will explain this term fully. Briefly, the times of the Gentiles will be fulfilled when the LDS missionaries will be called out of the Gentile, or Christian, nations. This will be because of the unreceptive attitude and great wickedness which will characterize the Gentile people at that time. This event will be the beginning of great calamities throughout the world and a terrible internal war within the United States.

the Spirit of God will entirely withdraw from those Gentile nations, and leave them to themselves. Then they will find something else to do besides warring against the Saints in their midst — besides raising their sword and fighting against the Lamb of God; for then war will commence in earnest, and such a war as probably never entered into the hearts of men in our age to conceive of. No nation of the Gentiles upon the face of the whole earth but what will be engaged in deadly war, except the Latter-day Kingdom. They will be fighting one against another.[21]

At the time of this second stage of warfare, which could be termed "warfare of complete destruction," the majority of the righteous Saints will not remain among the Gentile nations, but "shall be gathered unto it [Zion] out of every nation under heaven."[22]

A careful analysis of Christ's explanation in the *Pearl of Great Price* of the events which are to happen in the last days will show that He recognized these two periods of warfare and differentiated between them. After telling His disciples of the impending destruction of Jerusalem (which took place in seventy A. D.) He began to explain the events which will precede His second coming. He told of false Christs and false prophets who would arise to deceive even the very elect, and then told of the period of preparatory wars:

Behold, I speak these things unto you for the elect's sake; and *you also shall hear of wars, and rumors of wars;* see that ye be not troubled, for all I have told you must come to pass; but the end is not yet.[23]

21. JD, 7:188.
22. D & C 45:69.
23. JS 1:23. The reader should note that the translation made by Joseph Smith (which is known as Joseph Smith chapter one in the *Pearl of Great Price*) has served to give chronological sequence to Christ's statements found in Matthew, chapter 24. In the Biblical chapter the chronology is indistinguishable but it becomes evident in the *Pearl of Great Price* rendition.
This chapter talks about two periods of time. The first portion is a prophecy of the fall of Jerusalem which was fulfilled 1900 years ago. The second portion deals with the events which will precede Christ's second coming. In his prophecy, the Savior compares the events of the two periods. Verse 21 from the *Pearl of Great Price* is the transition verse between the past and present: "Behold, these things I have spoken unto you *concerning the Jews:* and *again, after the tribulation* of those days which shall come upon Jerusalem . . ."

He warned them that during this period false reports of His coming would be given and cautioned them that such reports should not be accepted. He said that when He did come, His coming would be visible to all the earth. After this warning He began to speak of the second era of wars: the wars of complete destruction. His statement details the characteristics of this later period. He foretold the calling of the members out of the nations of the earth to Zion: "Mine elect [shall] be gathered from the four quarters of the earth."[24] Then the Savior, in prophesying of the second period of wars, also foretold the plagues and destruction which are to be poured out when the times of the Gentiles will have been fulfilled and which are to be a characteristic of the period of wars of complete destruction:

> Behold I speak for mine elect's sake; for nation shall rise against nation, and kingdom against kingdom; there shall be famines, and pestilences, and earthquakes, in divers places.[25]

The great wickedness which will have brought about the withdrawal of the missionaries and the members from the lands of the Gentiles is mentioned, for the Lord said that "because iniquity shall abound, the love of many shall wax cold."[26]

Nephi also contrasted these two eras of warfare as he expounded the prophecies of Isaiah. He referred to the era of preparatory war as the period when "the Lord God will proceed to make bare his arm in the eyes of all the nations, in bringing about his covenants and his gospel unto those who are of the house of Israel."[27] This period of preaching, as he foresaw, will be marked by nations who will fight against Israel and will persecute the Church.[28] Then he referred to the second stage of warfare, or period of complete destruction, in which the house of

---

24. JS 1:27.
25. JS 1:29.
26. JS 1:30. The Savior's prophecy continues on from this point giving a chronology of the events which will transpire until His final coming in glory. He foretells the preaching of the Gospel after the great world war (verse 31); He alludes to two events of the Battle of Armageddon (the abomination of desolation, or desecrating of the temple at Jerusalem; and the darkening of the heavens which will be seen to be a result of the earthquake at the time of His coming on the Mount of Olives) in verses 32-35. Then he tells of the appearance of the sign of the coming of the Son of Man and finally of his coming in glory with the hosts of heaven (verses 36 and 37).
27. I Ne. 22:11.
28. I Ne. 22:14.

Israel will be gathered out of captivity and the nations who warred against the Saints "shall war among themselves, and the sword of their own hands shall fall upon their own heads, and they shall be drunken with their own blood."[29] They shall be "turned one against another, and they shall fall into the pit which they digged to ensnare the people of the Lord."[30] All those who have fought against Zion "shall be destroyed."[31]

United States Warned of Conflict
During Period of Preparatory Wars —Third World War

Several prophecies have been recorded as having been uttered by the Prophet Joseph which deal with a future war of world wide dimensions. This war, according to the evidence to be cited, will fall during the period of preparatory wars, before the fulfilling of the times of the Gentiles and before the period of warfare of total destruction.

Mosiah Hancock, son of a close friend and bodyguard of Joseph Smith, recorded an important prophecy as having been made by the Prophet. According to his diary, this prophecy was made the day after Joseph made his final speech to the Nauvoo Legion (Wednesday, June 19, 1844; eight days before his martyrdom). After telling how the Prophet discussed a map of the West and foretold the route the Saints would follow in their western exodus, Hancock records Joseph Smith's statement to him that,

> There will be two great political parties in this country. One will be called the Republican, and the other the Democrat party. These two parties will go to war and *out of these two parties will spring another party which will be the Independent American Party. The United States will spend her strength and means warring in foreign lands until other nations will say, "Let's divide up the lands of the United States",* then the people of the U. S. will unite and swear by the blood of their fore-fathers, that the land shall not be divided. Then *the country will go to war, and they will fight until one half of the U. S. army will give up, and the rest will continue to struggle.* They will keep on until they are very ragged and discouraged, and almost ready to give up—when *the boys from the mountains will rush forth in time to save the American Army from defeat and ruin.* And they will say, 'Brethren, we are glad you have come; give us men, henceforth, who can talk with God'.

29. I Ne. 22:13.
30. I Ne. 22:14.
31. I Ne. 22:14.

Then you will have friends, but *you will save the country when it's* [sic] *liberty hangs by a hair, as it were.*[32]

In the light of recent events, it appears that the powers which will attack the U. S. after this nation has expended its strength in foreign wars will be the Communist powers under the leadership of Russia. In a conference address delivered on October 7, 1961, Elder Ezra Taft Benson spoke on the dangers of Communism and warned of the great danger to the United States which that force poses. He spoke of a Communist attempt to overthrow the United States Constitution and spoke of a prophecy similar to the above prophecy which was recorded by Mosiah Hancock:

> Concerning the United States, the Lord revealed to his prophets that its greatest threat would be a vast, world-wide secret combination which would not only threaten the United States but seek to overthrow the freedom of all lands, nations and countries. *In connection with the attack on the United States, the Lord told his prophet there would be an attempt to overthrow the country by destroying the Constitution. Joseph Smith predicted that the time would come when the Constitution would hang, as it were, by a thread, and at that time this people will step forth and save it from the threatened destruction. It is my conviction that the Elders of Israel, widely spread over the nation, will at that crucial time successfully rally the righteous of our country and provide the necessary balance of strength to save the institutions of constitutional government.* . . . The prophets in our day have continually warned us of these internal threats — that our greatest threat from Socialistic Communism lies within our country. . . . As the First Presidency pointed out in a statement signed in 1936, *if we continue to uphold Communism by not making it treasonable, our land shall be destroyed,* for the Lord has said that whatsoever nation shall uphold such secret combinations to get power and gain until they shall spread over the nation — behold, they shall be destroyed. *The Lord has declared that before the second coming of Christ, it will be necessary to destroy the secret works of darkness in order to preserve the land of Zion — the*

---

32. Mosiah Lyman Hancock, *Life Story of Mosiah Lyman Hancock,* p. 29. A typewritten copy of the original manuscript is available in the Brigham Young University library.

Americas. The world-wide secret conspiracy which has risen up in our day to fulfill these prophecies is easily identified.[33]

As both the Prophet and Elder Benson indicated above, this war is to come to a sudden and seemingly miraculous end through the instrumentality of members of the Church. President McKay, while speaking at a devotional assembly at Brigham Young University in May, 1960, also alluded to a miraculous overthrow of Communism:

> Russia enveloped with communism—a new religious freedom must come. *God will overrule it,* for that people must hear the truth, and truth in simplicity. Truly there is much for the Church to do in the coming century.[34]

Ezra Taft Benson, in his recent conference address, quoted President McKay as saying

> Men will be free! I have hoped for twenty years that the Russian system would break up. There is no freedom under it, and *sooner or later the people will rise against it.* They cannot oppose those fundamentals of civilization and of God. They cannot crush their people always. Men will be free![35]

Joseph Smith gave several prophetic warnings about the danger of attack from Communistic countries. In one prophecy, he warned of possible attack by the Chinese who are under com-

---

33. Ezra Taft Benson, General Conference Address, October 7, 1961. For a discussion of the prophecy which he quotes from Joseph Smith dealing with the Constitution hanging by a thread, see chapter five and the appendix.
34. CN, May 28, 1960.
35. Benson, *op cit.* The author has in his possession copies of two Patriarchal Blessings given by a Patriarch in St. Johns, Arizona, in which a war between Russia and the United States is prophesied. Because of their personal nature, and because the evidence in this work is limited to the scriptures and works of general authorities of the Church they are not quoted here. However, a brief summary of their message may not be improper and would serve to shed some light on the matter under consideration. They are in complete harmony with each other. Each term the war a Third World War. They speak of Russia and her allies and clearly state that they will be defeated by the United States and her allies. The United States is to be attacked by "a strong European power." The war will take place largely in the air and under the ocean, and both major powers will drop bombs on each other. Traitor after traitor will be detected and apprehended in this country. The God of Heaven will take over and bring the war to a speedy victory for America and her allies. Russia will never again be a great world power, and the United States will eventually arise to great heights among the nations of the world.

munist rule. He stated that "there is a land beyond the Rocky Mountains that will be invaded by the heathen Chinese unless great care and protection are given."[36] Ezra Taft Benson echoed this warning in General Conference October 9, 1960, when he said that "there is little doubt that the leaders of Red China view war as inevitable and await only the propitious moment in which to strike."[37]

Two other prophetic utterances attributed to Joseph Smith seem to shed further light on a possible war with Russia. The first deals with those who will be allied against that country:

> The Lord took of the best blood of the nations and planted them on the small islands now called England and Great Britain, and gave them great power in the nations for a thousand years and *their power will continue with them, that they may keep the balance of power and keep Russia from usurping her power over all the world. England and France are now bitter enemies, but they will be allied together and be united to keep Russia from conquering the world.*[38]

The other prophecy was made by the Prophet to the father of President John Taylor. After foretelling the United States' war with Mexico and also the War Between The States, Joseph commented that "When the great bear lays her paw on the lion the winding up scene is not far distant."[39] Since the bear is a symbol for Russia, and since the lion is a symbol for England, this seems to be a prophetic allusion to attack or persecution by Russia against England. It would seem to apply in the present context.

Four items of logic seem to establish the fall of Communism during the period of preparatory wars, before the period of wars of complete destruction begins. First, statements by various general authorities indicate that following Russia's collapse, the missionaries will penetrate into that area and preach the gospel there. President McKay's statement quoted above should be recalled in this context: "A new religious freedom must come. God will overrule it [Communism], *for that people must hear the*

---

36. Prophecy recorded by Edwin Rushton and Theodore Turley as having been made by Joseph Smith on May 6, 1843. For a detailed discussion of this prophecy see the appendix. Further references to this prophecy will be given as "Prophecy recorded by Edwin Rushton and Theodore Turley."
37. IE, December, 1960, p. 944.
38. Prophecy recorded by Edwin Rushton and Theodore Turley.
39. JI, March 15, 1890, p. 162.

truth and truth in simplicity. Truly there is *much for the Church to do in the coming century.*"[40]

Second, intense religious persecution against the Church in Russia is prophesied, yet in the era of wars of complete destruction the Church is to be ignored while its enemies fight among themselves. Said Orson Pratt,

> Even in Russia, that place where they would almost put you to death if you brought a printed work of religious nature into the empire, — in that country, where they will not suffer you to propagate the Bible unmolested, whose religion is established by law, has the Gospel of Jesus Christ to be preached. Yes, *the Church of the Saints is to be established there; and after it is established, there they are to gather together in multitudes, like other nations, to fight against it.*[41]

Third, Melvin J. Ballard, in a conference address in April, 1930, stated that the gospel would be carried to Russia soon, and associated that work with God's overthrow of a despotic government there, which is another characteristic of the period of preparatory war:

> I am sure also that God is moving in Russia. Much as we are disturbed over the tyranny and the oppression that is waged against religion in that land today, it is not a new thing, for that has been the order for ages. But I can see God moving also in preparing the way for other events that are to come. The field that has gone to wild oats needs to be plowed up and harrowed and prepared for a new seed. So in Russia. It may seem appalling to us, but *it is God breaking up and destroying an older order of things, and the process will be the accomplishment of God's purposes within a very short period of time, which normally may have taken generations.* But that people will come back, for *I bear witness that there are thousands of the blood of Israel in that land, and God is preparing the way for them.*[42]

Fourth, it will be seen in a coming chapter that the fulfilling of the times of the Gentiles (the line of demarcation between the two eras of war) will commence at the outbreak of an internal war in the United States.[43] In this internal war, mob rule will prevail and the U. S. state and federal government will

---

40. CN, May 28, 1960.
41. JD, 7:185-86.
42. CR, April, 1930, p. 157.
43. See chapter four.

completely collapse, along with all its defensive forces. Only the Saints who gather to the mountains will be free from this struggle. The fulfillment of the prophecies cited pertaining to war with Russia must *precede* the civil war in the United States, for after that internal war there will be no United States government to be opposed by Communism.

Summary

This chapter has dealt with the following chronological events:

1. There is a period of preparatory wars, which began with the rebellion of South Carolina in 1861. This period of wars has as its purpose the overthrow of despotic governments which prohibit the preaching of the gospel. It is in progress now and will continue for an unknown time until the times of the Gentiles are fulfilled.

   A. The slaves are to rise against their masters. This seems to be in the process of being fulfilled now.

   B. The United States will spend her strength and means warring in foreign lands. Other nations (which appear to be Russia and her allies) will attack her and war will be waged. This war will end with the United States emerging victorious, after help is provided for the U. S. Army in a miraculous fashion by the Elders of the Church.

   C. The gospel will be carried to Russia and other countries where the word has not yet penetrated.

   D. As more and more of the countries become receptive to the Church's missionary efforts, converts will be made within them. These converts will be instructed to remain in those countries. There they will be subjected to varying degrees of persecution because of their religious beliefs.

2. There is to be a period of terrible wars of destruction.

   A. The times of the Gentiles will be fulfilled. The Gentiles, because of their wickedness, will have the missionaries taken from them. The time of fulfillment of the times of the Gentiles is the time when God's judgments of plagues, famine, pestilence, earthquakes, tidal waves, etc. will begin to sweep the wicked off the earth with greatly increased violence.

   B. The converts and members of the Church living in other countries will be called out and instructed to come to Zion in America when the times of the Gentiles are fulfilled.

C. An internal war will rage within the United States which will bring about the collapse of national and state government.

D. A world war or wars of terrible destruction will be fought which will lay waste the Gentile world. The Saints will, for the most part, escape the impact of this war.

The items mentioned in the second division of the summary above will be discussed in detail in coming chapters.

CHAPTER II

Missionary Work Among the Gentiles

The Gospel Must Be Taught to Every Nation

A basic tenet in Latter-day Saint theology is that the members have been commanded by God to carry His word to all the nations of the earth. *The Doctrine and Covenants* records just such a commandment in the Lord's own words:

> Wherefore, I the Lord, knowing the calamity which should come upon the inhabitants of the earth, called upon my servant Joseph Smith, Jun., and spake unto him from heaven, and gave him commandments;
>
> And also gave commandments to others, that *they should proclaim these things unto the world; and all this that it might be fulfilled, which was written by the prophets—*[1]

In the same section the assertion is made that the fulness of the gospel must be proclaimed "unto the ends of the world, and before kings and rulers."[2] Earlier the section states that "the voice of warning shall be unto all people, by the mouths of my disciples. . . ."[3]

Thus the responsibility of a world-wide proselyting effort has been laid upon the Church which is momentous in its scope and challenge. Thousands of missionaries have gone into the world each year to preach the news of the restored gospel. Recently the quota of full-time missionaries was increased to 12,000. The Church is striving to prepare its youth to accept this important calling.

Four Periods of Missionary Labor

The prophecies which deal with the missionary work in the last days often speak in terms of nations and groups other than individuals, which will hear the gospel. For instance, Christ said that "this Gospel of the Kingdom shall be preached in all the world, for a witness *unto all nations*, and then shall the end

1. D & C 1:17-8.
2. D & C 1:23.
3. D & C 1:4.

come, or the destruction of the wicked."[4] While the ultimate aim of the missionary labor is that every individual throughout the world will receive the gospel message personally, it does not appear that that aim will be accomplished until after the second advent of the Savior. Instead there seem to be four periods of missionary labor outlined in the prophecies. These periods are *distinguished by the kinds of nations to whom the missionaries will be directed.* Undoubtedly there will be some overlapping, and those of the later periods will be prepared to receive the missionary message during the preceding periods. The periods, along with the era of warfare into which they will fall, are as follows:

1. Mission to the Gentile nations. (Preparatory Wars)
2. Mission to the House of Israel. (Wars of Complete Destruction)
3. Mission to the Heathen nations. (After the Battle of Armageddon)
4. Final Mission to All Mankind. (Immediately preceding and during the Millennium)

This chapter is devoted to a consideration of the first of these four periods. The others will be treated in their chronological sequence in later chapters.

Who Are The Gentiles?

There are many meanings of the word Gentile, and the term is used in different ways by the various religious groups. In its original sense, it was used to differentiate those who were not descendants of Abraham and were not partakers of the Abrahamic covenant from those who were of the lineage of Abraham. Latter-day Saints often use it in this sense today. They use it also as a general term of reference to those who are not adherents to Mormonism.

In the prophetic sense, however, the word takes on a more limited, nationalistic denotation. It appears to refer to those nations which embraced Christianity. Such, for instance, was the way Orson Pratt used it when he spoke of wars "which will rage among all the nations and kingdoms of the Gentiles, or, in other words, among the nations of Christendom."[5] These nations are

4. JS, 1:31.
5. JD, 7:186.

considered to be the nations formed from the ancient Roman Empire plus the nations which have grown out of those countries through immigration and colonization. The Gentile or Christian nations are often contrasted with the "heathen nations," or nations which have not accepted Christianity.[6] The reader should understand that this is the sense in which the terms "Gentile" and "Heathen" are used in this discussion.

What Are The "Times of The Gentiles"?

According to the traditional Christian viewpoint, the "times of the Gentiles" is the period during which the House of Israel is to be scattered and persecuted among the nations of the earth. With the destruction of Jerusalem in 70 A.D. the Jewish people were scattered and began to suffer a period of persecution which continues to the present day. To other churches, then, the "times of the Gentiles" is the era during which the Gentile nations have embraced Christianity and hold full power over Israel and over all the nations of the earth. The Church of Christ did become a church made up of converts from outside of the house of Israel and the Gospel was truly taken from the Jews.

The Latter-day Saints have a different understanding of the term. They recognize that the Gospel was taken, to a certain degree, to the Gentiles through the work of Paul and other Christian missionaries of the first century, and that at the same time it was taken from the Jewish people and they were dispersed among the nations. But a fundamental belief of the church is that an apostasy took place during the first centuries A. D. in which Christianity became corrupt and the Gospel was taken from the earth. Thus there was an extended period in which the true doctrines of Christ were not found among the Gentile nations.

Instead of accepting the traditional Christian view, the Latter-day Saints hold that the "times of the Gentiles" in our modern day commenced with the restoration of the Gospel through Joseph Smith. In 1831, a revelation, alluding to the spiritual light that broke forth through the revelations to Joseph Smith and others stated, "And when the times of the Gentiles is come in, a light shall break forth among them that sit in darkness, and it shall be the fulness of my gospel."[7] *Thus Latter-day*

---

6. For instance, see JD, 18:339-40.
7. D & C 45:28.

Saints understand the "times of the Gentiles" to be the period (which began in 1830) in which the Gospel is to be preached to the people of the Gentile nations.[8]

What is The Fulness of The Gentiles?

Another term which pertains to the Gentiles was introduced by the Angel Moroni, who informed Joseph Smith, in 1823, that "the fulness of the Gentiles was soon to come in;"[9] that is, that their *full opportunity to receive the Gospel in the latter-days was about to begin.*

Orson Pratt defined the "fulness of the times of the Gentiles" as the period in which the gospel will be preached to every nation, kindred and tongue among the Gentile nations:

> The great object of the angel in restoring the Gospel was, in the first place, to fulfil the times of the Gentiles. Inquires one — "What do you mean by that?" I mean that *God will send this Gospel, restored by an angel, to every nation, kindred, people and tongue in the Gentile world before he will permit his servants to go to the scattered remnants of Israel.*[10]

It is now during the fulness of the times of the Gentiles, however, that the House of Israel will begin to be prepared to accept the Gospel. Paul wrote to the Romans that "blindness in part is happened to Israel, *until the fulness* of the Gentiles be come in."[11] It appears that this is the period spoken of by the prophet Zenos in which he said that people of Israel will "no more turn aside their hearts against the Holy One of Israel,"[12] in preparation for their being gathered in from the four quarters of the earth and their restoration to the covenants which God made with their fathers. The present success in proselyting the Lamanites is regarded as being a preparatory stage preceding the major period of conversion of the House of Israel.

Conditional Promises Made to The Gentiles in The Americas

Much difficulty has been encountered by various students of the Book of Mormon over numerous conditional promises which

---

8. An explanation of how and when the Gospel will be carried to the Jews is found in chapter seven.
9. JS, 2:41.
10. JD, 18:176-77.
11. Ro. 11:25.
12. I Ne. 19:15.

the *Book of Mormon* prophets make to the Gentiles who are to come to this land of America. Typical of these prophecies are the following:

> But, said he [Lehi], notwithstanding our afflictions, we have obtained a land of promise, *a land which is choice above all other lands;* a land which the Lord God hath covenanted with me should be a land for the inheritance of my seed. Yea, the Lord hath covenanted this land unto me, and to my children forever, *and also all those who should be led out of other countries by the hand of the Lord.*
>
> Wherefore, this land is consecrated unto him whom he [God] shall bring. *And if it so be that they shall serve him according to the commandments which he hath given, it shall be a land of liberty unto them; wherefore they shall never be brought down into captivity; if so, it shall be because of iniquity;* for if iniquity shall abound cursed shall be the land for their sakes, but unto the righteous it shall be blessed forever.[13]

Again:

> And blessed are the Gentiles, they of whom the prophet has written; for behold, *if it so be that they shall repent and fight not against Zion, and do not unite themselves to that great and abominable church,* they shall be saved; for the Lord God will fulfil his covenants which he has made unto his children; and for this cause the prophet has written these things.[14]

And also:

> And I say unto you, that *if the Gentiles do not repent after the blessing which they shall receive,* after they have scattered my people . . . *the sword of my justice shall hang over them at that day*; and except they repent it shall fall upon them, saith the Father, *yea, even upon all the nations of the gentiles.*[15]

A problem in understanding these passages arises from trying to consider all the Gentiles as belonging to one group. The Book of Mormon speaks of two groups of Gentiles. One group is to be blessed "because of their belief" in God and will have the fulness of the gospel made known unto them. But the second group, "the unbelieving of the Gentiles," shall "be filled

---

13. II Ne. 1:5, 7.
14. II Ne. 6:12.
15. III Ne. 20:15, 20. For an interesting commentary on these passages by B. H. Roberts see HC, 5:552-53.

with all manner of lyings, and of deceits, and of mischiefs, and all manner of hypocrisy, and murders, and priestcrafts, and whoredoms, and of secret abominations." And the Lord says that if they do these things, He will "bring the fulness of my [His] gospel from among *them*."[16]

Most of The Gentiles Will Reject The Gospel

The Doctrine and Covenants states that in the main the Gentiles will not receive the Gospel:

> And when the times of the Gentiles is come in, a light shall break forth among them that sit in darkness, and it shall be the fulness of my gospel;
>
> But *they receive it not;* for they perceive not the light, and they turn their hearts from me because of the precepts of men.
>
> *And in that generation shall the times of the Gentiles be fulfilled.*[17]

Orson Pratt also makes it clear that the Gentile nations in general will reject the Gospel, even though there will be converts among them:

> Having established his kingdom, he offers it first to these Gentile nations, if they will receive it; and *when they shall account themselves unworthy of the kingdom, unworthy of eternal life, unworthy of the message which God has sent to them, and shall persecute his servants and his people all the day long, and shall close up their sanctuaries, their Churches, their chapels, their meeting houses, and their places of worship against this message, and when it can no longer find place among them,* so as to bring them to a knowledge and understanding of the truth, the Lord will, after a while, designate by revelation, and say unto his servants, "It is enough. You have been faithful in laboring in my vineyard, for the last time;" for it was the decree of heaven, that this shall be the last time, that he will labor in his vineyard. It is the eleventh hour, the last warning that will be given to the nations of the earth, first to the Gentiles, and then to the House of Israel.[18]

The Fulfilling of The Times of The Gentiles: The Gospel Will Be Taken Instead To The House of Israel

According to the prophecies, there is to come a time when the people of the Gentile nations who will accept the Gospel

---

16. III Ne. 16:6-15.
17. D & C 45:28-30.
18. JD, 20:146.

will have come into the Church and those who are left will, to a large degree, refuse to allow the beliefs of the Church to be preached to them. When this has happened among all the Gentile nations the times of the Gentiles will be fulfilled or completed. The Gospel will be taken from them.

Orson Pratt spoke repeatedly of the time when, after the Gentile nations had been taught the Gospel, the Lord will tell his servants to

> Come home, come out from the midst of these Gentile nations, where you have labored and borne testimony for so long a period; come out from among them, for *they are not worthy; they do not receive the message that I have sent forth*, they do not repent of their sins; come out from their midst, *their times are fulfilled*.[19]

After the Gentile nations reject the Gospel the Church will recall its missionaries from among them and they will be later reassigned to search out the remnants of the House of Israel. Explained Orson Pratt:

> *Then, when the Gentile nations shall reject this Gospel*, and count themselves unworthy of eternal life, as the Jews did before them, the Lord will say—"It is enough, come away from them, my servants, I will give you a new commission, *you shall go to the scattered remnants of the house of Israel. I will gather them in from the four quarters of the earth, and bring them again into their own lands. They shall build Jerusalem on its own heap; they shall rear a Temple on the appointed place in Palestine*, and they shall be grafted in again." Now that, in short, is the nature of this great latter-day preparatory work for the coming of the Son of Man.[20]

The Gentiles, who were the last to receive the Gospel in the meridian of time, have been the first to receive it in this dispensation, while Israel, who received the Gospel first in the time of Christ, must wait until last to receive it. This was the intent of Christ's statement that "the last shall be first and the first last."[21]

---

19. JD, 18:64.
20. JD, 18:177.
21. Matt. 20:16.

Signs of The Approaching Fulfillment of The Times of The Gentiles

Down through the history of the Church since its restoration, various events have been interpreted as signs of the nearing completion of the times of the Gentiles.

Joseph Fielding Smith, for example, commented that the liberation of the Jewish people in the First World War is a sign which indicates that this is a transition period leading to a termination of the times of the Gentiles:"

> The Lord said they [the Jews] should remain scattered among the nations *until* the times of the Gentiles were fulfilled. Moroni said the times of the Gentiles were about to be fulfilled. *Today we are living in the transition* period; the day of the Gentiles has come in, and the day of Judah and the remnant of downtrodden Israel is now at hand. *The sign for the fulfillment of this prophecy has been given.*[22]

According to Orson Pratt, even after the Gospel is taken from the Gentiles and missionaries are no longer carrying their message among them, Gentiles will continue to seek out the Church:

> *Will the Gentiles be entirely cut off? Oh no, there will be a great many, even when Israel are gathering, who will come along and say, "Let us be numbered with Israel,* and be made partakers of the same blessings with them; let us enter into the same covenant and be gathered with them and with the people of God." Though the testimony is bound, and though the law is sealed up, yet there will be an opening for you to come in. *But you will have to come of your own accord, there will be no message sent to you, no ministration of the servants of God expressly directed to you.*[23]

The continuing increase of wickedness on the earth has been taken as another sign that the fulfilling of the times of the Gentiles is imminent, and it is the message of the prophets that the earth will not become more righteous. The Lord has said, "I, the Lord, am angry with the wicked; I am holding my Spirit from the inhabitants of the earth."[24] Joseph Smith foretold the effect of this withdrawal of the Holy Spirit:

---

22. Joseph Fielding Smith, *Doctrines of Salvation* (Salt Lake City: Bookcraft, 1956), III, 258-59.
23. JD, 14:64.
24. D & C 63:32.

I prophesy, in the name of the Lord God of Israel, anguish and wrath and tribulation and the withdrawing of the Spirit of God from the earth await this generation, until they are visited with utter desolation. *This generation is as corrupt as the generation of the Jews that crucified Christ;* and if He were here to-day, and should preach the same doctrine He did then, they would put Him to death.[25]

Wilford Woodruff made this statement about the increasing wickedness of the world:

The angels of God are waiting to fulfill the great commandment given forty-five years ago, to go forth and reap down the earth because of the wickedness of men. How do you think eternity feels today? *Why there is more wickedness, a thousand times over, in the United States now, than when that revelation was given. The whole earth is ripe in iniquity,*[26]

The trend toward wickedness has become even more pronounced now. Even the casual observer is aware of the tremendous increases in crime which have taken place in America and Europe since World War II.[27]

---

25. HC, 6:58.
26. JD, 18:128.
27. To illustrate the recent increase in crime, the following article is quoted from *The Idaho Challenge* issue for October, 1961:
NEWEST FBI CRIME RATE FIGURES MAKE GRIM READING FOR US
WASHINGTON — The Federal Bureau of Investigation has just put out a 141-page report on "Crime in the United States—1960." It makes grim reading.
This "land of the free, and home of the brave," even a glance at the report makes clear, also is the home of a disturbing number of criminals and criminally inclined.
FBI Director J. Edgar Hoover makes the following assertions:
  (1) "Serious crime in the United States last year reached a new all-time high, with an astounding 98 percent increase over 1950, while the population increase during this decade was only 18 percent";
  (2) "There were 1,861,300 serious crimes of murder, forcible rape, robbery, aggravated assault, burglary, larceny $50 and over, and auto theft reported in 1960 — 14 percent higher than in 1959." (The number was undoubtedly larger as these were only cases "reported.")
  (3) "During 1960 a serious crime was committed every 15 seconds in the United States; a murder, forcible rope [sic], or assault to kill occurred every three minutes, a murder every 58 minutes, a forcible rape every 34 minutes, and an aggravated assault every 4 minutes."

It has been prophesied, too, that during this period such wickedness is to enter into areas where the Church is well established, and many of the Church members will be affected by it. According to Heber C. Kimball,

> After a while the Gentiles will gather to this place by the thousands and *Salt Lake will be classified among the wicked cities of the world.* A spirit of speculation and extravagance will take possession of the Saints, and the result will be financial bondage.
>
> Persecution comes next, and all true Latter-day Saints will be tested to the limit. Many will apostatize, and others will stand still, not knowing what to do. *"Darkness will cover the earth and gross darkness the minds of the people."*[28]

Mosiah Hancock recorded a dream of which Brigham Young spoke while they were conversing which had much the same message:

> He conversed freely on the situation of the Saints in the mountains, and said that he dreaded the time when the Saints would become popular with the world; for he had seen in sorrow, in a dream, or in dreams, this people clothed in the fashions of

---

(4) "Arrests of juveniles more than doubled since 1950, while the population of youths aged 10 to 17 increased by less than one half."

(5) "Crime, for the past five years, has been rising over four times faster than the population."

(6) "Direct property losses averaged $256 for every robbery; $183 for every burglary; $74 for every larceny; and $830 for every auto theft. In 1960 thieves stole loot amounting to over $570,000,000. The police recovered 52 percent of this stolen property."

(7) "Law enforcement agencies in the United States handled 15,000,000 violations of traffic and motor vehicle laws, and city police alone issued 31,000,000 parking citations in 1960.00 [sic]."

(8) "During 1960 48 police officers were killed in the line of duty, 8 at the hands of killers. Six of these were slain by vicious killers then benefiting from leniency granted after conviction for crimes of murder, robbery, aggravated assault, burglary, and forgery . . . In addition more than 9,600 city police were assaulted while performing their duties."

These are only some of the grimmer figures and records found in this compilation that devotes over 100 of its pages to tables on the nation, state and city level.

The report leaves one halfway persuaded that crime in the United States may be more dangerous to the nation's well-being and security than anything being plotted in the Kremlin or in Peking.

28. *Prophetic Sayings of Heber C. Kimball to Amanda H. Wilcox.* A copy of this prophecy is available in the Brigham Young University library.

Babylon and drinking in the spirit of Babylon until one could hardly tell a Saint from a black-leg. And he felt like shouting, "To your tents, Oh Israel!" because it was the only thing that could keep this people pure . . . *Many of this people for the sake of riches and popularity, will sell themselves for that which will canker their souls and lead them down to misery and despair.* It would be better for them to dwell in wigwams among the Indians than to dwell with the gentiles and miss the glories which God wishes them to obtain.[29]

In connection with the growth of the Saints, past Church leaders have prophesied and taught concerning the wealth which the Saints will eventually attain in the mountains. Said Brigham Young, "I do not worry about the Saints in poverty but when the Lord sees fit to open the great oil reserves in Utah, I tremble for them."[30]

Yet before the times of the Gentiles are fulfilled, Latter-day Saint missionaries must penetrate into many areas which are yet untouched and preach the gospel there. The accompanying maps and charts indicate the major religions located in the areas of the world and the extent of Latter-day Saint mission organization in the corresponding places.

The Fulfilling of The Times of The Gentiles Is An Important Chronological Event

The reader should be aware of the important chronological significance of the fulfilling of the times of the Gentiles. Both the prophecies made by Latter-day Saint general authorities and the prophecies of the scriptures use it as a point of reference to establish the order of things yet future. Some of the events to follow this change in the missionary program are listed here:

First, the fulfilling of the times of the Gentiles is to mark the end of the period of preparatory wars and will *begin the period of wars of devastation,* as was seen in the preceding chapter.

---

29. Mosiah Lyman Hancock, *The Life Story of Mosiah Lyman Hancock,* p. 73. A typewritten copy of this diary is available in the Brigham Young University library.
30. Prediction attributed to Brigham Young. It was apparently made in St. George, Utah, and was commonly known in that community several decades ago. It was repeated to Ben H. Bullock, who recorded it, by an Elder Holt about thirty years ago. Exact dates and further verification are unknown.

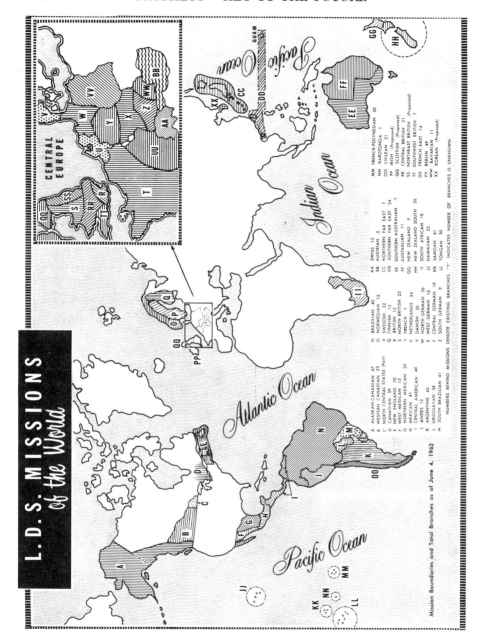

L.D.S. Missions of The World.

Used by permission of *The Instructor* magazine.

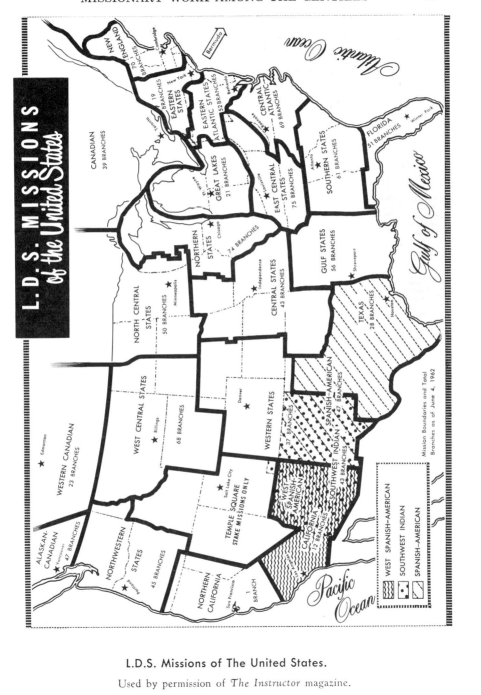

L.D.S. Missions of The United States.

Used by permission of *The Instructor* magazine.

NATIONS of the WORLD and their FAITHS

... Behold the field is white already to harvest ... D. & C. 4:4.

The following table lists the major religions of the world and gives approximate figures for current membership totals. The figures given, including the total world population, are estimates.[1] Precise figures are not available.

Religion	Membership	Religion	Membership
Roman Catholic	498,000,000	Confucianism	301,000,000
Eastern Orthodox	130,000,000	Buddhism	150,000,000
Protestantism	210,000,000	Taoism	50,000,000
Jewish	12,000,000	Shinto	30,000,000
Islam	421,000,000	Primitive religions	122,000,000
Hinduism	323,000,000	Other religions or none	403,000,000
		Total	2,650,000,000

Total membership of Church of Jesus Christ of Latter-day Saints as of December 31, 1958 (latest available figure). 1,555,799

[1]Based on figures shown in *The World Almanac*, 1959, (publisher, New York World-Telegram and Sun) and taken from the *Encyclopedia Brittanica's 1958 Book of the Year.*

These maps give a broad picture of how the major religions of the world are distributed geographically. The shadings indicate the predominant religions in the various areas. Where necessary, detail has been restricted or slightly modified.

Since the maps are concerned with positive religious faiths no attempt has been made to indicate the boundaries of the Communist empire where, in general, belief in God is officially discouraged though privately accepted by some.

For map of L.D.S. Missions see Instructor, July 1959, pages 222, 223.

Legend:

- Roman Catholic (Western Rite)
- Eastern Orthodox Churches (Orthodox, Armenian, Coptic, Jacobite, Nestorian and Roman Catholic of Eastern Rites)
- Protestantism
- Christianity (sect not distinguished)
- Jewish (State of Israel, plus important minorities chiefly in cities)
- Islam (covers Sunni Moslems and Shiah Moslems)
- Hinduism
- Buddhism (includes Lamaism)
- Chinese Religion (mixture of Confucianism, Taoism and Buddhism)
- Japanese Religion (Shinto and Buddhism superimposed)
- Tribal Religions
- Religions Undifferentiated (composition not known to Instructor compilers)

0   500   1000   1500
ONE INCH TO 1200 MILES

[2]Based upon map appearing in *Goode's World Atlas*, compiled by J. Paul Goode, edited by Edward B. Espenshade, Jr. Copyright by Rand McNally & Company, R. L. 60 S 1.

Compiled by Dr. H. Bowman Hawkes, professor and head of the department of Geography, University of Utah; and H. George Bickerstaff, *Instructor* research editor.

Nations of The World and Their Faiths.

Second, the fulfilling of the times of the Gentiles will *mark the real beginning of the great punishments and judgments which God is to pour out upon the earth.* This is the message of the Lord to Joseph Smith when he said,

> That through your administration they may receive the word, and through their administration the word may go forth unto the ends of the earth, unto the Gentiles first, and then behold, and lo, they shall turn unto the Jews.
>
> *And then cometh the day when the arm of the Lord shall be revealed in power in convincing the nations, the heathen nations, the house of Joseph, of the gospel of their salvation.*[31]

Among those who have expounded the importance of this relationship is Wilford Woodruff, who said,

> By and by the testimony of the Gospel will be sealed among the Gentiles, and the Gospel will turn to the whole house of Israel, and the *judgments of God will back up the testimony of the elders of this Church,* and the Lord will send messengers who will go forth and reap down the earth.[32]

Apparently this will happen because of the great wickedness of the Gentile people. The Lord said that his indignation is "soon to be poured out without measure upon all nations; and this will I [the Lord] do when the cup of their iniquity is full."[33]

The Angel Moroni said these terrible judgments are to come upon the earth in this generation. Joseph Smith reported,

> He commenced, and again related the very same things which he had done at his first visit, without the least variation; which having done, he informed me of great judgments which were coming upon the earth, with great desolations by famine, sword, and pestilence; and that these grievous judgments would come on the earth in this generation.[34]

Third, a revelation contained in the *Doctrine and Covenants* tells us that though a remnant of Israel be scattered among all nations "they shall be gathered again; but they shall remain until the times of the Gentiles be fulfilled."[35] The present gathering appears to be of small import in terms of numbers of

---

31. D & C 90:9-10.
32. JD, 18:38.
33. D & C 101:11.
34. JS, 2:45.
35. D & C 45:25.

participants when compared to the *gathering of Israel which must yet take place after the times of the Gentiles are fulfilled.*

Fourth, the times of the Gentiles will be fulfilled *before the Saints return to build the New Jerusalem in Jackson County, Missouri.* A prophecy made by Heber C. Kimball says,

> The judgments of God will be poured out upon the wicked to the extent that our elders from far and near will be called home. Or, in other words, *the gospel will be taken from the Gentiles and later on will be carried to the Jews* . . . Then the Prophet Joseph and others will make their appearance and *those who have remained faithful will be selected to return to Jackson County, Missouri,* and take part in the upbuilding of that beautiful city, the new Jerusalem.[36]

About this chronological relationship, Orson Pratt commented in 1875:

> There is one thing which I am now about to read which has not yet been fulfilled, and which *we must fulfill before Zion is redeemed.* I will read it — "Behold, saith the Father, *I will bring the fulness of my Gospel from among them* [*the Gentiles*] *and then I will remember my covenant which I have made unto my people, O house of Israel, and I will bring my Gospel unto them.*[37]

Fifth, the fulfilling of *the times of the Gentiles will precede the coming of the Ten Tribes from the North to the New Jerusalem.* Orson Pratt told of the time when instead of trying to convert the Gentile nations, the missionaries would be instructed to

> Go unto the remnants of the house of Israel that are scattered in the four quarters of the earth. Go and proclaim to them that the times of their dispersion are accomplished; that the *times of the Gentiles are fulfilled*; that the time has arrived for my people Israel, who have been scattered for generations in a dark and cloudy day, to gather unto their own homes again, and to build up old Jerusalem on its former heap. *And then will commence the gathering of the Jews to old Jerusalem; then the ten tribes in the northern regions, wherever they may be, after having been concealed from the nations for twenty-five hundred years, will come forth and will return.*[38]

---

36. *Prophetic Sayings of Heber C. Kimball to Amanda H. Wilcox.* A copy of this prophecy is available in the Brigham Young University library.
37. JD, 17:299.
38. JD, 18:64.

The Prophet Joseph Smith implied that the times of the Gentiles must be fulfilled and the judgments which will then be poured out must come some time before the coming of the Ten Tribes, for he stated that "pestilence, hail, famine, and earthquake will sweep the wicked of this generation from off the face of the land, to open and prepare the way for the return of the lost tribes of Israel from the north country."[39]

Summary

This chapter has dealt with the following important points:

1. The Lord has commanded that the gospel be preached unto every nation. This will be done in four periods of proselyting activity:

   A. Mission to the Gentile Nations.

   B. Mission to the House of Israel.

   C. Mission to the Heathen Nations.

   D. Final mission to all mankind.

   The first of these periods has already begun and the last will be immediately preceding and during the Millennium.

2. Five terms were defined in the sense in which they are usually used in prophecies:

   A. Gentiles—The nations which have embraced Christianity.

   B. Heathen Nations — The nations which have not embraced Christianity.

   C. Times of the Gentiles—The period which began with the restoration of the Church in which the Gentile nations are to hear the gospel.

   D. Fulness of the Gentiles—The period during which the Gentile Nations will have a full opportunity to have the gospel preached to them.

   E. Fulfilling of the times of the Gentiles—The ending of the missionary labor to the Gentiles because of their wickedness and refusal to accept the Gospel. When this event takes place, the second missionary period will begin, in which the gospel will be carried to those of the house of Israel.

3. Certain signs indicate the nearness of the fulfilling of the times of the Gentiles, yet there are many Gentile nations

---

39. HC, 1:315.

who must still be reached by our missionaries before their times are fulfilled.

4. The members of the Church have been warned of the wickedness which will penetrate their ranks if they adopt the ways of their non-member neighbors.

5. The fulfilling of the times of the Gentiles is an important item in the chronology of the future. The teachings and prophecies of the scriptures and of general authorities indicate that the following happenings will definitely come after this event:

A. Wars of complete destruction will begin.

B. God's judgments will be poured out on the world.

C. Israel will be gathered to Palestine.

D. The Saints will go back to build up the New Jerusalem.

E. The Lost Tribes will come down from the North.

CHAPTER III

God Will Pour Out His Judgments

Great Calamities Are To Come After The Gospel Is Taken From The Gentiles

It was on the night of September 21, 1823, that the prophet Joseph Smith was first visited by Moroni, an angelic being. Moroni told Joseph many important truths during his three visits that night. Among the most significant of his statements was the following warning which the Prophet recorded:

> He informed me of great judgments which were coming upon the earth, with great desolations by famine, sword, and pestilence; and that these grievous judgments would come on the earth in this generation.[1]

Similar warnings have been given by the Lord repeatedly. While he was still on the earth He foretold to his apostles the events which would come to pass in the last days:

> Behold I speak for mine elect's sake; for nation shall rise against nation, and kingdom against kingdom; there shall be famines, and pestilences, and earthquakes, in divers places.[2]

Modern day revelations have indicated the time when judgments caused by the elements will begin to take their toll. Although earthquakes, tidal waves, great storms and other calamities have been increasing in number over the years, yet the time of the full onslaught of these disasters is to be the period after the times of the Gentiles have been fulfilled. The Lord made this clear in Section 88 of the *Doctrine and Covenants* when He told how the saints are

> To go forth among the Gentiles for the last time, as many as the mouth of the Lord shall name, to bind up the law and seal up the testimony, and to prepare the saints for the hour of judgment which is to come.[3]

---

1. JS 2:45.
2. JS 1:29.
3. D & C 88:84.

He then proclaimed that "after your testimony cometh wrath and indignation upon the people."[4] What calamities did the Lord say would come upon the earth in this period?

> For after your testimony cometh the testimony of earthquakes, that shall cause groanings in the midst of her, and men shall fall upon the ground and shall not be able to stand.
>
> And also cometh the testimony of the voice of thunderings, and the voice of lightnings, and the voice of tempests, and the voice of the waves of the sea heaving themselves beyond their bounds.
>
> And all things shall be in commotion; and surely, men's hearts shall fail them; for fear shall come upon all people.[5]

Nephi, the great *Book of Mormon* prophet, foresaw the wickedness which would characterize the Gentiles after their times had been fulfilled. He said his prophecy applies both to those Gentiles "who shall come upon this land [America] and those who shall be upon other lands,"[6] and would be fulfilled when "they will be drunken with iniquity and all manner of abominations."[7] Then he foretold of God's judgments which would come upon them:

> And when that day shall come they shall be visited of the Lord of Hosts, with thunder and with earthquake, and with a great noise, and with storm, and with tempest, and with the flame of devouring fire.[8]

Nephi's brother, Jacob, also foresaw this period of destruction and said that it would come when "the Messiah will set himself again the second time to recover"[9] his people of Israel who still wait for the coming of the Messiah. As was seen in the preceding chapter, the major gathering of Israel will come after the times of the Gentiles are fulfilled, or in the time spoken of by Nephi above. Jacob's prophecy was similar to his brother's:

> And they that believe not in him shall be destroyed, both by fire, and by tempest, and by earthquakes, and by bloodsheds, and by pestilence, and by famine.[10]

---

4. D & C 88:88.
5. D & C 88:89-91.
6. II Ne. 27:1.
7. II Ne. 27:1.
8. II Ne. 27 2.
9. II Ne. 6:14.
10. II Ne. 6:15.

Part of the message of the Prophecy on War is that, beginning with the period after the slaves will have risen against their masters throughout the world

> . . . with the sword and by bloodshed the inhabitants of the earth shall mourn; and *with famine, and plague, and earthquake, and the thunder of heaven, and the fierce and vivid lightning* also, shall the inhabitants of the earth be made to feel the wrath, and indignation, and chastening hand of an Almighty God, until the consumption decreed hath made a full end of all nations.[11]

Thus the period of great and natural disasters and calamities is identified as being after the times of the Gentiles are fulfilled and during the period of wars of total destruction. President Brigham Young warned of the calamities which nature would hold for the world in this period:

> *When the testimony of the Elders ceases to be given, and the Lord says to them, "Come home;* I will now preach my own sermons to the nations of the earth," *all you now know can scarcely be called a preface to the sermon that will be preached with fire and sword, tempests, earthquakes, hail, rain, thunders and lightnings, and fearful destruction.* What matters the destruction of a few railway cars? You will hear of *magnificent cities, now idolized by the people, sinking in the earth, entombing the inhabitants. The sea will heave itself beyond its bounds, engulphing* [sic] mighty cities. *Famine will spread* over the nations, and *nation will rise up against nation,* kingdom against kingdom, and states against states, in our own country and in foreign lands; and *they will destroy each other,* caring not for the blood and lives of their neighbours, of their families, or for their own lives.[12]

The Lord's Desolating Scourge

Of special note is the series of prophecies which deal with a terrible sickness which God will pour out upon the earth during this period. After telling of the times of the Gentiles and stating that they will turn their hearts from him because of the precepts of men, the Lord said,

> . . . in that generation shall the times of the Gentiles be fulfilled.

---

11. D & C 87:6.
12. JD, 8:123.

And there shall be men standing in that generation, that
shall not pass until they shall *see an overflowing scourge; for
a desolating sickness shall cover the land.*

But my disciples shall stand in holy places, and shall not
be moved; but among the wicked, men shall lift up their voices
and curse God and die.

*And there shall be earthquakes also in divers places, and
many desolations;* yet men will harden their hearts against me,
and *they will take up the sword,* one against another, and they
will kill one another.[13]

Even before the Church was organized the Savior proclaimed
that the testimony of the three witnesses would go forth and
would be for the condemnation of this generation if they rejected it. He then said what that condemnation would embrace:

For a desolating scourge shall go forth among the inhabitants of the earth, and shall continue to be poured out from
time to time, if they repent not, until the earth is empty, and
the inhabitants thereof are consumed away and utterly destroyed by the brightness of my coming.[14]

In 1832 the Lord gave the warning that

I, the Almighty, have laid my hands upon the nations,
to scourge them for their wickedness.

And plagues shall go forth, and they shall not be taken
from the earth until I have completed my work, which shall
be cut short in righteousness — [15]

A prophecy in Isaiah has been interpreted by various general authorities of the L.D.S. Church as having reference to a
future calamity in the Americas. The population is compared to
a grape vine and the prediction is made that God will

. . . both cut off the sprigs with pruning hooks, and take
away and cut down the branches.

They shall be left together unto the fowls of the mountains,
and to the beasts of the earth; and the fowls shall summer
upon them, and all the beasts of the earth shall winter upon
them.[16]

The time of this event is identified as following the fulfilling
of the times of the Gentiles, for it will be when Israel (and pos-

---

13. D & C 45:30-3.
14. D & C 5:19.
15. D & C 84:96-7.
16. Is. 18:5-6.

sibly the reference refers to the return of the Ten Tribes) is being gathered:

> In that time shall the present be brought unto the Lord of hosts of a people scattered and peeled, and from a people terrible from their beginning hitherto; a nation meted out and trodden under foot, whose land the rivers have spoiled, to the place of the name of the Lord of hosts, the mount Zion.[17]

Orson Pratt spoke on this prophecy and clearly interpreted it as referring to a future destruction in America. He said that God will visit the American continents

> . . . with judgments that are terribly severe that will cause them to *lie by hundreds and thousands unberied* [sic], *from one end of the land to the other*, to be meat for the fowls of the air and the beasts of the earth. Why? Because the judgments will be swift, giving no time for burial.
>
> Inquires one — "Do you really believe that such judgments are coming upon our nation?" I do not merely believe, but I know it.[18]

This scourge was expected to come in some measure upon the *Saints if they are not righteous as well as the Gentiles*. A revelation given in 1832 stated that "vanity and unbelief have brought the whole church under condemnation," and that "they shall remain under this condemnation until they repent . . . otherwise there remaineth a scourge and judgment to be poured out upon the children of Zion."[19] A revelation given the following year said,

> The Lord's scourge shall pass over by night and by day, and the report thereof shall vex all people; yea, it shall not be stayed until the Lord come;
>
> For the indignation of the Lord is kindled against their abominations and all their wicked works.
>
> Nevertheless, *Zion shall escape if she observe to do all things* whatsoever I have commanded her.
>
> *But if she observe not to do whatsoever I have commanded her, I will visit her according to all her works, with sore affliction, with pestilence, with plague, with sword, with vengeance, with devouring fire.*[20]

---

17. Is. 18:7.
18. JD, 17:319. See also JD, 2:295.
19. D & C 84:55-9.
20. D & C 97:23-6.

The Prophet Joseph taught that many of the Saints, even though they are righteous may fall prey to the diseases and pestilences which are predicted:

> Explained concerning the coming of the Son of Man; also that *it is a false idea that the Saints will escape all the judgments whilst the wicked suffer; for all flesh is subject to suffer,* and the "righteous shall hardly escape;" still many of the Saints will escape, for the just shall live by faith; yet many of the righteous shall fall a prey to disease, to pestilence, etc., by reason of the weakness of the flesh, and yet be saved in the Kingdom of God. So that *it is an unhallowed principle to say that such and such have transgressed because they have been preyed upon by disease or death,* for all flesh is subject to death; and the Savior has said, "Judge not, lest ye be judged."[21]

Famine and Drought

Closely connected with the coming danger of disease and pestilence is the great danger from famine. In addition to the many prophetic warnings of famine already cited in this chapter, several passages call to mind ways in which the Lord may cause famine to come upon the people of the world.

A prophecy is given in the Doctrine and Covenants of an important event which is yet future. It will take place at an unspecified time before the coming of the Lord. The Lord proclaimed that *"there shall be a great hailstorm sent forth to destroy the crops of the earth."*[22] Perhaps it was this revelation which influenced the prayer offered by the Prophet Joseph Smith as he dedicated the Kirtland Temple. While speaking of the unrepentant among those who are enemies of the Church, he asked the Lord "that all their works may be brought to naught, and *be swept away by the hail,* and by the judgments which thou wilt send upon them in thine anger."[23]

Another way in which the Lord may send famines upon the lands is by changing the seasons. While replying to the Prophet's despairing prayer which he offered while he was a prisoner in Liberty Jail, the Lord revealed that

> *God hath set his hand and seal to change the times and seasons,* and to blind their minds, that they may not under-

21. HC, 4:11.
22. D & C 29:16.
23. D & C 109:30.

stand his marvelous workings; that he may prove them also, and take them in their own craftiness;[24]

But perhaps the greatest threat as a possible cause of famine is the danger from drought. The Lord also warns that drought can play an important part in the events of the last days:

> Behold, at my rebuke I dry up the sea. I make the rivers a wilderness; their fish stink, and die for thirst.
>
> I clothe the heavens with blackness, and make sackcloth their covering.
>
> And this shall ye have of my hand — ye shall lie down in sorrow.[25]

Even now the problem of water shortage in the United States is critical. President Kennedy, just previous to his inauguration said:

> In fifteen years we will need twice as much water as we do now. . . . Today 40 million Americans are on the edge of a serious water shortage and water tables are falling almost everywhere. Today nearly every major waterway in the United States is polluted.[26]

In a recent government-sponsored study meteorologists and conservation workers reported that the United States

> Will be in serious difficulty in about ten years unless it can turn salt water into fresh water economically. . . . A report prepared by the House Science Committee said that the nation already is using every available drop of its fresh water supply. . . . The study found 'a likelihood that the United States will be the first of the high civilized, technologically advanced nations to find itself in real difficulty due to fresh water shortages.' It predicted the difficulty will materialize by 1970 or before, as much as 10 years earlier than previous studies have indicated.[27]

An independent research group, Resources for the Future, Inc., outlined the tremendous cost necessary to even temporarily solve this nation's water problem:

> Unless many areas begin water development programs forthwith, they face economic deterioration. The study calls for

---

24. D & C 121:12.
25. D & C 133:68-70.
26. *This Week Magazine,* January 15, 1961.
27. *The Oregonian,* Portland, Oregon, January 30, 1961.

gigantic measures costing $228 billion over 20 years to fore-
stall a critical shortage estimated for 1980. A drought could
push the date up several years.[28]

Even now, many communities have severe water shortages.
An article written in Arizona in 1960, stated that

> *One of every seven U. S. communities suffered last year
> from water shortage rated as moderate to severe. No less than
> 79% of Illinois communities were short of water for at least a
> part of 1959.* But the American people have refused to pay
> any attention to a problem that is already with them, is grow-
> ing more acute and one of these days will have practically the
> whole nation in desperate straits. Awakening the people to
> their danger is an imperative necessity, according to William
> E. Richards of Holdrege, Nebraska, president of the National
> Association of Soil Conservation Districts.[29]

Look Magazine added,

> To many in the United States, the problem is already here.
> *More than 1000 communities were forced to curtail the use of
> water in one recent year,* according to the U. S. Geological
> Survey. *Forty-five states felt shortages.* Today, the Geolog-
> ical Survey notes, no area of the country is without some form
> of water problem![30]

One of the most serious aspects to the water problem is the
greatly increased danger of water pollution. President Kennedy
said that water pollution has reached "alarming proportions"
and that "current corrective efforts are not adequate."[31] Con-
tamination of the water supply is increasing faster than man has
been able to devise water purification methods, and some diseases are being transmitted even though the water has been
"purified." The noted columnist, Drew Pearson, warned,

> Government doctors have traced paralytic polio in Camden,
> N. J., typhoid fever in Milwaukee, dysentery in Cincinnati,
> and *yellow jaundice in Utah, all to polluted water!* . . . The
> Columbia River is so contaminated in some areas that mere
> motorboat spray can cause disease. In Washington, D. C., resi-
> dents have been warned against eating fish caught in the Poto-
> mac, and swimming in the Potomac is now almost non-exist-
> ent.[32]

---

28. *Look,* July 19, 1960.
29. *Arizona Farmer-Ranchman,* December 3, 1960.
30. *Look, op. cit.*
31. *UPI* Release, February 23, 1961.
32. *Grand Forks Herald,* February 13, 1960.

The Los Angeles Times states that

Two-thirds of the nation's people get their drinking water from sources into which are discharged disease-carrying bacteria, viruses and toxic material.[33]

A statement in the *New Republic* warns that

More than 70 million Americans, out of 117 million having public water supplies, now drink water that has been through a sewage or industrial plant 'at least once.'[34]

Of particular interest to Latter-day Saints who are acquainted with prophecies concerning the cleansing of Jackson County, Missouri, (to prepare the way for the return of the Saints to build the New Jerusalem) is this statement recently made in the *St. Louis Globe-Democrat*:

The Missouri River below Kansas City *"is the worst polluted source of water supply in the United States."* Bacteriological counts of its water average 25 times the allowable level for human consumption. Its fish "taste like coal oil." The Public Health Service reported finding floating debris, garbage, blood and manure from packing plants, feathers, oil, chemicals and domestic sewage in the river. All this threatens to turn the Missouri into an open sewer.[35]

The above quotations dealing with the dangers of water shortage and disease carrying water supplies are meaningful in the present context. Here is evidence of the nearness of potential famines and pestilence. Surely, in the light of the Lord's constant warning about approaching famine, Church members would do well to follow the counsel of their leaders and lay in adequate supplies.

An Earthquake in America

The prophecies already cited in this chapter have made frequent reference to various earthquakes and storms. Future chapters will deal with three specific earthquakes of great importance which have been prophesied,[36] but Latter-day Saint prophets have given indications of at least one earthquake which will have far-reaching effects on the people of the United States.

---

33. *Los Angeles Times,* February 24, 1960.
34. *New Republic,* June 6, 1960.
35. *St. Louis Democrat,* November 29, 1960.
36. These earthquakes will take place at the coming of the Ten Tribes, the Battle of Armageddon, and Christ's final coming in Glory.

An important prophecy was uttered by Wilford Woodruff in a sermon delivered in Logan, Utah, on August 22, 1863, in which he prophesied the manner in which the cities of New York, Boston, and Albany would be destroyed:

> You are to become men and women, fathers and mothers; yea, the day will come, after your fathers, and these prophets and apostles are dead, you will have the privilege of going into the towers of a glorious Temple built unto the name of the Most High (pointing in the direction of the bench), east of us upon the Logan bench; and *while you stand in the towers of the Temple and your eyes survey this glorious valley filled with cities and villages, occupied by tens of thousands of Latter-day Saints*, you will then call to mind this visitation of President Young and his company. You will say: That was in the days when Presidents Benson and Maughan presided over us; *that was before New York was destroyed by an earthquake. It was before Boston was swept into the sea, by the sea heaving itself beyond its bounds; it was before Albany was destroyed by fire*; yea, at that time you will remember the scenes of this day. Treasure them up and forget them not. President Young followed and said: 'What Brother Woodruff has said is revelation and will be fulfilled'.[37]

Orson Pratt also alluded to the destruction of New York on two occasions. While speaking of the people of America, he said,

> They must perish, unless they repent. *They will be wasted away, and the fulness of the wrath of Almighty God will be poured out upon them, unless they repent. Their cities will be left desolate. A time is coming when the great and populous city of New York—the greatest city of the American Republic, will be left without inhabitants. The houses will stand*, some of them, not all. They will stand there, but unoccupied, no people to inherit them. *It will be the same in regard to numerous other cities.*[38]

Several years before, Elder Pratt had given a similar prophecy:

> *The great, powerful and populous city of New York, that may be considered one of the greatest cities of the world, will*

---

37. DN, 33:678. See also JD, 21:299. This prophecy is of special interest when viewed in the light of the message of warning found in the *Doctrine and Covenants*: "Let the bishop go unto the city of New York, also to the city of Albany, and also to the city of Boston, and warn the people of those cities with the sound of the gospel, with a loud voice, of the desolation and utter abolishment which await them if they do reject these things. For if they do reject these things the hour of their judgment is nigh, and their house shall be left unto them desolate. D & C 84:114-15.

38. JD, 20:152.

in a few years become a mass of ruins. The people will wonder while gazing on the ruins that cost hundreds of millions to build, what has become of its inhabitants. *Their houses will be there, but they will be left desolate.* So saith the Lord God. *That will be only a sample of numerous other towns and cities on the face of this continent.*[39]

The Lord seems to be preparing the earth to send great earthquakes upon it. The frequency and severity of earthquakes throughout the world is increasing. The strongest earthquake ever recorded took place on May 21, 1960, in Chile. It has been estimated that it would take the combined force of 25,000 atomic bombs of the Hiroshima class to begin to release the equivalent energy of only one of the major shocks in this disaster.

Jackson County To Be Swept Clean

It seems that during this tumultuous period Jackson County, Missouri, will be purged as a preparation for the Saints. Prophecy has not defined how this will take place, but it has made it very clear that the entire area where the New Jerusalem is to be built will be swept clean. President Brigham Young spoke of the time when the Lord will "purge the land . . . cut off the evil doer, and prepare a way for the return of my [His] people to their inheritance," and added that "if our enemies do not cease their oppression upon this people, as sure as the Lord lives it will not be many days before we will occupy that land [of Zion] and there build up a Temple to the Lord."[40]

Perhaps it was in reference to this statement that Heber C. Kimball said that the western boundaries of the state of Missouri "will be swept so clean of its inhabitants that, as President Young tells us, when we return to that place, 'There will not be left so much as a yellow dog to wag his tail.' "[41]

Orson Pratt also stated that before the Saints return to Jackson County, God will visit that area *"in judgment, and there will be no owners left to occupy the country."*[42]

Will the Saints Escape Judgments?

Prophecy paints both a pessimistic and a bright picture in telling whether the Saints will be permitted to escape the judgments predicted for this land. A revelation given to Joseph

---

39. JD, 12:344.
40. JD, 9:270.
41. *Prophetic Sayings of Heber C. Kimball to Amanda H. Wilcox.* A copy of this prophecy is available in the Brigham Young University library.
42. DEN, 8:265, October 2, 1875.

Smith warns that they will come upon the wicked and unfaithful members of the Church before spreading to other people:

> Behold, vengeance cometh speedily upon the inhabitants
> of the earth, a day of wrath, a day of burning, a day of desola-
> tion, of weeping, of mourning, and of lamentation; and as a
> whirlwind it shall come upon all the face of the earth, saith
> the Lord.
>
> *And upon my house shall it begin, and from my house
> shall it go forth, saith the Lord;*
>
> *First among those among you, saith the Lord, who have
> professed to know my name and have not known me,* and have
> blasphemed against me in the midst of my house, saith the
> Lord.[43]

Though this prophecy has been interpreted at various times to
have seen partial fulfillment by the Saints as they underwent
various trials, it would appear in light of the evidence contained
in this chapter that its real fulfillment is yet future.

Wilford Woodruff proclaimed that the judgments of God
would "come to both Jew and Gentile, Zion and Babylon."[44]
Another revelation given to Joseph Smith states:

> I have sworn in my wrath, and decreed wars upon the face
> of the earth, and the wicked shall slay the wicked, and fear
> shall come upon every man;
>
> And the *saints also shall hardly escape;* nevertheless, I,
> the Lord, am with them, and will come down in heaven from the
> presence of my Father and consume the wicked with unquench-
> able fire.[45]

It will be seen in the next chapter that the beginning of
these judgments will be accompanied by an internal war within
the United States. Heber C. Kimball foretold that this period
of civil strife will be preceded by a time of great persecution
when "all true Latter-day Saints will be tested to the limit.
Many will apostatize, and others will stand still, not knowing
what to do." He then spoke of the judgments which will sweep
clean the western portion of Missouri and said "Before that day
come, however, the Saints will be put to a test that will try the
integrity of the best of them. The pressure will become so great

43. D & C 112:24-6.
44. JD, 18:122.
45. D & C 63:33-4.

that the more righteous among them will cry unto the Lord day and night until deliverance comes."[46]

But the Prophets have made it clear that righteous living is the criterion which will allow the Saints to escape the worst of the judgments. According to Wilford Woodruff, the only ones who have a right to be shielded from the judgments are worthy priesthood holders:

> Can you tell me where the people are who will be shielded and protected from these great calamities and judgments which are now at our doors? I'll tell you. *The priesthood of God who honor their priesthood, and who are worthy of their blessings are the only ones who shall have this safety and protection. They are the only mortal beings. No other people have a right to be shielded from these judgments.* They are at our very doors; not even this people will escape them entirely. They will come down like the judgments of Sodom and Gomorrah. And none but the priesthood will be safe from their fury.[47]

And finally, it was taught by Brigham Young that as long as the majority of the Saints live the commandments of God, the curses and judgments of the Almighty will never come upon them, though they will still have trials of many kinds:

> There is one principle I would like to have the Latter-day Saints perfectly understand — that is, of blessings and cursings. For instance, we read that war, pestilence, plagues, famine, etc., will be visited upon the inhabitants of the earth; but *if distress through the judgments of God comes upon this people, it will be because the majority have turned away from the Lord.* Let the majority of the people turn away from the Holy Commandments which the Lord has delivered to us, and cease to hold the balance of power in the Church, and we may expect the judgments of God to come upon us; *but while six-tenths or three-fourths of this people will keep the commandments of God, the curse and judgments of the Almighty will never come upon them, though we will have trials of various kinds,* and the elements to contend with — natural and spiritual elements. While this people will strive to serve God according to the best of their abilities, they will fare better, have more to eat and to wear, have better houses to live in, better associations, and enjoy themselves better than the wicked ever do or ever will do.[48]

---

46. *Prophetic Sayings of Heber C. Kimball to Amanda H. Wilcox.* A copy of this prophecy is available in the Brigham Young University library.
47. *Young Womens Journal,* Vol. 5, number 11, August, 1894.
48. JD, 10:335-36.

Summary

Great calamities and disasters caused by nature are predicted to come upon the earth beginning at the time when the missionaries are called home and the times of the Gentiles are fulfilled. It appears that these disasters have already begun but will be sent by God with greatly increased intensity at that time. These judgments can be classed under three general headings:

1. Pestilences.
    A. A desolating sickness is to cover the United States.
    B. It will come rapidly and will cause people to lie by the hundreds and thousands unburied.
    C. The sickness will come mainly upon the wicked, but some of the Saints who are righteous will also suffer and die.
    D. Pestilence will continue to be poured out, from time to time "until the earth is empty."
2. Famines.
    A. The Lord has said that a great hailstorm will destroy the crops of the earth. Famines may also be caused by the changing of seasons (which will affect growing periods), and by lack of water.
    B. A serious lack of water already exists in the United States. Government specialists predict that by 1970 the problem of water shortage will be of disaster proportions in many areas.
    C. Water pollution is also a serious problem and is increasing in intensity. The purification processes in use today do not remove all dangerous elements from the water supply and some diseases have already been found to have been transported through the culinary water supply.
3. Earthquakes, Floods, Tidal Waves, Storms, etc.
    A. Prophecies say that New York will be destroyed by earthquake, Albany by fire, Boston by tidal wave, and that many other cities on the American continent will be destroyed or left desolate.
    B. Earthquakes are increasing in number and intensity. They are happening frequently in the United States. They are far more destructive than atomic bombs.
    C. Although the manner of its destruction has not been revealed, Jackson County, Missouri, the site for the New Jerusalem, is to be swept clean of its inhabitants.

The Saints will suffer from these calamities to a degree, but will, in general, escape the worst of these disasters to the extent that they are righteous.

CHAPTER IV

Internal Wars and the Collapse of United States Government

Future War and Strife Within The United States

Even though they knew of the impending Civil War which had been prophesied by Joseph Smith, the early leaders of the Church often spoke of another time of terrible war, destruction, famine, and plague within the United States, subsequent to that struggle. As early as 1833 the Prophet wrote the following in a letter directed to N. E. Seaton, a newspaper editor, and requested that it be published:

> And now I am prepared to say by the authority of Jesus Christ, that not many years shall pass away before *the United States shall present such a scene of bloodshed as has not a parallel in the history of our nation; pestilence, hail, famine, and earthquake will sweep the wicked of this generation from off the face of the land, to open and prepare the way for the return of the lost tribes of Israel from the north country.*[1]

On July 1, 1839, Joseph Smith met in a special meeting with the Twelve Apostles and with some of the Seventies who were about to leave on overseas missions. It was at this time that the pattern for the coming war began to be clarified. The war is expected to be an internal war, not a war with other nations. It will not be a war of two opposing factions like the Civil War, but it will be many local wars characterized by mob rule and strife between families, cities, and states. This pattern was explained by the Prophet to the other Church leaders:

> . . . Some may have cried peace, but the Saints and the world will have little peace from henceforth . . . .
>
> *I saw men hunting the lives of their own sons, and brother murdering brother, women killing their own daughters, and daughters seeking the lives of their mothers. I saw armies arrayed against armies. I saw blood, desolation, fires. The Son of Man has said that the mother shall be against the daughter,*

---

1. HC, 1:315.

*and the daughter against the mother. These things are at our
doors. They will follow the Saints of God from city to city.*
Satan will rage, and the spirit of the devil is now enraged. I
know not how soon these things will take place; but with a view
of them, shall I cry peace? No! I will lift up my voice and testify of them. How long you will have good crops, and the
famine be kept off, I do not know; When the fig tree leaves,
know then that the summer is nigh at hand.[2]

Though many details have not been revealed concerning the
coming internal strife, its general characteristics can be identified by a careful consideration of the prophecies which have been
given. Orson Pratt, speaking in 1879, also described the war
and emphasized the same characteristics:

But what about the American nation. *That war that destroyed
the lives of some fifteen or sixteen hundred thousand people*
[Civil War] *was nothing, compared to that which will eventually devastate that country.* The time is not very far distant
in the future, when the Lord God will lay his hand heavily
upon that nation. . . . What then will be the condition of that
people, when this great and terrible war shall come? *it will be
very different from the war between the North and the South.*
Do you wish me to describe it? I will do so. *It will be a war of
neighborhood against neighborhood, city against city, town
against town, county against county, state against state, and
they will go forth, destroying and being destroyed and manufacturing will, in a great measure, cease, for a time among the
American nation.* Why? Because in these terrible wars, they
will not be privileged to manufacture, there will be too much
bloodshed, too much mobocracy, *too much going forth in bands
and destroying and pillaging the land to suffer people to pur-
sue any local vocation with any degree of safety. What will
become of millions of the farmers upon that land? They will
leave their farms and they will remain uncultivated, and they
will flee before the ravaging armies from place to place; and
thus will they go forth burning and pillaging the whole country; and that great and powerful nation, now consisting of
some forty millions of people, will be wasted away, unless they
repent.*

Now these are predictions you may record. You may let
them sink down into your hearts. And if the Lord your God shall

2. HC, 3:390-391. Others have referred to this and other statements by the
Prophet and interpreted them as having a fulfillment which is yet future.
See, for instance, statements in JD, 2:146-47; 20:150-151; and DEN, Vol.
8, No. 265, October 2, 1875.

permit you to live, you will see my words fulfilled to the very letter. They are not my words, but the words of inspiration — the words of the everlasting God, who has sent forth his servants with this message to warn the nations of the earth.[3]

In his description of the war Brigham Young stressed the idea that there will not be a definite series of tactical advances and retreats, but instead men will flee before pillaging mobs from one area to another without organization:

I heard Joseph Smith say, nearly thirty years ago, "They shall have mobbing to their hearts content, if they do not redress the wrongs of the Latter-day Saints. *Mobs will not decrease, but will increase until the whole government becomes a mob, and eventually it will be State against State, city against city, neighborhood against neighborhood.*" . . . it will be Christian against Christian, and man against man, and those who will not take up the sword against their neighbors, must flee to Zion.[4]

In a General Conference address delivered in 1879, President John Taylor taught that this war would be more terrible and devastating than anything this nation has ever experienced:

Were we surprised when the last terrible war [Civil War] took place here in the United States? No; . . . You will see worse things than that, for *God will lay his hand upon this nation, and they will feel it more terribly than ever they have done before. There will be more bloodshed, more ruin, more devastation than ever they have seen before.* Write it down! You will see it come to pass; it is only just starting in. . . . there is yet to come a sound of war, trouble and distress, in which *brother will be arrayed against brother, father against son, son against father*, a scene of desolation and destruction that will permeate our land until it will be a vexation to hear the report thereof.[5]

In 1868 Orson Pratt stated that the death toll from this anticipated war will be "many hundreds of thousands of souls," and pointed out that it will not be one war, but *civil wars*:

"What! this great and powerful nation of ours to be divided one part against the other and *many hundreds of thousands of souls to be destroyed by civil wars!*" Not a word of it would they

3. JD, 20:151.
4. DN, Vol. 11, No. 9, May 1, 1861.
5. JD, 20:318.

believe. They do not believe what is still in the future. . . .
*The time will come when there will be no safety in carrying on
the peaceable pursuits of farming or agriculture. But these
will be neglected, and the people will think themselves well off
if they can flee from city to city, from town to town and escape
with their lives.* Thus will the Lord visit the people, if they
will not repent.[6]

A prophecy by Wilford Woodruff seems to link these wars
with the same period as the natural disasters spoken of in the
preceding chapter:

> The judgments of God will now begin to rest more fully
> upon this nation and will be increased upon it, year by year.
> Calamities will come speedily upon it and it will be visited with
> thunder, lightning, storms, whirlwinds, floods, pestilence,
> plagues, war and devouring fire; *the wicked will slay the
> wicked until the wicked are wasted away.*[7]

The Government of The United States Will
Completely Collapse

According to the prophecies, the government and national
identity of the United States as it now exists will be completely
demolished during these internal wars. Joseph Smith several
times referred to the collapse of the federal government. To
Judge Stephen A. Douglas he said:

> I prophesy in the name of the Lord God of Israel, unless
> the United States redress the wrongs committed upon the
> Saints in the state of Missouri and punish the crimes committed
> by her officers that *in a few years the government will be ut-
> terly overthrown and wasted,* and there will not be so much as
> a potsherd left.[8]

Half a year later the Prophet recorded a similar prophecy:

> While discussing the petition to Congress, I prophesied,
> by virtue of the holy Priesthood vested in me, and in the name
> of the Lord Jesus Christ, that, *if Congress will not hear our
> petition and grant us protection, they shall be broken up as a
> government.*[9]

He also spoke of "the end of this nation, if she continues to
disregard the cries and petitions of her virtuous citizens, as

---

6. JD, 12:344.
7. Matthias F. Cowley, *Wilford Woodruff* (Salt Lake City: Deseret News,
   1916), p. 393.
8. HC, 5:394.
9. HC, 6:116.

she has done and is now doing."[10] It is significant that after the Civil War the Saints still looked forward to the fulfillment of these prophecies and to the final reduction of America to chaos.

Another prophetic statement apparently made by Joseph Smith was that

> A terrible revolution will take place in the land of America, such as has never been seen before; for *the land will be literally left without a supreme government,* and every species of wickedness will run rampant. Father will be against son, and son against father, mother against daughter, and daughter against mother. *The most terrible scenes of murder and bloodshed and rapine that have ever been looked upon will take place.*[11]

Wilford Woodruff recorded a vision which was given to him in 1880 which indicated the coming destruction of this nation:

> The Lord then poured out His spirit upon me and opened the vision of my mind so that I could comprehend in a great measure the mind and will of God concerning the nation and concerning the inhabitants of Zion. *I saw the wickedness of the nation, its abominations and corruptions and the judgments of God and the destruction that awaited it. . . .* On January 28th I was again given a vision. It concerned the destiny of our nation and of Zion. *My pillow was again wet by a fountain of tears as I beheld the judgments of God upon the wicked.* I was strongly impressed that the Apostles and elders should warn the inhabitants of the earth.[12]

Moses Thatcher, another of the early apostles, also anticipated the end of this nation. While speaking in Franklin, Idaho, on June 16, 1882, he said:

> *I have seen the end of this nation* and it is terrible . . . I will tell you in the name of the Lord that a *secret band* will sap the life of this nation:[13]

10. HC, 4:89.
11. Prophecy recorded by Edwin Rushton and Theodore Turley.
12. Cowley, *op cit.,* pp. 530-31.
13. *Franklin Ward Historical Record,* Franklin, Idaho. June 16, 1882. A comparison of this prophecy with the statements of Ezra Taft Benson in chapter one would raise the question of whether this secret combination is Communism. In that chapter it is seen that Russia will go down to defeat during the period of Preparatory Wars. Nevertheless, just as elements of Naziism lingered after World War II in various countries, it is possible that Communist elements could linger in the United States after the war with Russia until they caused the collapse of the American government. On the other hand, the secret combination may be the combined effect of many of the criminal elements which now exist and which will continue to increase, according to prophecy.

Brigham Young commented that strife and opposition within the communities "is the knife that will cut down this government."

> The nations will consume each other, and the Lord will suffer them to bring it about. It does not require much talent or tact to get *up opposition in these days. You see it rife in communities, in meetings, in neighbourhoods, and in cities. That is the knife that will cut down this Government.* The axe is laid at the root of the tree, and every tree that bringeth not forth good fruit will be hewn down.[14]

Because of the wasting away of the national government, it is expected that the Saints will find it necessary to maintain their own government so that law and order can be preserved. This matter was explained by Orson Pratt in 1875:

> God has sent forth his warning message in the midst of this nation, but they have rejected it and treated his servants with contempt; the Lord has gathered out his people from their midst, and has planted them here in these mountains; and *he will speedily fulfill the prophecy in relation to the overthrow of this nation, and their destruction. We shall be obliged to have a government to preserve ourselves in unity and peace; for they, through being wasted away, will not have the power to govern;* for state will be divided against state, city against city, town against town, and the whole country will be in terror and confusion; mobocracy will prevail and their [sic] will be no security, through this great Republic, for the lives or property of the people. *When that time shall arrive, we shall necessarily want to carry out the principles of our great constitution and as the people of God, we shall want to see those principles magnified, according to the order of union and oneness which prevails among the people of God.* We can magnify it, and all will be united without having democrats or republicans and all kinds of religions; we can magnify it according to the spirit and letter of the constitution, though we are united in politics, religion, and everything else.[15]

War Will Spread from America to Other Lands

Comments by the Prophets on the destruction of this nation are often linked with prophetic statements regarding the

14. JD, 8:143.
15. DEN, Vol. 8, No. 265, October 2, 1875.

collapse of other nations. Said Orson Pratt, while describing the effects of the internal wars within the United States:

> If a war of this description should take place, who could carry on his business in safety? Who would feel safe to put his crops in the ground, or to carry on any enterprise? *There would be fleeing from one State to another, and general confusion would exist throughout the whole Republic. Such eventually is to be the condition of this whole nation,* if the people do not repent of their wickedness; and *such a state of affairs means no more or less than the complete overthrow of the nation, and not only of this nation, but the nations of Europe.*[16]

Wilford Woodruff taught that the coming destruction of this nation, and of other nations as well, would surely come to pass:

> When I contemplate the condition of our nation, and see that wickedness and abominations are increasing, so much so that the whole heavens groan and weep over the abominations of this nation and the nations of the earth, *I ask myself the question, can the American nation escape? The answer comes, No; its destruction, as well as the destruction of the world, is sure;* just as sure as the Lord cut off and destroyed the two great and prosperous nations that once inhabited this continent of North and South America, because of their wickedness, so will he them destroy, and *sooner or later they will reap the fruits of their own wicked acts, and be numbered among the past.*[17]

There seems to be no specific prophecies which have been made concerning the chronological relationship between the collapse of the United States government and the destruction of other governments, except that peace will be taken from other nations during the period when the United States undergoes internal wars. Said the Prophet Joseph:

> Peace will be taken from the earth and there will be no peace only in the Rocky Mountains. This will cause many hundreds and thousands of the honest in heart to gather there; not because they would be saints but for safety and because they would not take up the sword against their neighbor.[18]

However, a pattern does seem to emerge. The conflict in the United States seems to begin the period of wars of complete de-

16. JD, 18:341.
17. JD, 21:301.
18. Prophecy recorded by Edwin Rushton and Theodore Turley.

struction. During the struggle in which this nation collapses a political kingdom will be established by the Saints and they will then return to build the New Jerusalem. The power of opposing nations will diminish as they succumb to the ravages of various wars and natural destruction which will begin while the United States is falling. The Kingdom of God will increase in dominion.

A Remnant of Jacob to Tread Down The Gentiles

The "Prophecy on War" speaks of a time long after the United States Civil War, in which "slaves shall rise up against their masters, who shall be marshaled and disciplined for war," and also predicts that "the remnants who are left of the land will marshall themselves, and shall become exceedingly angry, and shall vex the Gentiles with a sore vexation."[19] The Savior, in the *Book of Mormon*, also speaks of a remnant in the land of America which will rise up to vex the Gentiles,[20] and identifies this remnant as a remnant of Jacob (a phrase usually interpreted to mean the Lamanites or Indians):

> And my people who are a remnant of Jacob shall be among the Gentiles, yea, in the midst of them as a lion among the beasts of the forest, as a young lion among the flocks of sheep, who, if he go through both treadeth down and teareth in pieces, and none can deliver.
>
> Their hand shall be lifted up upon their adversaries, and all their enemies shall be cut off.
>
> Yea, woe be unto the Gentiles except they repent: for it shall come to pass in that day, saith the Father, that I will cut off thy horses out of the midst of thee, and I will destroy thy chariots;
>
> And I will cut off the cities of thy land, and throw down all thy strongholds;
>
> And I will cut off witchcrafts out of thy land, and thou shalt have no more soothsayers;
>
> Thy graven images I will also cut off, and thy standing images out of the midst of thee, and thou shalt no more worship the works of thy hands;
>
> And I will pluck up thy groves out of the midst of thee; so will I destroy thy cities.
>
> And it shall come to pass that all lyings, and deceivings, and envyings, and strifes, and priestcrafts, and whoredoms, shall be done away.

---

19. D & C 87:4-5.
20. See chapter two for a discussion of the conditional aspects of these prophecies.

For it shall come to pass, saith the Father, that at that day *whosoever will not repent and come unto my Beloved Son, them will I cut off from among my people, O house of Israel;*

And I will execute vengeance and fury upon them, even as upon the heathen, such as they have not heard.[21]

The Lord stated to the Nephite people that when the remnant of Jacob is allowed to go through the Gentiles like "a lion among the beasts of the forest" it will be because the Gentiles will have become like "salt that hath lost its savor, which is thenceforth good for nothing but to be cast out, and to be trodden under foot of [His] people." In other words, this will be "at that day when the Gentiles shall sin against [His] gospel," and the Lord will bring the fulness of His gospel from among them. This is to occur in the period in which "the Gentiles shall not have power over you; but I [the Lord] will remember my covenant unto you, O house of Israel, and ye shall come unto the knowledge of the fulness of my gospel."[22]

Mormon also issued a warning to the Gentiles who could live on this land in the last days. He told them they could not withstand the power of God unless they would repent and then added:

Therefore, repent ye, and humble yourselves before him, lest he shall come out in justice against you—*lest a remnant of the seed of Jacob shall go forth among you as a lion, and tear you in pieces, and there is none to deliver.*[23]

An uprising of the Lamanite peoples of the American continents against the Gentile inhabitants is thus anticipated by the Latter-day Saints. As has been seen above, such an uprising is to take place when the times of the Gentiles are fulfilled, and before the majority of the Lamanites and the rest of the House of Israel have come to a knowledge of the Gospel. It apparently falls, therefore, during the period of internal wars which the United States must suffer.

It should be emphasized, however, that this prophecy was made conditional. The Gentiles can escape this judgment if they will repent and not sin against the Gospel, but it appears in the light of prophecy and current trends that such will not be the course which they will choose.

---

21. III Ne. 21:12-21. See also III Ne. 20:15-17.
22. III Ne. 16:10-15.
23. Mor. 5:24.

The Gathering of The Saints to The Mountains

Although the present policy of the Church is to establish its membership in organized groups throughout the world, when the warfare and distress come upon the United States this policy will be reversed and the instructions will be to "Let them, therefore, who are among the Gentiles flee unto Zion."[24]

The Lord also spoke of a "gathering together" upon the land of Zion as a "refuge from the storm, and from wrath" and said it would be in a period when the *"wrath of God shall be poured out without mixture upon the whole earth."*[25]

Brigham Young told of the future gathering of the Saints to the western United States:

> An inland Empire will be established in these valleys of the mountains, which will be *a place of refuge for millions of people to gather to, when the great day of the judgments of God comes upon the earth, and the righteous come here for safety.* Our people will go East, West, North and South, but the day will come, when they will be glad to come back. We will be shut out from the rest of the world.[26]

On another occasion he described the coming internal wars and taught that those who will not take up the sword against their neighbor must flee to the mountains. It was President Young's teaching, also, that the western mountains were especially prepared by God to serve as a shelter for the Saints:

> It will be the same with other denominations of professing Christians, and it will be Christian against Christian, and man against man, and *those who will not take up the sword against their neighbors, must flee to Zion.*
>
> We are blessed in these mountains; this is the best place on earth for the Latter-day Saints. Search for the history of all nations and every geographical position on the face of the earth, and you cannot find another situation so well adapted

---

24. D & C 133:12. For assurance that this is the proper chronological fulfillment of this passage compare D & C 88:84-92 with D & C 133:8-12. Note that the cry that the "Bridegroom cometh, go ye out to meet him" is to follow the pouring out of God's judgments, yet it marks the time when the Saints will be called to gather to Zion.
25. D & C 115:6.
26. Statement made by Brigham Young to Benjamin Kimball Bullock as recorded by the latter's son, Ben H. Bullock. The author has a copy of notarized statements pertaining to the validity of this and other prophecies recorded by Bullock on file.

for the Saints as are these mountains. *Here is the place in which the Lord designed to hide His people. . . It has been designed, for many generations, to hide up the Saints in the last days, until the indignation of the Almighty be over. His wrath will be poured out upon the nations of the earth.*[27]

Orson Pratt also taught that although the Saints would previously have been blessed by God and enabled to spread throughout the land, that in the time of the Lord's judgments the place of safety would be in the heart of the American continent:

> The hand of the Lord will be over us to sustain us, and we will spread forth. He will multiply us in the land; He will make us a great people, and strengthen our borders, and send forth the missionaries of this people to the four quarters of the earth to publish peace and glad tidings of great joy and *proclaim that there is still a place left in the heart of the American continent where there are peace and safety and refuge from the storms, desolations and tribulations coming upon the wicked.*[28]

President J. Golden Kimball, of the First Council of Seventy, prophesied in 1926 of a time to come when many will have a burning desire to return to the West:

> I prophesy that before many of you go to the other side you will have a burning desire in your hearts to return to the place where the leaders of the Church have counseled the Saints to settle, and you will give anything in the world to be able to live there.[29]

The great influx of people into the area will be a source of growth to the Latter-day Saints in the West. Several prophecies deal with this growth, although it cannot be determined if they are indicative of the period during the internal wars or afterward. A prophecy attributed to Brigham Young asserts that

> . . . The day will come when there will be large places of manufacture and storage constructed West of the Jordan River and *there will be over three millions of people living there and Jordan River will practically run through the center of Salt Lake City.*[30]

27. DN, Vol. 11, No. 9, May 1, 1861.
28. JD, 12:345.
29. CR, October, 1926, p. 58.
30. Prophecy made by Brigham Young to William B. Armstrong and recorded by Ben H. Bullock. The author has a copy of notarized statements pertaining to the validity of this and other prophecies recorded by Bullock on file.

Another prophecy, this time concerning the Logan area, was made by Wilford Woodruff: In a discourse delivered on August 22, 1863, in Logan, Utah, he predicted the construction of the Logan Temple. He then spoke of a time which is yet future when the valley in which Logan is situated will be filled with cities and villages, and will be filled with tens of thousands of Latter-day Saints:

> Now, my young friends, I wish you to remember these scenes you are witnessing during the visit of President Young and his brethren. . . . The day will come, after your fathers and these prophets and apostles are dead, you will have the privilege of going into the towers of a glorious Temple built unto the name of the Most High (pointing in the direction of the bench), east of us upon the Logan bench; and while you stand in the towers of the Temple and your eyes *survey this glorious valley filled with cities and villages, occupied by tens of thousands of Latter-day Saints*, you will then call to mind this visitation of President Young and his company.[31]

What is expected to happen during this internal war in the United States to those Saints who refuse to gather to safety in the Rocky Mountains? The Prophet Jospeh said in 1839 that there would be Stakes here and there but when wars come, the Saints will have to flee to Zion. He commented that the time is soon coming when no man will have any peace but in Zion and her stakes, and it appears that this is a reference to the stakes located near the center of the Church in the west, as is indicated by the statements cited above. He then told of the Saints who will be followed by mobs from city to city. The above statements seem to indicate that these Saints will not be located in the mountains, but will be the Saints who remained in outlying areas. This is the Prophet's statement:

> There will be here and there a Stake [of Zion] for the gathering of the Saints. *Some may have cried peace, but the Saints and the world will have little peace from henceforth.* Let this not hinder us from going to the Stakes; *for God has told us to flee, not dallying, or we shall be scattered, one here, and another there.* There your children shall be blessed, and you in the midst of friends where you may be blessed. The Gospel net gathers of every kind.

---

31. DN, Vol. 33, p. 678. The unofficial census count for the 1960 Census shows the population for the city of Logan as 17,464 and of the entire Cache Valley as 35,688. *The Deseret News and Telegram,* May 12, 1960.

I prophecy, that that man who tarries after he has an opportunity of going, will be afflicted by the devil. Wars are at hand; we must not delay; but are not required to sacrifice. We ought to have the building up of Zion as our greatest object. *When wars come, we shall have to flee to Zion.* The cry is to make haste.

. . . The time is soon coming when no man will have any peace but in Zion and her stakes. . . . These things are at our doors. *They will follow the Saints of God from city to city.*[32]

The Righteous Gentiles Will
Also Gather to The Mountains

Millions of Gentiles also are expected to gather to the West at this time to escape the warfare which is to rage throughout the rest of the nation and other nations of the world. Orson Pratt said that at this time other governments would be crumbling, and gave this description of the coming of Gentile peoples to the West from foreign lands:

A flowing stream is one that runs continually; and *the Gentiles will, in that day, come to us as a flowing stream,* and we shall have to set our gates open continually, they will come as clouds and as doves in large flocks. Do you suppose that the Gentiles are going to be ignorant of what is taking place? "Now this will not be the case, they will perfectly understand what is taking place. The people will see that the hand of God is over this people; they will see that He is in our midst, and that He is our watchtower, that He is our shield and our defense, and therefore, they will say, "Let us go up and put our riches in Zion, for there is no safety in our own nations."

Those nations are trembling and tottering and will eventually crumble to ruin, and those men of wealth will come here, not to be baptized, but many of them will come that have never heard the servants of God; but they will hear that peace and health dwell among us, and that our officers are all peace officers, and our tax-gatherers men of righteousness.[33]

Heber C. Kimball, at the time of the arrival in Salt Lake City of a second of the handcart companies, prophesied of a time when enormous amounts of people will come fleeing to the West without even so much as handcarts:

---

32. HC, 3:390-91.
33. JD, 3:16.

I am very thankful that so many of the brethren have come in with handcarts; my soul rejoiced, my heart was filled and grew as big as a two-bushel basket. Two companies have come through safe and sound. Is this the end of it? No; *there will be millions on millions that will come much in the same way, only they will not have handcarts, for they will take their bundles under their arms, and their children on their backs, and under their arms, and flee.*[34]

George Q. Cannon also raised his voice to explain that when strife came, men would have to "flee to the Mormons" for safety:

I expect to see the day when the Latter-day Saints will be the people to maintain constitutional government on this land. Men everywhere should know that we believe in constitutional principles, and that we expect that it will be our destiny to maintain them. That the prediction will be fulfilled that was made forty-four years ago the seventh of last March, wherein God said to Joseph Smith—"Ye hear of wars in foreign lands; but behold I say unto you, they are nigh, even at your doors, and not many years hence ye shall hear of wars in your lands;" *but the revelation goes on to say that the day will come among the wicked, that every man that will not take his sword against his neighbor, must needs flee unto Zion for safety. A portion of that revelation has been fulfilled, the remainder will be.* The causes are in operation to bring it about. We are not alone in the thought that the republic is drifting steadily in that direction; that we are leaving the old constitutional landmarks, and that the time is not far distant when there will be trouble in consequence of it, when there will be civil broils and strife; and to escape them, we believe, *men will be compelled to flee to the "Mormons,"* despised as they are now.[35]

The Saints Will Eventually Be
Cut Off From The Rest of The Land

The early leaders of the Church taught that during this era of internal strife the Saints in the West would be isolated from the rest of the United States. Brigham Young, speaking in 1868, asserted that

By and by there will be a gulf between the righteous and the wicked so that they cannot trade with each other and national intercourse will cease.[36]

34. JD, 4:106.
35. JD, 18:10.
36. JD, 12:284.

Their theme was always the necessity for home manufacture so that the Saints would be prepared for the time when they would be cut off from the rest of the United States. This was Heber C. Kimball's admonition:

> Lay up your stores, and take your silks and fine things, and exchange them for grain and such things as you need, and the *time will come when we will be obliged to depend upon our own resources;* for the time is not far distant *when the curtain will be dropped between us and the United States.* When that time comes, brethren and sisters, you will wish you had commenced sooner to make your own clothing. I tell you, God requires us to go into home manufacture; and, prolong it as much as you like, you have got to do it.[37]

Orson Pratt also advocated this principle. He made this statement on the necessity for the Saints to be prepared and to be self-sustaining when "the gate will be shut down:"

> And the time will come, when we shall find ourselves restricted, and when it will be very important indeed for us to patronize home productions, and cease sending our millions abroad for importations, *for the gate will be shut down, and circumstances will be such that we cannot bring things from abroad;* and hence the necessity of the exhortation that we have received from time to time, *to engage with all our hearts in the various branches of industry necessary to make us self-sustaining,* and to carry them out with all the tact and wisdom which God has given to us, that we may become free and independent in all these matters, free before the heavens, and free from all the nations of the earth and their productions, so far as being dependent upon them is concerned.[38]

A prophecy attributed to the Prophet Joseph Smith summarizes these problems and adds material of an international nature. It holds that the wars in America will be so inhuman and so terrible that England will try to stop them:

> *While the terrible revolution of which I have spoken has been going on,* England will be neutral until it becomes so inhuman that she will interfere to stop the shedding of blood. England and France will unite together to make peace, not to subdue the nations; *they will find the nations so broken up*

---

37. JD, 5:10.
38. DEN, Vol. 8, No. 265, October 2, 1875.

and so many claiming government, till there will be no re-sponsible government. Then it will appear to the other na-tions or powers as though England had taken possession of the country. . . . *Peace and safety in the Rocky Mountains will be protected by a cordon band of the White Horse [the Church] and the Red Horse.*[39]

The Influx of People Will Bring Danger of Famine in The West

It is logical that such a period, when no food can be im-ported and when the population in central areas will have under-gone great increases in only a short period, there will be great danger from famine, lack of housing and sanitation preparations, etc. The Prophet Joseph, while telling of the influx of the Gen-tiles to the western communities during the internal wars, warned,

> *You will be so numerous that you will be in danger of famine,* but not for the want of seed time and harvest, but *because of so many to be fed.* Many will come with bundles under their arms to escape the calamities, and there will be no escape except by fleeing to Zion.[40]

Heber C. Kimball warned that "The day will come when the people of the United States will come lugging their bundles under their arms, coming to us for bread to eat."[41] The same sermon contained the statement that

> *The day will come that you (strangers) will have to come to us for bread to eat; and we will be your saviours here upon Mount Zion.* You don't believe it now; but wait a little while, and you will see that it will come to pass.[42]

On another occasion Heber C. Kimball told of a strange dream which seems to emphasize the need for food which the Saints will feel at this time:

> I will tell you a dream which Brother Kesler had lately. He dreamed that there was a sack of gold and a cat placed before him, and that he had the privilege of taking which he pleased, whereupon he took the cat, and walked off with her. Why did he take the cat in preference to the Gold? Because *he could eat*

39. Prophecy recorded by Edwin Rushton and Theodore Turley.
40. *Ibid.*
41. JD, 5:10.
42. JD, 5:9.

the cat, but could not eat the gold. You may see about such times before you die.[43]

Wilford Woodruff taught the Saints that they must be prepared, for "the Lord is not going to disappoint either Babylon or Zion, with regard to famine, pestilence, earthquakes or storms," and he admonished them to "lay up your wheat and other provision against a day of need, for the day will come when they will be wanted, and no mistake about it." He said that *"we shall want bread, and the Gentiles will want bread, and if we are wise we shall have something to feed them and ourselves when famine comes."*[44] President Brigham Young asserted that the Saints would not feel the effect of famine if they would lay in their supply of food and be continually prepared:

> I have never promised a famine to the Latter-day Saints, if we will do half right. You have never heard it drop from my lips that a famine would come upon this people. There never will, if we will only do half right, and we expect to do better than that.[45]

Summary

Latter-day Saint prophets have made many prophecies concerning a series of internal wars which will bring about the collapse of the government and dominion of the United States. The wars are to have the following characteristics and results:

1. The wars will involve family strife. Fathers will be pitted against their sons and mothers will fight against their daughters.
2. Instead of one general war, there will be many local wars involving neighborhoods, cities, and states.
3. Instead of battles between armies, the struggles will be between mobs which will roam from one location to another intent on destroying their opposition.
4. Farming and manufacturing will cease. The farmers will flee before the pillaging mobs. This will, undoubtedly, cause famine and starvation in many areas.
5. It appears that the Lamanites, or Indians of North, Central, and South America will also rise up and challenge the Gentile people during this period of internal wars.

43. JD, 3:262.
44. JD, 18:121.
45. JD, 12:241.

6. The struggle in the United States will take place after the times of the Gentiles are fulfilled—in the same period as earthquakes, droughts, great storms, and pestilence are being poured out upon that nation and the other nations of the world.

7. Wars will also rage during this period in foreign lands.

8. The Saints will gather to the tops of the mountains for protection. Those members of the Church who remain in other areas of the country will be persecuted and driven by the mobs.

9. Righteous non-members will also come to the tops of the mountains for protection.

10. The Saints and Gentiles in the tops of the mountains will eventually be completely cut off from the rest of the country.

11. The great increase in population in the West will place the people in danger of famine unless the Saints have sufficient food supplies stored to provide for the newcomers as well as for themselves.

12. The wars will cause the complete collapse of national and state governments in the United States.

CHAPTER V
The Establishment of the Kingdom of God

**When The United States Government Fails,
The Saints Will Uphold The Constitution**

As was seen in the preceding chapter, the internal conflict in the United States will be so extensive that governmental power will cease and law enforcement will become ineffective. Because of the wasting away and collapse of the national government, the Saints will find it necessary to maintain their own government so that law and order can be preserved. This matter was explained by Orson Pratt:

> God has sent forth his warning message in the midst of this nation, but they have rejected it and treated his servants with contempt; the Lord has gathered out his people from their midst, and has planted them here in these mountains; and *he will speedily fulfill the prophecy in relation to the overthrow of this nation, and their destruction. We shall be obliged to have a government to preserve ourselves in unity and peace; for they, through being wasted away, will not have power to govern;* for state will be divided against state, city against city, town against town, and the whole country will be in terror and confusion; mobocracy will prevail and their [sic] will be no security, through this great Republic, for the lives or property of the people. *When that time shall arrive, we shall necessarily want to carry out the principles of our great constitution and, as the people of God, we shall want to see those principles magnified, according to the order of union and oneness which prevails among the people of God.* We can magnify it, and all be united without having democrats or republicans and all kinds of religions; we can magnify it according to the spirit and letter of the constitution, though *we are united in politics, religion, and everything else.*[1]

The early Church leaders taught that the government the Saints were to establish was to be apart from the Church. For instance, Elder George Q. Cannon, in reply to the question "is

1. DEN, 8:265, October 2, 1875.

the Church of God, and the kingdom of God the same organization?" said,

> We are informed that some of the brethren hold that they are separate.
>
> This is the correct view to take. *The Kingdom of God is a separate organization from the Church of God.*[2]

A problem in terminology arises because of the political organization being called the "Kingdom of God." In many instances reference is made to Christ's Church on the earth as the "kingdom of God" and the term is contrasted with the term "kingdom of Heaven," or the state of exaltation. The reader should understand that the term "kingdom of God" has been used in the quotations cited in this chapter as having reference to a political organization and not to the Church.

When the United States government ceases to exist the Elders of Israel will assume the responsibility for governing the remainder of the people of this nation. They will sustain the Constitution and hold it inviolate. Church leaders have commented upon this principle in clarifying a prophesy attributed to Joseph Smith. Said Brigham Young,

> Will the Constitution be destroyed? No: it will be held inviolate by this people; and, as Joseph Smith said, *"The time will come when the destiny of the nation will hang upon a single thread. At that critical juncture, this people will step forth and save it from the threatened destruction."* It will be so.[3]

Orson Hyde gave further clarification to the matter:

> It is said that brother Joseph in his lifetime declared that the Elders of this Church should step forth at a particular time when the Constitution should be in danger, and rescue it, and save it. This may be so; but I do not recollect that he said exactly so. *I believe he said something like this — that the time would come when the Constitution and the country would be in danger of an overthrow; and said he, if the Constitution be saved at all, it will be by the Elders of this Church.* I believe this is about the language as nearly as I can recollect it.
>
> The question is whether it will be saved at all, or not. I do not know that it matters to us whether it is or not: the Lord will provide for and take care of his people, if we do every duty,

---

2. HC, 7:382.
3. JD, 7:15.
   For further consideration of the Constitution's "hanging by a thread," see the appendix.

and fear and honour him, and keep his commandments; and *he will not leave us without a Constitution.*[4]

In 1879, President John Taylor alluded to the strain which will be placed on the Constitution and the manner in which the Saints will come forward to uphold it:

> *When the people shall have torn to shreds the Constitution of the United States the Elders of Israel will be found holding it up to the nations of the earth and proclaiming liberty and equal rights to all men,* and extending the hand of fellowship to the oppressed of all nations. This is part of the programme, and as long as we do what is right and fear God, he will help us and stand by us under all circumstances.[5]

The Church looks upon the United States Constitution as a preparation for the Kingdom of God which will someday bear universal rule. John Taylor thought of it as "the entering wedge for the introduction of a new era, and in it were introduced principles for the birth and organization of a new world."[6] Orson Pratt said the Constitution is a "stepping stone to a form of government infinitely greater and more perfect—a government founded upon Divine laws, with all its institutions, ordinances, and officers appointed by the God of heaven."[7]

The Foundation for The Kingdom of God Was Laid through Revelation to Joseph Smith

The political "Kingdom of God," the government which the Saints will find it necessary to establish during this period of stress, will not be a new organization. Instead, it will be the re-establishment of a government which was first established by the Lord through the instrumentality of Joseph Smith. The keys of the Kingdom of God are said to have been on the earth since the early days of the Church. Said a revelation in 1831:

> *The keys of the kingdom of God are committed unto man on the earth,* and from thence shall the gospel roll forth unto the ends of the earth, as the stone which is cut out of the mountain without hands shall roll forth, until it has filled the whole earth. . . .

4. JD, 6:152.
5. JD, 21:8.
6. JD, 21:31.
7. JD, 7:215.

Call upon the Lord, that his kingdom may go forth upon the earth, that the inhabitants thereof may receive it, and be prepared for the days to come, in the which the *Son of Man shall come down in heaven, clothed in the brightness of his glory, to meet the kingdom of God which is set up on the earth.*

Wherefore, may the kingdom of God go forth, that the kingdom of heaven may come.[8]

Brigham Young stated that the Prophet Joseph Smith established the kingdom during the last few months before his martyrdom and said that the constitution of this kingdom was given by revelation:

The Prophet gave a full and complete organization to this kingdom the Spring before he was killed. . . . I shall not tell you the names of the members of this kingdom, neither shall I read to you its constitution, but *the constitution was given by revelation. The day will come when it will be organized in strength and power.*[9]

The Prophet apparently recorded the organization of this council and stated its earliest aims in the minutes of a meeting he held on March 11, 1844:

Present—Joseph Smith, Hyrum Smith, Brigham Young, Heber C. Kimball, Willard Richards, Parley P. Pratt, Orson Pratt, John Taylor, George A. Smith, William W. Phelps, John M. Bernhisel, Lucien Woodworth, George Miller, Alexander Badlam, Peter Haws, Erastus Snow, Reynolds Cahoon, Amos Fielding, Alpheus Cutler, Levi Richards, Newel K. Whitney, Lorenzo D. Wasson, and William Clayton, *whom I organized into a special council*, to take into consideration the subject matter contained in the above letters, and also the best *policy for this people to adopt to obtain their rights from the nation and insure protection for themselves and children; and to secure a resting place in the mountains, or some uninhabited region*, where we can enjoy the liberty of conscience guaranteed to us by the Constitution of our country, rendered doubly sacred by the precious blood of our fathers, and denied to us by the present authorities who have smuggled themselves into power in the States and Nation.[10]

The council grew and was termed the "General Council" or the "Council of Fifty." Brigham Young alluded to the early

8. D & C 65:2, 5-6.
9. JD, 17:156-57.
10. HC, 6:260-61.

stage of the political Kingdom of God in a letter he wrote on May 3, 1844, in which he said,

> The kingdom is organized; and although as yet no bigger than a grain of mustard seed, the little plant is in a flourishing condition and our prospects brighter than ever.[11]

An event shortly after the death of the Prophet serves to establish the relationship between the Council of Fifty and the Church. At this time, there was confusion among some members of the Church because of the Prophet's martyrdom. Bishop George Miller and Alexander Badlam wanted the Council of Fifty to meet and put the Church in order. The *History of the Church* records the reply their request received:

> *They were told that the Council of Fifty was not a church organization, but was composed of members irrespective of their religious faith,* and organized for the purpose of consulting on the best manner of obtaining redress of grievances from our enemies, and to devise means to find and locate in some place where we could live in peace; and that *the organization of the church belonged to the priesthood alone.*[12]

It was partly under the direction of the General Council, or the Council of Fifty, that the Saints undertook their westward exodus. Brigham Young recorded on March 1, 1845 that he "met with the 'General Council' at the Seventies Hall. We decided to send nine brethren westward, to search out a location for the Saints."[13] On September 9, 1845, he recorded,

> General Council [Council of Fifty] met. Resolved that a company of 1500 men be selected to go to Great Salt Lake valley and that a committee of five be appointed to gather information relative to emigration, and report the same to the council.[14]

However, the brethren seemed to realize that the time for the rise to power of the Kingdom of God was not yet ripe, and that the Council in that day was fulfilling only a preparatory function. Brigham Young said in 1885,

> As was observed by Brother Pratt [this morning] that kingdom [i.e. of God] is actually organized and the inhabitants of

---

11. HC, 7:381.
12. HC, 7:213.
13. HC, 7:379.
14. HC, 7:439.

the earth do not know it. If this people know anything about it, all right; *it is organized preparatory to taking effect in the due time of the Lord,* and in the manner that shall please him.[15]

The Council of Fifty, like the practice of plural marriage, was a cause of antagonism between the members and non-members during the early years of the Church in Utah. Because of these difficulties, both the ideology and the practice of the political Kingdom of God were discontinued until the time approached for their future need. This time will begin when state and federal government collapses in the United States and the Saints will have to establish a government of their own.

The Future Policy of The Kingdom of God

If the assumption is valid that the Council of Fifty will be organized on the same principles in the coming period as it was originally, then the membership will not be limited to Latter-day Saint Church members. Brigham Young stated,

> As observed by one of the speakers this morning *that kingdom grows out of the Church of Jesus Christ of Latter-day Saints, but it is not the church; for a man may be a legislator in that body which will issue laws to sustain the inhabitants of the earth in their individual rights and still not belong to the Church of Jesus Christ at all.* And further though a man may not even believe in any religion it would be perfectly right, when necessary, to give him the privilege of holding a seat among that body which will make laws to govern all the nations of the earth and control those who make no profession of religion at all.[16]

This was also taught by George Q. Cannon, who said,

> *There may be men acting as officers in the Kingdom of God who will not be members of the Church of Jesus Christ of Latter-day Saints. On this point the Prophet Joseph gave particular instructions before his death,* and gave an example, which he asked the younger elders who were present to always remember. It was to the effect that men might be chosen to officiate as members of the Kingdom of God who had no standing in the Church of Jesus Christ of Latter-day Saints.[17]

---

15. HC, 7:381.
16. HC, 7:381-82.
17. HC, 7:382.

According to Brigham Young, the Kingdom of God will be dependent upon revelation from God to sustain it. Such a Government is called a theocracy, or "God-guided" government:

> Few, if any, understand *what a theocratic government is. . . . its subjects will recognize the will and dictation of the Almighty.* The kingdom of God circumscribes and comprehends the municipal laws for the people in their outward government, to which pertain the Gospel covenants, by which the people can be saved; and those covenants pertain to fellowship and faithfulness.[18]

He said also:

> What do I understand by a theocratic government? *One in which all laws are enacted and executed in righteousness, and whose officers possess that power which proceedeth from the Almighty.* That is the kind of government I allude to when I speak of a theocratic government, or the kingdom of God upon the earth. It is, in short, the eternal powers of the Gods.[19]

According to John Taylor, before men will accept the dominion of the Kingdom of God, the Church must preach the first principles to all nations to prepare them:

> *Before there could be a kingdom of God, there must be a Church of God, and hence the first principles of the Gospel were needed to be preached to all nations,* as they were formerly when the Lord Jesus Christ and others made their appearance on the earth. And why so? Because of the impossibility of introducing the law of God among a people who would not be subject to and be guided by the spirit of revelation.[20]

The change from the United States Government to the rule of the Council of Fifty and the political Kingdom of God may not be too great. According to President Young, the theocratic government

> Is a republican government, and differs but little in form from our National, State, and Territorial Governments. . . .
>
> *The Constitution and laws of the United States resemble a theocracy more closely than any government now on the earth,* or that ever has been, so far as we know, except the

---

18. JD, 6:342.
19. JD, 6:346-47.
20. JD, 18:137.

government of the children of Israel to the time when they elected a king.[21]

The Kingdom of God will rule fairly and will allow all men to follow the dictates of their own conscience. George Q. Cannon said,

> The Kingdom of God when established will not be for the protection of the Church of Jesus Christ of Latter-day Saints alone, but for the protection of all men, whatever their religious views or opinions may be. Under its rule, no one will be permitted to overstep the proper bounds or to interfere with the rights of others.[22]

Brigham Young said that the political Kingdom of God will serve to protect all men in their rights, regardless of their creed. However, he contrasted this policy with that of the Church, which is designed for the perfection of only those who hold membership in it:

> *This kingdom is the kingdom that Daniel spoke of, which was to be set up in the last days; it is the kingdom that is not to be given to another people; it is the kingdom that is to be held by the servants of God, to rule the nations of the earth*, to send forth those laws and ordinances that shall be suitable and that shall apply themselves to the Church of Jesus Christ of Latter-day Saints; that will apply themselves to the mother Church, "the holy Catholic Church;" they will commend themselves to every Protestant Church upon the earth; they will commend themselves to every class of infidels, and *will throw their protecting arms around the whole human family, protecting them in their rights.* If they wish to worship a white dog, they will have the privilege, if they wish to worship the sun they will have the privilege, if they wish to worship a man they will have the privilege, and if they wish to worship the "unknown God" they will have the privilege. *This kingdom will circumscribe them all and will issue laws and ordinances to protect them in their rights* — every right that every people, sect and person can enjoy, and the full liberty that God has granted to them without molestation.
>
>   Can you understand me? *This Church of Jesus Christ of Latter-day Saints is organized for the building up of this Church alone; it is not for the building up of Catholicism, it it is not for promoting any or all the dissentients from the*

---

21. JD, 6:342.
22. HC, 7:382.

Mother Church, it is alone for the Church of Jesus Christ of Latter-day Saints and for no other body of people. When we organize according to these laws and ordinances we make this people one, but we do not bring in the Methodists, Presbyterians or Calvinists, they are independent of themselves.[23]

The Kingdom of God Will Eventually Gain World-Wide Dominion

The future growth of the Kingdom of God can be described as having three stages:

1. The beginning stage, when it will be organized in the West;
2. The growth stage, during which it will rise in power as wars and disasters cause the dominion of other nations to diminish;
3. The world-ruling stage, when it will be the political kingdom through which Christ will rule during the millennium.

In the beginning stage the Kingdom of God will be small and will function only in the area controlled by the Saints in the tops of the Western Mountains. Elder Parley P. Pratt spoke of the smallness of the political kingdom of God as it will exist in this stage and said it will function only where the Saints are in the majority:

> Hence the gathering of the Saints; *the organization of the kingdom of God, religiously and politically,* if you will; . . . *It will be one of the smallest of governments upon this earth,* to which a grain of mustard seed is brought as a comparison. *When we see the signs in the sun, moon, and stars, and among different nations, it proves that the kingdom of God is nigh at hand;* we may then begin to look around for it. We must not look to Russia, or to England, to become this kingdom, but to the smallest of the governments in this world, one so small that it is compared to a grain of mustard seed. Where must we look for it? . . . *among the Saints right here, where they compose the majority,* where there is not another larger government, where they are hemmed in with mountains, and can establish peace, and a kingdom, and a government, and a law.[24]

But even before it can be established at this time, the Saints will have to be prepared to receive the responsibility of govern-

23. JD, 17:156.
24. JD, 1:180-82.

ing properly. Daniel H. Wells, when telling how he would answer the question "When will the kingdom be given into the hands of the Saints of the most high God?" said that it would be

> *Just as soon as the Lord finds that He has a people upon the earth who will uphold and sustain that kingdom, who shall be found capable of maintaining its interests and of extending its influence upon the earth.* When he finds that he has such a people, a people who will stand firm and faithful to him, a people that will not turn it over into tbe [sic] lap of the devil, then, and not until then, will he give "the kingdom" into the hands of the Saints of the most high, in its power and influence when it shall fill the whole earth. . . it depends, in a great measure, upon the people themselves, as to how soon the kingdom spoken of by Daniel shall be given into the hands of the Saints of God. *When we shall prove ourselves faithful in every emergency that may arise, and capable to contend and grapple with every difficulty that threatens our peace and welfare, and to overcome every obstacle that may tend to impede the progress of the Church and kingdom of God upon the earth*, then our heavenly Father will have confidence in us, and then he will be able to trust us.[25]

The opportunity to "prove ourselves faithful in every emergency that may arise," of which he spoke, will no doubt have presented itself in the warfare and judgments which will have taken place in the United States and other nations by that time. According to John Taylor, the great conflicts of that day will provide the Kingdom of God with a definite objective:

> The Almighty has established this kingdom with order and laws and every thing pertaining thereto, that we might understand his will and operate in his kingdom, that we might be taught of God and understand correct principles, that *when the nations shall be convulsed, we may stand forth as saviours, and do that which will be best calculated to produce the well-being of the human family and finally redeem a ruined world, not only in a religious but in a political point of view.*[26]

After its organizational period in the West in which it will be reestablished in a similar state to the way it previously functioned, the Kingdom of God will enter its second stage. In this era it will be carried by the Saints back to Jackson County,

---

25. JD, 23:305.
26. JD, 9:342.

Missouri. There it will begin to take on the aspects of a world power. John Taylor told of the struggle which it would undergo:

> Now as to the great future what shall we say? Why, a little stone has been cut out of the mountains without hands, and this little stone is becoming a great nation, and it will eventually fill the whole earth. How will it fill it, religiously? Yes, *and politically too, for it will have the rule, the power, the authority, the dominion in its own hands. This is the position that we are destined to occupy. . . . I expect one nation after another to rise against us until they will all be broken to pieces.* We have a great many things to accomplish; we need not think that we have no business to attend to or that the world has gone through its regeneration for *it has got to be struggle after struggle, and power after power will be arrayed against us,* and then, if we have not learned it we shall learn that God is our strength and that in him only can we trust.[27]

Parley P. Pratt told how other kingdoms will be collapsing as the Kingdom of God rises:

> Now, *when the times of the Gentiles are fulfilled there will be an uprooting of their governments and institutions,* and of their civil, political, and religious polity. There will be a shaking of nations, a downfall of empires, an upturning of thrones and dominions, as Daniel has foretold, and the kingdom and power, and *rule on the earth will return to another people,* and exist under another polity, as Daniel has further foretold.[28]

According to the proclamation issued by the Quorum of the Twelve Apostles shortly after the Prophet Joseph's death, the leaders of nations will recognize the rise in power of the Kingdom of God. The proclamation states that they will not be able to remain neutral, but will either support it or attack it:

> There is also another consideration of vast importance to all the rulers and people of the world in regard to this matter. It is this: — *as this work progresses in its onward course, and becomes more and more an object of political and religious interest and excitement, no king, ruler, or subject — no community or individual will stand neutral; all will at length be influenced by one spirit or the other,* and will take sides either for or against the kingdom of God, and the fulfillment of the

27. JD, 9:343.
28. JD, 3:135.

Prophets in the great restoration and return of His long-dis-
persed covenant people. . .

You cannot, therefore, stand as idle and disinterested spec-
tators of the *scenes and events which are calculated, in their
very nature, to reduce all nations and creeds to one political
and religious standard*, and thus put an end to Babel forms and
names, and to strife and war. You will, therefore, either be led
by the good Spirit to cast in your lot, and to take a lively interest with the Saints of the Most High, and the covenant
people of the Lord; or, on the other hand, you will become
their inveterate enemy, and oppose them by every means in your
power.[29]

Joseph Smith detailed the manner in which some nations
will react to the rise of the Kingdom of God. Said he in 1843,

In these days God will set up a kingdom, never to be
thrown down, for other kingdoms to come unto. And these
kingdoms that will not let the Gospel be preached will be
humbled until they will.

*England, Germany, Norway, Denmark, Sweden, Switzer-
land, Holland, and Belgium* have a considerable amount of
blood of Israel among their people which must be gathered.
*These nations will submit to the kingdom of God. England will
be the last of these kingdoms to surrender, but when she does
she will do it as a whole* in comparison as she threw off the
Catholic power.[30]

During this period the Kingdom of God will become a standard unto the nations. Parley P. Pratt says that it will be the standard to which the Ten Tribes will come when they return from
the North:

This government has to maintain its character, *and become a
standard*, having developed in it every principle for the salvation of the living and the dead; to hold the keys of the Priesthood that bear rule in heaven, on earth, and in hell, and maintain a people built upon it, which is all necessary in order to
become a standard. *To this the Ten Tribes will look*, to this
will look the scattered remnants that are aware of the promise
to Abraham, that in his seed, and not in some other Priesthood
and lineage, shall all the nations and people of the earth be
blessed.[31]

29. *Millennial Star,* October 22, 1845.
30. Prophecy recorded by Edwin Rushton and Theodore Turley.
31. JD, 1:182.

The Second Coming of Christ will initiate the third stage of progress for the Kingdom of God. It will be in that stage that it will bear universal rule. At that time it will function with capitals both in the New Jerusalem (Missouri) and in the old Jerusalem (Palestine). Brigham Young commented on this government and the rule it would extend:

> We have a nation here in the mountains that will be a kingdom by-and-by, and be governed by pure laws and principles. What do you call yourselves? some may ask. Here are the people that constitute the kingdom of God. *It may be some time before that kingdom is fully developed, but the time will come when the kingdom of God will reign free and independent.*
>
> There will be a kingdom on the earth, that will be controlled upon the same basis, in part, as that of the Government of the United States; and it will govern and protect in their rights the various classes of men, irrespective of their different modes of worship; *for the law must go forth from Zion, and the word of the Lord from Jerusalem, and the Lord* Jesus will govern every nation and kingdom upon the earth.[32]

Orson Pratt said that the day will come

> When the United States government, and all others, will be uprooted and the kingdoms in this world will be united in one, and the kingdom of God will govern the whole earth.
>
> The nucleus of such a government is formed and its laws have emanated from the throne of God.[33]

He also spoke of the respect which this government will hold from the nations of the world:

> The law for the government of all nations will go forth from Zion as the laws for the government of the United States now go forth from Washington. *Zion will be the seat of government and her officers will be far more respected, and have far more influence, than those of any government on earth; all nations will yield perfect obedience to their command and counsels.*[34]

Charles W. Penrose summed up the world rule which the Kingdom of God would exercise under the direction of Christ during the Millennium:

> Now, we look for the coming of our Lord Jesus Christ, and we expect it just as much as when the sun goes down we expect

---

32. JD, 5:329-30.
33. Orson Pratt, *The Seer,* Vol. I, October, 1853, pp. 147-48.
34. *Ibid.,* Vol. II, pp. 266-67.

it to rise above the hill tops in the morning. And when He comes we expect it will be Himself—Jesus of Nazareth, our Elder Brother, the firstborn of God in the spirit world, the Only Begotten of God in the flesh. *We expect that He will come and reign over the earth as King of kings and lord of lords, and we expect that all kingdoms, all governments, and all institutions that men have set up will be broken down,* and as Nebuchadnezzar saw them in the vision which Daniel interpreted, they will become as the chaff of the summer threshing floor, and be swept away, and no place found for them upon the face of the whole earth; because *the Kingdom of God and of His Christ will prevail everywhere, and it will cover the earth.* For it is the kingdom that was spoken of by the Prophets, and we are told that "the kingdom and the dominion and the greatness of the kingdom under the whole heavens"—that is over all the earth, is it not? —shall be His kingdom and *shall "be given into the hands of the people of the Saints of the Most High, and their kingdom shall be an everlasting kingdom."* Now, we expect the fulfillment of all these things, and when they come to pass they will occur just as they are written, like other prophecies have been accomplished.[35]

Further explanation of this era will be made in the chapter entitled "The Millennium."

Summary

When law, order, and government collapse in the United States, the Church will be compelled to establish a government to preserve peace in the Western United States. This government will be known as the "Kingdom of God." Much has been said about the history, characteristics, and future of this kingdom:

1. *History*
   A. The Kingdom of God was first organized by Joseph Smith shortly before his death.
   B. It was to be governed by a "General Council" which was also called the "Council of Fifty."
   C. This organization played an important part in the Westward exodus of the Church, but became a source of antagonism to the non-members in the West and so it was discontinued by the Church.

---

35. JD, 25:222.

2. *Characteristics* (When it is organized in the future.)

  A. The Kingdom of God will be led by a Council of Fifty. Some of them might not be Latter-day Saints.

  B. It will uphold the rights of men of all creeds and will be dedicated to rule justly.

  C. The Kingdom will be a theocracy.

  D. It will uphold the principles of the United States Constitution and be somewhat similar in method of operation to the present United States Government.

  E. In the Kingdom will be included people of all nations.

3. *Future* (The future Kingdom of God will progress through three stages of growth.)

  A. *The beginning stage* — The Saints will be in the West. Here the influence of the Kingdom will be relatively limited and unknown.

  B. *The growth stage* — During this period many of the Saints will journey from the West to Missouri to establish the New Jerusalem. There the Kingdom of God will rise in power, not by waging war on other nations, but by being a standard of peace and lawfulness while other governments collapse through corruption and war.

  C. The world-ruling stage — This period will commence with the second coming of Christ and will take place during the Millennium.

CHAPTER VI
Establishment of the New Jerusalem

During the internal conflict in the United States, but after many of the cities have fallen and mobocracy has gained control, it is expected that the Saints in the Rocky Mountains will prepare to journey eastward and redeem the promised land of Zion. This land, centering at Independence, Jackson County, Missouri, has been regarded as the final gathering place for the Latter-day Saints since the early days of the Church. Though they were driven from their homes in Missouri over a hundred years ago, the Saints still anticipate the time when they will be called to return and reclaim their lost possessions and establish a city of Zion in righteousness.

A Leader Like Unto Moses Is To Be Chosen

The *Doctrine and Covenants* speaks of a leader like unto Moses who will be chosen by God to lead the people in the redemption of Zion:

> Behold, I say unto you, *the redemption of Zion must needs come by power;*
>
> *Therefore, I will raise up unto my people a man, who shall lead them like as Moses led the children of Israel.*
>
> For ye are the children of Israel, and out of the seed of Abraham, and ye must needs be let out of bondage by power, and with a stretched-out arm.[1]

During the early days of the Church, and especially during the period shortly after the Saints came to the West, there was a great deal of speculation concerning the identity of this future leader. A statement by Orson Pratt demonstrates the possibilities which have been considered:

> Indeed, before we can go back to inherit this land in all its fulness of perfection, *God has promised that he would raise up a man like unto Moses. Who this man will be I do not know;* it may be a person with whom we are entirely unacquainted;

1. D & C, 103:15-17.

it may be one of our infant children; it may be some person not yet born; it may be some one of middle age. But suffice it to say, that God will raise up such a man, and he will show forth his power through him, and through the people that he will lead forth to inherit that country, as he did through our fathers in the wilderness.[2]

While discussing the *Doctrine and Covenants* prophecy of the man who would be raised up by God, Pratt stated on another occasion that

Whether that man is now in existence, or whether it is some one yet to be born; or whether it is our present leader who has led us forth into these valleys of the mountains, whether God will grant unto us the great blessing to have his life spared to lead forth his people like a Moses, we perhaps may not all know. He has done a great and wonderful work in leading forth this people into this land and building up these cities in this desert country; and I feel in my heart to say, Would to God that his life may be prolonged like Moses, in days of old, who, when he was eighty years old, was sent forth to redeem the people of Israel from bondage. God is not under the necessity of choosing a young man, he can make a man eighty years of age full of vigor, strength and health, and he may spare our present leader to lead this people on our return to Jackson County. But whether it be he or some other person, *God will surely fulfill this promise. . . .* whether President Young is the man, or whether the Lord shall hereafter raise up a man for that purpose, *we do know that when that day comes the Lord will not only send his angels before the army of Israel, but his presence will also be there.*[3]

Some of the leaders of the Church have raised the question of the possibility of Joseph Smith being resurrected to fulfill this mission. In connection with his discussion of the matter which was just cited, Orson Pratt stated,

This was given before our Prophet Joseph Smith was taken out of our midst. Many of us no doubt thought when that revelation was given that Joseph would be the man. . . . *I do not know but he will yet. God's arm is not shortened that he cannot raise him up even from the tomb.* We are living in the dispensation of the fullness of times, the dispensation of the resurrection, and *there may be some who will wake from their tombs for*

---

2. JD, 21:153.
3. JD, 15:362-63.

certain purposes and to bring to pass certain transactions on the earth decreed by the Great Jehovah; and if the Lord sees proper to bring forth that man just before the winding up scene to lead forth the army of Israel, he will do so. And if he feels disposed to send him forth as a spiritual personage to lead the camp of Israel to the land of their inheritance, all right.[4]

Another of the early apostles, Erastus Snow, was of the opinion that Joseph would be resurrected long before Christ's coming in glory. In 1884, after telling how the Prophet and others had filled a mission preaching in the Spirit World, he spoke of a future mission they would fulfill:

The next mission will be to come and prepare the way in Zion, and in her Stakes, and in the temples of our God for turning the key of the resurrection of the dead, to bring forth those that are asleep, and to exalt them among the Gods. *And who will be first and foremost? Why, he whom God has chosen and placed first and foremost to hold the keys of this last dispensation.* How long will it be? It is not given to me to say the month, the day, or the hour; but it is given unto me to say that that time is nigh at hand. *The time is drawing near (much nearer than scarcely any of us can now comprehend) when Joseph will be clothed upon with immortality, when his brother Hyrum will be clothed upon with immortality, when the martyrs will be raised from the dead, together with their faithful brethren* who have performed a good mission in the spirit world — they, too, will be called to assist in the work of the glorious resurrection. The Lord Jesus, who was the first fruits of the dead, the first fruit of them that sleep, and who holds the keys of the resurrection, *will bring to pass the resurrection of the Prophet Joseph and his brethren, and will set them to work in bringing about the resurrection of their brethren* as he has set them to work in all the other branches of the labor from the beginning.[5]

After telling of his belief that the resurrection of the Prophet was not too far away Elder Snow emphasized that this would be before the Lord appears in the temple[6] before the Savior's coming in glory:

---

4. JD, 15:362-63.
5. JD, 25:33-34.
6. This is apparently Christ's appearance in the Temple at the New Jerusalem. For a discussion of this appearance see the next chapter.

*And the Lord Jesus will appear and show Himself unto His
servants in His temple in holy places, to counsel and instruct
and direct.* He will appear in the glory of His Father, in His
resurrected body, among those who can endure His presence
and glory. And *all this I expect long before He will waste away
and destroy the wicked from off the face of the earth.*[7]

Heber C. Kimball also believed and prophesied that Joseph
Smith would return before the second coming of the Lord and
associated his return with this period. After prophesying of the
destruction which would sweep the western portion of Missouri,
he foresaw that

The pressure will become so great that the more righteous
among them will cry unto the Lord day and night until deliverance comes.

*Then the Prophet Joseph and others will make their ap-
pearance and those who have remained faithful will be se-
lected to return to Jackson County, Missouri,* and take part in
the upbuilding of that beautiful city, the New Jerusalem.[8]

Thus the authorities of the Church have anticipated the
raising up of a leader who will guide the Saints in their establishment of the New Jerusalem, and several have expressed the
thought that this person may be Joseph Smith as a resurrected
being. Suffice it to say that Latter-day Saints expect to return
to Jackson County under inspired leadership and with power.

The Eastward Journey of The Saints While
Strife Continues in The United States

After the decision to return to Jackson County has been
made, it is anticipated that the Saints will make the eastward
journey as a group. Orson Pratt gave a colorful description of the
Saints' return:

We shall go back to Jackson County. . . . when we go back,
there will be a very large organization consisting of thousands,
and tens of thousands, and they will march forward, *the glory
of God overshadowing their camp by day in the form of a
cloud, and a pillar of flaming fire by night, the Lord's voice
being uttered forth before his army. . . .*

*Will not this produce terror upon all the nations of the
earth?* Will not armies of this description, though they may

---

7. JD, 25:34.
8. *Prophetic Sayings of Heber C. Kimball to Amanda H. Wilcox.*

not be as numerous as the armies of the world, cause a terror to fall upon the nations? The Lord says the banners of Zion shall be terrible.[9]

It would appear that his description is an interpretation of Isaiah 4:5-6. This interpretation is perhaps inappropriate as a description of the journey. At least, though, his comment indicates the magnitude of the undertaking and that the members of the Church will be organized into a single group. On another occasion he said that "there may be a few individuals go to prepare the way, to purchase a little more land and get things in order; but when that is accomplished, *this people as a body will return to that land*, the Lord going with them."[10]

A vision recorded by Joseph Smith was given to his scribe in the Kirtland Temple, in which "the armies of heaven protecting the Saints in their return to Zion"[11] were seen. It would seem that if the Saints will need the protection of a heavenly army the eastward journey will take place during the period of internal strife. This was certainly Orson Pratt's belief:

> Well then, to return to the prophesying, *when the time shall come that the Lord shall waste away this nation, he will give commandment to this people to return* and possess their own inheritance which they purchased some forty-four years ago in the state of Missouri.[12]

A statement apparently made by Joseph Smith in 1843 seems to fix the time of the Saints' return to Missouri as during the era of internal strife. He said, "when you see this land bound with iron you may look toward Jackson County."[13] Joseph F. Smith expressed his view also that this will be a time of strife and that the saints may have to defend themselves from foes on the right hand and on the left.

> When God leads the people back to Jackson County, how will he do it? Let me picture to you how some of us may be gathered and led to Jackson County. *I think I see two or three hundred thousand people wending their way across the great plain enduring the nameless hardships of the journey, herding and guarding their cattle by day and by night, and defending*

---

9. JD, 15:364.
10. JD, 17:304.
11. HC, 2:381.
12. DEN, Vol. 8, No. 265, Oct. 2, 1875.
13. Prophecy recorded by Edwin Rushton and Theodore Turley.

Location of Jackson County, Missouri.

*themselves and little ones from foes on the right hand and on
the left, as when they came here.* They will find the journey
back to Jackson County will be as real as when they came out
here. Now, mark it. And though you may be led by the power
*of God "with a stretched out arm," it will not be more mani-
fest than the leading the people out here to those that participate in it. They will think there are a great many hardships
to endure in this manifestation of the power of God,* and it
will be left, perhaps to their children to see the glory of their
deliverance, just as it is left for us to see the glory of our
former deliverance from the hands of those that sought to destroy us.[14]

It would seem, then, that the return to Jackson County will
be during the period of internal wars, and that the Saints will
encounter opposition during their journey. Of interest also is
the fact that though this prophetic description was uttered long
after the coming of the railroad, he does not envision modern
transportation methods as being used in the journey. Instead, the
people will be "herding and guarding their cattle" by the way.
This prediction might be regarded as an indication of a great
destruction of this nation's roads and transportation system during the period of internal strife. This interpretation is borne out,
perhaps, by a vision attributed to Wilford Woodruff in which he
purportedly saw various sections of the United States as it was
being engulfed by a terrible disease. Speaking of the area just
west of Omaha, Nebraska, the account states,

As I passed along upon my way east, I saw the road full of
people, mostly women, with just what they could carry in
bundles on their backs traveling to the mountains on foot.

I wondered how they could get through with such a small
pack on their back. It was remarkable to me that there were
so few men among them. *It did not seem to me as though the
cars were running. The rails looked rusty and abandoned.*[15]

Though the trip eastward is expected to be a perilous journey, the following statement by Orson Pratt describes the peaceable manner in which he expects the Saints will proceed. He
also explains that the group returning will be made up of the
wives and children, as well as the Elders of Israel:

---

14. JD, 24:156-57.
15. Vision attributed to Wilford Woodruff, as quoted in Robert W. and
    Elizabeth A. Smith, *The Last Days* (Salt Lake City: Pyramid Press, 1948)
    Tenth Edition, p. 78.

Perhaps you may inquire if we expect to return as a majority. Yes. *Do we expect to return as a great people? Yes. Do we expect to return with our wives and our children? Yes.* Do we expect to return in a peaceable manner? Of course. Have you ever seen any other feeling on the part of the Latter-day Saints, only to promote peace wherever they may settle? What has been our object from the commencement? Peace and good-will to all men.[16]

Many Saints Will Remain in The West

Although it is anticipated that "tens of thousands" of the Saints will travel eastwards, Brigham Young made it clear that not all will journey to Jackson County. Many members of the Church will remain behind and maintain their homes in the western mountains:

Are we going back to Jackson County? Yes. When? As soon as the way opens up. Are we all going? O no! of course not. The country is not large enough to hold our present numbers. When we do return there, *will there be any less remaining in these mountains than we number today? No, there may be a hundred then for every single one that is there now.* It is folly in men to suppose that we are going to break up these our hard earned homes to make others in a new country.[17]

Orson Pratt agreed that there will be Saints in both places:

We do not expect that when the time shall come, that all Latter-day Saints, who now occupy the mountain valleys, will go in one consolidated body, leaving this land totally without inhabitants. We do not expect any such thing. But we do expect, that there will be a period in the future history of the Church when many hundreds of this people — our youth, for

---

16. JD, 24:23.
17. JD, 18:355-56. Herein seems to lie the explanation for a prophetic statement made by Joseph Smith:
"It [the Church] will fill the Rocky Mountains. There will be tens of thousands of Latter-day Saints who will be gathered in the Rocky Mountains and there they will open the door for the establishing of the Gospel among the Lamanites who will receive the Gospel and their endowments, and the blessings of God. This people will go into the Rocky Mountains; they will there build temples to the Most High. They will raise up a posterity there, and the Latter-day Saints who dwell in these mountains will stand in the flesh until the coming of the Son of Man. The Son of Man will come to them while in the Rocky Mountains." CR, April, 1898, p. 57.

instance, who will grow up in those days, when they will be consolidated as a body, and will go to the eastern portions of the state of Kansas, and also to the western portions of the state of Missouri to settle.[18]

But he also said that "we expect that these mountains will not be the residence of all the Latter-day Saints; *we expect that the great majority of the people will emigrate.*"[19]

Those chosen to make the journey are expected to be the most worthy and the best prepared, who, as Heber C. Kimball said, "do right and honour their calling."[20]

Establishing The New Jerusalem
Under The Law of Consecration

It is expected by many that the Saints, as they arrive in Kansas and Missouri, will find the site of their New Jerusalem desolate, barren, and uninhabited. In the chapter dealing with the judgments which God will pour out upon the earth [Chapter three] prophecies were cited that God will visit that area in judgment and that "there will be no owners left to occupy the country,"[21] and that Jackson County "will be swept so clean of its inhabitants that . . . there will not be left so much as a yellow dog to wag his tail."[22] In a vision attributed to Wilford Woodruff, he was shown the condition of this area of land at the time of the laying of the New Jerusalem temple cornerstone, and recorded that "I seemed to be standing on the left bank of the Missouri and Illinois and all of Iowa were a complete desert with no living being there."[23] The repopulating of this land with a group of many thousands of the Saints arriving all at once will undoubtedly be a great challenge to the leadership of the Church. The dividing up of the land and apportionment of sites will need to be carefully governed and directed.

It appears that this will be carried out under the communal living system known in the Church as the *United Order* or the *Law of Consecration.*

In the Law of Consecration, every participating Latter-day Saint recognizes that the earth is the Lord's and consecrates him-

18. JD, 21:149.
19. JD, 24:23.
20. JD, 9:27.
21. DEN, Vol. 8, No. 265, Oct. 2, 1875.
22. *Prophetic Sayings of Heber C. Kimball to Amanda H. Wilcox.*
23. Robert W. Smith, *op cit.,* p. 80.

self and all his property to God. He then becomes a steward over a portion of the Lord's property and as an heir in the system has the right to draw upon the storehouse to develop and expand his stewardship. An allotment of land and other materials is apportioned to him to develop on the basis of the size of his family, his branch of business, and so forth. The Church gives him financial help to establish and expand his farm or business, but his progress is subject to yearly supervision and review by the Bishop. People live in family units and eat at their own tables. It is held by Latter-day Saints that a faithful and wise steward of the Lord's property will eventually receive his stewardship as an eternal inheritance.[24]

According to Orson Pratt, when the return to Missouri takes place, the Law of Consecration will immediately be put into full force and will be used in the distribution of property:

> There is one thing certain — something that you and I may depend upon, with as much certainty as we expect to get our daily food, and that is, that *the Lord our God will take this people back, and will select from among this people, a sufficient number, to make the army of Israel very great. And when that day comes, he will guide the forces of those who emigrate to their possessions in those two states,* that I have mentioned. And the land thus purchased will be no doubt, as far as possible, located in one district of country, which will be settled very differently from the way we now settle up these mountain regions. You may ask, in what respect we shall differ in settling up those countries when we go there to fulfill the commandments of the Lord? I will tell you. *No man in those localities will be permitted to receive a stewardship on those lands, unless he is willing to consecrate all his properties to the Lord. That will be among the first teachings given.* . . . *in that day the whole of our properties, amounting to a very much larger sum, will be held in trust. For whom? For the Church of Jesus Christ of Latter-Saints* [sic], *and for all this great company that will be gathered together.*[25]

The combined resources of the Saints, when they consecrate it to the Church at this time, will, it seems, be a great sum. The Latter-day Saints will apparently have more than sufficient funds to purchase additional lands for settlement and build their cities. In the words of Orson Pratt,

24. See JD, 21:150-53.
25. JD, 21:149-50.

Now, when the time comes for purchasing this land, we will have means. How this means will be brought about it is not for me to say. Perhaps the Lord will open up mines containing gold and silver, or in some other way as seemeth to him best, wealth will be poured into the laps of the Latter-day Saints till they will scarcely know what to do with it. *I will here again prophesy on the strength of former revelation that there are not people on the face of the whole globe, not even excepting London, Paris, New York, or any of the great mercantile cities of the globe—there are no people now upon the face of the earth, so rich as the Latter-day Saints will be in a few years to come.* Having their millions; therefore they will purchase the land, build up cities, towns, and villages, build a great capital city, at headquarters, in Jackson County, Missouri.[26]

Joseph Smith also reported that

The Temple in Jackson County will be built in this generation. The saints will think there will not be time to build it, but with all the help you will receive you can put up a great temple quickly. They will have all the gold, silver, and precious stones; for these things only will be used for the beautifying of the temple; all the skilled mechanics you want.[27]

A conflict seems to exist between these statements and the prophecies quoted in chapter three which say that Jackson County at that time will be without inhabitants. It would appear that in any instance in which the Saints will be able to find owners to whom they can make restitution, they will be ready and willing to do so. It should be remembered, of course, that much of the land originally belonged to the Saints.

The establishment of the Law of Consecration will apparently be a necessity, for it is a celestial law and the Lord has said that "Zion cannot be built up unless it is by the principles of the law of the celestial kingdom; otherwise I cannot receive her unto myself."[28]

Though the Law will not be established in full until the New Jerusalem is established, Orson Pratt taught that before the Saints go back to Missouri "there will be an approximation to it, here in these mountains. We will learn a great many pure

---

26. JD, 21:136.
27. Prophecy recorded by Edwin Rushton and Theodore Turley.
28. D & C 105:5.

principles to enable us to carry out the law as far as we possibly can, under the circumstances that we are placed in here."[29] On another occasion he explained that while the Lord will help the Saints to prepare to live the Law of Consecration while they are still in the West he did not feel the full law would be lived until the Saints arrive in Missouri:

> If you cannot deal justly in relation to these small accounts, how is it to be expected you will perform the pure law of God — the law of consecration? I tell you, we have got to begin and attend faithfully to these small things. But when we are first born into His kingdom we cannot run alone; we are not able to prance, and trot, and caper about; He has therefore ordained certain helps, and governments, and laws to govern us while we are in the creeping state, and trying to advance into a more perfect order of things. This Perpetual Emigrating Fund is one of those helps, ordained to assist us in our imperfect and weak state: *by and bye, when the full law of God comes in force, these helps can then be dispensed with. When that will be, I do not know, but I have an idea that it will not be until we get back to Jackson County, for the Lord has told us, in one revelation, in substance as follows—"Let these laws I have given concerning my people in Jackson County be fulfilled after the redemption of Zion."*[30]

Lorenzo Snow also taught that an approximation of the Law of Consecration would be necessary while the Saints are still in the mountains, and said that they "shall not be permitted to enter the land from whence we were expelled, till our hearts are prepared to honor this law, and we become sanctified through the practice of the truth."[31]

The United Order into which the Saints will enter in Missouri will provide not only for the needs of individuals and families, but also for public construction and community purposes. In describing this facet of the benefits of living the Law of Consecration Orson Pratt explained,

> The revelation says: "They shall give into the storehouse all that is not needed for the support of the needy families." In this way the Lord's storehouse will be full and in great abundance; and *these means will be used for public purposes, and also by way of providing farming implements,*

---

29. DEN, Vol. 8, No. 265, Oct. 2, 1875.
30. JD, 2:57.
31. JD, 16:276.

books, etc., for the remnants of Joseph who will come into the *covenant in those days,* that they may also have their steward- ships in the midst of the people of God. There will be a portion of the avails of these stewardships that will be consecrated to the Lord's storehouse, and which will be *used for the building* *of Temples, and for beautifying public places in the city of* *the New Jerusalem, and making that a city of perfection as* *near as we possibly can.*[32]

An Inspired Plan for The
City and for The Temple

Two years after the location for the City of Zion was re- vealed in 1831, Joseph Smith drew up a plan for the city and sent it, together with a detailed explanation of the lay-out, to the Church members then residing in Missouri. It was his in- tention that all the cities founded by the Saints would follow this plan, and "so fill up the world in these last days."[33] Though the Saints were driven from their homes before this city could be constructed, this general plan has served as a guide for many of the western communities which the Church has established. Four years later, in recording the conference held April 6, 1837, Wilford Woodruff stated that the plan was given by revelation and will be carried out when the New Jerusalem is built:

> He also presented us in some degree with the plot of the city of Kirtland, which is the stronghold of the daughter of Zion. *The plan which he presented was given to him by vision,* *and the future will prove that the visions of Joseph concern-* *ing Jackson County, all the various stakes of Zion and the re-* *demption of Israel will be fulfilled in the time appointed of the* *Lord.*[34]

Attention should be called to several items of particular im- portance in this plan. The plan[35] dealt with the establishment of a city plat with 49 blocks which would provide for from fif- teen to twenty thousand people. The wide streets (132 feet) were to be more than enough to accommodate the advanced means of transportation which are known to man today. The blocks were to be laid off in squares but the houses were to face in alternating directions from block to block. The farm land was

32. JD, 21:152-53.
33. HC, 1:358.
34. *Journal History,* April 6, 1837.
35. The plan which the Prophet Joseph drew up is printed in the appendix.

to be located outside the city to the North and South and the city was to be kept free from unsightly buildings. The central portions of the plat were reserved for public buildings and in this manner the city was set up so that no one would live more than six blocks from the center of town. As the population increased, other plats similar to the one the Prophet describes were to be set up in adjoining sections.

In the center of the plat of Zion Joseph Smith prepared are two blocks with numbered sections where it is anticipated that a large temple will be built. The temple, according to the Prophet's plan, will have twenty-four sections or buildings which will each serve a certain part of the Church's priesthood leadership.[36]

Joseph Smith also gave detailed instructions for one of the twenty-four Temple compartments.[37] It appears, however, that this temple compartment was to be of a temporary nature and it was not anticipated that it would be a part of the final temple edifice which would stand forever. A description given by Orson Pratt of the Temple which will be built when the Saints return to redeem Zion differs from the plan drawn up by the Prophet, for he speaks of twenty-four rooms built in a circular form and arched over the center. He alludes to this description as being the result of a revelation given forty years before (which

---

36. The Names of the temples to be built on the painted squares as repre-·sented on the plot of the city of Zion, . . . numbers 10, 11, and 12, are to be called, House of the Lord, for the Presidency of the High and most Holy Priesthood, after the order of Melchizedek, which was after the order of the Son of God, upon Mount Zion, City of the New Jerusalem. Numbers 7, 8, and 9, the Sacred Apostolic Repository, for the use of the Bishop. Numbers, 4, 5, and 6, the Holy Evangelical House, for the High Priesthood of the Holy Order of God. Numbers 1, 2, and 3, the House of the Lord, for the Elders of Zion, an Ensign to the Nations. Numbers 22, 23, and 24, House of the Lord for the Presidency of the High Priesthood, after the Order of Aaron, a Standard for the People. Numbers 19, 20, and 21, House of the Lord, the Law of the Kingdom of Heaven, and Messenger to the People; for the Highest Priesthood after the Order of Aaron; Numbers 16, 17, and 18, House of the Lord for the Teachers in Zion, Messenger to the Church. Numbers 13, 14, and 15, House of the Lord for the Deacons in Zion, Helps in Government. Underneath must be written on each house—HOLINESS TO THE LORD.   HC, 1:359.

37. This house of the Lord was to be a two-story brick edifice, 87 feet long and 61 feet wide, which would rest on a raised foundation of stone. There was to be a shingled Gothic-style roof with a belfry containing a large bell at the east end. On the inside, the two stories were to be made on an identical plan, with raised pulpits at each end, and with reversible pews on which the backs would move, thereby allowing the congregation to sit facing either end. HC, 1:359-62.

would be in 1839), but says that the names of the compartments were given "some forty-five or forty-six years ago" (which would be in 1833-34, the time of the Prophet's giving of the plat of Zion):

> There, however, we expect to build a temple different from all other temples in some respects. It will be built much larger, cover a larger area of ground, far larger than this Tabernacle covers, and this Tabernacle will accommodate from 12,000 to 15,000 people. We expect to build a temple much larger, very much larger, *according to the revelation God gave to us forty years ago in regard to that Temple.* But you may ask in what form will it be built? Will it be built in one large room, like this Tabernacle! No; there will be 24 different compartments in the Temple that will be built in Jackson County. *The names of these compartments were given to us some forty-five or forty-six years ago;* the names we still have, *and when we build these twenty-four rooms, in a circular form and arched over the centre, we shall give the names to all these different compartments just as the Lord specified through Joseph Smith. . . .* Perhaps you may ask for what purpose these twenty-four compartments are to be built. I answer not to assemble the outside *world in, nor to assemble the Saints all in one place, but these buildings will be built with a special view to the different orders, or in other words, the different quorums or councils of the two Priesthoods that God has ordained on the earth. . . .* But will there be any other buildings excepting those 24 *rooms that are all joined together in a circular form and arched over the center* — are there any other rooms that will be built — detached from the Temple? Yes. *There will be tabernacles, there will be meeting houses for the assembling of the people on the Sabbath day. There will be various places of meeting so that the people may gather together; but the Temple will be dedicated to the Priesthood of the Most High God, and for most sacred and holy purposes.*[38]

Even though the appearance of the temple has apparently been seen in vision, further revelation at the time it is being built is anticipated. While speaking of the men who would be raised up by the Lord to lead the Saints to Zion in power Orson Pratt commented in 1879,

> I expect, when that time comes, that man will understand all the particulars in regard to the Temple to be built in Jackson County. Indeed, *we have already a part of the plan revealed,*

---

38. JD, 24:24-25.

and also the plat explaining how the city of Zion is to be laid off. . . . This house will be reared, then according to a certain plan, *which God is to make known to his servant whom he will, in his own due time, raise up.*[39]

At the time Zion is redeemed revelation is expected to guide the construction of the entire city as well as the temple. Elder Pratt continued:

And *he will have to give more revelation* on other things equally as important, for we shall need instructions how to build up Zion; how to establish the centre city; how to lay off the streets; the kind of ornamental trees to adorn the sidewalks, as well as everything else by way of beautifying it, and making it a city of perfection, as David prophetically calls it.[40]

This control from heaven is expected to extend so far as to indicate the style of architecture adapted throughout the city. Orson Pratt stated that "we shall erect in that county a beautiful city *after the order and pattern that the Lord shall reveal,* part of which has already been revealed," and added that God "will point out the pattern and show the order of architecture."[41]

That the construction of the Temple, and of the city as well, will be carried out under the direction of the Lord, and will not be left merely to man's ingenuity, also was clearly taught by President John Taylor:

We talk of returning to Jackson County to build the most magnificent temple that ever was formed on the earth and the most splendid city that was ever erected; yea, cities, if you please. *The architectural designs of those splendid edifices, cities, walls, gardens, bowers, streets, &c., will be under the direction of the Lord, who will control and manage all these matters; and the people, from the President down, will all be under the guidance and direction of the Lord in all the pursuits*

---

39. JD, 21:154.
40. JD, 21:154.
41. JD, 15:365. When asked how he reconciled Orson Pratt's description of the Temple with an arched roof with Joseph Smith's plan for a Gothic-styled structure, President Joseph Fielding Smith stated that "we don't know how the Temple will be built or what it will look like." This discussion followed an address by President Smith to Seminary and Institute teachers, June 27, 1960, on the Campus of the Brigham Young University, and was held in the presence of a group of teachers. Roy W. Doxey and Ray C. Colton were members of the group and heard President Smith's answer to the above question.

of human life; until eventually they will be enabled to erect cities that will be fit to be caught up—that when Zion descends from above, Zion will also ascend from beneath, and be prepared to associate with those from above.[42]

Who Will Build The New Jerusalem

In connection with the divine help which is expected during the construction of the New Jerusalem, some Church leaders have anticipated the presence of Joseph Smith and others, apparently as resurrected beings, at that time. Commented Heber C. Kimball in 1861,

> You will be blessed, and you will see the day when *Presidents Young, Kimball, and Wells, and the Twelve Apostles will be in Jackson County, Missouri laying out your inheritances. In the flesh? Of course.* We should look well without being in the flesh! We shall be there in the flesh, and all our enemies cannot prevent it. *Brother Wells, you may write that: You will be there, and Willard will be there, and also Jedediah, and Joseph and Hyrum Smith and David, and Parley;* and the day will be when I will see those men in the general assembly of the Church of the First-Born, in the great council of God in Jerusalem, too.[43]

Brigham Young explained that although the Lord will direct the work by revelation, men will have to perform the actual labor:

> *He* [the Lord] *will not send His angels to gather up the rock to build up the New Jerusalem. He will not send His angels from the heavens to go to the mountains to cut the timber and make it into lumber to adorn the city of Zion. He has called upon us to do this work;* and if we will let Him work by, through, and with us, He can accomplish it; otherwise we shall fall short, and shall never have the honor of building up Zion on the earth. Is this so? Certainly. Well, then let us keep the commandments.[44]

The Book of Mormon defines the working force that will build the temple by saying that "They [the Gentiles, who come into the Church after the internal strife in America] shall assist my people, the remnant of Jacob, and also as many of the house of Israel as shall come, that they may build a city, which shall be called the New Jerusalem."[45]

---

42. JD, 10:147.
43. JD, 9:27.
44. JD, 13:313.
45. III Ne. 21:23.

Thus three groups are listed who will participate in building this city:

1. The Gentiles,
2. The Lamanites, and
3. As many of the house of Israel as shall come.

This third group seems to be a reference to the coming of the Ten Tribes and to those who will already be members of the Church, and therefore of the house of Israel, at that time. The leadership in the construction work will naturally remain with the Church and with the political kingdom.

It will be seen in the next two chapters that all three groups mentioned will take part, but that perhaps the list is in reverse order chronologically. To fully understand this matter it must be realized that the City of Zion is expected to grow over a period of many years until it becomes a great world metropolis. In the earliest stage of its development most of the work will apparently be done by the members of the Church (the third group) who will be joined early in the construction program by the arrival of the Ten Tribes from the North. A great missionary program among the Lamanites (the second group) will then be inaugurated and they will come by the millions to the new Zion. The brunt of the construction effort will then apparently fall to them. As the New Jerusalem grows into a world power, and strife draws to an end in the United States the Gentiles (the first group) will also flock to the city and they will assist in aiding the growth also.

The commentary given by Orson Pratt on this subject is of interest:

> They [the Lamanites] will also be instructed to cultivate the earth, to build buildings as we do, instructed how to build Temples and in the various branches of industry practised [sic] by us; and then, after having received this information and instruction, *we shall have the privilege of helping them to build the New Jerusalem.* The Lord says, — "They," the Gentiles, who believe in the Book of Mormon, "shall assist my people, the remnant of Jacob, that they may build a city, which shall be called the New Jerusalem."
>
> *Now, a great many, without reading these things, have flattered themselves that we are the ones who are going to do all this work. It is not so; we have got to be helpers,* we have got to be those who co-operate with the remnants of Joseph in

accomplishing this great work; for the Lord will have respect unto them, because they are of the blood of Israel, and the promises of their fathers extend to them, and they will have the privilege of building that city, according to the pattern that the Lord shall give.[46]

Apparently it is the Lord's will that kings and rulers among the Gentile nations will eventually contribute to the upbuilding of Zion. The *Doctrine and Covenants* records a revelation in which the Prophet was commanded to issue a proclamation to "all the kings of the world, to the four corners thereof, to the

---

46. JD, 17:301. President Joseph Fielding Smith, however, does not concur in this interpretation. Says he:

My attention has been called to statements in the *Book of Mormon* which some interpret to mean that the Lamanites will take the lead in building the temple and the New Jerusalem in Missouri. But I fail to find any single passage which indicates that this is to be the order of things when these great events are to be fulfilled.

Most of the passages used as evidence, in an attempt to prove that the Lamanites will take the lead and we are to follow, seem to come from the instruction given by our Lord when He visited the Nephites after his resurrection. Chapters 20 and 21 of Third Nephi are the main sources for this conclusion. But I fail to find in any of the words delivered by our Savior any declaration out of which this conclusion can be reached. It all comes about by a misunderstanding and an improper interpretation.

In these chapters the Lord is speaking throughout of the *remnant of Jacob.* Who is Jacob whose *remnant* is to perform this great work in the last days? Most assuredly *Jacob is Israel. Then again, when he speaks of the seed of Joseph, who is meant? Those who are descendants of Joseph, son of Israel, and this includes, of course, the Lamanites as well as the Ephraimites who are now being assembled and who are taking their place, according to prophecy, at the head to guide and bless the whole house of Israel.*

In his discourse, the Savior states that the gentiles who are upon this land will be blessed, if they will receive the gospel, and they will be numbered with the house of Israel. The gentiles were to be a scourge to the remnant upon this land. Again, they were to be nursing fathers to them, and this they are beginning to be in these latter-days, after the terrible scourging in former days:

The gentiles were promised that they would be entitled to have all the blessings which were given to Israel, if they would repent and receive the gospel. All this was seen in vision by Nephi and was stated by the Savior on the occasion of his visit to the Nephites.

He also said that if the gentiles, *not only upon this land, but also of all lands,* did not repent he would bring the fulness of the gospel from among them. The *remnant of the house of Israel spoken of in First Nephi, chapter 13, and Third Nephi, chapters 16, 20, and 21, does not have reference only to the descendants of Lehi, but to all the house of Israel, the children of Jacob, those upon this land and those in other lands. Reference to the gentiles also is to all the gentiles on this land and in other lands. Doctrines of Salvation,* II, 247-48.

honorable president-elect, and the highminded governors of the nation in which you live, and to all the nations of the earth scattered abroad." The revelation stated that the Lord was about to call these rulers "to give heed to the light and glory of Zion, for the set time has come to favor her," and stated that He would "visit and soften their hearts, many of them for your good, that . . . they may come to the light of truth, and the Gentiles to the exaltation or lifting up of Zion."[47] It has already been seen that governments will have been raised up in several areas which will prove more receptive to the missionary effort and the cause of Zion than present governments. Although persecution prevented the Prophet from writing this proclamation during his lifetime, it was penned and published by the Quorum of the Twelve shortly after his death. It spoke of many important events, but significant in this context is the following invitation to rulers and kings:

> And now, O ye kings, rulers, and the people of the Gentiles, hear ye the word of the Lord, for this commandment is for you. *You are not only required to repent and obey the Gospel in its fulness, and thus become members or citizens of the kingdom of God; but you are also hereby commanded, in the name of Jesus Christ, to put your silver and your gold, your ships and steam-vessels, your railroad trains and your horses, chariots, camels, mules, and litters, into active use for the fulfillment of these purposes.* For be it known unto you, that the only salvation which remains for the Gentiles, is for them to be identified in the same covenant, and to worship at the same altar with Israel. In short, they must come to the same standard; for there shall be one Lord, and His name one, and He shall be king over all the earth.[48]

Life Within The New Jerusalem

Latter-day Saint Church leaders have been very descriptive in telling of life in the New Zion. The following quotations are typical of their many descriptions of the life which the Saints will lead. Orson Pratt spoke of varied pursuits which the Saints will follow and of the educational opportunities which will be found in the City of Zion:

---

47. D & C 124:2, 3, 6, 9.
48. "Proclamation of the Twelve Apostles of the Church of Jesus Christ of Latter-day Saints," *Millennial Star,* October 22, 1845.

But perhaps you may still further inquire concerning our emigration to the eastern boundaries of the State of Kansas, and to the western boundaries of the State of Missouri, what we intend to do in that part of the country? *We expect to be farmers, a great many of us. We expect to introduce all kinds of machinery and manufactures. We expect to build mills. We expect to become a very industrious, frugal, economical people. We expect to have our merchandise and our stores and storehouses in that land.* We expect to build a great many hundred school-houses in that country, just the same as we have already done in this country and in the two adjacent Territories, Idaho in the north and Arizona in the south. We do not calculate to neglect our children in regard to their education. We expect to build a great number of academies or the higher schools and besides a great many school-houses. We expect to erect universities for the still higher branches to be taught. We expect to build many hundreds of meeting-houses, and *we expect to be a people very densely located there — not one man taking up six or eight miles of land and calling it his farm; we don't expect to live in that way, but we expect to settle a very dense settlement in that region by country.*[49]

He also spoke of the cosmopolitan background of the many Saints who will gather there, and of the peaceful life they will lead:

Not many years hence — I do not say the number of years — you will look forth to the western counties of the State of Missouri, and to the eastern counties of the State of Kansas, and in all that region round about *you will see a thickly populated country, inhabited by a peaceful people, having their orchards, their fruit trees, their fields of grain, their beautiful houses and shade trees, their cities and towns and villages.* And you may ask — Who are all these people? The answer will be — Latter-day Saints! Where have they come from? *They have come from the nations of the earth! They have come from the mountains of Utah, from Arizona, from Idaho, and from the mountainous territories of the North American Continent,* they have come down here, and are quietly cultivating the lands of these States! Now, this will all come to pass, just as sure to come to pass as there is a God that reigns in yonder heavens, and not many years hence either.[50]

49. JD, 24:23.
50. JD, 21:135.

Elder John Taylor told of his expectation that the Saints will excel in the arts, science, and manufacturing, that they will rear magnificent edifices, and that they will have divine direction to guide them:

> We believe, moreover, that God, having commenced his work, will continue to reveal and make manifest his will to his Priesthood, to his Church and kingdom on the earth, and that among this people there will be an embodiment of virtue, of truth, of holiness, of integrity, of fidelity, of wisdom and of the knowledge of God. *We believe that there will be a temporal kingdom of God organized that will be under the direction and auspices of the Lord of Hosts*, and that in all our affairs, whether they relate to things temporal or things spiritual, as we have been in the habit of calling them, we shall be under the direction of the Lord, as the Scriptures say, "It shall come to pass that all people shall be taught of the Lord." This is part and parcel of our creed. *We believe that we shall rear splendid edifices, magnificent temples and beautiful cities that shall become the pride, praise and glory of the whole earth. We believe that this people will excel in literature, in science and the arts and in manufactures.* In fact, there will be a concentration of wisdom, not only of the combined wisdom of the world as it now exists, but men will be inspired in regard to all these matters in a manner and to an extent that they never have been before, and *we shall have eventually, when the Lord's purposes are carried out, the most magnificent buildings, the most pleasant and beautiful gardens, the richest and most costly clothing, and be the most healthy and the most intellectual people that will reside upon the earth.* This is part and parcel of our faith; in fact, Zion will become the praise of the whole earth; and as the Queen of Sheba said anciently, touching the glory of Solomon, the half of it had not been told her, so it will be in regard to Israel in their dwelling places. *In fact, if there is anything great, noble, dignified, exalted, anything pure, or holy, or virtuous, or lovely, anything calculated to exalt or ennoble the human mind to dignify and elevate the people, it will be found among the people of the Saints of the most High God.*[51]

Summary

The following items have been considered in connection with the establishment of the New Jerusalem:

1. When the time comes for the Saints to return to Jackson County, Missouri, the Lord will raise up a man "who shall

---

51. JD, 10:146-47.

lead them like as Moses." There has been speculation as to the identity of this man which includes the possibility of the Prophet Joseph being raised from the dead to guide the Saints in their return.

2. The Saints will make the journey eastward during the period when internal strife is still raging in the United States. They will have to defend themselves against their enemies and will apparently be denied the more modern means of transportation because of the poor condition of the roads and facilities.

3. Many of the Saints are expected to remain in the West although the center of Church influence will remove to Jackson County.

4. The Saints, as they begin to lay out the city, will organize themselves under the United Order. There will be an approximation of this program in the West as a preparatory measure.

5. The Saints will have great wealth and will purchase those lands which they do not already own.

6. The land, as the Saints arrive, will be in a desolate and abandoned condition.

7. The plan for the city was given to Joseph Smith by revelation. It is anticipated that further revelation will be given directing the construction of the city and the temple.

8. The city will be built by three groups of people over an extended period of time. These groups are

    A. The members of the Church and those of the House of Israel including the Ten Tribes.

    B. The Lamanites, or Indians.

    C. The Gentiles who will come into the Church after the period of internal strife in the United States.

    The relationship between these three groups will become more apparent in coming chapters.

9. The Saints expect to grow and prosper there and to construct a mighty city. Their activities will be designed to sanctify and exalt the people.

CHAPTER VII

Four Important Events in America

In the period following the beginning of the city of New Jerusalem, four important events are indicated by prophecy as being prepared to come to pass. They are

1. The intensive proselyting and conversion of the Lamanites, or Indians of North, Central and South America;
2. The appearance of the Lord Jesus Christ in the New Jerusalem;
3. The coming of the Ten Tribes from the North to the New Jerusalem;
4. The calling of 144,000 high priests to minister the Gospel in the last days.

The Conversion of The Lamanites

According to Orson Pratt, after the Temple in the City of Zion has been completed and the city itself is beginning to develop and flourish, the time will come for the gospel to be taught with great emphasis to the Lamanites. A remnant of that people will have been converted before Zion is redeemed, but the time for the main body of the Lamanite people to hear the Gospel will be after the establishment of the New Jerusalem:

> The coming of Christ seems to be near at hand, yet Zion must be redeemed before that day; the temple must be built upon the consecrated spot, the cloud and glory of the Lord rest upon it, *and the Lamanites, many of them, brought in, and they must build up the NEW JERUSALEM!* It is true, so says the Book of Mormon, that inasmuch as the Gentiles receive the Gospel, they shall assist my people the remnant of Jacob, saith the Lord, to build the New Jerusalem. And when they have got it built, then we are told that they shall assist my people who are of Jacob to be gathered unto the New Jerusalem.
>
> *Only a few thousand or hundreds of thousands, then, are to be engaged in this work, and then, after it is done, we are to assist the Lamanites to gather in; and then shall the powers of heaven be in your midst; and then is the coming of Christ.*

It will not be before the Lamanites come in, nor before the temple is constructed in Jackson County; but there is a great people to do the work.[1]

He also explained that the Gospel will be taken to the Lamanites after the foundation of the city has been laid and the temple has been built, and that the gathering of the Lamanites to the New Jerusalem would involve an extended period of time:

Do not misunderstand me, *do not think that all the Lamanite tribes are going to be converted and receive this great degree of education and civilization before we can return to Jackson County. Do not think this for a moment, it will be only a remnant; for when we have laid the foundation of that city and have built a portion of it, and have built a Temple therein,* there is another work which we have got to do in connection with these remnants of Jacob whom we shall assist in building the city. What is it? We have got to be sent forth as missionaries to all parts of this American continent. *Not to the Gentiles, for their times will be fulfilled;* but we must go to all those tribes that roam through the cold regions of the north— British America, to all the tribes that dwell in the Territories of the United States, also to all those who are scattered through Mexico, and Central and South America, and the object of our going will be to declare the principles of the Gospel unto them, and bring them to a knowledge of the truth. *"Then shall they assist my people who are scattered on all the face of the land, that they may be gathered in to the New Jerusalem."*

Will not this be a great work? *It will take a good while to gather all these tribes of South America*, for some of them will have to come from five to eight thousand miles in order to reach the New Jerusalem. *This will be quite a work, and yet we shall have to perform it after the city is built.*[2]

The proclamation issued by the Twelve Apostles shortly after the martyrdom of the Prophet Joseph Smith also referred to the gathering of the Lamanites and said they would be made one nation in this glorious land:

We also bear testimony that the "Indians" (so-called) of North and South America are a remnant of the tribes of Israel, as is now made manifest by the discovery and revelation of their ancient oracles and records.

1. JD, 3:18.
2. JD, 17:301-02.

And that *they are about to be gathered, civilized, and made one nation in this glorious land.* They will also come to the knowledge of their forefathers, and of the fulness of the Gospel; and they will embrace it and become a righteous branch of the house of Israel.[3]

Benjamin F. Johnson stated that the prophet had spoken of a time yet future *"when a path will be opened for the Saints through Mexico, South America, and to the center Stake of Zion."*[4]

This great work will apparently begin shortly before the coming of the Savior to His Temple in New Jerusalem and the appearance of the Ten Tribes from the North. It will probably continue to some extent after these great events transpire. This order of events was emphasized by Orson Pratt:

First, a [Lamanite] remnant will be converted; second, Zion will be redeemed, and all among the Gentiles who believe will assist this remnant of Jacob in building the New Jerusalem; third, a vast number of missionaries will be sent throughout the length and breadth of this great continent, to gather all the dispersed of his people in unto the New Jerusalem; fourth, the power of heaven will be made manifest in the midst of this people, and the Lord also will be in their midst.[5]

The missionary work among the Lamanites marks the beginning of the gathering of a mighty group of the blood of Israel. This gathering process involves three groups: (1) the Lamanites in the Americas, (2) the ten lost tribes of Israel, and (3) the Jews who are scattered throughout the world. Third Nephi 21:23-22:3 gives a panoramic view of the order in which the gathering of these groups will take place. After the New Jerusalem is built (v. 23) the Lamanites are to be gathered in (v. 24), and then the Savior will appear in their midst (v. 25). The work will then commence among the lost tribes which will return at this time (v. 26), and then will Israel be gathered out from among all nations (v. 27-29). As Israel is gathered in, the desolate cities formerly possessed by the Gentiles on this hemisphere will be inhabited by those of Israel (22:1-3). The passage is here quoted:

3. "Proclamation of the Twelve Apostles of the Church of Jesus Christ of Latter-day Saints," *Millennial Star,* October 22, 1845.
4. Benjamin F. Johnson, *My Life's Review* (Independence, Missouri: Zion's Printing and Publishing Company, 1947), p. 101.
5. JD, 17:302.

And they [the Gentiles, if they repent so as to be given this blessing] shall assist my people, the remnant of Jacob, and also as many of the House of Israel as shall come, that they may *build a city, which shall be called the New Jerusalem.*

And then shall they *assist my people that they may be gathered in,* who are scattered upon all the face of the land, in unto the New Jerusalem.

And then shall the power of heaven come down among them; and *I also will be in the midst. And then shall the work of the Father commence at that day, even when this gospel shall be preached among the remnant of this people.* Verily I say unto you, *at that day shall the work of the Father commence among all the dispersed of my people, yea, even the tribes which have been lost,* which the Father hath led away out of Jerusalem.

Yea, the *work shall commence among all the dispersed of my people,* with the Father, to prepare the way whereby they may come unto me, that they may call on the Father in my name.

Yea, and *then shall the work commence, with the Father among all nations,* in preparing the way whereby his people may be gathered home to the land of their inheritance.

And *they shall go out from all nations;* and they shall not go out in haste, nor go by flight, for I will go before them, saith the Father, and I will be their rearward.

And then shall that which is written come to pass: Sing, O barren, thou that didst not bear; break forth into singing, and cry aloud, thou that didst not travail with child [Israel, in her scattered conditon, who is here likened unto a barren woman who under the conditions of her estrangement begets no children to the Lord]; for more are the children of the desolate [Israel] than the children of the married wife [the Gentiles when they are favored as the Lord's people, with the opportunity to do His work], saith the Lord.

Enlarge the place of thy tent, and let them stretch forth the curtains of thy habitations; spare not, lengthen thy cords and strengthen thy stakes;

For thou [Zion during the future times of Israel] shalt break forth on the right hand and on the left, and thy seed shall inherit the Gentiles and *make the desolate cities to be inhabited.*

Orson Pratt made it clear that these desolate Gentile cities would be inhabited by latter-day Israel before the coming of the Savior with the hosts of heaven. This seemingly will be done in a continually extending circle surrounding Jackson County. More and more of the vacated cities will be inhabited as the Lamanites and others gather to Zion:

> Now that order of things will continue and *will spread forth from that nucleus in Jackson County* and the western counties of Missouri and the eastern counties of Kansas, where this people will be located, and *it will spread abroad for hundreds and hundreds of miles,* on the right hand and the left, east, west, north and south from the great central city and all the people will be required to execute the law in all their stewardships, and then there will be a oneness and union which will continue, and *it will spread wider and wider, and become greater and greater, until the desolate cities of the Gentiles will be inhabited by the Saints.* Then will be fulfilled the prophecy of Isaiah, in which he says, "Thy seed shall inherit the Gentiles and make the desolate cities to be inhabited," *for God will visit them in judgment, and there will be no owners left to occupy the country.* Then the land will be filled up with Saints, those who will keep the celestial law; and they will receive their stewardships according to the appointment of heaven.
>
> *By and by the time will come for Jesus to appear,* and he will bring the heavenly society which has been engaged for thousands of years in that celestial world in carrying out these principles. They will come down here, and they will find a society just like themselves, so far as union is concerned; they will find a people perfected and carrying out the principles here on earth, as they are carried out in the heavens.[6]

For purposes of discussion it may be said that there will be two periods of conversion for the Lamanite people. The first occurs before the return of the Saints to redeem Zion, and seems, to some extent, to be taking place now. The second, and most important period of Lamanite conversion, will commence in the early days of the New Jerusalem. It appears that it is in this era that the "Lamanites shall blossom as the rose,"[7] and the scales of darkness will fall from their eyes and "they shall be a white and delightsome people."[8]

The 1845 proclamation of the Twelve Apostles described the eventual state of the Lamanite people and said that God

> *Will assemble the natives, the remnants of Joseph in America, and make of them a great, and strong, and powerful nation;*

---

6. DEN, Vol. 8, No. 265, October 2, 1875.
7. D & C 49:24.
8. II Ne. 30:6.

and he will civilize and enlighten them, and will establish a holy city, and temple, and seat of Government among them, which shall be called Zion. . . .

The despised and degraded son of the forest, who has wandered in dejection and sorrow, and suffered reproach, shall then drop his disguise and stand forth in manly dignity, and exclaim to the Gentiles who have envied and sold him— "I am Joseph; does my father yet live?" or in other words, I am a descendant of that Joseph who was sold into Egypt. You have hated me, and sold me, and thought I was dead; but lo! I live and am heir to the inheritance, titles, honours, priesthood, sceptre, crown, throne, and eternal life and dignity of my fathers, who live for evermore.

He shall then be ordained, washed, anointed with holy oil, and arrayed in fine linen, even the glorious and beautiful garments and royal robes of the high priesthood, which is after the order of the Son of God; and shall enter into the congregation of the Lord, even into the Holy of Holies, there to be crowned with authority and power which shall never end.

The spirit of the Lord shall then descend upon him like the dew upon the mountains of Hermon, and like refreshing showers of rain upon the flowers of Paradise.

His heart shall expand with knowledge, wide as eternity, and his mind shall comprehend the vast creations of his God, and his eternal purpose of redemption, glory, and exaltation, which was devised in heaven before the worlds were organized; but made manifest in these last days, for the fulness of the Gentiles, and for the exaltation of Israel.[9]

The Lord Shall Come to His Temple in Zion

Four specific appearances of the Lord are prophesied during the last days. Three of these appearances are local appearances in which his coming will be known only to those in the immediate vicinity. The fourth appearance will be His coming in glory (which is often called the second coming of Christ) which will be witnessed by all mankind. These appearances are

1. Christ's appearance in the temple in the New Jerusalem, at which time He will give his laws to Zion and minister unto the people.

2. Christ's appearance at Adam-ondi-Ahman, Missouri, at which time He will receive the keys of the kingdom and hold judgment on the nations of the earth.

---

9. "Proclamation of the Twelve Apostles of the Church of Jesus Christ of Latter-day Saints," *Millennial Star,* October 22, 1845.

3. Christ's appearance on the Mount of Olives and in the temple at Jerusalem, Palestine, at which time He will save Israel from defeat in the battle of Armageddon.
4. Christ's appearance in glory to an unspecified place, at which time He will be accompanied by the hosts of Heaven and will cleanse the earth by fire.

Brigham Young, in a discourse in which he addressed himself to the Jews, differentiated between Christ's coming in Palestine and his coming in America:

When he comes again he will not come as he did when the Jews rejected him; neither will he appear first at Jerusalem when he makes his second appearance on the earth; but he will appear first on the land where he commenced his work in the beginning, and planted the garden of Eden, and that was done in the land of America.[10]

Joseph Smith also commented on the Lord's coming to the people in the newly established Zion in Missouri:

The coming of the Messiah among this people will be so natural, that only those who see Him will know that He has come, but He will come and give His laws unto Zion, and minister unto His people. *This will not be His coming in the clouds of heaven to take vengeance on the wicked of the world.*[11]

In an article entitled *The Second Advent*, President Charles W. Penrose describes three of the major appearances which comprise the Second Coming of the Messiah. In doing so he tells of the Lord's coming to the City of Zion, as the first of the Lord's series of appearances, and states that the world at large will be unaware of His appearance at this time:

Among the first-mentioned of these three classes of men, *the Lord will make his appearance first;* and that appearance will be unknown to the rest of mankind. *He will come to the Temple prepared for him, and his faithful people will behold his face, hear his voice, and gaze upon his glory.* From his own lips they will receive further instructions for the development and beautifying of Zion and for the extension and sure stability of his Kingdom.[12]

---

10. JD, 11:279.
11. Prophecy recorded by Edwin Rushton and Theodore Turley.
12. *Millennial Star,* September 10, 1859.

This appearance will be sudden,[13] and the Lord has stressed the importance of the Saints being gathered "in one" at that time.[14]

The Proclamation issued by the Twelve Apostles tells how the Lamanites will be present and prepared to meet with the Savior at this time:

> And *there the Messiah will visit them in person; and the old Saints, who will then have been raised from the dead, will be with Him;* and He will establish His kingdom and laws over all the land. . . .
>
> He [the Lamanites personified as a single individual] shall also behold his Redeemer, and be filled with His presence, *while the cloud of His glory shall be seen in His temple.*[15]

Though according to President Penrose the world at large will be unaware that the Lord has appeared, they will apparently know of His glory which will come upon the city. The *Doctrine and Covenants* states that "the glory of the Lord shall be there, and the terror of the Lord also shall be there," to the extent that "the wicked will not come unto it," and will express their fear that "the inhabitants of Zion are terrible, wherefore we cannot stand.[16] The prophet Isaiah described the glory that would be upon Mount Zion:

> And the Lord will create upon every dwelling place of mount Zion, and upon her assemblies, a *cloud and smoke by day, and the shining of a flaming fire by night; for upon all the glory shall be a defense.*
>
> And there shall be a tabernacle for a shadow in the daytime from the heat, and for a place of refuge, and for a covert from storm and from rain.[17]

This Isaiah passage seems to be accepted by Latter-day Saints as a direct reference to the New Jerusalem as a revelation given to Joseph Smith speaks specifically of the "gathering of his saints to stand upon Mount Zion, which shall be the city of New Jerusalem."[18] The Savior states in the *Book of Mormon* that "the

---

13. D & C 36:8.
14. D & C 42:36.
15. "Proclamation of the Twelve Apostles of the Church of Jesus Christ of Latter-day Saints," *Millennial Star,* October 22, 1845.
16. D & C 45:66-70.
17. Is. 4:5-6.
18. D & C 84:2.

powers of heaven shall be in the midst of this people; yea, even I will be in the midst of you."[19] He is also reported as stating that:

> Inasmuch as my people build a house unto me in the name of the Lord, and do not suffer any unclean thing to come into it, that it be not defiled, *my glory shall rest upon it;*
>
> *Yea, and my presence shall be there, for I will come into it,* and all the pure in heart that shall come into it shall see God.[20]

According to Orson Pratt this light and glory will be extremely conspicuous and will cause great excitement throughout the world:

> The *light will shine so conspicuously from that city, extending to the very heavens,* that it will in reality be like unto a city set upon a hill that cannot be hid, and *it will have quite a tendency to strike terror to all the nations of the earth.* Will all see it? No, some may be too far off, beyond the ocean, to behold that miraculous light that will shine forth in this city, but I will tell you the effect it will have upon the kings, queens, rulers, congressmen and judges of the earth—they will hear of it by telegraph; the news will be flashed over the civilized nations of the earth, but they will not believe it. They will say, "Let us cross the ocean, and let us see this thing that is reported to us by telegraph; let us sea [sic] whether it is so or not." Well when they get within a day or two's journey of the city they will be alarmed. Some of these kings and nobles, *when they see the light shining forth like the northern lights in the arctic regions, illuminating the whole face of the heavens*—when they see this light shining forth long before they reach the city, fear will take hold of them there, says the Psalmist, in the 48th Psalm, they will become weak, and their knees will smite together like the knees of Belshazzar. *They will try to haste away from the glory of God and from the power of God, and to get out of the country as soon as possible.* Fear and terror will be upon them. It will have an effect upon many other kings and nobles, more pure in heart, more honest, that are willing to receive the truth; it will have a different effect upon them, so much so, that they will say with Isaiah, "Arise, shine, for thy light is come, and the glory of the Lord is risen upon thee. For, behold, darkness covers the earth and gross darkness the people; but the Lord shall arise upon thee, and His glory shall be seen

---

19. III Ne. 20:22.
20. D & C 97:15-16.

from thee. *And the gentiles shall come to thy light, and kings to the brightness of thy rising.*"[21]

Not only will the glory of God be conspicuous for many miles around, this glory is expected to affect the materials from which the temple is built and keep them from decaying. Thus the presence of God will cause the buildings to become immortal. This is expected to happen both in the New and Old Jerusalem, according to Orson Pratt:

> Now, in this world there will be Temples, and these Temples will be constructed according to the most perfect law of the celestial kingdom, for the world in which they are built or in which they stand will be a celestial body. This last Temple that I am speaking of, or this last one to be built in Jackson County, Missouri, will be constructed after that heavenly pattern in all particulars. Why? Because it will never perish, it will exist forever. . . I do not ask you to think that this Temple and the city round about it will defy the rough hand of time, and the work of the elements of our globe, and exist forever, so far as natural laws are concerned; but there is a principle higher than these natural laws. Did you never think of it — a higher principle, a higher kingdom that governs all these laws of nature, such as you and I have been accustomed to understand ever since our youth. *I say there is a higher law, a controlling power over all the laws of nature, that will prevent these buildings from decaying;* and I wish while dwelling upon this subject to say a little about another subject; that is, the building up of Palestine with the New Jerusalem. It will be the old Jerusalem rebuilt upon its former site. Now, will that city ever be destroyed; will it ever decay? *Will the Temple to be built in Palestine ever be thrown down or ever be furrowed with hail, rain, snow and frost—will these ever have any effect upon it?* No, not in the least.
>
> hy? [sic] Because God will be there. So He will be in the temple of Zion on this continent, and by His power, by His laws — which are superior to all those grosser laws of nature — *He will preserve both of these cities, one on the western hemisphere, and one on the eastern hemisphere, from any decay whatever.*[22]

When the Lord makes his appearance in the Temple all those among the Saints who are worthy will be privileged to enter and see Him. According to Orson Pratt:

---

21. JD, 24:29.
22. JD, 24:25-26.

It shall come to pass that every man and every woman who is pure in heart, who shall go inside of that [New Jerusalem] temple, will see the Lord. Now, *how great a blessing it will be to see the Lord of Hosts as we see one another in the flesh.* That will take place, but *not till after the temple is built.*[23]

Not only will the Saints see the Savior in the Temple, but He will come into their homes and mingle with them according to Lorenzo Snow:

Many of you will be living in Jackson County and there you will be assisting in building the Temple; and if you will not have seen the Lord Jesus at that time you may expect Him very soon, *to see Him, to eat and drink with Him, to shake hands with Him and to invite Him to your houses as He was invited when He was here before.* I am saying things to you now, which I know something of the truth of them.[24]

Coming of The Ten Tribes

It appears that the long anticipated coming of the Ten Tribes from the north will take place shortly after or possibly just before Zion has been sanctified and the Lord has come to the temple. Oliver Cowdery stated that the Angel Moroni instructed Joseph Smith that after the Church "shall be *sanctified and receive an inheritance where the glory of God shall rest upon them . . .* and all things are prepared, *the ten tribes of Israel will be revealed in the north country, whither they have been for a long season.*"[25]

It should be recalled also that the order shown in III Nephi 21:22-22:3 which was discussed earlier in the chapter showed that first the building of the New Jerusalem would have begun, then the Lamanites would be gathered in, then the Savior would appear and "at that day shall the work of the Father commence among all the dispersed of my people, yea, *even the tribes which have been lost.*"[26] However a revelation attributed to Joseph Smith speaks of the building of the New Jerusalem and says that "the Ten Tribes of Israel will help you build it."[27] It is very

23. JD, 21:330.
24. Remarks made at a reunion of the authorities of the Priesthood in the Weber Stake, held on June 12, 1901, in the Fifth Ward Assembly Hall, as quoted in N. B. Lundwall, *Temples of the Most High* (tenth edition; Salt Lake City: Bookcraft) p. 259.
25. *Messenger and Advocate,* October, 1835.
26. III Ne. 21:26.
27. Prophecy recorded by Edwin Rushton and Theodore Turley.

possible, since there are to be not one, but twenty-four temple areas, that the Savior may appear in a completed portion and yet, when the lost tribes come, there will be other areas which will require their labor.

Another factor that helps to identify the time the Ten Tribes are expected to return is that their coming is to be preceded by a great upheaval of the earth's surface which will cast up a highway in the midst of the great deep and will cause the boundaries of the everlasting hills to tremble.[28] The revelation of John apparently alludes to this great upheaval, and says that when the mountains and islands are moved from their places the great change will have been precipitated by an earthquake which will be so powerful that it will make the sun appear to be black and the moon to appear red as blood:

> And I beheld when he had opened the sixth seal, and, lo, *there was a great earthquake; and the sun became black as sackcloth of hair, and the moon became as blood;*
> And *the stars of heaven fell unto the earth,* even as a fig tree casteth her untimely figs, when she is shaken of a mighty wind.
> And the heaven departed as a scroll when it is rolled together; and *every mountain and island were moved out of their places.*[29]

The *Doctrine and Covenants* tells of the coming of the Ten Tribes from the north. It seems that their coming will not be without incident for they have to deal with enemies during their advance. Note also the indication that the land to which they will come will at that time be barren and parched and that

---

28. D & C 133:27. Care must be taken while studying the 133rd section of the Doctrine and Covenants not to confuse the time of the return of the lost tribes with the time when the great deep shall be driven back to the north and the lands of Jerusalem and of the New Jerusalem shall be joined together. A careful reading of the entire section will show that it is a recording of many varied events and that they are not recorded in order chronologically. See JD, 18:346.

29. Rev. 6:12-14. It will be noted that this earthquake takes place at the end of the sixth thousand years since the beginning of the earth's temporal existence (D & C 77:6-7), which according to Bishop Ussher's chronology, ends somewhere near the end of the twentieth century. The close proximity to the calling of the 144,000 in the Revelation account seems to identify this earthquake with the upheaval which will precede the coming of the Ten Tribes.

the boundaries or entire land of the everlasting hills (a term used to identify the American continents) will shake and tremble when they come:

> And they who are in the north countries shall come in re-membrance before the Lord; and *their prophets shall hear his voice, and shall no longer stay themselves;* and they shall *smite the rocks, and the ice shall flow down at their presence.*
>
> And an *highway shall be cast up in the midst of the great deep.*
>
> *Their enemies shall become a prey unto them,*
>
> *And in the barren deserts there shall come forth pools of living water; and the parched ground shall no longer be a thirsty land.*
>
> And they shall bring forth their rich treasures unto the children of Ephraim, my servants.
>
> *And the boundaries of the everlasting hills shall tremble at their presence.*
>
> And there shall they fall down and be crowned with glory, even in Zion, by the hands of the servants of the Lord, even the children of Ephraim.
>
> And they shall be filled with songs of everlasting joy.
>
> Behold, this is the blessing of the everlasting God upon the tribes of Israel, and the richer blessing upon the head of Ephraim and his fellows.[30]

Although there will be prophets laboring at that time among the Ten Tribes, it appears that the majority of these people will not yet hold the priesthood. This power will be conferred upon them by the Saints in the city of Zion. Said Orson Pratt:

> Having spoken concerning the gathering of the ten tribes, I will refer again to their Prophets. "Their Prophets shall hear his voice." Do not think that we are the only people who will have prophets. God is determined to raise up Prophets among that people, but *he will not bestow upon them all the fulness of the blessings of the Priesthood. The fulness will be reserved to be given to them after they come to Zion. But Prophets will be among them while in the north, and a portion of the Priesthood will be there; and John the Revelator will be there,* teaching, instructing and preparing them for this great work.[31]

---

30. D & C 133:26-34.
31. JD, 18:25. During the conference of June 2-6, 1831, the Prophet Joseph Smith stated that John the Revelator was at that time laboring among the lost tribes. See HC, 1:176.

Wilford Woodruff also taught that the Ten Tribes would receive Priesthood authority and their endowments in the land of Zion.[32]

It is prophesied that the records of the lost tribes will be combined with the *Bible* and the *Book of Mormon*:

> For behold, I shall speak unto the Jews and they shall write it; and I shall also speak unto the Nephites and they shall write it; and *I shall also speak unto the other tribes of the house of Israel, which I have led away, and they shall write it;* and I shall also speak unto all nations of the earth and they shall write it.

> And it shall come to pass that the Jews shall have the words of the Nephites, and the Nephites shall have the words of the Jews, and the *Nephites and the Jews shall have the words of the lost tribes of Israel; and the lost tribes of Israel shall have the words of the Nephites and the Jews.*

> And it shall come to pass that my people, which are of the house of Israel, shall be gathered home unto the lands of their possessions; and *my word also shall be gathered in in one.* And I will show unto them that fight against my word and against my people, who are of the house of Israel, that I am God, and that I covenanted with Abraham that I would remember his seed forever.[33]

These records will, perhaps, be combined with records from the American continents written during *Book of Mormon* times, which Orson Pratt says will be brought at some future time from the Hill Cumorah to the temple in the New Jerusalem:

> The Prophet Mormon, the father of Moroni, had been entrusted with all the sacred records of his forefathers, engraved on metallic plates. New plates were made by Mormon, on which he wrote, from the more ancient books, an abridged history of the nation, incorporating therewith many revelations, prophecies, the Gospel, etc. These new plates were given to Moroni on which to finish the history. *All the ancient plates Mormon deposited in Cumorah, about three hundred and eighty-four years after Christ. When Moroni, about thirty-six years after, made the deposit of the book entrusted to him, he was, without doubt, inspired to select a department of the hill separate from the great sacred depository of the numerous volumes hid up by his father.* The particular place on the hill,

---

32. JD, 4:231-32.
33. II Ne. 29:12-14.

where Moroni secreted the book, was revealed, by the angel, to the Prophet Joseph Smith, to whom the volume was delivered in September, A. D. 1827. *But the grand depository of all the numerous records of the ancient nations of the western continent was located in another department of the hill, and its contents under the charge of Holy angels, until the day should come for them to be transferred to the sacred temple of Zion.*[34]

Calling of The 144,000

It appears that after the Ten Tribes come from the north, a force of 144,000 High Priests will be established which will minister to the Church and will seek out the House of Israel from the nations of the world and gather them to the lands of their inheritance. Twelve thousand are to be chosen from each of the tribes of Israel to participate in this great proselyting program, which would seem to indicate that their calling must follow the coming of the Ten Tribes, since only a minor representation from many of the tribes would be available before that time. Says the Biblical account:

> And after these things I saw four angels standing on the four corners of the earth, holding the four winds of the earth, that the wind should not blow on the earth, nor on the sea, nor on any tree.
> And I saw another angel ascending from the east, having the seal of the living God: and he cried with a loud voice to the four angels, to whom it was given to hurt the earth and the sea,
> Saying, *Hurt not the earth, neither the sea, nor the trees, till we have sealed the servants of our God in their foreheads.*
> And I heard the number of them which were sealed: *and there were sealed an hundred and forty and four thousand of all the tribes of the children of Israel.*
> Of the tribe of *Juda* were sealed twelve thousand. Of the tribe of *Reuben* were sealed twelve thousand. Of the tribe of *Gad* were sealed twelve thousand.
> Of the tribe of *Aser* were sealed twelve thousand. Of the tribe of *Nepthalim* were sealed twelve thousand. Of the tribe of *Manasses* were sealed twelve thousand.
> Of the tribe of *Simeon* were sealed twelve thousand. Of the tribe of *Levi* were sealed twelve thousand. Of the tribe of *Issachar* were sealed twelve thousand.

---

34. *Millennial Star,* 28:417-19. See also JD. 19:38.

Of the tribe of *Zabulon* were sealed twelve thousand. Of the tribe of *Joseph* were sealed twelve thousand. Of the tribe of *Benjamin* were sealed twelve thousand.[35]

This passage is interpreted in the *Doctrine and Covenants*, where it is stated that the angels who hold control over earth life are kept from bringing destruction on the earth by Elias, who admonishes them to "hurt not the earth, neither the sea, nor the trees, till we have sealed the servants of our God in their foreheads." The sealing of the 144,000 is then defined:

We are to understand that *those who are sealed are high priests, ordained unto the holy order of God, to administer the everlasting gospel,* for they are they who are *ordained out of every nation, kindred, tongue, and people,* by the angels to whom is given power over the nations of the earth, *to bring as many as will come to the church of the Firstborn.*[36]

This sealing process was further explained by Orson Pratt, who stated that the recipients would undergo physical changes which would serve to preserve their lives when they encounter pestilence and earthquakes:

When the Temple is built the sons of the two Priesthoods, that is, those who are ordained to the Priesthood of Melchizedec, that Priesthood which is after the order of the Son of God, with all its appendages; and those who have been ordained to the Priesthood of Aaron with all its appendages, the former called the sons of Moses, the latter the sons of Aaron, will enter into that Temple . . . and *all of them who are pure in heart will behold the face of the Lord and that too before he comes in his glory in the clouds of heaven,* for he will suddenly come to his Temple, and *he will purify the sons of Moses and of Aaron, until they shall be prepared to offer in that Temple an offering that shall be acceptable in the sight of the Lord. In doing this, he will purify not only the minds of the Priesthood in that Temple, but he will purify their bodies until they shall be quickened, and renewed and strengthened, and they will be partially changed,* not to immortality, but changed in part that they can be filled with the power of God, and they can stand in the presence of Jesus, and behold his face in the midst of that Temple.

This will prepare them for further ministrations among the nations of the earth,—it will prepare them to go forth in

---

35. Rev. 7:1-8.
36. D & C 77:7-11.

the days of tribulation and vengeance upon the nations of the wicked, when God will smite them with pestilence, plague and earthquake, such as former generations never knew. Then the servants of God will need to be armed with the power of God, they will need to have that sealing blessing pronounced upon their foreheads that *they can stand forth in the midst of these desolations and plagues and not be overcome by them. When John the Revelator describes this scene* he says he saw four angels sent forth, ready to hold the four winds that should blow from the four quarters of heaven. Another angel ascended from the east and cried to the four angels, and said, "Smite not the earth now, but wait a little while." "How long?" "Until the servants of our God are sealed in their foreheads." What for? *To prepare them to stand forth in the midst of these desolations and plagues, and not be overcome. When they are prepared, when they have received a renewal of their bodies in the Lord's temple, and have been filled with the Holy Ghost and purified as gold and silver in a furnace of fire, then they will be prepared to stand before the nations of the earth and preach glad tidings of salvation in the midst of judgments that are to come like a whirlwind upon the wicked.*[37]

The Prophet Joseph Smith taught that this sealing "signifies sealing the blessing upon their heads, meaning the everlasting covenant, thereby making their calling and election sure."[38]

Orson Pratt gives this further commentary on the sealing of the 144,000 and emphasizes that they will be chosen after the appearance of the Ten Tribes:

The Ten Tribes will have to come forth and come to this land, to be crowned with glory in the midst of Zion by the hands of the servants of God, even the children of Ephraim; and twelve thousand High Priests will be elected from each of these ten tribes, as well as from the scattered tribes, and sealed in their foreheads, and will be ordained and receive power to gather out of all nations, kindreds, tongues and people as many as will come unto the general assemblage of the Church of the first-born. Will not that be a great work? *Imagine one hundred and forty-four thousand High Priests going forth among the nations,* and gathering out as many as will come to the Church of the first-born. *All that will be done, probably, in the morning of the seventh thousand years.* The work is of

37. JD, 15:365-66. See Mal. 3:1-4; D & C 128:24.
38. HC, 5:530.

great magnitude, Latter-day Saints, and we are living almost upon the eve of it.[39]

The Prophet Joseph Smith made a comment of special note concerning the 144,000, in which he pointed out that those chosen groups will be accompanied by a large host. His comment seems to be a further commentary on *Revelation* chapter seven:

> I am going on in my progress for eternal life. It is not only necessary that you should be baptized for your dead, but you will have to go through all the ordinances for them, the same as you have gone through to save yourselves. *There will be 144,000 saviors on Mount Zion, and with them an innumerable host that no man can number.* Oh! I beseech you to go forward, go forward and make your calling and your election sure; and if any man preach any other Gospel than that which I have preached, he shall be cursed.[40]

This statement seems to indicate that not all of the 144,000 will function as missionaries, but that some will labor in the temples doing work for the dead. It should be noted that the *Doctrine and Covenants* states that the 144,000 will be called to "administer the everlasting gospel," and whether their function is limited to missionary work is not indicated. It appears that they may also function in the wards, stakes, and temples of Zion. Some Latter-day Saints understand the innumerable host mentioned by the Prophet as a reference to those who come into the Church of the Firstborn through the ministrations of these High Priests. Joseph Smith further commented that the selection of persons to be among the 144,000 high priests had already begun in his day:

> I attended prayer-meeting with the quorum in the assembly room, and made some remarks respecting the hundred and forty-four thousand mentioned by John the Revelator, showing that the selection of persons to form that number had already commenced.[41]

Several journals kept by early brethren in the church contain statements saying that they are to be among the 144,000. This raises the possibility that some of the 144,000 will be resurrected beings.

---

39. JD, 16:325-26.
40. HC, 6:365.
41. HC, 6:196.

Orson Pratt stated that sealing the servants of God in their foreheads was necessary to prepare them "so that the power of death and pestilence and plague that will go forth in those days sweeping over the nations of the earth will have no power over them."[42] This statement infers that there are great judgments which are to come upon the nations of the earth after this time, and that they will come during the period in which the 144,000 high priests are laboring to gather the house of Israel.

Joseph Smith taught that the 144,000 would not only receive divine help by being sealed up against plagues and pestilence, but that in the gathering process, "Righteousness and truth are going to sweep the earth as with a flood," and "men and angels are to be co-workers in bringing to pass this great work."[43]

Summary

Four important events are anticipated in the early days of the New Jerusalem:

1. The Gospel will be taken to the Lamanites.
    A. While a relatively small number of the Lamanites have been and will be converted before the return to the New Jerusalem, the main period of their conversion will begin in the early days of that city.
    B. Millions of Lamanites are expected to come into the Church. They will gather to the area surrounding Jackson County and inhabit the nearby cities which will have been left desolate.
2. The Lord will visit the Saints in the New Jerusalem.
    A. The faithful Saints will be able to see Him in the Temple. His stay will be prolonged and He will enter into the homes of the members of the Church.
    B. The city will glow because of the presence of God's glory. The light will be visible for many miles around. The presence of God will work some change in the temple to make it resistant to decay—it will become immortal.

42. JD, 18:25. Joseph Smith made a statement which is highly significant in that it shows that the length of time from the choosing of the 144,000 to the building of the temple in old Jerusalem will be less than a generation, for he "remarked that the hundred and forty-four thousand sealed are the priests who should be anointed to administer in the daily sacrifice." (HC, 5:326) For information concerning these priests in the Palestine temple service, see Ezek. 44 and 45.
43. HC, 2:260.

3. The Ten Tribes will be revealed in the North and will come to the New Jerusalem.

   A. A great earthquake will accompany their coming.

   B. They will settle in the New Jerusalem area and will receive their priesthood and ordinances there.

4. A group of 144,000 High Priests will be chosen to administer the gospel.

   A. There will be 12,000 from each of the Twelve Tribes of Israel.

   B. These men will undergo physical changes which will protect them against the ravages of severe plagues which God will pour out after they are called.

CHAPTER VIII

The Gathering of the House of Israel to Palestine

In an earlier chapter it was seen that the missionary effort during the last days is to take place in four periods which are differentiated by the groups who are to be recipients of the proselyting. The first period, that of the missionary work among the Gentiles, is to end when the internal strife in the United States begins and God sends his judgments on the nations. The second part of the missionary work, in which the Gospel is to be carried to the people of the House of Israel, will begin when the Gospel is taken to the Lamanites during the early days of the New Jerusalem. The two earliest portions of the missionary work among the House of Israel (the conversion of the Lamanites and the restoration of the Ten Tribes) were discussed in the previous chapter. This chapter will consider another aspect of God's work with the House of Israel— the gathering of the Jews to their native land of Palestine.

Time of The Gathering of The Jews

In a revelation given to Joseph Smith on March 7, 1831, the Lord revealed the time in which the gathering of the Jewish people is to be anticipated. The revelation told of the destruction of the Jewish temple in ancient times and of the scattering of that people. Then the promise was given that "they shall be gathered again; *but they shall remain until the times of the Gentiles be fulfilled.*"[1]

During his visit to the Nephite people after his resurrection, the Savior had made the same message clear and emphatic. In speaking of the Gentiles he referred to the time when they would harden their hearts against him, and said that then he would remember his covenant to gather Israel to Palestine:

> And they shall be a scourge unto the people of this land. Nevertheless, *when they shall have received the fulness of my*

---

1. D & C 45:25.

gospel, then if they shall harden their hearts against me I will return their iniquities upon their own heads, saith the Father.

And I will remember the covenant which I have made with my people; and I have covenanted with them that I would gather them together in mine own due time, that I would give unto them again the land of their fathers for their inheritance, which is the land of Jerusalem, which is the promised land unto them forever, saith the Father.[2]

The Lord further identifed the time of the gathering of the Jews to Palestine as following in a chronological sequence. The New Jerusalem is to be built, the Lamanites to be gathered in to it, Christ is to appear there, the Gospel will be preached to the Ten Tribes, and after these events take place,

Yea, and then shall the work commence, with the Father, among all nations; in preparing the way whereby his people may be gathered home to the land of their inheritance.

And they shall go out from all nations; and they shall not go out in haste, nor go by flight, for I will go before them, saith the Father, and I will be their rearward.[3]

The Lord, then, has been careful to identify the true period of the gathering of the Jewish people as being a considerable distance in the future of the present era, after the fulfilling of the times of the Gentiles and the return of the Ten Tribes.

The Present — A Period of Preparatory Gathering

But though the actual period of gathering is yet future, the Lord is now preparing the way for that gathering. Just as the way is being prepared for the conversion of the Lamanites by the present success in the missions—, just as God is increasing the number of natural disasters from year to year in preparation for the time when He will pour out His judgments without measure—, so he is bringing to pass a preliminary gathering of the Jews to Palestine.

Latter-day Saints find much more meaning in this movement than does the world at large, for they claim the restoration of the keys of the gathering of Israel to the Prophet Joseph

2. III Ne. 20:28-29.
3. III Ne. 21:28-29.

Smith and to Oliver Cowdery by Moses in 1836.[4] Shortly after that event Orson Hyde, one of the twelve apostles, was commissioned to travel to Palestine where he dedicated that land for the return of the Jews.[5] On October 24, 1841,[6] he stood on the Mount of Olives and prayerfully petitioned God for the return of Judah's scattered remnants and for the rebuilding of the city of Jerusalem and the temple there.

Since that time the Church has witnessed many events which have indicated the spread of the spirit of gathering throughout the earth. The following brief outline is presented as a summary of important historical events which, according to Latter-day Saints, have marked the progress in the preparation for the great gathering in Palestine:

1. 1836—The keys for the gathering of Israel were restored in the Kirtland Temple.

2. 1841—The land of Palestine was dedicated for the return of the dispersed remnants of Israel by Orson Hyde.

3. 1896—The Zionist Organization was organized. It held its first conference in Basel, Switzerland, in 1897, and has done a great deal to establish the spirit of nationalism among the Jewish people.

---

4. D & C 110:11.

5. The following comment made by B. H. Roberts in the *History of the Church* is interesting in connection with Orson Hyde's mission:

   The mission appointed to Elders Orson Hyde and John E. Page, of the quorum of the Twelve, to Jerusalem, was second in importance only to that appointed to the rest of the Twelve to Great Britain. John E. Page utterly failed to fulfill his appointment, notwithstanding the frequent urging and reproofs of the Prophet. He never left the shores of America, and finally returned to Nauvoo to be severely censured for his lack of faith and energy. Orson Hyde, on the contrary, in the midst of many hardships, persevered in his journey to the Holy Land, until he succeeded in accomplishing that which had been appointed unto him. Elder Hyde it appears, was a descendant of the tribe of Judah; and sometime after the Prophet had become acquainted with him, most probably in the year 1832, in the course of pronouncing a blessing upon him, said: "In due time thou shalt go to Jerusalem, the land of thy fathers, and be a watchman unto the house of Israel; and by thy hand shall the Most High do a great work, which shall prepare the way and greatly facilitate the gathering together of that people." It was in fulfillment of this prediction upon his head that he had been called upon this mission to Jerusalem, to dedicate the land of Palestine by apostolic authority, preparatory to the return of the Jews and other tribes of Israel to that land of promise. This mission he fully accomplished. HC, 4:xxxi.

6. The land of Palestine was also dedicated by President George A. Smith in March, 1873. This was just five years before the Jewish organization of the "Lovers of Zion" was formed.

4. 1917—British forces, under the direction of General Allenby, conquered Palestine and wrested it from the grasp of the Turkish empire, which had controlled it for four centuries. England, in the armistice agreement, received the mandate of Palestine, and an Englishman of Jewish descent, Sir Herbert Samuel, was set up as governor. The Balfour Declaration, a proclamation inviting the Jews to return to Palestine, was issued by England, and Palestine became a Jewish place of gathering. The Jews began to return to their native land. Large amounts of money were spent by England in helping to build up the land and its resources.

5. 1922—Because of the discovery of oil within the borders of the Arab nation, and because of her fear of driving the Arab nations into the camp of her enemies, England, under the direction of Sir Winston Churchill, issued a White Paper which seriously weakened the effects of the Balfour Declaration. The White Paper detached Trans-Jordan from the area of Zionist operations and spoke of forming a legislative council to direct affairs in Palestine. Though it still maintained that a Jewish National Home was to be formed in Palestine, it limited Jewish immigration by stating that immigration "will not exceed the economic capacity of the country to absorb new arrivals." Nevertheless, the bitterness of Arab leaders toward the immigrating Jews grew.

6. 1930—The English Lord Passfield announced that "no margin of land available for agricultural settlement for immigrants remained," and it became the duty of Great Britain as the Mandatory power to suspend immigration until the unemployed portion obtained work.

7. 1939—A British statement of policy known as the 1939 White Paper further retarded the efforts of the Jews to gather to their new home. This paper, based on the strong anti-Jewish feelings manifested by the Arabs, prohibited Jewish immigration to Palestine after a five year period "unless the Arabs of Palestine are prepared to acquiesce in it," and proposed that a joint Jewish-Arab government be set up within ten years. To the Jews this meant the defeat of the Zionist movement and the end of a Jewish home in Palestine, for they could see that the Jews would have a very restricted part in such an arrangement.

8. 1939-1944—During World War II the Jews fought on the side of Great Britain while the Arab Mufti of Jerusalem became a tool of Adolph Hitler and lent his influence towards the destruction of the Jews throughout all of the area controlled by the Axis powers. This destruction is said to have reduced the world Jewish population from seventeen million to eleven million.[7]

9. 1947—The United Nations Special Committee on Palestine called for a separation of Palestine into an Arab state, a Jewish state, and the city of Jerusalem. The United Nations General Assembly voted to partition Palestine by October 1, 1948. A Jewish and an Arab state were to be created. In addition, the City of Jerusalem (with 100,000 Jews and 105,000 Arabs, and a territory of 289 square miles) was to be governed by the United Nations Trusteeship Council with a U. N.-appointed governor. A five-nation commission was to supervise the partition.

10. 1948—The British forces withdrew, and the British mandate ended. The Republic of Israel was proclaimed on May 14 and 15, 1948. The area assigned to Israel comprized about 5,500 square miles and had a total population of 935,000 (538,000 were Jews, 397,000 were Arabs). The Arab territory consisted of 4,500 square miles and had a population of 814,000 (804,000 were Arabs, 10,000 were Jews). A provisional president was chosen for the Jewish republic.

On May 15 units of the regular armed forces of Transjordan, Syria, Lebanon, Iraq and Egypt, together with token troops from Saudi Arabia, were sent to Palestine by the Arabs to fight against Israel. After a short period of warfare and a temporary truce, the U. N. Security Council effected a permanent truce on July 16, 1948. Breaches of the truce by both Jews and Arabs were common. Jewish immigration immediately in-

7. CR, April 1950, pp. 77-78.

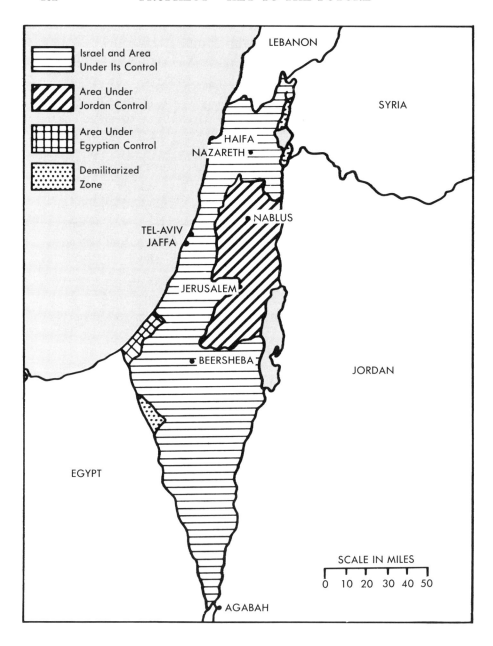

Israel and The Surrounding Nations After Armistice Agreements of 1949.

Used by permission of W. W. Norton & Company, Inc., from the book, **The Struggle For Palestine,** by **J.** C. Hurewitz. Original artist was David de Porte.

creased.[8] A final truce was effected by the U. N. by July of 1949. "The Armistice lines left in Israel's *de facto* possession almost all the territory occupied by its troops within the boundaries of the former Palestine Mandate: the entire Galilee, the Negeb (including Beersheba but excluding al-'Awja and the Gaza strip), the Coastal Plain, and a sizable corridor to Jewish Jerusalem."[9]

11. 1949—The Republic of Israel chose its first president and formed its first constituent assembly on February 14. It was admitted to membership in the United Nations on May 11, 1949.

---

8. J. C. Hurewitz in his book, *The Struggle for Palestine,* (New York: W. W. Norton and Company, Inc., 1950), pp. 27-28, made the following comment on the population growth in Palestine:

The Jewish population of Palestine grew steadily in the second half of the nineteenth century through the arrival of immigrants, drawn to the country for religious reasons. After 1882 the persecution of Jews in eastern Europe, principally Russia, and the beginnings of Zionism increased the rate of influx. The number of Jews had enlarged from about 12,000 in 1845, double that in 1882, and 47,000 in 1895 to nearly 85,000 in 1914. During World War I the Jewish population declined to an estimated 65,000 in 1919 or roughly 10 per cent of the total in the country. Between September 1920 and December 1936 some 280,000 Jews migrated to Palestine with mandatory authorization, bringing the number of Jews to 404,000 or close to 30 per cent of the over-all population. Jews from Poland headed the list of newcomers. The influx reached its peak after 1932, when the sharpening anti-Jewish feeling caused an abrupt rise in the immigration from central Europe. Between 1933 and 1936 the size of the Jewish Community, or *Yishuv* (settlement), as it had come to be known, expanded by 83 per cent as a result of the arrival of 166,000 settlers. Among the immigrants were also Jews from the near-by Arab and more remote Oriental countries, attracted to the national home because of the greater economic opportunities. . . .

At first, the immigrants had settled chiefly in the four "holy cities" of Jerusalem, Hebron, Safed, and Tiberias. But by 1914 the Jews had founded forty-four villages, whose 12,000 inhabitants, or 14 per cent of the Jewish total, continued unchanged throughout World War I. As a result of the centralized planning of the postwar years, the number of villages multiplied to 203 in 1936 and their population to 98,000, or 24 per cent of the total. Aside from Jerusalem and its immediate suburbs, the area of Jewish settlement was mainly confined to a small district southeast of Jaffa, the Coastal Plain from that city to Haifa, the Valley of Jezreel, and eastern Galilee. Two-thirds lived in Tel-Aviv, Jerusalem, and Haifa. Indeed Tel-Aviv, which started out as a northern suburb of Jaffa in 1909, had become the largest city in the country by 1936, with an all-Jewish population of about 150,000. The Jewish population expanded by almost 400 per cent between 1914 and 1936; the area of Jewish-owned land enlarged by less than 200 per cent, from approximately 110,000 acres to 308,000. This represented about 4.6 per cent of the country's over-all land area.

9. Hurewitz, *Ibid,* p. 319.

12. The events which have taken place since the formation of the Republic of Israel are summarized in this brief statement taken from *Business Week*:

> In only 10 years, the country has converted an unproductive semi-wilderness into a modern state. It has absorbed 1.3-million immigrants. It has tripled its industrial and agricultural output (the gross national product now is about $1.6-billion). Per capita income has multiplied from $200 to $600. And Israel has constructed over 450 new towns, added 200,000 units of housing, expanded land transport sixfold, and built up a merchant fleet of 200,000 tons.
>
> These demonstrations of growth, coupled with the Sinai military campaigning during the Suez crisis—when Israel's forces swept into Egypt—have made Israel confident. Even so, the nation's problems seem formidable. Continuing pressure from Egypt and other Arab neighbors is forcing Israel to spend more for defense. There is little relief in sight, barring a complete turnabout in Middle East politics.[10]

How many Jews are to be gathered? The Jewish Statistical Bureau estimates that at present [1961] there are approximately 12,650,000 Jews living throughout the world. About one seventh of them are in Palestine at present. The accompanying chart indicates the distribution of Jewish people throughout the world. The persecutions of World War II greatly reduced the population of this people, but their numbers are now increasing steadily. Prophecy gives no indication of the percent or number of the Jews who will return to Palestine.

JEWISH POPULATION BY COUNTRIES AND CITIES

Country or Continent	Jewish Population
United States	5,370,000
Canada	250,000
South America	681,150
Europe (includes Asiatic USSR and Turkey)	3,714,850
Asia	2,016,650
Australia and New Zealand	68,500
Africa	551,180
Total Jewish Population	12,652,330

10. "Israel Hurdles Its First 10 Years," *Business Week*, May 3, 1958, p. 80.

European Country:

Austria	10,500
Czechoslovakia	18,000
France	350,000
Germany	30,000
Great Britain	450,000
Hungary	100,000
Italy	32,000
Poland	41,000
Soviet Union	2,268,000
Switzerland	19,000
Turkey	60,000

Country:

Argentina	400,000
Brazil	125,000
India	26,800
Iran	80,000
Israel	1,880,000
Japan	1,000
Lebanon	6,000
Syria	5,500

City:

Jerusalem	152,000
London	280,000
Montreal	102,000
New York City	2,020,000
Paris	175,000
Tel Aviv-Jaffa	380,000

Source: *The World Almanac 1961,* p. 466 as quoted in the unpublished Master's thesis of Ross W. Warner, *The Fulfillment of Book of Mormon Prophecies,* (Provo, Utah: Brigham Young University, 1961), p. 159. Original source for the Almanac—Jewish Statistical Bureau, Dr. H. S. Linfield, Director. Figures are 1961 estimates.

The scriptures are explicit in stating that the Lord will "gather together the dispersed of Judah from the four corners of the earth."[11] But it is also of interest to note that several passages speak of specific areas from which the remnant of the House of Israel will come. Isaiah says that the remnant will be gathered from "Assyria, and from Egypt, and from Pathros, and from Cush, and from Elam, and from Shinar, and from Hamath, and from the islands of the sea"[12] He also states

11. Is. 11:12. See I Ne. 22:25; III Ne. 16:5.
12. Is. 11:11.

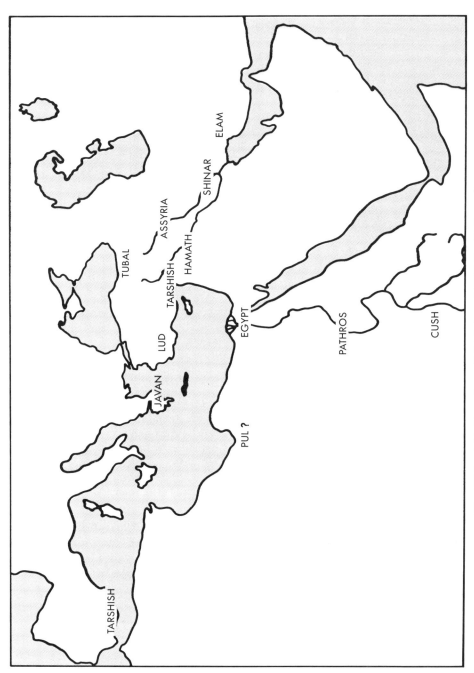

The Biblical Nations From Which Israel Will Be Gathered in The Last Days According to The Prophet Isaiah.

that missionaries will be sent "to Tarshish, Pul, and Lud, that draw the bow, to Tubal, and Javan, to the isles afar off"[13] to bring in the scattered remnants of Israel. The location of these ancient lands can be identified by comparison of the accompanying historical map with a map of the Mediterranean area as it is today.

The ancient prophets also spoke of a highway which in the last days will extend "out of Egypt to Assyria, and the Assyrian shall come into Egypt, and the Egyptian into Assyria."[14] It is not clear if all the Biblical references deal with the same highway, but they speak of "the way of holiness,"[15] and proclaim to the people that it will be made "straight in the deseret."[16] Jeremiah speaks of the route of the highway as being the same as the route by which the tribes of Israel were carried northward through Assyria:

> Is Ephraim my dear son? is he a pleasant child? for since I spake against him, I do earnestly remember him still: therefore my bowels are troubled for him; I will surely have mercy upon him, saith the Lord.
>
> Set thee up waymarks, make the high heaps: *set thine heart toward the highway, even the way which thou wentest*: turn again, O virgin of Israel, turn again to these thy cities.[17]

The swiftness of the travel of the Jews in their gathering was envisioned by Isaiah, who also saw that they would "lay hold of the prey," or in other words, bring with them the wealth of other countries which those nations will not be able to regain. Yet Isaiah also envisions sorrow and conflict in the land as they return to it:

> And he will lift up an ensign to the nations from far, and will hiss unto them from the end of the earth; and, behold, *they shall come with speed swiftly;*
>
> None shall be weary nor stumble among them; none shall slumber nor sleep; neither shall the girdle of their loins be loosed, nor the latchet of their shoes be broken:
>
> *Whose arrows are sharp, and all their bows bent, their horses' hoofs shall be counted like flint, and their wheels like a whirlwind:*

13. Is. 66:18-21.
14. Is. 19:23.
15. Is. 35:8-10.
16. Is. 40:3.
17. Jer. 31:20-21.

Their roaring shall be like a lion, they shall roar like young lions: yea, they shall roar, and *lay hold of the prey, and shall carry it away safe*, and none shall deliver it.

And in that day they shall roar against them like the roaring of the sea: and if one look unto the land, *behold darkness and sorrow*, and the light is darkened in the heavens thereof.[18]

Time of The Conversion of The Jews

Orson Pratt commented on the return of the Jews to Palestine and described the various attitudes which will characterize those who will return:

The *Jews dispersed among the Gentiles will not come and sing in the height of Zion*, or but very few of them, they will go to Jerusalem. *Some of them will believe in the true Messiah, and thousands of the more righteous, whose fathers did not consent to the shedding of the blood of the Son of God, will receive the Gospel before they gather from among the nations. Many of them, however, will not receive the Gospel, but seeing that others are going to Jerusalem they will go also;* and when they get back to Palestine, to the place where their ancient Jerusalem stood, and see a certain portion of the believing Jews endeavoring to fulfill and carry out the prophecies, they also will take hold and assist in the same work. *At the same time they will have their synagogues, in which they will preach against Jesus of Nazareth, "that imposter," as they call him, who was crucified by their fathers.*[19]

His statement seems to be a summary of various views held by Church members as to the time of the conversion of the Jewish people. The scriptures speak of three periods of conversion when portions of the Jews will accept the Savior before returning to Palestine. Jacob states that when the Jews "shall come to the knowledge of their Redeemer, they shall be gathered together again to the lands of their inheritance,"[20] and he records a statement by the Savior that "when the day cometh that they shall believe in me, that I am Christ, then have I covenanted with their fathers that they shall be restored in the flesh, upon the earth, unto the lands of their inheritance."[21] Nephi teaches

18. Is. 5:26-30.
19. JD, 18:64.
20. II Ne. 6:11.
21. II Ne. 10:7.

that others of the House of Israel, a second group, will not accept the Gospel before returning to Palestine, but that God "will bring them again out of captivity, and they shall be gathered together to the lands of their inheritance; and they shall be brought out of obscurity and out of darkness; and they shall know that the Lord is their Savior and their Redeemer, the Mighty One of Israel."[22] Others of the Jews will not be converted until Christ appears on the Mount of Olives:

> And then shall the Jews look upon me and say: What are these wounds in thine hands and in thy feet?
>
> *Then shall they know that I am the Lord;* for I will say unto them: These wounds are the wounds with which I was wounded in the house of my friends. I am he who was lifted up. I am Jesus that was crucified. I am the Son of God.[23]

The conversion of the Jews thus cannot be identified as happening at one single time, but must be accepted as a continuing, three-stage process, which will culminate in the coming of Christ during the Battle of Armageddon.

Summary

1. The Gathering of the Jews was identified by the Savior as being a process which will follow the fulfilling of the times of the Gentiles and the construction of the New Jerusalem.
2. However, Latter-day Saints recognize the hand of the Lord in the preparation of the Jewish people to return to Palestine. Beginning with the restoration of the keys for the gathering of Israel in 1836, a series of important events have led to the recent establishment of the nation of Israel in Palestine and an increased Jewish population in that country.
3. When the time for the gathering of the Jews arrives, they will be brought from throughout the world to Palestine in varying conditions of religious belief.
   A. Some Jews will accept the gospel before gathering to Palestine.
   B. Others will be converted in Palestine after gathering there.
   C. A large group, if not the majority, will not accept the gospel until Christ manifests himself to them on the Mount of Olives.

Other prophecies dealing with the gathering to Palestine will be considered in chapter thirteen.

---

22. I Ne. 22:12.
23. D & C 45:51-52.

CHAPTER IX

Plagues and the Book of Revelation

Chronological Importance of The
Choosing of The 144,000 High Priests

In the opinion of Latter-day Saints, the book of Revelation contains a prophetic account of many important events leading up to Christ's coming in glory. Of particular interest to them is the material found in chapters six through eleven of that book.[1] A series of questions and answers recorded by Joseph Smith and known to the Church as Section Seventy-seven of the *Doctrine and Covenants* provides a detailed key to this section of John's prophetic work and forms the basis for Latter-day Saint understanding of many future events.

In the seventy-seventh section the Prophet records that the earth is to pass through seven thousand years of temporal existence.[2] The present time is regarded as being near the end of the sixth thousand-year period since the time of Adam, who is thought to have been placed on the earth about 4,000 B. C. An important event or characteristic of each of the thousand-year periods is described in the Book of Revelation for each era from the time of Adam to the end of the Millennium. These eras are marked by the opening of seals—a seal for each thousand-year period.

The sixth seal tells of two important events which will take place on the earth during the present thousand-year period. The first of the two events is a great earthquake, while the second event is the calling of 144,000 men who will be sealed up against great plagues which will be poured out. Since the sixth thousand years are held to be almost completed, and since these two events have not yet taken place they will apparently take place in close proximity to each other. The anticipated nearness of the earthquake to the latter event seems to identify

1. A detailed consideration of interpretations of the Book of Revelation made by Latter-day Saint General Authorities has been collected by the author for publication in the near future.
2. D & C 77:6.

the earthquake as the quake which will take place when the Ten Tribes come from the North.[3]

In the *Revelation* account, the seventh seal, signifying the seventh thousand years, is opened after the 144,000 are called. It apparently follows soon after their call because the plagues against which they are sealed up take place during the beginning of that Millennial era. Since the Book of Revelation carefully details events during an extensive portion of the seventh thousand-years, it makes the calling of the 144,000 an important connecting link between those events and the events already considered.

The calling of the 144,000 marks a pivotal point between two types of prophecy. The reader has probably noted that a large portion of the prophecies cited have been statements of the modern Latter-day Saint General Authorities rather than statements found in the ancient scriptures. The calling of the 144,000 is the point where a transition will be made into areas which will be more extensively discussed in the scriptures themselves. It is at this point that prophecy shifts its gaze from the Americas to the world in general, with particular emphasis on future events in Palestine.

The Beginning of The Seventh Thousand-year Period

The majority of the next, or seventh thousand-year period, is expected to be occupied by the millennial reign of Christ as the King and Lawgiver upon the earth. Following his explanation in the *Doctrine and Covenants* of events to transpire in the sixth thousand-years, Joseph Smith made reference to those events to take place immediately after the beginning of the seventh thousand-years as he answered the question "What are we to understand by the sounding of the trumpets, mentioned in the eighth chapter of Revelation?" Said he,

> We are to understand that as God made the world in six days, and on the seventh day he finished his work, and sanctified it, and also formed man out of the dust of the earth, even so, *in the beginning of the seventh thousand years will the Lord God sanctify the earth, and complete the salvation of man, and judge all things, and shall redeem all things*, except

---

3. For a discussion of these two events, see chapter seven.

that which he hath not put into his power, when he shall have sealed all things, unto the end of all things; and *the sounding of the trumpets of the seven angels are the preparing and finishing of his work, in the beginning of the seventh thousand years—the preparing of the way before the time of his coming.*[4]

From this statement it is apparent that Joseph Smith held that the final events ushering in the millennial reign of Christ would not transpire until after the commencement of the seventh thousand-years of the earth's temporal existence. John's Revelation indicates that at that time great destruction will be poured out upon the earth.[5] The Prophet also specified by inspiration that the things spoken of in chapter nine of *Revelation* "are to be accomplished after the opening of the seventh seal [in the beginning of the seventh thousand-years], *before the coming of Christ.*"[6] It appears, then, that the series of seven trumps which John the Revelator outlines in chapters eight through eleven, encompasses a period of the future which begins after the time the 144,000 are chosen and sealed in Zion, and continues until after the Battle of Armageddon. They will be culminated when "the Lord God [will] sanctify the earth, and complete the salvation of man, and judge all things, and shall redeem all things, except that which he hath not put into his power,"[7] at the time of His coming in glory.

Trumps and Plagues Are Literal

It is the understanding of Latter-day Saints that the various trumps, plagues, voices of storms, and so forth, which are mentioned in the scriptures, are to be regarded as receiving a literal fulfillment. A key to such matters may be contained in the account found in the *Doctrine and Covenants*, concerning the resurrection of the righteous. Therein a revelation declares that "a trump shall sound both long and loud, *even as upon Mount Sinai*, and all the earth shall quake."[8] This statement is obviously an allusion to the Biblical account wherein God spoke to the Children of Israel on Mount Sinai through Moses and gave them the Ten Commandments. The Children of Israel were instructed that "when the trumpet soundeth long, they

---

4. D & C 77:12.
5. See Rev. 8.
6. D & C 77:13.
7. D & C 77:12.
8. D & C 29:13.

shall come up to the mount." Three days later, when there were thunders and lightnings and a thick cloud upon the mount, the people heard "the voice of the trumpet exceeding loud; so that all the people that was in the camp trembled." This trump served as a signal for Moses to assemble the people. "When the voice of the trumpet sounded long, and waxed louder and louder,"[9] Moses spake and communicated with the Lord. These trumps were not man-made, but were of a supernatural nature, and so loud that they caused the people to tremble. So also will be the trump which will bring forth the righteous dead.

Orson Pratt was very emphatic in his insistence that the trumpet blasts and the plagues of *Revelation* are to be interpreted literally. Said he:

> *The time will come, when the seven angels having the seven last trumps will sound their trumps literally, and the sound thereof will be heard among the nations,* just preparatory to the coming of the son of man; and *all the judgments foretold by John, which are to succeed the sound of each of the seven trumpets, will be fulfilled literally* upon the earth in their times and seasons.[10]

The period of plagues during the ministry of the 144,000 seems to be the period in which the Lord will testify to the people of the earth through earthquakes, lightnings, and tempests which will speak with actual voices. A revelation to Joseph Smith asked what man would say when

> The day cometh when the *thunders shall utter their voices from the ends of the earth, speaking to the ears of all that live, saying — Repent, and prepare for the great day of the Lord?*
> Yea, and again, when the lightnings shall streak forth from the east unto the west, and *shall utter forth their voices* unto all that live, and make the ears of all tingle that hear, *saying these words — Repent ye, for the great day of the Lord is come?*
> And again, the *Lord shall utter his voice out of heaven,* saying: Hearken, O ye nations of the earth, and hear the words of that God who made you.[11]

Elder Pratt held that these storms will speak actual words, calling men to repentance:

---

9. Ex. 19:13-19.
10. JD, 18:227.
11. D & C 43:21-23. See D & C 88:89-91.

It is true that the Lord has not yet spoken by the voice of thunders, calling upon the people from the ends of the earth, saying, "Repent and prepare for the great day of the Lord," but such an event will come; and when it does come *it will not be a mere ordinary, common thunderstorm, such as we experience occasionally, extending only over a small extent of country, but the Lord will cause the thunders to utter their voices from the ends of the earth until they sound in the ears of all that live, and these thunders shall use the very words here predicted —* "Repent O ye inhabitants of the earth and prepare the way of the Lord, prepare yourselves for the great day of the Lord." *These words will be distinctly heard by every soul that lives, whether in America, Asia, Africa, Europe, or upon the islands of the sea.* And not only the thunders, but the lightnings will utter forth their voices in the ears of all that live, saying, "Repent, for the great day of the Lord is come." *Besides the voices of thunder and lightning, the Lord himself, before he comes in his glory, will speak by his own voice out of heaven in the ears of all that live, commanding them to repent and to prepare for his coming.*[12]

The thunderings, lightnings, and tempests previously alluded to in the *Doctrine and Covenants* seem to fit into the *Revelation* timetable just before the series of seven angels sound their trumps to bring the plagues and destruction:

And the angel took the censer, and filled it with fire of the altar, and cast it into the earth: and *there were voices, and thunderings, and lightnings, and an earthquake.*

And the seven angels which had the seven trumpets prepared themselves to sound.[13]

There may be a continuation of these messages from heaven at the time of the earthquake which will interrupt the Battle of Armageddon:

And there were voices, and thunders, and lightnings; and there was a great earthquake, such as was not since men were upon the earth, so mighty an earthquake, and so great.[14]

These messages from heaven are expected also at the time of Christ's coming in glory:

And the temple of God was opened in heaven, and there was seen in his temple the ark of his testament: *And there*

---

12. JD, 15:332-33.
13. Rev. 8:5-6.
14. Rev. 16:18.

were lightnings, and voices, and thunderings, and an earth-quake, and great hail.[15]

The Plagues

The plagues which will accompany the sounding of the first five trumps (prophesied in *Revelation* chapters eight to eleven) fall in John's prophetic chronology after the choosing of the 144,000.

The first plague will cause all the earth's grass to be burned, as well as a third of the trees. It is thus characterized by great heat, though whether it is from fire, or from drought and the scorching effects of the sun is not revealed.

The second plague will turn a third of the sea to blood, and will kill a third of the creatures of the sea.

In the third plague, some change in the water will make it bitter and will kill many men.

The sounding of the fourth trump reveals no damage that will be done to the earth, but tells that a third part of the sun, the moon, and the stars will be darkened. (It should be noted that in both of the other two instances where prophecies say the sun will be darkened, an earthquake is involved.) These are the earthquakes which apparently precede or accompany the coming of the Lost Tribes from the north and the earthquake which interrupts the Battle of Armageddon.[16]

The fifth plague will consist of locusts, which will not hurt the grass, trees, nor other green things, but will attack only those men which have not the seal of God in their foreheads. They will torment men for five months. They are described by John like an army coming to battle, and it is stated that the devil is their leader.

These, then, are the plagues which the earth will witness after the Saints have established the New Jerusalem and the 144,000 have been chosen.[17]

It appears that an allusion to these same plagues is made in the *Doctrine and Covenants*, which states that sometime before the coming of the Lord in glory

---

15. Rev. 11:19.
16. See Joel 2:10, 31; 3:12-15; Rev. 6:12-14.
17. The Revelation account of these plagues is quoted in the left-hand column of the next section.

The sun shall be darkened, and the moon shall be turned into blood, and the stars shall fall from heaven, and there shall be greater signs in heaven above and in the earth beneath;

And there shall be *weeping and wailing* among the hosts of men;

And *there shall be a great hailstorm sent forth to destroy the crops of the earth.*

And it shall come to pass, because of the wickedness of the world, that I will take vengeance upon the wicked, for they will not repent; for the cup of mine indignation is full; for behold, my blood shall not cleanse them if they hear me not.

Wherefore, I the *Lord God will send forth flies upon the face of the earth, which shall take hold of the inhabitants thereof, and shall eat their flesh, and shall cause maggots to come in upon them;*

And *their tongues shall be stayed that they shall not utter against me; and their flesh shall fall from off their bones, and their eyes from their sockets;*

And *it shall come to pass that the beasts of the forest and the fowls of the air shall devour them up.*[18]

Comparison With Other Series of Seven Angels in The Book of Revelation

A second report of seven angels, also pouring out vials of destruction, is prophesied by John the Revelator, but the time of the fulfillment of their missions is not clear. It can be determined that their work will terminate with the Battle of Armageddon, but the time in which they will begin is open to question. It appears that the work of these seven angels is either (1) a restatement of the plagues treated in the section above (though in a different order), or else they (2) begin after the sixth plague and take place in the interim between the sixth plague and the battle of Armageddon. The evidence for each interpretation is given below. To demonstrate that these may be considered as identical with the plagues in Revelation chapters eight to eleven, they are presented in parallel columns. Note that the order is greatly changed at the coming of the sixth and seventh angels. The right-hand column is not in chronological order, as contained in John's Revelation, but is adjusted to show a comparison of events as given in the left-hand column.

18. D & C 29:14-20.

Revelation 16

First Trump

The first angel sounded, and there followed hail and fire mingled with blood, and they were cast upon the earth; and the *third part of trees was burnt up, and all green grass was burnt up.* (8:7)

Second Trump

And the second angel sounded, and as it were a great mountain burning with fire was cast into the *sea; and the third part of the sea became blood;*

And the third part of the creatures which were in the sea, and had life, died; and the third part of the ships were destroyed. (8:8-9)

Third Trump

And the third angel sounded, and there fell a great star from heaven, burning as it were a lamp, and *it fell upon the third part of the rivers, and upon the fountains of waters;*

And the name of the star is called Wormwood: and the third part of the waters became wormwood; and many men died of the waters, *because they were made bitter.* (8:10-11)

Fourth Trump

And the fourth angel sounded, and the third part of the sun was smitten, and the third part of the moon, and the third part of the stars; so as *the third part of them was darkened,* and the day shone not for a third part of it, and the night likewise. (8:12)

Fifth Trump

And the fifth angel sounded, and I saw a star fall from heaven unto the earth: and to him was given the key of the bottomless pit.

And he opened the bottomless pit; and there arose a smoke out of the pit, as the smoke of a great furnace; and the *sun and the air*

Revelation 8-11

Fourth Plague

And the fourth angel poured out his vial upon the *sun; and power was given unto him to scorch men with fire.*

And men were scorched with great heat, and blasphemed the name of God, which hath power over these plagues: and they repented not to give him glory. (16: 8-9)

Second Plague

And the second angel poured out his vial upon the *sea; and it became as the blood of a dead man: and every living soul died in the sea.* (16:3)

Third Plague

And the third angel poured out his vial upon the *rivers and fountains of waters; and they became blood.* (16:4)

Fourth Plague

And the fifth angel poured out his vial upon the seat of the beast; and *his kingdom was full of darkness;* and they gnawed their tongues for pain,

And blasphemed the God of heaven because of their pains and their sores, and repented not of their deeds. (16:10-11)

were darkened by reason of the smoke of the pit.

And there came out of the smoke locusts upon the earth: and unto them was given power, as the scorpions of the earth have power.

And it was commanded them that they should not hurt the grass of the earth, neither any green thing, neither any tree; but *only those men which have not the seal of God in their foreheads.*

And to them it was given that they should not kill them, but that *they should be tormented five months: and their torment was as the torment of a scorpion, when he striketh a man.*

And in those days shall men seek death, and shall not find it; and shall desire to die, and death shall flee from them.

And the shapes of the locusts were like unto horses prepared unto battle; and on their heads were as it were crowns like gold, and their faces were as the faces of men.

And they had hair as the hair of women, and their teeth were as the teeth of lions.

And they had breastplates, as it were breastplates of iron; and the sound of their wings was as the sound of chariots of many horses running to battle.

And they had tails like unto scorpions, and there were stings in their tails: and their power was to hurt men five months.

And they had a king over them, which is the angel of the bottomless pit, whose name in the Hebrew tongue is Abaddon, but in the Greek tongue hath his name Apollyon. (9:1-11)

Sixth Trump

And the sixth angel sounded, and I heard a voice from the four horns of the golden altar which is before God,

Saying to the sixth angel which had the trumpet, *Loose the four angels which are bound in the great river Euphrates.*

Fifth Plague

And the first went, and poured out his vial upon the earth; and *there fell a noisome and grievous sore upon the men which had the mark of the beast, and upon them which worshipped his image.* (16:2)

Sixth Plague

And the sixth angel poured out his vial upon the *great river Euphrates; and the water thereof was dried up, that the way of the kings of the east might be prepared.* (16:12)

And the four angels were loosed, which were prepared for an hour, and a day, and a month, and a year, for to slay the third part of men.

And the number of the army *of the horsemen were two hundred thousand*: and I heard the number of them.

And thus I saw the horses in the vision, and them that sat on them, having breastplates of fire, and of jacinth, and brimstone: and the heads of the horses were as the heads of lions; and out of their mouths issued fire and smoke and brimstone.

By these three was the third part of men killed, by the fire, and by the smoke, and by the brimstone, which issued out of their mouths. (9:13-18)

First Intermediate Event Between the Sixth and Seventh Trump

And the voice which I heard from heaven spake unto me again, and said, Go and take the little book which is open in the hand of the angel which standeth upon the sea and upon the earth.

And I went unto the angel, and said unto him, Give me the little book. And he said unto me, Take it, and eat it up; and it shall make thy belly bitter, but it shall be in thy mouth sweet as honey.

And I took the little book out of the angel's hand, and ate it up; and it was in my mouth sweet as honey: and as soon as I had eaten it, my belly was bitter.

And he said unto me, *Thou must prophesy again b e f o r e many peoples, and nations, and tongues, and kings.* (10:8-11)

First Intermediate Event

And I saw *three unclean spirits* like frogs come out of the mouth of the dragon, and out of the mouth of the beast, and out of the mouth of the false prophet.

For *they are the Spirits of devils, working miracles, which go forth unto the kings of the earth and of the whole world, to gather them to the battle of that great day of God Almighty.*

And behold, I come as a thief. Blessed is he that watcheth, and keepeth his garments, lest he walk naked, and they see his shame.

And *he gathered them together into a place called in the Hebrew tongue Armageddon.* (16:13-16)

Second Intermediate Event Between the Sixth and Seventh Trump

And there was given me a reed like unto a rod: and the angel stood, saying, Rise, and *measure the temple of God, and the altar, and them that worship therein.*

But the court which is without the temple leave out, and measure it not; for it is given unto the Gentiles: and *the holy city shall they tread under foot for forty and two months.*

And *I will give power unto my two witnesses, and they shall prophesy a thousand two hundred and threescore days,* clothed in sackcloth.

These are the two olive trees, and the two candlesticks standing before the God of the earth.

And if any man will hurt them, fire proceedeth out of their mouth, and devoureth their enemies: and if any man will hurt them, he must in this manner be killed.

These have power to shut heaven, that it rain not in the days of their prophecy: and have power over waters to turn them to blood, and to smite the earth with all plagues, as often as they will.

And when they shall have finished their testimony, the beast that ascendeth out of the bottomless pit shall make war against them, and *shall overcome them, and kill them.*

And *their dead bodies shall lie in the street of the great city,* which spiritually is called Sodom and Egypt, where also our Lord was crucified.

And *they of the people and kindreds and tongues and nations shall see their dead bodies three days and a half,* and shall not suffer their dead bodies to be put in graves.

And they that dwell upon the earth shall rejoice over them, and make merry, and shall send gifts one to another; because these two prophets tormented them that dwelt on the earth.

And after three days and a half the Spirit of life from God entered into them, and they stood upon their feet; and great fear fell upon them which saw them.

And they heard a great voice from heaven saying unto them, Come up hither, And *they ascended up to heaven in a cloud; and their enemies beheld them.*

And the same hour was there a great earthquake, and the tenth part of the city fell, and in the earthquake were slain of men seven thousand: and the remnant were affrighted, and gave glory to the God of heaven. (11:1-13)

Seventh Trump

And the seventh angel sounded; and there were great voices in heaven, saying, *The kingdoms of this world are become the kingdoms of our Lord, and of his Christ, and he shall reign for ever and ever.*

And the four and twenty elders, which sat before God on their seats, fell upon their faces, and worshipped God.

Saying, We give thee thanks, O Lord God Almighty, which art, and wast and art to come; because thou hast taken to thee thy great power, and hast reigned.

Seventh Plague

And the seventh angel poured out his vial into the air; and there came a great voice out of the temple of heaven, from the throne saying, It is done.

And there were voices, and thunders, and lightnings; and there was a great earthquake, such as was not since men were upon the earth, so mighty an earthquake, and so great.

And the great city was divided into three parts, and the cities of the nations fell: and great Babylon came in remembrance before God, to give unto her the cup of the wine of the fierceness of his wrath.

And every island fled away, and the mountains were not found.

And there fell upon men a great hail out of heaven, every stone about the weight of a talent: and men blasphemed God because of the plague of the hail; for the plague thereof was exceeding great. (16:17-21)

And the nations were angry, and
*thy wrath is come, and the time
of the dead, that they should be
judged, and that thou shouldest
give reward unto thy servants the
prophets, and to the saints, and
them that fear thy name, small and
great; and shouldest destroy them
which destroy the earth.*
And the temple of God was
opened in heaven, and there was
seen in his temple the ark of his
testament; *and there were lightnings, and voices, and thunderings,
and an earthquake, and great hail.*
(11:15-19)

The interpretation that the plagues of Revelation sixteen
will follow the sounding of the sixth trump, which will introduce a period of extreme devastation, would cause the time sequence to be arranged in the following manner:

Revelation 8 to 11   **Revelation 16**

First Trump (8:7)
Second Trump (8:8-9)
Third Trump (8:10-11)
Fourth Trump (8:12)
Fifth Trump (9:1-11)
Sixth Trump (9:13-18)

                                          First Plague (16:2)
                                          Second Plague (16:3)
                                          Third Plague (16:4)
                                          Fourth Plague (16:8-9)
                                          Fifth Plague (16:10-11)
                                          Sixth Plague (16:12)

Gathering of Tribes to Israel (10:8-11)   Gathering to the Battle of Arma-
geddon (16:13-16)
Battle of Armageddon (11:1-13)   Seventh Plague (16:17-21)
Seventh Trump (11:15-19)

It may be seen that no conclusive decision can be made as
to how these two series of angels will come chronologically.
However, the message of *Revelation* can be generalized as saying that a series of terrible plagues will come upon the earth
following the choosing of the 144,000 and before the Battle of
Armageddon.

Comparison With Angels With Trumpets in the Doctrine and Covenants

Another report of seven angels is spoken of in *Doctrine and
Covenants* 88:95-110. In this chapter the angels sound their

trumps and then sound them in the same order a second time.
Though their message is discussed later in this work, the time
of their coming will be considered here. They begin to function
at the Savior's final coming—after the curtain of heaven is unfolded, the face of the Lord has been unveiled, the living saints
have been caught up, and the righteous dead have been raised.

> And there shall be *silence in heaven for the space of half
> an hour;* and immediately after shall the *curtain of heaven be
> unfolded,* as a scroll is unfolded after it is rolled up, and the
> face of the Lord shall be unveiled;
> And the *saints that are upon the earth, who are alive,
> shall be quickened and be caught up to meet him.*
> And they who have slept in their graves shall come forth,
> for their *graves shall be opened; and they also shall be caught
> up to meet him* in the midst of the pillar of heaven.
> They are Christ's, the first fruits, *they who shall descend
> with him first,* and they who are on the earth and in their
> graves, who are first caught up to meet him, and all this by
> the voice of the sounding of the trump of the angel of God.
> And after this *another angel shall sound, which is the
> second trump; and then cometh the redemption of those who
> are Christ's at his coming;* who have received their part in
> that prison which is prepared for them, that they might receive
> the gospel, and be judged according to men in the flesh.[19]

Orson Pratt thought that the first seven trumps in section
eighty-eight of the *Doctrine and Covenants* were the same
trumps as those of *Revelation* eight to eleven. While explaining
the resurrection as related in *Doctrine and Covenants* section
eighty-eight, he held that there would be quite an extended
period of months or even years between the time when the
Saints would be raised from their graves and the actual coming
of the Savior. He then described what would have to take place
during the interim period:

> We might bring up, also, the declaration of John in relation
> to the two witnesses who are to prophecy about that period.
> They are to prophecy three and a half years, and their field of
> labor will be Jerusalem, after it shall have been rebuilt by the
> Jews. By means of their prophecies and the power of God
> attending them, the nations who are gathered together against
> Jerusalem will be kept at bay, these Prophets will hold them
> in check by their faith and power. By and by these nations over-

19. D & C 88:95-99.

come the two witnesses and, having finished their mission they are slain, and their bodies will lie three days and a half in the streets of the city. Then a great earthquake will take place, and these two witnesses will be caught up to heaven.

All this takes place after these trumps begin to sound [Doctrine and Covenants 88:95-110]; and if these two witnesses are to fulfill a mission of three and a half years, *it shows that the sounding of the trumpets does not take place, as many have supposed, in rapid succession, but certain events have to be accomplished between their respective soundings. By and by the whole seven will have sounded, and then they commence to sound a second time.* According to the revelation from which I have read, the second sounding of the trumpets is not to produce destruction among the nations, but the sound of the first one will reveal the secret acts of God, his purposes and doings on the earth during the first thousand years; the sounding of the second will reveal the doings and purposes of the Great Jehovah during the second thousand years, and so on, until the seventh shall sound the second time, and pronounce the work of God finished, so far as the great preparation needful for his second coming is concerned.

Notice, now, that it is the first sounding of the first of these seven [Doctrine and Covenants 88:95-110] *when the first resurrection takes place; and all these great works are to be performed on the earth, and years elapse before Jesus descends with all his Saints;* that is, if we understand these things correctly, by what little is revealed upon the subject.[20]

His interpretation was apparently based on the assumption that the silence in heaven for the space of half an hour in *Doctrine and Covenants* 88:95 is the same period as the half hour of silence mentioned in *Revelation* 8:1. But this interpretation is probably unacceptable due to the great difference in the messages and missions of the several angels of the account in the *Doctrine and Covenants,* as compared to the work performed by the angels in *Revelation* chapters eight through eleven. If the *Doctrine and Covenants* series of angels with trumps is different than the angels spoken of in *Revelation,* then the correlation between the two accounts would seem to be as follows:

20. JD, 16:329.

Revelation 8-11

Half Hour of Silence in Heaven (interlude between the calling of the 144,000 and the beginning of the plagues.) (8:1)

First Trump. (8:7)

Second Trump. (8:8-9)

Third Trump. (8:10-11)

Fourth Trump. (8:12)

Fifth Trump. (9:1-11)

Sixth Trump. (9:13-18)

Battle of Armageddon (11:1-13)

Seventh Trump. (11:15-9)

Doctrine and Covenants 88:95-110

Half Hour of Silence in Heaven (interlude between the Battle of Armageddon and Christ's Coming in Glory.) (88:95)

Curtain of Heaven Unrolled. (88:95)

Face of the Lord Unveiled. (88:95) Living Saints Caught Up into Heaven. (88:96)

Dead Caught Up to Heaven. (88:97) This is the first trump.

Second Trump. (Christ's Coming.) (88:99)

Trumps Three to Seven. (88:100-106)

Seven Trumpets Again Sound. (88:108-110)

Summary

1. The choosing of the 144,000 is an important chronological link because it relates the many prophecies concerning America and the New Jerusalem with the Biblical prophecies of later happenings. It also represents a shifting point from prophecies which have been made predominantly by modern prophets in the last days back to prophecies found in the Bible.

2. The calling of the 144,000 is an event which is prophesied to take place during the sixth thousand-year period of the earth's temporal existence. Chronologies indicate that the end of this thousand-year period is near.

3. The *Revelation* account also describes a great earthquake which will happen during the sixth thousand-year era. Since we know of no fulfillment of this prophecy in the past it is expected to transpire in the future. The nearness of the end of the thousand-year period seems to indicate that the earthquake will immediately precede the calling of the 144,000. This links the earthquake with the earthquake which will accompany the return of the Ten Tribes, whose coming will of necessity need to precede the calling of the 144,000 since many of the 144,000 will be taken from the returning tribes.

4. The seventh thousand-year period will encompass the Millennium. Beginning shortly after the calling of the 144,000, this period will be prefaced by a series of plagues which were prophesied by John the Revelator.

5. These plagues will be introduced by angels sounding trumps. These will be literal trumpet blasts and will be heard throughout the world.

6. It appears that the plagues spoken of in *Revelation* 8-11 may be the same plagues prophesied in *Revelation* chapter 16. If they are not, then the plagues of *Revelation* 16 begin after the sixth trump of the plagues prophesied in Revelation 8-11.

7. It appears that the angels sounding the trumps in Revelation 8-11 are different than the angels spoken of in Doctrine and Covenants 88:95-110. Apparently the angels mentioned in the Doctrine and Covenants fulfill their responsibilities after those mentioned in *Revelation*.

CHAPTER X

Universal Conflict and the Fall of the Christian Nations

It has been shown that before the times of the Gentiles are fulfilled, wars and revolutions are expected in some measure to overthrow those despotic governments that do not allow the Gospel to be preached within their borders. Such warfare has been regarded by Latter-day Saints as a factor aiding governments to be established that will more readily allow "Mormon" missionaries to enter their respective countries and carry their message to those who will receive it. During the time of these wars the Saints are not expected to gather out of their homelands in large numbers, but will apparently remain in their homes even though they may be called upon to suffer harsh persecution and much tribulation. When the times of the Gentiles are fulfilled, however, many nations are expected to crumble, to rise no more.

In America, except the Gentiles repent, it is forseen that internal strife, resulting largely from spiritual decay, will plunge society into chaos. During that period of turmoil the place of greatest safety throughout the land is expected to be among the Saints in the Rocky Mountains. During this era it is believed that the Center Place of Zion will be redeemed and built up. When that building program begins and the Lamanites and the Ten Tribes come to Zion, the time will arrive for 144,000 ministers to be called from among the tribes of Israel and sealed with power to administer the Gospel to the nations of the earth. These High Priests are expected to be endowed with special powers to withstand the plagues to be poured out in that day.

World-wide Conflict —Fourth World War

Five of these plagues prophesied by John the Revelator were discussed in the previous chapter. The sixth is to be a great war which will apparently originate near the river Euphrates and which will apparently destroy a third of all mankind:

> And the sixth angel sounded, and I heard a voice from the four horns of the golden altar which is before God,

Saying to the sixth angel which had the trumpet, *Loose the four angels which are bound in the great river Euphrates.*

And the four angels were loosed, which were prepared for an hour, and a day, and a month, and a year, for to slay the third part of men.

And the number of the army of the horsemen were two hundred thousand thousand: and I heard the number of them.

And thus I saw the horses in the vision, and them that sat on them, having breastplates of fire, and of jacinth, and brimstone: and the heads of the horses were as the heads of lions; and out of their mouths issued fire and smoke and brimstone.

By these three was the third part of men killed, by the fire, and by the smoke, and by the brimstone, which issued out of their mouths.[1]

A revelation to Joseph Smith, that makes reference to the New Jerusalem in that era, emphasizes that this conflict will be worldwide, for it reports that "there shall be gathered unto it out of every nation under heaven; and it shall be the only people that shall not be at war one with another."[2] This will probably be because of the glory of God which will have encompassed the city.

Orson Pratt taught that in that future day, when the Spirit of the Lord will have been withdrawn from the Gentiles and the missionaries of Zion will have been sent to seek out Israel, the Lord's judgments will be poured out. At that time the missionaries will give greater emphasis to the Lord's proclamation of universal judgments:

It is not only a Gospel to be preached to all the nations of the earth, but in connection with it *you will have to make proclamation connected with it, to all people, to fear God and give glory to him, for the hour of his judgment is come.* And as these judgments come, *kingdoms and thrones will be cast down and overturned. Empire will war with empire, kingdom with kingdom, and city with city, and there will be one general revolution throughout the earth, the Jews fleeing to their own country,* desolation coming upon the wicked, with the swiftness of whirlwinds and fury poured out.[3]

On another occasion Orson Pratt spoke of a great war of desolation upon the earth, after the times of the Gentiles are

---

1. Rev. 9:13-18.
2. D & C 45:69.
3. JD, 14:65-66.

fulfilled and the Lord has withdrawn His servants from among them. With particular reference to the European scene he explained:

> When that day shall come [when the missionaries will be called home] there shall be wars, not such wars as have come in centuries and years that are past and gone, but *a desolating war. When I say desolating, I mean that it will lay these European nations in waste. Cities will be left vacated, without inhabitants. The people will be destroyed by the sword of their own hands.* Not only this but *many other cities will be burned;* for when contending armies are wrought up with the terrible anger, without the Spirit of God upon them, when they have not that spirit of humanity that now characterizes many of the wars amongst the nations, when they are left to themselves, there will be no quarter given, no prisoners taken, but *a war of destruction, of desolation, of the burning of the cities and villages, until the land is laid desolate.*[4]

Elder Pratt also spoke of the universal nature of this conflict and said that the Jews who have remained scattered among the nations will flee in great numbers to Palestine at that time:

> By-and-by the Spirit of God will entirely withdraw from those Gentile nations, and leave them to themselves. *Then they will find something else to do besides warring against the Saints in their midst — besides raising their sword and fighting against the Lamb of God; for then war will commence in earnest,* and such a war as probably never entered into the hearts of men in our age to conceive of. *No nation of the Gentiles upon the face of the whole earth but what will be engaged in deadly war, except the Latter-day Kingdom.* They will be fighting one against another. And when that day comes, *the Jews will flee to Jerusalem, and those nations will almost use one another up,* and those of them who are left will be burned; for that will be the last sweeping judgment that is to go over the earth to cleanse it from wickedness.[5]

His comments seem to provide the answer to the problem of what will be the influence which will cause the Jews to gather to Palestine. On the other hand, the gathering of the Jews to Jerusalem serves to indicate that the universal conflict will take place after the coming of the Ten Tribes and the calling of the 144,000 high priests.

---

4. JD, 20:150-51.
5. JD, 7:188.

The Christian Nations Will Fall

Orson Pratt foretold the downfall of England after the righteous have been gathered out of that nation. From other statements which he made it seems that he expected this prophecy to be fulfilled during this period of universal devastation:

> But if you will not, as a nation, repent, and unite yourselves with God's kingdom, then the days are near at hand, when the righteous shall be gathered out of your midst; and woe unto you when that day shall come! For it shall be a day of vengeance upon the British nation; and your armies shall perish; your maritime forces shall cease; your cities shall be ravaged, burned, and made desolate, and your strongholds shall be thrown down; the poor shall rise against the rich, and their storehouses and their fine mansions shall be pillaged, their merchandise, and their gold, and their silver, and their rich treasures, shall be plundered; then shall the Lords, the Nobles, and the merchants of the land, and all in high places, be brought down, and shall sit in the dust, and howl for the miseries that shall be upon them; and they that trade by sea shall lament and mourn; for their traffic shall cease. And thus shall the Lord Almighty visit you, because of your great wickedness in rejecting His servants and His kingdom; and *if you continue to harden your hearts, your remnants which shall be left, shall be consumed as the dry stubble before the devouring flame,* and all the land shall be cleansed by the fire of the Lord, that the filthiness thereof may no more come up before Him.[6]

Charles W. Penrose also spoke of this era of universal warfare and gave a warning of the many manifestations of destruction and distress that would then occur. He explained that

> Through the rejection of this Gospel, which "shall be preached to all the world as a witness" of the coming of Christ, *the world will increase in confusion, doubt, and horrible strife. As the upright in heart, the meek of the earth, withdraw from their midst, so will the Spirit of God also be withdrawn from them.* The darkness upon their minds in relation to eternal things will become blacker, nations will engage in frightful and bloody warfare, the crimes which are now becoming so frequent will be of continual accurrence, the ties that bind together families and kindred will be disregarded and violated, the passions of human nature will be put to the vilest uses, the very elements around will seem to be affected by the na-

---

6. *Millennial Star,* Vol. 19, pp. 680-681, October 24, 1857.

tional and social convulsions that will agitate the world, and *storms, earthquakes, and appalling disasters by sea and land will cause terror and dismay among the people; new diseases will silently eat their ghastly way through the ranks of the wicked;* the earth, soaked with gore and defiled with the filthiness of her inhabitants, will begin to *withhold her fruits in their season; the waves of the sea will heave themselves beyond their bounds,* and all things will be in commotion; and in the midst of all these calamities, the *masterminds among nations will be taken away,* and fear will take hold of the hearts of all men.[7]

A prophecy uttered by the Prophet Daniel speaks of the period of universal conflict and foretells the outcome of that strife. He prophesied of four beasts, which are understood by Latter-day Saints to be references to four great world powers in various periods of history. The first was Babylonia; the second, the Medes and Persians; the third, Greece; and the fourth, Rome and the kingdoms that emerged from the Roman Empire. Though each of these powers fell to the onslaught of the next, their people still continued in existence and their descendants have come down to the present day. Daniel foretold of the eventual downfall of the descendants of each of these four kingdoms in a time which is yet future. Apparently speaking of the destruction of the nations which have their origin in the Roman Empire, he said:

> I beheld till the thrones were cast down, . . . I beheld even till *the beast was slain, and his body destroyed, and given to the burning flame.*
>
> *As concerning the rest of the beasts, they had their dominion taken away: yet their lives were prolonged* for a season and a time.[8]

Orson Pratt, in commenting on Daniel's prophecy, explained its message that the universal conflict would result in the destruction of the nations which have descended from the Roman Empire:

> *The fourth beast, represented by the Roman Empire and the kingdoms that have grown out of it, will be* "slain and his body destroyed and given to the burning flame." Here then we can read the destiny of that portion of the inhabitants of the earth constituting the fourth beast: or, in other words, *the destiny*

---

7. *Millennial Star,* Vol. 21, p. 582, September 19, 1859.
8. Dan. 7:9, 11-12.

of the kingdoms of Europe, who were to arise and grow out of that fourth power. *We can read the final destiny of the kingdoms of Europe, namely, Germany, France, Italy, Spain, Portugal, Scandinavia, and the great northern power Russia, Austria and Prussia,* and all those various nations, that more particularly pertain to this great iron power that once so cruelly oppressed the people; its "body shall be destroyed and given to the burning flame," which signifies the nature of the judgment that will befall them. *According to other prophecies, contained in Daniel, a succession of judgments, great and terrible in their nature, will overtake them, before the fire spoken of comes. Nation will rise against nation in war, kingdom against kingdom:* or in the language of Isaiah, "Behold, the Lord will come with fire, and with his chariots like a whirlwind, to render his anger with fury, and his rebuke with flames of fire. For by fire and by his sword will the Lord plead with all flesh; and the slain of the Lord shall be many."

It seems then that the body of the fourth power is to be given to the burning flame, that signifies the utter extinction of that power from the face of the earth. *The heathen nations representing the other three beasts, will not then be destroyed: but their lives are to be prolonged, and their dominion is to be taken away. Though their lives will be prolonged, yet they will not have power to rule and govern, only as they are permitted.* If you will read from the beginning of the 36th to the end of the 39th chapters of Ezekiel, you find much said, in regard to the heathen nations. "And the heathen shall know that I am the Lord," etc. But the fourth power represents the nations of modern Christendom. They have not the privilege of the heathen, in having their lives prolonged. Why? Does the speaker mean to say that modern Christendom is more wicked than the heathen? Yes; *the people of Christendom possess more light and knowledge than the heathen, and therefore, they are under the greater condemnation; for according to the light and knowledge they severally have, will they be judged.* The more enlightened nations, so called, are rejecting the Gospel message which is being sent to them by divine authority; and for that reason their utter destruction is inevitable, and, as had been decreed, they must pass away. Their lives will not be prolonged. *Not only the kingdoms and governments of Europe, and the western portions of Asia are to be thus visited, but also those who have grown out of these kingdoms, that have emigrated to this western hemisphere, and elsewhere.*[9]

---

9. JD, 18:339-40. Repeated lines in the text have been omitted by the author.

Thus Elder Pratt taught Daniel's message: that in a time yet future the nations which have originated from the Roman Empire, or the nations which have embraced Christianity, will be overcome. Those people who are descended from Babylonia, Media, Persia, and Greece will lose their dominion and political power in the same conflict, but that they will not lose their cultural identity as nations until a later period.

It was his teaching, however, that all governments will eventually be destroyed:

> This prophecy of Daniel will give a true understanding of the matter to our wise men and statesmen, and all who desire to know the *future destiny of the American government, the European governments, and all the kingdoms of the earth. Their destiny is total destruction* from our earth, no matter how great or powerful they may become. Though our nation may grasp on the right hand and on the left; though it may annex the British possessions, and extend its dominions to the south and grasp the whole of this great western hemisphere, *and although our nation shall become as powerful in population as in extent of territory, its destiny is foretold in the saying of the Prophet Daniel,* "They shall become like the chaff of the summer threshing floor, the wind shall carry them away and no place shall be found for them." *So with the kingdoms of Europe, so with the kingdoms of Western Asia and Eastern Europe.*[10]

Summary

1. There is to be a period of universal conflict when terrible war will engulf the world. It will come after the New Jerusalem is built and during the period in which Israel will be gathering to Palestine.
2. The only place which will be free from war at this time will be the New Jerusalem—apparently because of the glory of God which will be radiating from it.
3. The conflict will apparently serve as a force which will cause many Jewish people who otherwise would have remained in other lands to gather to Palestine.
4. The conflict will destroy, as political entities, the nations which have descended from the Roman Empire. Since these are the nations which have accepted Christian principles, this represents a major judgment upon present-day Christianity.

---

10. JD, 15:72-73.

5. Non-Christian, or heathen nations, will also be affected by the war. They will loose their power and dominion but will maintain their national identities.

6. The war will be far more devastating than any war which has yet been fought, for it will cause the death of one-third of the world's population. The survivors will be left in a disorganized condition in lands filled with rubble and chaos.

CHAPTER XI

Christ's Appearance in the Council at Adam-Ondi-Ahman

Adam is The Ancient of Days

Sometime during the period of universal conflict an important council meeting is expected to be held on the American continent. Latter-day Saints accept Daniel's report of a prophetic vision of this event as an important statement pertaining to this great assemblage. Said the Hebrew prophet,

> *I beheld till the thrones were cast down,* and the Ancient of days did sit, whose garment was white as snow, and the air of his head like the pure wool: his throne was like the fiery flame, and his wheels as burning fire.
> A fiery stream issued and came forth from before him: thousand thousands ministered unto him, and *ten thousand times ten thousand stood before him: the judgment was set, and the books were opened.*[1]

This prophecy by Daniel interrupts his prophecy of the destruction of the Christian nations spoken of in the preceding chapter. Two items seem to indicate the chronological position of this event: first before it happens, Daniel reports, thrones will be cast down. Apparently the universal conflict will be well underway. Yet at the council the judgment is set. This second point, it will be seen, will be the judging of the nations and their future fate. This apparently will take place before the universal conflict is over, since it will cause the downfall of many nations.

Joseph Smith and other prominent Latter-day Saint leaders spoke repeatedly of this event and its importance to the picture of latter-day events. In identifying the Ancient of days, the Prophet said:

> Daniel in his seventh chapter speaks of the Ancient of days; *he means the oldest man, our Father Adam, Michael, he will call his children together and hold a council with them to prepare them for the coming of the Son of Man.* He (Adam)

---

1. Dan. 7:9-10.

is the father of the human family, and presides over the spirits of all men, and *all that have had the keys must stand before him in this grand council.* This may take place before some of us leave this stage of action. *The Son of Man stands before him, and there is given him glory and dominion. Adam delivers up his stewardship to Christ,* that which was delivered to him as holding the keys of the universe, but retains his standing as head of the human family.[2]

Joseph Smith said a great deal about Adam and the role he is held to play in the affairs of this earth. On another occasion he stated that Adam holds the keys of the dispensation of the fullness of times:

> Commencing with *Adam, who was the first man, who is spoken of in Daniel as being the "Ancient of Days," or in other words, the first and oldest of all,* the great, grand progenitor of whom it is said in another place he is Michael, because he was the first and father of all, not only by progeny, but the first to hold the spiritual blessings, to whom was made known the plan of ordinances for the salvation of his posterity unto the end, and to whom Christ was first revealed, and through whom Christ has been revealed from heaven, and will continue to be revealed from henceforth. *Adam holds the keys of the dispensation of the fullness of times:* i.e., *the dispensation of all the times have been and will be revealed through him from the beginning to Christ, and from Christ to the end of all the dispensations that are to be revealed.* "Having made known unto us the mystery of His will, according to His good pleasure which He hath purposed in Himself: that in the dispensation of the fullness of times He might gather together in one all things in Christ, both which are in heaven, and which are on earth; even in him." (Ephesians, 1st chap., 9th and 10th verses.)
>
> *Now the purpose in Himself in the winding up scene of the last dispensation is that all things pertaining to that dispensation should be conducted precisely in accordance with the preceding dispensations.*
>
> And again. *God purposed in Himself that there should not be an eternal fullness until every dispensation should be fulfilled and gathered together in one,* and that all things whatsoever, that should be gathered together in one in those dispensations unto the same fullness and eternal glory, should be in Christ Jesus; therefore He set the ordinances to be the same forever and ever, and *set Adam to watch over them, to reveal them from heaven to man, or to send angels to reveal them.*

---

2. HC, 3:386-87.

"Are they not all ministering spirits, sent forth to minister for them who shall be heirs of salvation?" (Hebrews, i, 14).

These angels are under the direction of Michael or Adam, who acts under the direction of the Lord. From the above quotation we learn that Paul perfectly understood the purposes of God in relation to His connection with man, and that glorious and perfect order which He established in Himself, whereby he sent forth power, revelations, and glory. . . .

This, then, is the nature of the Priesthood; *every man holding the Presidency of his dispensation, and one man holding the Presidency of them all, even Adam; and Adam receiving his Presidency and authority from the Lord,* but cannot receive a fullness until Christ shall present the Kingdom to the Father, which shall be at the end of the last dispensation.[3]

Location and Description of The Council at Adam-ondi-Ahman

In 1838 the Prophet pointed out that this anticipated assembly will be held at a place known to Latter-day Saints as Adam-ondi-Ahman. Of the location of that place in the State of Missouri and how it was initially designated, Joseph Smith wrote,

> In the afternoon I went up the river about half a mile to Wight's Ferry, accompanied by President Rigdon, and my clerk, George W. Robinson, for the purpose of selecting and laying claim to a city plat near said ferry in Daviess County, township 60, ranges 27 and 28, and sections 25, 36, 31, and 30, which the brethren called *"Spring Hill," but by the mouth of the Lord it was named Adam-ondi-Ahman, because, said He, it is the place where Adam shall come to visit his people, or the Ancient of Days shall sit, as spoken of by Daniel the Prophet.*[4]

Those present in the council of Adam-ondi-Ahman are expected to include all those who, in past ages of the earth's history, have held keys of priesthood and responsibility, and also many who will then be living in mortality on the earth. The council is to be attended by a great multitude of the mortal and immortal beings. Orson Pratt marvelled at the vast number Daniel reported would be present at that meeting:

> *How much is ten thousand times ten thousand? Only a hundred millions, but that would make quite a large congregation.* All the inhabitants of the United States only number about forty millions, counting men, women and children.

3. HC, 4:207-09.
4. HC, 3:35. See D & C 116.

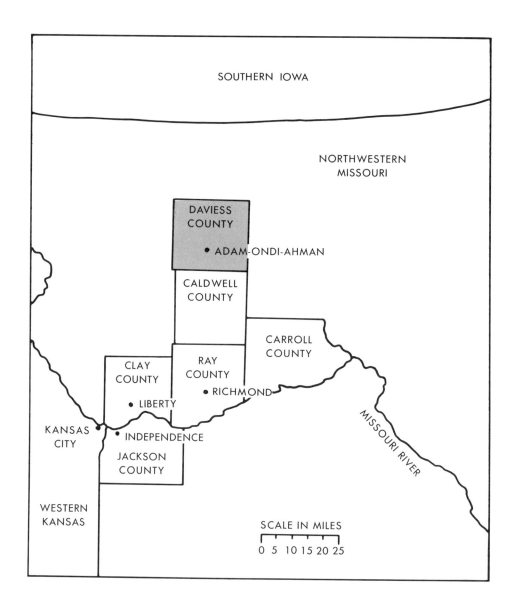

Location of Adam-ondi-Ahman, Missouri.

The Hill of Adam-ondi-Ahman Rising Above the Ruins of a Cabin Built by an Early Member of the Church, Lyman Wight.

If they were assembled in one place, it would present a grand spectacle; but suppose we double that number, making it eighty millions, what a vast congregation that number of people would make, we can hardly grasp in our comprehension its extent; and still we will add to it another twenty millions so as to equal the size of the congregation which the Prophet Daniel saw standing before the Ancient of Days. *Such a body of people must extend over a great many miles of country, however closely they may be collected together.* I doubt whether the extremes of such a congregation could be seen by the natural eyes of mortals; they would be lost in the distance.[5]

However, Joseph Fielding Smith believes that this meeting, even though it will be gigantic in its scope, will be held in secret:

When this gathering is held, the world will not know of it; the members of the Church at large will not know of it, yet it shall be preparatory to the coming in the clouds of glory of our Savior Jesus Christ as the Prophet Joseph Smith has said. The world cannot know it. *The Saints cannot know it —except those who officially shall be called into this council—* for it shall precede the coming of Jesus Christ as a thief in the night, unbeknown to all the world.[6]

Purposes of The Council at Adam-ondi-Ahman

Latter-day Saints hold that the council at Adam-ondi-Ahman will serve several major purposes. Orson Pratt explained that the council would be held to organize the Priesthood of all the dispensations so that each man and his family will know their assigned place:

Who was this personage called the Ancient of Days? We are told by the Prophet Joseph Smith — the great Prophet of the last days, whom God raised up by his own voice and by the ministration of angels to introduce the great and last dispensation of the fullness of times — the last dispensation on the earth so far as the proclamation of mercy is concerned; I say we are told by this Prophet that the Ancient of Days is the most ancient

5. JD, 18:338-39.
6. Joseph Fielding Smith, *The Way to Perfection* (Fifth Edition, Utah: the Genealogical Society, 1943), p. 291. This seems to be his interpretation of I Thessalonians 5:2. There appears to be nothing that would indicate that this passage is referring to the Council at Adam-ondi-Ahman, or that the council will be held in secret. It would seem that a council of this magnitude would involve a considerable number of the members of the Church. Even, then, the vast majority of participants seemingly would have to come from behind the veil.

personage that ever had an existence in days here on the earth. And who was he? Why, of course, Old Father Adam, he was the most ancient man that ever lived in the days that we have any knowledge of. He comes, then, as a great judge, to assemble this innumerable host of which Daniel speaks. He comes in flaming fire. The glory and blessing and greatness of his personage it would be impossible even for a man as great as Daniel fully to describe. He comes as a man inspired from the eternal throne of Jehovah himself. *He comes to set in order the councils of the Priesthood pertaining to all dispensations, to arrange the Priesthood and the councils of the Saints of all former dispensations in one grand family and household.*

What is all this for? Why all this arrangement? Why all this organization? Why all this judgment and the opening of the books? *It is to prepare the way for another august personage whom Daniel saw coming with the clouds of heaven, namely the Son of Man, and these clouds of heaven brought the Son of Man near before the Ancient of Days.* And when the Son of Man came to the Ancient of Days, behold *a kingdom was given to the Son of Man, and greatness and glory, that all people, nations and languages should serve him,* and his kingdom should be an everlasting kingdom, a kingdom that should never be done away.

This explains the reason why our father Adam comes as the Ancient of days with all these numerous hosts, and organizes them according to the records of the book, every man in his place, preparatory to the coming of the Son of Man to receive the kingdom. *Then every family that is in the order of the Priesthood, and every man and every woman, and every son or daughter whatever their kindred, descent or Priesthood, will know their place.*[7]

Continuing, Pratt spoke again of the purpose and nature of that meeting, saying that in the Council the Priesthood quorums from the various dispensations will each take its place. He also intimated that some of the participants in the meeting will be resurrected, and not just spirit beings:

This man, will sit upon his throne, and ten thousand times ten thousand immortal beings—his children—will stand before him, with all their different grades of Priesthood, according to the order which God has appointed and ordained. *Then every quorum of the Priesthood in this Latter-day Saint Church will find its place and never until then.* If we go behind the vail

7. JD, 17:185-86.

[sic] we will not see this perfect organization of the Saints of all generations until that period shall arrive. *That will be before Jesus comes in his glory.* Then we will find that there is a place for the First Presidency of this Church; for the Twelve Apostles called in this dispensation; for the twelve disciples that were called among the remnants of Joseph on this land in ancient times; for the Twelve that were called among the ten tribes of Israel in the north country; for the Twelve that were called in Palestine, who administered in the presence of our Savior; *all the various quorums and councils of the Priesthood in every dispensation that has transpired since the days of Adam until the present time will find their places,* according to the callings, gifts, blessings, ordinations and keys of Priesthood which the Lord Almighty has conferred upon them in their several generations. This, then, will be one of the grandest meetings that has ever transpired upon the face of our globe. What manner of persons ought you and I, my brethren and sisters, and all the people of God in the latter-days to be, that we may be counted worthy to *participate in the august assemblies that are to come from the eternal worlds, whose bodies have burst the tomb and come forth immortalized and eternal in their nature.*[8]

Another purpose of this council is revealed in the original quotation from Daniel which stated that "the judgment was set, and the books were opened." The Prophet Joseph made it clear that this meant giving the power of judgment to the Saints. In clarifying the matter he stated that wars, fires, pestilence and earthquakes would continue in succession "until the Ancient of Days comes, then judgment will be given to the Saints."[9] Elder Pratt explained that this will include the power to judge the nations which will then exist:

The records of the nations — their rise and decadence, with everything pertaining to them, in a national capacity, will be written. Then there will be the records of the families and of individuals, even of all people and tongues of the earth. The books will be opened, and the judgment will sit. What Judgment? *Not the final judgment, because that is to take place more than a thousand years after this. This judgment refers to the nations that will then exist, and it is out of these records and*

---

8. JD, 17:187-88.
9. HC, 3:391.

by this judgment will they be judged. The calamities spoken of will take place in fulfillment of the Scriptures, and of the great purposes of Jehovah.[10]

Christ's Appearance and Acceptance of Dominion

It appears that during the Council at Adam-ondi-Ahman, Christ will make the second of his series of four prophesied appearances. While telling of the coming of the Ancient of Days and of the universal conflict, Daniel prophesies that

> I saw in the night visions, and, behold, one like the Son of Man came with the clouds of heaven, and came to the Ancient of Days, and they brought him near before them.
> And there was given him dominion and glory, and a kingdom, that all people, nations, and languages, should serve him: his dominion is an everlasting dominion, which shall not pass away, and his kingdom that which shall not be destroyed.[11]

A major purpose of the Council at Adam-ondi-Ahman will be to conduct the turning over of the keys of the world power to the Savior. Each leader is to deliver his authority to Adam who will, in turn, give them to the Savior. Note that complete world-wide control will be relinquished to the Savior and he will be given "dominion, and glory, and a kingdom, that all people, nations, and languages, should serve him."[12] From this time forward, then, Christ will stand as the literal head of the kingdom of God. That kingdom will cease to be a preparatory kingdom and will assert itself as the power by which the world is to be governed. Those nations that will not unite with it, from this time forward, will perish. To quote Orson Pratt,

> The kingdoms of the world have waxed old; and, because of wickedness, they are destined to be speedily broken to pieces; but the kingdom of God will endure forever. It is destined to increase in strength, power, and dominion, and to bear rule over all the earth. *Those nations and kingdoms which will not unite themselves with the kingdom of God, and become one with it, honoring its laws and institutions, will utterly perish, and no place will be found for them.*[13]

10. JD, 18:342.
11. Dan. 7:13-14.
12. Dan. 7:14. B. H. Roberts definitely associated this passage with Dan. 7:9-10., thereby including it as part of the events of the Council at Adam-ondi-Ahman. See HC, 3:35.
13. *Millennial Star,* Vol. 19, pp. 680-681, October 24, 1857.

The council at Adam-ondi-Ahman is expected to mark the end of persecution against the Saints in the last days. The Prophet Joseph Smith, in commenting on the book of Daniel, said,

> The "Horn" made war with the Saints and overcame them, until the Ancient of Days came; judgment was given to the Saints of the Most High from the Ancient of Days; the time came that the Saints possessed the Kingdom. This not only makes us ministers here, but in eternity.[14]

The council is expected to be an important turning point which will eventually affect the attitude of the entire world towards the Church.

Summary

1. During the period of universal conflict an important council will be held at Adam-ondi-Ahman, Missouri.
2. The Council will be under the direction of the Ancient of Days, who is Adam.
3. According to Daniel, there is to be a vast number of participants in the Council. Some of them will be mortal beings, but the majority of participants will apparently be from beyond the veil.
4. The Savior is to appear to Adam and receive the dominion which comes through the acceptance of the Kingdom of God.
5. The Council at Adam-ondi-Ahman will fulfill five purposes:
   A. The keys for each dispensation will be turned over to Adam.
   B. The members of the Church will be organized into one grand family with Adam as the patriarch.
   C. Each priesthood quorum which has existed down through the ages will be assigned its place in the government of the Church.
   D. Judgment will be set. In addition to judging affairs within the Church, the Saints are expected to judge the nations then in existence and determine their fate.
   E. Power, glory, and dominion will be turned over to the Savior.

---

14. HC, 3:389. See Dan. 7:21-22.

CHAPTER XII

Growth and Development in Zion and Palestine After the Era of Universal Conflict

It has been seen that during the ministration of the 144,000 High Priests, the world is expected to witness a great outpouring of plagues, conflict, and devastation. Included among the plagues will be a terrible war which will bring desolation to the European continent. The overall length of these judgments is not known. However, both the scriptures and comments by General Authorities of the Church indicate certain conditions and events which will apparently take place in a more peaceful atmosphere following the universal conflict and yet before Christ appears on the Mount of Olives during the Battle of Armageddon. In this chapter it will be seen that this intermediate era will be a time of growth and development for both the New Jerusalem and for the land of Palestine.

Growth of Zion in America

It is anticipated that the city of the New Jerusalem on the American continent will experience a great increase in both population and importance as the world recognizes its progress and stability.

Orson Pratt indicated that after the other nations have been broken up many people will gladly accept the cause and rule of Zion:

> When that day comes that the Lord shall cut off such people, when the day comes that he will fulfill the revelations of Isaiah, as well as many other revelations that have been given, Zion will have to go forth in her strength and power, and the inhabitants of the nations that are afar off will say, "Surely, Zion is the city of our God, for the Lord is there, and His glory is there, and the power and the might of His terror is there,"—terror to the wicked, terror to those who commit sin: and *many people will say, "Come, let us be subject to her laws." That will be after the Lord has broken up the nations, after He has destroyed and*

*wasted them away, so far as the wicked portions are con-
cerned. Those who are left will gladly acknowledge Zion,* will
acknowledge God and His people, and will acknowledge the laws
that will be literally sent forth from Zion to the nations of
the earth.[1]

It appears that as these people come to the New Jerusalem
that city and the surrounding area will experience great growth,
and Zion will undergo a period of great expansion. Elder Pratt
stated that many of the desolate cities of this nation will be re-
populated, and Zion will begin to expand until it will cover the
two American continents:

> Then will be fulfilled another saying in this same chapter which
> I have read—"For thou shalt break forth on the right hand
> and on the left; and thy seed shall inherit the Gentiles, and make
> the desolate cities to be inhabited." Now, *there are a great
> many cities in the United States that will not be totally de-
> stroyed when the inhabitants are swept off the surface of the
> earth. Their houses, their desolate cities will still remain un-
> occupied until Zion in her glory and strength shall enlarge the
> place of her tents,* and stretch forth the curtains of her habi-
> tations. That is the destiny of this nation, and the destiny of
> the Latter-day Saints.[2]

The Proclamation issued by the Quorum of the Twelve shortly
after the Prophet's death made the following reference to the
expansion of Zion on both the American continents and the unity
which will then exist between their peoples:

> The city of Zion, with its Sanctuary and Priesthood, and
> the glorious fulness of the Gospel, will constitute a standard
> which will put an end to jarring creeds and political wran-
> glings, by *uniting the republics, states, provinces, territories,
> nations, tribes, kindreds, tongues, people, and sects of North
> and South America in one great and common bond of brother-
> hood;* while truth and knowledge shall make them free, and love
> cement their union.[3]

This proclamation was apparently based on the teachings of the
Prophet, for the following is recorded concerning his instruction
by Elder Benjamin F. Johnson,

---

1. JD, 22:36.
2. JD, 24:31-32.
3. "Proclamation of the Twelve Apostles of the Church of Jesus Christ of
   Latter-day Saints," *Millennial Star,* Oct. 22, 1845.

He taught us that the Saints would fill the great West, and through Mexico and Central and South America we would do a great work for the redemption of the remnant of Jacob, and he taught us relating to the kingdom of God as it would become organized upon the earth through "all nations learning war no more," and all adopting the God-given Constitution of the United States as a paladium of liberty and equal rights.[4]

The period following the universal conflict is thus regarded by Latter-day Saints as an epoch when the influence of the Gospel will be greatly extended and when the political dominion of the Kingdom of God will expand because of the recognition which it will receive as a source of stability, strength, and righteous rule. It will be shown hereafter that this work will reach its ultimate fulfillment in the Millennium.

David, The Prince

Joseph Smith spoke, on one occasion, of David, the ancient leader of Israel, and indicated that he lost part of his glory because of transgression. The Prophet then explained, as to his eternal priesthood that *"the throne and kingdom of David is to be taken from him and given to another by the name of David in the last days, raised up out of his lineage.[5]* It appears that during the period immediately preceding the Battle of Armageddon this new leader for Israel will emerge. Like his ancient predecessor, he will rule as a prince and his name will be David. Jeremiah said that the Lord will raise up a David as king of Israel in the time when that people shall serve the Lord their God.[6] Zechariah referred to him as the BRANCH, and while comparing him with a priest named Joshua who was living at that time, told of the great responsibility David would have in Palestine in the last days. The Prophet said that *"he shall build the temple of the Lord;* and he shall bear the glory, and shall sit and rule upon His throne; and he shall be a priest upon his throne."[7] Ezekiel said that the Lord "will set up one shepherd over them [Israel], and he shall feed them, even my [the Lord's] servant David; he shall feed them, and he shall be their shepherd."[8]

---

4. "An Interesting Letter," unpublished letter of Benjamin F. Johnson to George S. Gibbs, 1903, Brigham Young University Library, p. 8.
5. HC, 6:253. See D & C 132:38-39.
6. Jer. 30:9.
7. Zech. 6:11-13. See 3:8-9; Jer. 23:5-6, Hosea 3:4-5.
8. Ezek. 34:23-24.

Many of the Old Testament prophets speak of the David who will be raised up in this future period. Isaiah taught that he will be "a witness to the people, a leader and commander to the people," and said that he shall call a nation that he does not know, and nations that he does not know will run unto him because the Lord will glorify him.[9]

It seems quite possible that Isaiah's prophecy can be interpreted by another portion of his teachings. Chapter eleven of Isaiah tells of an important person who is called both a "rod" and a "Branch":

> And there shall come forth *a rod out of the stem of Jesse, and a Branch shall grow* out of his roots;
>
> And the spirit of the Lord shall rest upon him, the spirit of wisdom and understanding, the spirit of counsel and might, the spirit of knowledge and of the fear of the Lord;
>
> And shall make him of quick understanding in the fear of the Lord: and he shall not judge after the sight of his eyes, neither reprove after the hearing of his ears:
>
> But with righteousness shall he judge the poor, and reprove with equity for the meek of the earth: and he shall smite the earth with the rod of his mouth, and with the breath of his lips shall he slay the wicked.
>
> And righteousness shall be the girdle of his loins, and faithfulness the girdle of his reins.[10]

Section 113 of the *Doctrine and Covenants* says that this individual is

> A servant in the hands of Christ, who is partly a descendant of Jesse as well as of Ephraim, or of the house of Joseph, on whom there is laid much power.[11]

After telling of the righteous judgment and power which this individual will hold Isaiah then describes the peaceful atmosphere which will prevail during the Millennium (Isaiah 11:6-9) and then, speaking of that period, says,

> And in that day there shall be a root of Jesse, which shall stand for an ensign of the people; to it shall the Gentiles seek: and his rest shall be glorious.[12]

9. Is. 55:3-5.
10. Is. 11:1-5.
11. D & C 113:4.
12. Is. 11:10.

The *Doctrine and Covenants* identifies the "root" as being

> A descendant of Jesse, as well as of Joseph, unto whom rightly belongs the priesthood, and the keys of the kingdom, for an ensign, and for the gathering of my people in the last days.[13]

Thus it appears that the individual referred to by Isaiah as the "rod", "Branch", and "root" will have certain characteristics:

1. He will live during a period (apparently just before the beginning of the Millennium) when he can both judge the poor with righteousness and yet cause the wicked to be slain. (Is. 11:1-5)
2. He will live on into the Millennium. (Is. 11:6-10)
3. He will stand as an ensign of the people (Is. 11:10) and to him will the Gentiles seek (this could be as the Gentiles covet the wealth of Palestine and cause the Battle of Armageddon).
4. He will be an important and powerful servant in the hands of Christ. (Doctrine and Covenants 113:4)
5. He will be a descendant of both Judah (through Jesse) and Joseph (through Ephraim). (Doctrine and Covenants 113: 4, 6)

It is significant to note that this prophecy (Isaiah 11) was quoted by the Angel Moroni to Joseph Smith when that heavenly being made his first appearance to the Prophet. Moroni said that the prophecy "was about to be fulfilled."[14]

Ezekiel also held that Prince David is to play an important part in Israel's worship in the last days:

> And it shall be the prince's part to give burnt offerings, and meat offerings, and drink offerings, in the feasts, and in the new moons, and in the sabbaths, in all solemnities of the house of Israel: he shall prepare the sin offering, and the meat offering, and the burnt offering, and the peace offerings, to make reconciliation for the house of Israel.[15]

The same Hebrew seer taught that David will be the prophet who will be privileged to approach the Lord when He comes to the Temple in Jerusalem, and a special door in that temple will be reserved for his use when the Lord is there.[16] Ezekiel further stated that two tracts of ground, one on the east and one on the

---

13. D & C 113:6.
14. JS 2:40.
15. Ezek. 45:17. See 46:2, 12.
16. Ezek. 44:1-3.

west outside of the city limits of Jerusalem, will be given by the people unto the Prince as an inheritance, and they will also give him an oblation of a portion of their crops and herds.[17]

It appears, then, that the David of the last days will hold both religious and political control over Palestine in the period just before the beginning of the Millennium and during the early days of that era. He will oversee the gathering of Israel and the construction of the Jerusalem temple, and will receive the Savior at the time of His coming to Palestine.

Removal of The Ten Tribes
From Zion to Palestine

Another important event which will apparently take place during this period following the universal conflict will be the removal of the Ten Tribes from an area near the New Jerusalem to the land of Palestine. Even though the Americas have been set apart as the land of inheritance for the descendants of Joseph,[18] yet it appears that some from the tribes of both Manasseh and Ephraim will return to Palestine and settle there, as Ezekiel includes them in his apportionment of the land in Palestine in the last days.[19]

According to Orson Pratt, however, these tribes will linger quite some time (at least until after the selection of the 144,000) in the area of the New Jerusalem before journeying to Palestine:

> How long will they who come from the north countries tarry in the heights of Zion? Some time. They have got to raise wheat, cultivate the grape, wine and oil, raise flocks and herds, and their souls will have to become as a watered garden. *They will dwell in Zion a good while, and during that time, there will be twelve thousand chosen out of each of these ten tribes, besides twelve thousand that will be chosen from Judah, Joseph, and the remaining tribes, one hundred and forty-four thousand in all.* Chosen for what? To be sealed in their foreheads. For what purpose? So that the power of death and pestilence and plague that will go forth in those days sweeping over the nations of the earth will have no power over them.[20]

It appears that although the tribes will linger in the latter-day Zion for some time, they nevertheless may return to Palestine

---

17. Ezek. 45:7, 13-16.
18. See I Ne. 5:5, Alma 46:23-24.
19. Ezek. 48:1-5.
20. JD, 18:25.

in time to assist in rebuilding the city of Jerusalem and the temple before the Lord appears. Orson Pratt taught that "the whole of the twelve tribes of Israel are to return back to Palestine in Asia and rebuild their city of Jerusalem and a temple within that city before, and preparatory to the coming of the Lord."[21] That the Lord's coming to which Pratt referred was the coming on the Mount of Olives is made clear by another statement which he made. Note also that he speaks of the tribes returning to Palestine after the era of universal conflict:

> It is because of this, of the light that the nations have in their midst, which they will not receive that the Lord will visit them first; *and when he has visited and overthrown them, he will lay his hand heavily upon the heathen nations in Asia, and also those who are in Africa, and they will be visited with severe judgment, but they will not be utterly destroyed. A portion of the heathen nations will be redeemed. Why? They will see the power and glory of God that will be manifested among the tribes of Israel, who will be gathered out from their midst and return to their own land.* They will see the glory of God manifested as in ancient times and they will say, "surely Jaggernaut is no longer my God." "Surely I will not worship crocodiles, nor serpents; neither will I worship the sun, or the moon, for there is a God manifested among that people, Israel, who is worthy of the natures and attributes of a God. I will cast my Gods to the moles and bats, and I will worship the God of Israel. Then will be fulfilled that which was spoken by the prophet Ezekiel, "then shall the heathen know that I the Lord am God." *And it will come to pass, after that period, when Jesus shall have raised all the righteous from their graves, that he will descend with all the hosts of heaven accompanying him, and will stand upon the Mount of Olives, and he will go out of Jerusalem, and the Jews will go out to the mount to meet him and will acknowledge him as their Messiah and King; and then it shall come to pass, that the heathen nations will also more fully recognize him as the true and only God.* Then will be fulfilled that which is written in the last chapter of Zachariah [sic], that every nation round about Jerusalem, shall come up from year to year, to worship the King, the Lord of hosts, at Jerusalem, and also to keep the Feast of Tabernacles. There will be a great many of those solemn assemblies and feasts that were commanded in ancient times, that will be re-established in the midst of Israel when they shall return.[22]

---

21. JD, 14:349-50.
22. JD, 20:153.

Several scriptural passages seem to support Pratt in his view that the Ten Tribes will return to Palestine before the battle of Armageddon and Christ's coming to the Mount of Olives. John's Revelation appears to indicate that a temple will have been erected before the battle of Armageddon for as he prophecies of the battle he speaks of the "temple of God, and the altar, and them that worship therein." He comments also that the court which is without the temple will be "given unto the Gentiles, and the holy city shall they tread under foot forty and two months."[23] It has also been seen that an Israelite leader, a prince by the name of David, will be raised up in the last days and that "he shall build the temple of the Lord"[24] which is to be established. Since the temple will probably be constructed before the battle of Armageddon, and since David is to be responsible for its construction, it would seem that David will rise to power before the time of Christ's appearance on the Mount of Olives. Ezekiel stated that both Israel and Judah would be returned to Palestine and David would be established as their king, and then the Lord would set his sanctuary, or temple, among them. In doing so he spoke of a "stick" of Judah and another "stick" for "Joseph, the stick of Ephraim, and for all the house of Israel his companions." Then he recorded that the Lord would make them "one stick, and they shall be one in mine [His] hand." And then Ezekiel clarified his prophecy by stating:

> Thus saith the Lord God; Behold, I will take the children of Israel from among the heathen, whither they be gone, and will gather them on every side, and bring them into their own land:
>
> And I will make them one nation in the land upon the mountains of Israel; and *one king shall be king to them all: and they shall be no more two nations, neither shall they be divided into two kingdoms any more at all:* . . .
>
> *And David my servant shall be king over them;* . . . *and my servant David shall be their prince for ever.*
>
> Moreover I will make a covenant of peace with them; it shall be an everlasting covenant with them: and I will place them, and multiply them, and *will set my sanctuary in the midst of them for evermore.*

---

23. Rev. 11:1-13.
24. Zech. 6:12-13. For assurance that the BRANCH is Prince David, compare this passage with Ezek. 44:2-4.

> My tabernacle also shall be with them: yea, I will be their God, and they shall be my people.[25]

It appears that the timing of this event may be further verified by a combination of two scriptural references. The Apostle John, in his vision of the events of the last days, foresaw a period of world warfare in which a third of men are to be slain, and he was also shown the Battle of Armageddon. But between these two revelations a voice from heaven spake to him and said:

> Go, and take the little book which is open in the hand of the angel which standeth upon the sea and upon the earth.
>
> And I went unto the angel, and said unto him, Give me the little book. And he said unto me, Take it, and eat it up; and it shall make thy belly bitter, but it shall be in thy mouth sweet as honey.
>
> And I took the little book out of the angel's hand, and ate it up; and it was in my mouth sweet as honey: and as soon as I had eaten it, my belly was bitter.
>
> And he said unto me, Thou must prophesy again before many peoples, and nations, and tongues, and kings.[26]

In interpreting the passage Joseph Smith recorded that "We are to understand that *it was a mission*, and an ordinance, for him *to gather the tribes of Israel*; behold, this is Elias, who, as it is written, must come and restore all things."[27] It appears then that John was prophesying that Israel would be gathered to Palestine between the sixth plague and the Battle of Armageddon.

---

25. Ezek. 37:15-27. It seems that Ezekiel established the following events in chronological order: (1) the Ten Tribes will be largely united with Judah in the land of Palestine, (2) David the Prince will rule over them, (3) the temple will be built or "set in the midst of them," and (4) the heathen will come to a knowledge of the power of God by seeing the downfall of the forces of Gog in the battle of Armageddon. See Ezek. 37:15-28, 38:16.

The Prophet Jeremiah also indicated that the captivity of Judah and of Israel will be ended and they will be restored to their inheritances in Jerusalem. He then tells how they will inhabit the desolate places of Palestine and make them blossom, and continues his account by telling how David will rule over them and execute judgment in righteousness in the land. In the days of his rule "shall Judah be saved." If this phrase is a reference to the Armageddon scene then his statement is also an indication of the chronology. See Jer. 33:7-16.

Statements of Zechariah and Isaiah seem to indicate that Israel and Judah will be united in battles against other nations, and these battles would apparently be before the Armageddon struggle. See Zech. 10:3-10 Is. 11:13-16.

26. Rev. 10:8-11.
27. D & C 77:14.

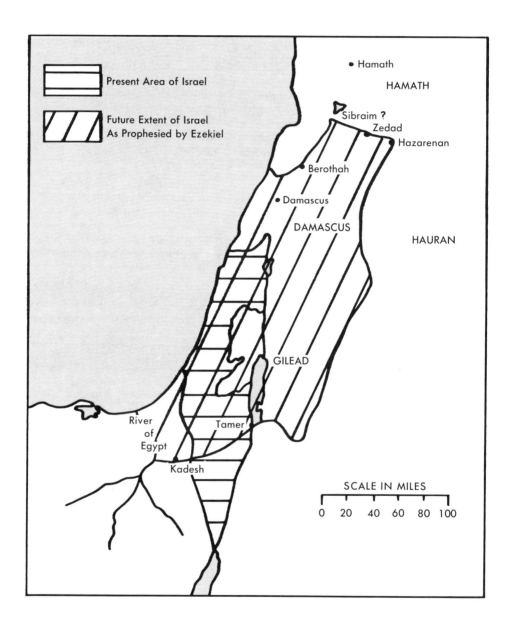

The Borders of Israel in The Last Days.

Distribution of Land Among The Tribes

In his vision Ezekiel saw and recorded the borders which will eventually encompass the land of Israel in the last days. These borders are to encompass a much larger area than the present territory of Palestine:

> And this shall be the border of the land toward the *north side*, from the great sea, the way of Hethlon, as men go to Zedad;
>
> Hamath, Berothah, Sibraim, which is between the border of Damascus and the border of Hamath; Hazarhatticon, which is by the coast of Hauran.
>
> And the border from the sea shall be Hazarenan, the border of Damascus, and the north northward, and the border of Hamath. And this is the north side.
>
> And the *east side* ye shall measure from Hauran, and from Damascus, and from Gilead, and from the land of Israel by Jordan, from the border unto the east sea. And this is the east side.
>
> And the *south side* southward, from Tamar even to the waters of strife in Kadesh, the river to the great sea. And this is the south side southward.
>
> The *west side* also shall be the great sea from the border, till a man come over against Hamath. This is the west side.
>
> So shall ye divide this land unto you according to the tribes of Israel.[28]

Ezekiel also saw (Ezekiel 47, 48) that a place of inheritance for each of the twelve tribes[29] will be established in parallel east-west strips across the land of Palestine. The Temple, an area for the priests, and a special area for the ruler will be set aside in the center. This distribution of land is summarized by Pfeiffer in his *Introduction to the Old Testament*:

> The twelve tribes are arranged in parallel strips, seven north (Dan, Asher, Naphtali, Manasseh, Ephraim, Reuben, Judah) and five (Benjamin, Simeon, Issachar, Zebulon, Gad) south of the sacred area (48:1-7, 48:23-29). This holy zone or "oblation" (45:1-8; 48:8-22) is a strip 25,000 cubits long and 10,000

---

28. Ezek. 47:15-21. See chart, next page.
29. Note that even though the continents of America have been promised as lands of inheritance for the descendants of Joseph, nevertheless there will be areas in Palestine which will be inherited by descendants of both Ephraim and Manasseh. Conceivably these could be the people who were with the lost tribes, and it is possible that they may prefer to go back to the land of Palestine with the rest of the tribes.

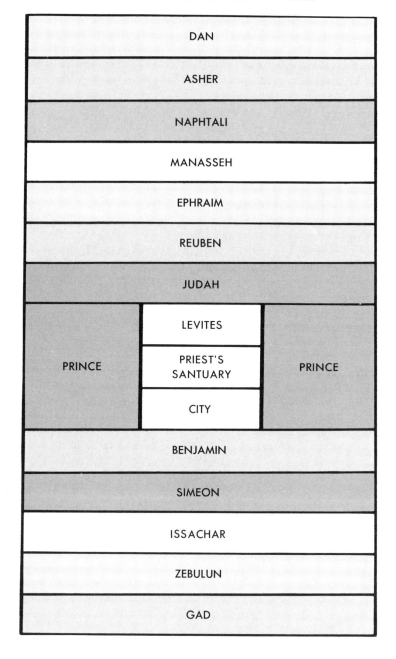

The Division of The Land of Palestine Among The Twelve Tribes
According to The Vision of Ezekiel.

wide comprising the domain of the priests with the Temple in the center; north of it is the Levite's domain (10,000 cubits wide), south of it the city, a square of 45,000 cubits per side all surrounded by a strip of open land 250 cubits wide; east and west of the city are its lands—two rectangles 5,000 by 10,000 cubits in size. The whole square, 25,000 cubits per side, comprising the domains of the Levites and priests and the city with its lands is surrounded by the tribal territories of Judah (north) and Benjamin (south), and by the domain of the prince (east and west).[30]

The prophet Jeremiah foretold of the area which the city of Jerusalem will eventually include:

> Behold, the days come, saith the Lord, that the city shall be built to the Lord from the tower of Hananeel unto the gate of the corner.
>
> And the measuring line shall yet go forth over against it upon the hill Gareb, and shall compass about to Goath.
>
> And the whole valley of the dead bodies, and of the ashes, and all the fields unto the brook of Kidron, unto the corner of the horse gate toward the east, shall be holy unto the Lord; it shall not be plucked up, nor thrown down any more for ever.[31]

Construction of The Temple in Jerusalem and The Restoration of Sacrificial Worship

It appears that the era after the universal conflict will also be the period when the temple will be built in Jerusalem and when Palestine will embark upon its greatest era of productivity. President Charles W. Penrose spoke of the removal of the Moslem mosque which now stands on the site where the temple will be built:

> The work is moving on for the gathering of the Jews to their own land that they may build it up as it was in former times; that the *temple may be rebuilt and the mosque of the Moslem which now stands in its place may be moved out of the way; that Jerusalem may be rebult* [sic] *upon its original site;* that the way may be prepared for the coming of the Messiah.[32]

---

30. Robert H. Pfeiffer, *Introduction To The Old Testament* (New York: Harper & Brothers, 1948), p. 556. According to Pfeiffer, a Hebrew cubit is the equivalent of 17.58 inches or 44.65 centimeters.
31. Jer. 31:38-40.
32. JD, 24:215.

The Prophet Ezekiel envisioned this temple and gave a detailed description of it. The following is a brief summary of Ezekiel's description, given by the Bible commentator Robert H. Pfeiffer:

> The sacredness of the Temple, entirely surrounded by the priests' domain, is further ensured by being enclosed within two courts, instead of the single court of Solomon's Temple. The external wall separating the holy from the common encloses a square 500 cubits per side (42:20), containing the outer court (40:28-37), a rectangle 350 by 200 cubits, within which stands the sanctuary. Laymen worship in the outer court (46:3, 9) and no longer take part in the sacrificial rites. The private sacrifices of the prince are slain by the priests (46:2), those of the people by the Levites (44:11), who also boil the meat (46:24) which the people eat in the outer court. Although Ezekiel's plan of having two courts instead of one was adopted in the postexilic Temple, the laymen did not renounce the immemorial custom of offering their own sacrifices in the inner court (cf. Lev. 1:5, 11, etc.).[33]

Ezekiel tells of a great river which will proceed out from under the temple, and he predicts that the water from this river will "issue out toward the east country, and go down into the desert, and go into the [Dead] sea: which being brought forth into the sea, the waters shall be healed."[34] Joseph Smith commented on this passage and said that:

> Judah must return, Jerusalem must be rebuilt, and the temple, and water come out from under the temple, and the waters of the Dead Sea be healed. *It will take some time to rebuild the walls of the city and the temple, &c.; and all this must be done before the Son of Man will make His appearance.* There will be wars and rumors of wars, signs in the heavens above and on the earth beneath, the sun turned into darkness and the moon to blood, earthquakes in divers places, the seas heaving beyond their bounds; then will appear one grand sign of the Son of Man in heaven. But what will the world do? They will say it is a planet, a comet, &c. But the Son of Man will come as the sign of the coming of the Son of Man, which will be as the light of the morning cometh out of the east.[35]

---

33. Pfeiffer, *op. cit.,* p. 556. This is a summary of Ezekiel's description recorded in Ezek. 40-42.
34. Ezek. 47:1-8.
35. HC, 5:337.

Ezekiel discusses the worship service of the temple which will be built and reveals that the principle of blood sacrifice will be restored:

And he said unto me, Son of man, thus saith the Lord God; *These are the ordinances of the altar in the day when they shall make it, to offer burnt offerings thereon, and to sprinkle blood thereon.*

And thou shalt give to the priests the Levites that be of the seed of Zádok, which approach unto me, to minister unto me, saith the Lord God, a young bullock for a sin offering.

And thou shalt take of the blood thereof, and put it on the four horns of it, and on the four corners of the settle, and upon the border round about; thus shalt thou cleanse and purge it.

Thou shalt take the bullock also of the sin offering, and he shall burn it in the appointed place of the house, without the sanctuary.

And on the second day thou shalt offer a kid of the goats without blemish for a sin offering; and they shall cleanse the altar, as they did cleanse it with the bullock.

When thou hast made an end of cleansing it, thou shalt offer a young bullock without blemish, and a ram out of the flock without blemish.

And thou shalt offer them before the Lord, and the priest shall cast salt upon them, and they shall offer them up for a burnt offering unto the Lord.

Seven days shalt thou prepare every day a goat for a sin offering: they shall also prepare a young bullock, and a ram out of the flock, without blemish.

Seven days shall they purge the altar and purify it; and they shall consecrate themselves.

And when these days are expired, it shall be, that upon the eighth day, and so forward, the priests shall make your burnt offerings upon the altar, and your peace offerings; and I will accept you, saith the Lord God.[36]

The Prophet Joseph Smith explained that the principle of sacrifice is eternal and that sacrifices are offered when the powers of the Melchizedek Priesthood are sufficiently manifest. However, he explained that the restoration of the principle of blood sacrifice does not mean that the Law of Moses, with its rites and ceremonies, will be re-established:

---

36. Ezek. 43:18-27.

It is generally supposed that sacrifice was entirely done away when the Great Sacrifice [i.e., the sacrifice of the Lord Jesus] was offered up, and that there will be no necessity for the ordinance of sacrifice in future: but those who assert this are certainly not acquainted with the duties, privileges and authority of the priesthood or with the Prophets.

The offering of sacrifice has ever been connected and forms a part of the duties of the Priesthood. It began with the Priesthood, and will be continued until after the coming of Christ, from generation to generation. . . .

These sacrifices, as well as every ordinance belonging to the Priesthood, will, when the Temple of the Lord shall be built, and the sons of Levi be purified, be fully restored and attended to in all their powers, ramifications, and blessings. This ever did and ever will exist when the powers of the Melchisedic [sic, early spelling] Priesthood are sufficiently manifest; else how can the restitution of all things spoken of by the Holy Prophets be brought to pass? *It is not to be understood that the law of Moses will be established again with all its rites and variety of ceremonies; this has never been spoken of by the Prophets; but those things which existed prior to Moses' day, namely, sacrifice, will be continued.*[37]

Prophecies Concerning Israel's Political Affairs

Isaiah seems to indicate that when the tribes of Israel return to Palestine they will live in peace among themselves and put away their ancient rivalry between the northern and southern kingdoms. He states that "the envy also of Ephraim shall depart, and the adversaries of Judah shall be cut off: Ephraim shall not envy Judah, and Judah shall not vex Ephraim."[38] However, several prophecies speak of the need for expansion which Israel will feel because of over-population stating that "place shall not be found for them,"[39] and that the Israelites as they gather will say, "The place is too strait for me: give place to me that I may dwell."[40]

Israel's political disputes with neighboring countries are also prophesied. A warfare against the surrounding nations is predicted for the period after the Ten Tribes have returned to Palestine:

37. HC, 4:211-12.
38. Is. 11:13.
39. Zech. 10:10.
40. Is. 49:20.

They [Ephraim and Judah] *shall fly upon the shoulders of the Philistines toward the west*; *they shall spoil them of the east together*; *they shall lay their hand upon Edom and Moab*; *and the children of Ammon shall obey them.*

And the Lord shall utterly destroy the tongue of the Egyptian sea; and with his mighty wind shall he shake his hand over the river, and shall smite it in the seven streams and make men go over dryshod.[41]

Of particular note is the repetition of prophecies concerning the eventual downfall of Egypt. Joel says that "Egypt shall be a desolation, and Edom shall be a desolate wilderness, for the violence against the children of Judah, because they have shed innocent blood in their land."[42] This apparently takes place before the battle of Armageddon, as Egypt is conspicuously absent from Ezekiel's list of those who will fight in that battle under the leadership of Gog. (See Ezekiel 38:16.)

Conflict with Egypt and with the nations that make up the area of ancient Assyria is also foretold by Zechariah. Apparently both of these areas will be overcome, though it is not clear what part Israel will play in their downfall:

Mine anger was kindled against the shepherds, and I punished the goats: for the Lord of hosts hath visited his flock the *house of Judah, and hath made them as his goodly horse in the battle.*

Out of him came forth the corner, out of him the nail, out of him the battle bow, out of him every oppressor together.

And *they shall be as mighty men, which tread down their enemies in the mire of the streets in the battle*; and they shall fight, because the Lord is with them, and the riders on horses shall be confounded.

And I will strengthen the house of Judah, and I will save the house of Joseph, and I will bring them again to place them; for I have mercy upon them: and they shall be as though I had not cast them off: for I am the Lord their God, and will hear them.

And *they of Ephraim shall be like a mighty man,* and their heart shall rejoice as through wine: yea, their children shall see it, and be glad; their heart shall rejoice in the Lord.

I will hiss for them, and gather them; for I have redeemed them; and they shall increase as they have increased.

41. Is. 11:14-15.
42. Joel 3:19.

And I will sow them among the people: and they shall remember me in far countries; and they shall live with their
children, and turn again.

*I will bring them again also out of the land of Egypt, and
gather them out of Assyria; and I will bring them into the
land of Gilead and Lebanon; and place shall not be found for
them.*

And he shall pass through the sea with affliction, and shall
smite the waves in the sea, and all the deeps of the river shall
dry up: and the *pride of Assyria shall be brought down, and
the sceptre of Egypt shall depart away.*[43]

Isaiah also speaks of the people gathering from Assyria
and Egypt in a time when they will be about to perish:

And it shall come to pass in that day, that the Lord shall
beat off from the channel of the river unto the stream of
Egypt, and ye shall be gathered one by one, O ye children of
Israel.

And it shall come to pass in that day, that the great
trumpet shall be blown, and *they shall come which were ready
to perish in the land of Assyria, and the outcasts in the land of
Egypt,* and shall worship the Lord in the holy mount at Jerusalem.[44]

And in another instance he speaks of the remnant of the
house of Israel "which shall be left," that will come "from Assyria,"[45] as if many of them had been destroyed. It is expected,
then, that Palestine will participate in a series of local wars between the time when Judah and the ten tribes will have returned
to Palestine and the time of the Battle of Armageddon.

Summary

In the era between the universal conflict and the battle of
Armageddon, both the New Jerusalem and the land of Palestine
will experience an important period of expansion.

1. The New Jerusalem will grow and extend its boundaries
   outward for many miles in all directions.

   A. The Lamanites and the Ten Tribes who will have re-
      cently gathered there will be joined by Gentiles from
      throughout the world who will come because their na-

---

43. Zech. 10:3-11.
44. Is. 27:12-13.
45. Is. 11:16.

tions will have been devastated. They will come because of the standard of peace and lawfulness which the New Jerusalem will maintain.

    B. The Kingdom of God will extend its rule throughout the two American continents and unite all the peoples of the Americas during this period.

2. This will be the period in which both Judah and the Ten Tribes of Israel will gather to Palestine. They will be apportioned parallel east-west strips of land on which the people from each of the twelve tribes will settle.

3. The boundaries of Israel will be much larger in that era than they are at the present time.

4. The temple will be rebuilt in Jerusalem and sacrificial worship will be restored there.

5. As the people of Israel return to Israel an important leader known as David, the Prince, will be raised up by God to lead them. He will:

    A. Be the ensign to which Israel will gather.

    B. Build the Jerusalem temple.

    C. Officiate in the temple services and receive the Messiah when he comes to the temple.

    D. Judge the people with righteousness.

    E. Live just before the beginning of the Millennium and into that period.

    F. Be a descendant of both Judah and Joseph.

6. Several wars or political disputes are prophesied which will seemingly involve Israel after all the tribes have gathered but before the battle of Armageddon. The present day counterparts of Egypt, Philistia, Edom, Moab, and Assyria are to be conquered.

CHAPTER XIII

The Battle of Armageddon and Christ's Appearance on the Mount of Olives

As the people of Judah and the Ten Tribes return to Israel and begin to prosper in the land, it is expected that they will excite the envy of the surrounding nations. These nations will come up to Palestine to wage war against them in an effort to satisfy their greed. This war, which is prophesied to continue for several years, is known as the Battle of Armageddon. Charles W. Penrose expressed this motive when he wrote that "the bankrupt nations, envying the wealth of the sons of Judah, will seek a pretext to make war upon them, and will invade the 'holy land' to 'take a prey and a spoil'."[1] Joel foretold the proclamation calling the nations up to war into the valley of decision:

> *Proclaim ye this among the Gentiles;* Prepare war, wake up the mighty men, let all the men of war draw near; let them come up:
> Beat your plowshares into swords, and your pruning hooks into spears: let the weak say, I am strong.
> Assemble yourselves, and come, *all ye heathen,* and gather yourselves together round about: thither cause thy mighty ones to come down, O Lord.
> *Let the heathen be wakened, and come up to the valley of Jehoshaphat: for there will I sit to judge all the heathen round about.*
> Put ye in the sickle, for the harvest is ripe: come get you down, for the press is full, the fats overflow; for their wickedness is great.
> *Multitudes, multitudes in the valley of decision: for the day of the Lord is near in the valley of decision.*[2]

Ezekiel envisioned Israel's latter-day establishment in the promised land, and saw that his people gathered out from among the nations would inhabit even the desolate places and cause them to flourish. He saw that this wealth would cause other nations

---

1. *Millennial Star,* Vol. XXI, p. 582, September 10, 1859.
2. Joel 3:9-14.

to rise up and try to spoil Palestine. In addressing these opposing nations he prophesied,

> Thou shalt ascend and come like a storm, *thou shalt be like a cloud to cover the land*, thou, and all thy bands, and many people with thee.
> Thus saith the Lord God; It shall also come to pass, that at the same time shall things come into thy mind, and *thou shalt think an evil thought*:
> *And thou shalt say, I will go up to the land of unwalled villages; I will go to them that are at rest, that dwell safely, all of them dwelling without walls, and having neither bars nor gates,*
> *To take a spoil, and to take a prey;* to turn thine hand upon the *desolate places that are now inhabited*, and upon the people that are gathered out of the nations, which have gotten cattle and goods, that dwell in the midst of the land.[3]

Orson Pratt made the observation that the gathering of Israel to Palestine may seriously affect the economy of some of the nations and they will seek to recover the wealth taken by the departing Israelites:

> When the Rothschilds and the great bankers among the Jewish nation shall return back to their own land to rebuild the city of Jerusalem, carrying their capital with them, it will almost ruin some of the nations, and the latter will go up against Jerusalem to take a spoil.[4]

Nations Which Will Attack Palestine

Who will the nations be that will attack Palestine? Ezekiel gave a detailed list:

> Son of man, set thy face against *Gog, the land of Magog, the chief prince of Meshech and Tubal*, and prophesy against *him*,
> And say, Thus saith the Lord God; Behold, I am against thee, O Gog, the chief prince of Meshech and Tubal:
> And I will turn thee back, and put hooks into thy jaws, and *I will bring thee forth, and all thine army*, horses and horsemen, all of them clothed with all sorts of armour, even a great company with bucklers and shields, all of them handling swords:
> *Persia, Ethiopia*, and *Libya* with them; all of them with shield and helmet:

---

3. Ezek. 38:9-12.
4. JD, 14:352.

> *Gomer*, and all his bands; the house of *Togarmah* of the north quarters, and all his bands: and *many people with thee*.[5]

It seems that Ezekiel's statement is referring to the descendants of the grandchildren of Noah, who spread out upon the face of the land after the time of the flood. Genesis chapter ten is known as the "Table of Nations," and furnishes some knowledge concerning these ethnic groups. Magog, Tubal, Meshech, and Gomer were all sons of Japheth, and Togarmah was the grandson of Japheth, through Gomer.[6] Ezekiel also mentions the land of Persia, which was also settled by descendants of Japheth, or what is classed by ethnologists as Indo-European people. Ethiopia and Libya, two countries settled by descendants of Ham, are included in the list too. While all of the ethnic groups mentioned in the Table of Nations are not known, each of the peoples mentioned by Ezekiel have been identified with relative certainty and thus the areas of which the prophet spoke are known. They are given in the accompanying source maps. The reader will recognize that this list actually includes the people who live in the present nations of Turkey, Persia, Ethiopia, Libya, and the southern tip of Russia just above the Caspian Sea. It will be noted that in Ezekiel's prophecy, Gog, the leader of the invaders, is identified by two clues which are seemingly of a conflicting nature. It appears that if Gog is to be an individual from the land of Magog (and Ezekiel's language is too vague to determine this point without doubt), then he will be a Russian. However, the prophet's repetition of the idea that Gog will be a chief prince of Meshech and Tubal would lend more credence to the thought that Gog will be a Turkish ruler. It is impossible to determine the matter for sure on the basis of the limited evidence now available.

Though Ezekiel said that these invading nations will have "many people with thee" [them], nevertheless it seems that these countries will very probably be the leaders of the attack upon Palestine, or else Ezekiel would not have named them.[7]

---

5. Ezek. 38:2-6.
6. Gen. 10:1-3.
7. It appears that in this instance the passage is not dealing with "the nations which are in the four quarters of the earth" (see Revelation 20:8) or else it would seem that Ezekiel would probably have given indication of it. It should be recalled that most of the nations of Europe are expected to be in a collapsed condition and that the American continents will be largely under the control of the Kingdom of God. Many of the heathen nations will not participate in the Armageddon struggle, for

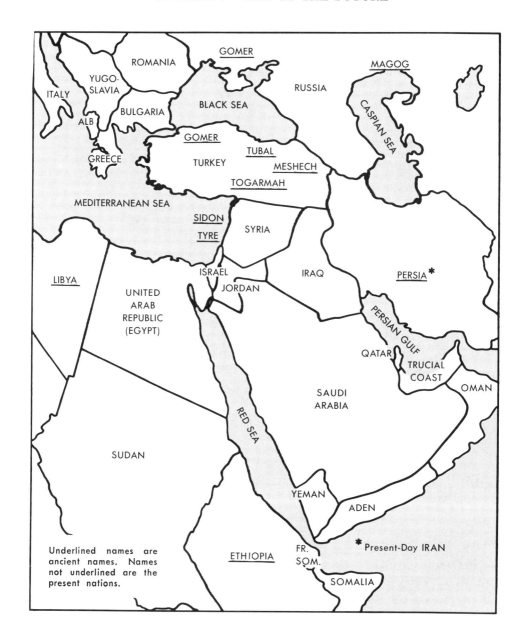

A Comparison of The Nations Identified by The Prophets
as Being Participants in The Battle of Armageddon with
The Nations of The Mediterranean Area Today.

The prophet Joel adds Tyre and Zidon to the list of opposing nations:

> For, behold, in those days, and in that time, when I shall bring again the captivity of Judah and Jerusalem,
> I will also gather all nations, and will *bring them down into the valley of Jehoshaphat, and will plead with them there for my people and for my heritage Israel,* whom they have scattered among the nations, and parted my land.
> And they have cast lots for my people; and have given a boy for an harlot, and sold a girl for wine, that they might drink.
> Yea, and *what have ye to do with me, O Tyre, and Zidon, and all the coasts of Palestine?* will ye render me a recompence? and if ye recompense me, swiftly and speedily will I return your recompense upon your own head;[8]

Orson Pratt states that the people of the world will not have repented after the many signs they will have been given, but instead will have given themselves over to the power of the devil, and that the forces which come against Palestine will number in the millions:

> After the kingdom of God has spread upon the face of the earth, and every jot and tittle of the prophecies have been fulfilled in relation to the spreading of the Gospel among the nations, — *after signs have been shown in the heavens above, and on the earth beneath, blood, fire, and vapour of smoke,—after the sun is turned into darkness, and the moon shall have the appearance of blood, and the stars have apparently been hurled out of their places, and all things have been in commotion, so great will be the darkness resting upon Christendom, and so great the bonds of priestcraft with which they will be bound,* that they will not understand, and they will be given up to the hardness of their hearts. *Then will be fulfilled that saying, That the day shall come when the Lord shall have power over his Saints, and the Devil shall have power over his own dominion.* He will give them up to the power of the Devil, and he will have power over them, and he will carry them about as chaff before a whirlwind. *He will gather up millions upon millions of people into the valleys around about Jerusalem in order to*

Ezekiel records that "all the heathen shall see my judgment that I have executed" after Gog and his forces are overcome. (Ezekiel 39:21-23). Nevertheless, the forces against Palestine are to be so great that Zechariah says "I will gather all nations against Jerusalem to battle." (Zech. 14:2)

8. Joel 3:1-4.

destroy the Jews after they have gathered. How will the Devil do this? He will perform miracles to do it. The Bible says the kings of the earth and the great ones will be deceived by these false miracles. It says there shall be three unclean spirits that shall go forth working miracles, and they are spirits of devils. Where do they go? To the kings of the earth; and what will they do? Gather them up to battle unto the great day of God Almighty. Where? Into the valley of Armageddon.[9]

Location of the Battlefield

The battle of the decadent nations against Israel will be centered in the valley of Armageddon, which is Esdraelon, a triangular plain about sixty miles northwest of Jerusalem:

> For they are the spirits of devils, working miracles which go forth unto the kings of the earth and of the whole world, to gather them to the battle of that great day of God Almighty.
>
> Behold, I come as a thief. Blessed is he that watcheth, and keepeth his garments, lest he walk naked, and they see his shame.
>
> And *he gathered them together into a place called in the Hebrew tongue Armageddon.*[10]

This place is also called the valley of Jehoshaphat or the Valley of Decision:

> Let the heathen be wakened, and *come up to the valley of Jehoshaphat*: for there will I sit to judge all the heathen round about.
>
> Put ye in the sickle, for the harvest is ripe: come get you down; for the press is full, the fats overflow; for their wickedness is great.
>
> *Multitudes, multitudes in the valley of decision; for* the day of the Lord is near in the valley of decision.[11]

---

9. JD, 7:188-89.
10. Rev. 16:14-16. In a discusion of the derivation of the word Armageddon, Andrew Zenos, of the Presbyterian Theological Seminary, states: "According to the commonly accepted view, Har-Magedon is simply a Greek transliteration of the Hebrew for 'mountain of Megiddon'. This does not occur in the O T, but the plain of Megiddo [n] [Plain of Esdraelon] was proverbially the scene of decisive contests (Zec. 12:11; Jg 5:19; IIK 9:27, 23:29), and Gunkel's theory may be correct in so far as it accounts for a change, under Babylonian influence of 'the plain of Megiddo' into 'a mountain of Megiddo.'" Funk and Wagnalls *Standard Bible Dictionary* (Third Revised Edition, Garden City, New York: Garden City Books, 1936), p. 331.
11. Joel 3:12-14.

The Valley of Armageddon (Plain of Esdraelon) in
Northwestern Palestine.

(Photo by Adelbert Bartlett)

As will be seen in the description of the battle which follows, the battlefield will apparently be extended until the war is waged within the precincts of Jerusalem, and until the dead are spread throughout the mountains of Israel.

The Battle

Joel describes the coming of the mighty throng to the attack as a well-disciplined army:

> A day of darkness and of gloominess, a day of clouds and of thick darkness, as the morning spread upon the mountains: a great people and a strong; *there hath not been ever the like, neither shall be any more after it, even to the years of many generations.*
>
> A fire devoureth before them; and behind them a flame burneth: the land is as the garden of Eden before them, and behind them a desolate wilderness; yea, and nothing shall escape them.
>
> The appearance of them is as the appearance of horses; and as horsemen, so shall they run.
>
> Like the noise of chariots on the tops of mountains shall they leap, like the noise of a flame of fire that devoureth the stubble, as a strong people set in battle array.
>
> Before their face the people shall be much pained: all faces shall gather blackness.
>
> *They shall run like mighty men: they shall climb the wall like men of war; and they shall march every one on his ways, and they shall not break their ranks:*
>
> *Neither shall one thrust another: they shall walk every one in his path: and when they fall upon the sword*, they shall not be wounded.
>
> *They shall run to and fro in the city*; they shall run upon the wall, they shall climb up upon the houses; they shall enter in at the windows like a thief.
>
> *The earth shall quake before them: the heavens shall tremble: the sun and the moon shall be dark, and the stars shall withdraw their shining:*[12]

During this terrible warfare most of the Jews will be slain, according to Zechariah, while the remainder will be purified by the Lord:

> Awake, O sword, against my shepherd, and against the man that is my fellow, saith the Lord of Hosts: smite the shep-

---

12. Joel 2:2-10.

THE BATTLE OF ARMAGEDDON

herd, and the sheep shall be scattered: and I will turn mine hand upon the little ones.

And it shall come to pass, that *in all the land, saith the Lord, two parts therein shall be cut off and die; but the third shall be left therein.*

And I will bring the third part through the fire, and will refine them as silver is refined, and will try them as gold is tried: they shall call on my name, and I will hear them: I will say, it is my people: and they shall say, The Lord is my God.[13]

The battle will apparently spread to Jerusalem, and that city will be surrounded and attacked for forty-two months. According to John, during this time two prophets will be preaching within the city. They will finally be slain, lie in the street for three and one-half days, and then be taken up into heaven:

And there was given me a reed like unto a rod: and the angel stood, saying, Rise, and measure the temple of God, and the altar, and them that worship therein.

But *the court which is without the temple leave out, and measure it not; for it is given unto the Gentiles: and the holy city shall they tread under foot forty and two months.*

And *I will give power unto my two witnesses,*[14] *and they shall prophesy a thousand two hundred and threescore days,*[15] clothed in sackcloth. These are the two olive trees, and the two candlesticks standing before the God of the earth.

And if any man will hurt them, fire proceedeth out of their mouth, and devoureth their enemies: and if any man will hurt them, he must in this manner be killed.

These have power to shut heaven, that it rain not in the days of their prophecy: and have power over waters to turn

---

13. Zech. 13:7-9.
14. Is. 51:19-20, Zech. 4:14, and D & C 133:58 are apparently allusions to these two prophets.
15. John's statement that the two prophets will labor for 1260 days, or forty-two months, would seem to indicate that the battle of Armageddon is separate and distinct from the period of universal conflict mentioned in an earlier chapter. The sixth trump (Rev. 9:13-21) apparently records the universal conflict in which a "third part of men [are] killed," and the time indication connected with the conflict is "an hour, and a day, and a month, and a year," or approximately thirteen months. Thus each of these eras differs in length and is also reported by John as being separate events. Whether there is continued strife between the two conflicts is a question unanswered by the evidence available. In some ways, however, it would seem that Armageddon might be considered the consumation of the universal conflict which will take place.

*them to blood, and to smite the earth with all plagues, as often
as they will.*

And when they shall have finished their testimony, the
beast that ascendeth out of the bottomless pit shall make war
against them, and shall overcome them, and *kill them.*

*And their dead bodies shall lie in the street of the great
city, which spiritually is called Sodom and Egypt,* where also
our Lord was crucified.

*And they of the people and kindreds and tongues and na-
tions shall see their dead bodies three days and an half, and
shall not suffer their dead bodies to be put in graves.*

And they that dwell upon the earth shall rejoice over them,
and make merry, and shall send gifts one to another; because
these two prophets tormented them that dwelt on the earth.

And *after three days and an half the Spirit of life from
God entered into them, and they stood upon their feet;* and
great fear fell upon them which saw them.

And they heard a great voice from heaven saying unto
them, Come up hither. *And they ascended up to heaven in a
cloud;* and their enemies beheld them.[16]

John's statement that the Gentiles will tread the holy city
under foot is supported by Zechariah's assertion that half of the
city will fall into captivity:

For I will gather all nations against Jerusalem to battle;
and *the city shall be taken, and the houses rifled, and the
women ravished; and half of the city shall go forth into captivity,* and the residue of the people shall not be cut off from
the city.[17]

Christ's Coming

According to Zechariah, after the city of Jerusalem has been
partly conquered, the Lord will appear on the Mount of Olives:

And his feet shall stand in that day upon the mount of
Olives, which is before Jerusalem on the east, and the mount
of Olives shall cleave in the midst thereof toward the east and
toward the west, and there shall be a very great valley; and
*half of the mountain shall remove toward the north, and half
of it toward the south.*

16. Rev. 11:1-12.
17. Zech. 14:2.

The Mount of Olives East of Jerusalem.

(The Mt. of Olives is the mount entering from the upper left.)

(Photo by Adelbert Bartlett)

And ye shall flee to the valley of the mountains; for the valley of the mountains shall reach unto Azal: yea, ye shall flee, like as ye fled from before the *earthquake* in the days of Uzziah king of Judah: and *the Lord my God shall come, and all the saints with thee.*[18]

John the Revelator gives a more vivid description of His coming. He describes the Lord as coming on a white horse, dressed in red garments, and followed by others who are also mounted:

> And I saw heaven opened, and behold a *white horse;* and he that sat upon him was called Faithful and True, and in righteousness he doth judge and make war.
>
> His eyes were as a flame of fire, and on his head were many crowns; and he had a name written, that no man knew, but he himself.
>
> And *he was clothed with a vesture dipped in blood*: and his name is called The Word of God.
>
> *And the armies which were in heaven followed him upon) white horses,* clothed in fine linen, white and clean.
>
> And out of his mouth goeth a sharp sword, that *with it he should smite the nations*: and he shall rule them with a rod of iron: and he treadeth the winepress of the fierceness and wrath of Almighty God.
>
> And he hath on his vesture and on his thigh a name written, KING OF KINGS, AND LORD OF LORDS.[19]

President Charles W. Penrose summarized the various appearances which the Savior will make in the last days. After describing Christ's appearance to the Saints in the New Jerusalem, he spoke of His second major appearance as being His coming on the Mount of Olives:

> His next appearance will be among the distressed and nearly vanquished sons of Judah. At the crisis of their fate, when the hostile troops of several nations are ravaging the city and all the horrors of war are overwhelming the people of Jeru-

---

18. Zech. 14:4-5.
19. Rev. 19:11-16. There is difficulty determining whether this is a description of Christ's coming on the Mount of Olives or his final coming in glory. It is assigned to its present context because:
   1. He comes to smite the nations. In his final coming in glory, judgment will be on an individual basis.
   2. His coming is followed by the "supper of the great god" in which the animals eat the bodies of those who are slain. Yet in his coming in glory the wicked will be consumed by fire. (Rev. 19:7-8)
   Descriptions of Christ's appearance at both times show him coming dressed in red. For information showing that the Coming on the Mount of Olives is not the final coming in glory, see the summary to this chapter.

salem, he will set his feet upon the Mount of Olives, which will cleave and part asunder at his touch. Attended by a host from heaven, he will overthrow and destroy the combined armies of the Gentiles, and appear to the worshiping Jews as the mighty Deliverer and Conquerer so long expected by their race.[20]

The Earthquake

It appears that the earthquake spoken of by Zechariah, which causes the Mount of Olives to split apart, is the same disaster which John prophesies will level a portion of the city of Jerusalem. In reporting his vision he states that just after the two prophets ascended into heaven "The same hour was there a great earthquake, and *the tenth part of the city fell,* and in the earthquake were slain of men seven thousand: and the remnant were affrighted, and gave glory to the God of heaven"[21] He then added the explanation that the earthquake was so far-reaching in its impact, that "the great city was divided into three parts, and the *cities of the nations fell."*[22]

Ezekiel also prophesied of this great earthquake:

> And it shall come to pass at the same time when Gog shall come against the land of Israel, saith the Lord God, that my fury shall come up in my face.
>
> For in my jealousy and in the fire of my wrath have I spoken, *Surely in that day there shall be a great shaking in the land of Israel;*
>
> So that the fishes of the sea, and the fowls of the heaven, and the beasts of the field, and all creeping things that creep upon the earth, and all the men that are upon the face of the earth, *shall shake at my presence, and the mountains shall be thrown down, and the steep places shall fall,* and every wall shall fall to the ground.[23]

The *Doctrine and Covenants* also speaks of an earthquake at the time of Christ's appearance on the Mount of Olives.

> Then shall the arm of the Lord fall upon the nations.
>
> And *then shall the Lord set his foot upon this mount, and it shall cleave in twain, and the earth shall tremble, and reel to and fro, and the heavens also shall shake.*

---

20. *Millennial Star,* Vol. XXI, p. 583, September 10, 1859.
21. Rev. 11:13.
22. Rev. 16:19.
23. Ezek. 38:18-20.

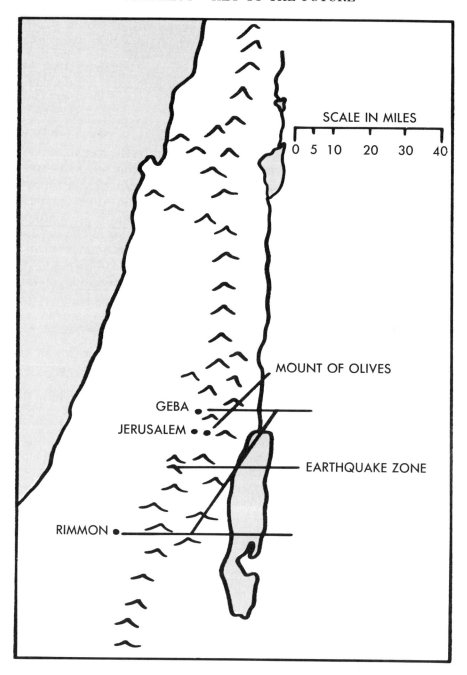

Map of Jerusalem, The Mount of Olives and The Earthquake Zone.

And the Lord shall utter his voice, and all the ends of the earth shall hear it; and the nations of the earth shall mourn, and they that have laughed shall see their folly.

And calamity shall cover the mocker, and the scorner shall be consumed; and they that have watched for iniquity shall be hewn down and cast into the fire.[24]

Joel's statement that "the sun and the moon shall be darkened, and the stars shall withdraw their shining"[25] during the struggle in the valley of decision may find its explanation in dust, ashes, and debris which will be thrown into the air by this earthquake.

It may be at this time also that the land from Geba (six miles north of Jerusalem) to Rimmon (twenty-eight miles south of Jerusalem), which is now extremely mountainous, "shall be turned as a plain."[26]

Conclusion of The Battle

When the Savior comes he will lend new courage to the children of Israel, and they will fight with the strength of David to drive away their enemies. Thus it would appear that the battle may continue after the Savior's appearance and not end at the exact time of his coming. Zechariah stated that "in that day shall the Lord defend the inhabitants of Jerusalem; and he that is feeble among them at that day shall be as David; and the house of David shall be as God, as the angel of the Lord before them."[27]

In addition to his renewing the strength of the Israelite armies at this time, it appears that God will also pour out his judgments on the attacking nations. Ezekiel recorded the Lord's promise that "I will plead against him [Gog] with *pestilence* and with *blood*; and I will rain upon him, and upon his bands, and upon the many people that are with him, an *over-flowing rain, and great hailstones, fire, and brimstone*,"[28] and also that "*I will*

---

24. D & C 45:47-50. The author is aware of certain problems which arise from this section in the matter of chronology. However, the majority of evidence does not seem to support its assertion that the coming on the Mount of Olives is the final coming in glory when the wicked will be destroyed.
25. Joel 3:15.
26. Zech. 14:10.
27. Zech. 12:8.
28. Ezek. 38:22.

send a fire on Magog, and among them that dwell carelessly in the isles: and they shall know that I am the Lord."[29]

In his vision of these judgments John recorded that *"there fell upon men a great hail out of heaven,* every stone about the weight of a talent: and men blasphemed God because of the plague of the hail; for the plague thereof was exceeding great."[30]

Zechariah told of yet another judgment which will be poured out:

> And this shall be the plague wherewith the Lord will smite all the people that have fought against Jerusalem; *Their flesh shall consume away while they stand upon their feet, and their eyes shall consume away in their holes, and their tongue shall consume away in their mouth. . . .*
>
> And so shall be the plague of the horse, of the mule, of the camel, and of the ass, and of all the beasts that shall be in these tents, as this plague.[31]

According to Ezekiel the army which has served under Gog will turn upon each other, "And I will call for a sword against him throughout all my mountains, saith the Lord God: *every man's sword shall be against his brother."*[32]

Zechariah recorded a similar prophecy, that "it shall come to pass in that day, that a great tumult from the Lord shall be among them; and they shall lay hold every one on the hand of his neighbour, and his hand shall rise up against the hand of his neighbour."[33]

Thus the prophets tell of the eventual downfall of the forces of Gog. Joel said the enemy will be driven back to a land barren and desolate:

> But I will remove far off from you the northern army, and will drive him into a land barren and desolate, with his face toward the east sea, and his hinder part toward the utmost sea,

---

29. Ezek. 39:6.
30. Rev. 16:21. A talent of silver weighs about 100 pounds, a talent of gold about 200 pounds. These hailstones, then, will be gigantic. Hailstones of these dimensions would certainly indicate the likelihood of great atmospheric disturbances during the Battle of Armageddon.
31. Zech. 14:12, 15. It is interesting to note that this plague will be of a similar nature to the strange disease which fell upon many of the mobocrats who participated in the murder of the Prophet Joseph Smith. See also D & C 29:18-19, Is. 66:23-24.
32. Ezek. 38:21.
33. Zech. 14:13.

and his stink shall come up, and his ill savour shall come up, because he hath done great things.[34]

Ezekiel described how only a sixth of the attacking armies will be spared, and how the animals will come and devour the remains of the slain. He foretells also the death of the enemy leader, Gog, upon the mountains of Israel:

Therefore, thou son of man, prophesy against Gog, and say, Thus saith the Lord God; Behold, I am against thee, O Gog, the chief prince of Meshech and Tubal:

And I will turn thee back, and *leave but the sixth part of thee*, and will cause thee to come up from the north parts, and will bring thee upon the mountains of Israel:

And I will smite thy bow out of thy left hand, and will cause thine arrows to fall out of thy right hand.

Thou shalt fall upon the mountains of Israel, thou, and all thy bands, and the people that is with thee: I will give thee unto the ravenous birds of every sort, and to the beasts of the field to be devoured.

Thou shalt fall upon the open field: for I have spoken it, saith the Lord God.[35]

And again:

And, thou son of man, thus saith the Lord God, Speak unto every feathered fowl, and to every beast of the field, Assemble yourselves, and come; gather yourselves on every side to my sacrifice that I do sacrifice for you, even a great sacrifice upon the mountains of Israel, that ye may eat flesh, and drink blood.

Ye shall eat the flesh of the mighty, and drink the blood of the princes of the earth, of rams, of lambs, and of goats, of bullocks, all of them fatlings of Bashan.

And ye shall eat fat till ye be full, and drink blood till ye be drunken, of my sacrifice which I have sacrificed for you.

Thus ye shall be filled at my table with horses and chariots, with mighty men, and with all men of war, saith the Lord God.[36]

John called this event the supper of the great God:

And I saw an angel standing in the sun; and he cried with a loud voice, saying to all the fowls that fly in the midst of heaven, Come and gather yourselves together unto the *supper of the great God*;

34. Joel 2:20.
35. Ezek. 39:1-5.
36. Ezek. 39:17-20.

That ye may eat the flesh of kings, and the flesh of captains, and the flesh of mighty men, and the flesh of horses, and of them that sit on them, and the flesh of all men both free and bond, both small and great.[37]

The task of burying the multitude of people who were slain in the Battle of Armageddon will apparently remain as a grim reminder of Israel's near-destruction:

And they that dwell in the cities of Israel shall go forth, and shall *set on fire and burn the weapons*, both the shields and the bucklers, the bows and the arrows, and the handstaves, and the spears, and *they shall burn them with fire seven years*:

So that they shall take no wood out of the field, neither cut down any out of the forests; for they shall burn the weapons with fire: and *they shall spoil those that spoiled them, and rob those that robbed them, saith the Lord God.*

And it shall come to pass in that day, that *I will give unto Gog a place there of graves in Israel*, the valley of the passengers on the east of the sea: and *it shall stop the noses of the passengers: and there shall they bury Gog and all his multitude: and they shall call it The valley of Hamon-gog.*

And *seven months shall the house of Israel be burying of them*, that they may cleanse the land.

Yea, all the people of the land shall bury them; and it shall be to them a renown the day that I shall be glorified, saith the Lord God.

And they shall *sever out men of continual employment, passing through the land to bury with the passengers those that remain upon the face of the earth, to cleanse it; after the end of seven months shall they search.*

And the passengers that pass through the land, when any seeth a man's bone, then shall he set up a sign by it, till the buriers have buried it in the valley of Hamon-gog.

And also the name of the city shall be Hamonah. Thus shall they cleanse the land.[38]

The Conversion of The Jews and Christ's Coming to The Jerusalem Temple

It will be at this coming of the Savior that the many Jews who have not yet believed in Jesus will recognize that He is the Christ:

37. Rev. 19:17-18.
38. Ezek. 39:9-16.

And then shall the Jews look upon me and say: What are these wounds in thine hands and in thy feet?

Then shall they know that I am the Lord; for I will say unto them: These wounds are the wounds with which I was wounded in the house of my friends. I am he who was lifted up. I am Jesus that was crucified. I am the Son of God.[39]

The knowledge that Jesus is the Christ will bring a sudden realization that their fathers slew the Messiah. According to Zechariah, this realization will cause great mourning among the Jews. They will also mourn because of the loved ones they will have lost during the war:

And I will pour upon the house of David, and upon the inhabitants of Jerusalem, the spirit of grace and of supplications: and *they shall look upon me whom they have pierced, and they shall mourn for him, as one mourneth for his only son,* and shall be in bitterness for him, as one that is in bitterness for his firstborn.

In that day shall there be a great mourning in Jerusalem, as the mourning of Hadadrimmon in the valley of Megiddon.

And the land shall mourn, every family apart; the family of the house of David apart, and their wives apart; the family of the house of Nathan apart, and their wives apart;

The family of the house of Levi apart, and their wives apart; the family of Shimei apart, and their wives apart;

All the families that remain, every family apart, and their wives apart.[40]

Ezekiel described the Savior's entrance into the Temple in Jerusalem:

Then he brought me back the way of the gate of the outward sanctuary which looketh toward the east; and it was shut.

Then said the Lord unto me; This gate shall be shut, it shall not be opened, and no man shall enter in by it; because *the Lord, the God of Israel, hath entered in by it, therefore it shall be shut.*

It is for the prince; the prince, he shall sit in it to eat bread before the Lord; he shall enter by the way of the porch of that gate, and shall go out by the way of the same.[41]

---

39. D & C 45:51-52. See Zech. 13:6.
40. Zech. 12:10-14.
41. Ezek. 44:1-3.

The Interval Between The Coming of Christ
to Palestine and Christ's Coming in Glory

Several passages of scripture seem to indicate that there will be an interval between Christ's coming on the Mount of Olives and his final coming in glory. Isaiah spoke of the Lord's coming to Jerusalem at a time when the "enemy shall come in like a flood" and of his glory resting upon that city as it rises in fame and beauty. He then tells of the coming of hosts of the Gentiles to worship there, and the gathering in of the people.[42] He also foretold the light which will emanate from the Lord while he is there, and of the rapid growth of the nation. Perhaps this scripture, in its broader sense, applies also to the Zion in America:

> So shall they fear the name of the Lord from the west, and his glory from the rising of the sun. When the enemy shall come in like a flood, the Spirit of the Lord shall lift up a standard against him.
>
> And the Redeemer shall come to Zion, and unto them that turn from transgression in Jacob, saith the Lord.
>
> As for me, this is my covenant with them, saith the Lord; My spirit that is upon thee, and my words which I have put in thy mouth, shall not depart out of thy mouth, nor out of the mouth of thy seed, nor out of the mouth of thy seed's seed, saith the Lord, from henceforth and for ever.
>
> Arise, shine; for thy light is come, and the glory of the Lord is risen upon thee.
>
> For, behold, the darkness shall cover the earth, and gross darkness the people: but the Lord shall arise upon thee, and his glory shall be seen upon thee.
>
> And the Gentiles shall come to thy light, and kings to the brightness of thy rising.
>
> Lift up thine eyes round about, and see: all they gather themselves together, they come to thee: thy sons shall come from far, and thy daughters shall be nursed at thy side.
>
> Then thou shalt see, and flow together, and thine heart shall fear, and be enlarged; because the abundance of the sea shall be converted unto thee, the forces of the Gentiles shall come unto thee.
>
> The multitude of camels shall cover thee, the dromedaries of Midian and Ephah; all they from Sheba shall come: they shall bring gold and incense; and they shall shew forth the praises of the Lord.

All the flocks of Kedar shall be gathered together unto thee, the rams of Nebaioth shall minister unto thee: they shall come up with acceptance on mine altar, and I will glorify the house of my glory.

Who are these that fly as a cloud, and as the doves to their windows?[42]

Surely the isles shall wait for me, and the ships of Tarshish first, to bring thy sons from far, their silver and their gold with them, unto the name of the Lord thy God, and to the Holy One of Israel, because he hath glorified thee.

And the sons of strangers shall build up thy walls, and their kings shall minister unto thee: for in my wrath I smote thee, but in my favour have I had mercy on thee.

Therefore thy gates shall be open continually; they shall not be shut day nor night; that *men may bring unto thee the forces of the Gentiles, and that their kings may be brought.*

For the nation and kingdom that will not serve thee shall perish; yea, those nations shall be utterly wasted.

The glory of Lebanon shall come unto thee, the fir tree, the pine tree, and the box together, to beautify the place of my sanctuary; and I will make the place of my feet glorious.

The sons also of them that afflicted thee shall come bending unto thee; and all they that despised thee shall bow themselves down at the soles of thy feet; and they shall call thee, the city of the Lord, the Zion of the Holy One of Israel.

Whereas thou hast been forsaken and hated, so that no man went through thee, I will make thee an eternal excellency, a joy of many generations.

Thou shalt also suck the milk of the Gentiles, and shalt suck the breast of kings: and thou shalt know that I the Lord am thy Saviour and thy Redeemer, the mighty One of Jacob.

For brass will I bring gold, and for iron I will bring silver, and for wood brass, and for stones iron: I will also make thy officers peace, and thine exactors righteousness.

Violence shall no more be heard in thy land, wasting nor destruction within thy borders; but thou shalt call thy walls Salvation, and thy gates Praise.

The sun shall be no more thy light by day; neither for brightness shall the moon give light unto thee: but *the Lord shall be unto thee an everlasting light, and thy God thy glory.*

Thy sun shall no more go down; neither shall thy moon withdraw itself: for the Lord shall be thine everlasting light, and the days of thy mourning shall be ended.

---

42. Verse eight is taken by some as an allusion to travel by air.

Thy people also shall be all righteous: they shall inherit the land for ever, the branch of my planting, the work of my hands, that I may be glorified.

A little one shall become a thousand, and a small one a strong nation: the Lord will hasten it in his time.[43]

Isaiah's comments that this era will be a time when "darkness shall cover the earth, and gross darkness the people"—his reference to a continued gathering when some will "fly as a cloud, and as the doves to their windows" and others will come by the "ships of Tarshish"—his allusion to nations which yet "shall be utterly wasted," and that "a small one [shall be] a strong nation" would seem to indicate that this is an era which still precedes the final appearance of the Savior when a time of world-wide peace will be inaugurated by the cleansing and purging out of the wicked of the earth by fire. Yet this passage definitely speaks of a time after the battle of Armageddon when the Savior will have come and redeemed the people of Israel, when "the glory of the Lord is risen upon thee," and the "Gentiles shall come to thy light, and kings to the brightness of thy rising," when "violence shall be no more heard in thy land, wasting nor destruction within thy borders;" and "thy people also shall be all righteous." This passage, then, seems to be an indication of the interval between the appearance of the Lord on the Mount of Olives and His final coming in glory. There seems to be no definite indication of the length of such an interval. It should be noted, however, that another generation will have raised up, for Isaiah said that "the sons also of them that afflicted thee shall come bending unto thee."

Other passages, also seem to speak of activities which are apparently to take place before the final cleansing of the earth when the elements will be cleansed by fervent heat and the wicked will be as stubble and yet after the battle of Armageddon has transpired. For instance, Zechariah told of a period after the coming of the Lord to the Mount of Olives when the nations will not only *be compelled* to leave Jerusalem in peace, but they will be *under obligation* to travel there and worship the Lord of Hosts:

And it shall come to pass, that *every one that is left of all the nations which came against Jerusalem shall even go up from*

---

43. Is. 59:19-21; 60:1-22.

year to year to worship the King, the Lord of hosts, and to keep the feast of tabernacles.

And it shall be, that *whoso will not come up of all the families of the earth unto Jerusalem to worship the King, the Lord of hosts, even upon them shall be no rain.*

And if the family of Egypt go not up, and come not, that have no rain; *there shall be the plague*, wherewith *the Lord will smite the heathen* that come not up to keep the feast of tabernacles.

This shall be the punishment of Egypt, and the punishment of all nations that come not up to keep the feast of tabernacles.[44]

It will be seen that such conditions are very much unlike the atmosphere which is prophesied to exist during the Millennium.

Just as it is prophesied that the Savior will tarry in the New Jerusalem after His appearance there, it is said that He will also tarry in the Old Jerusalem. Ezekiel revealed that God will be among the children of Israel and that they will see him face to face. He also foretold the effect which the miraculous sparing of Jerusalem will have on those who still remain among the heathen nations:

And *I will set my glory among the heathen, and all the heathen shall see my judgment that I have executed*, and my hand that I have laid upon them.

So the house of Israel shall know that I am the Lord their God from that day and forward.

And the heathen shall know that the house of Israel went into captivity for their iniquity: because they trespassed against me, therefore hid I my face from them, and gave them into the hand of their enemies: so fell they all by the sword.

According to their uncleanness and according to their transgressions have I done unto them, and hid my face from them.

Therefore thus saith the Lord God; Now will I bring again the captivity of Jacob, and have mercy upon the whole house of Israel, and will be jealous for my holy name;

After that they have borne their shame, and all their trespasses whereby they have trespassed against me, when they dwelt safely in their land, and none made them afraid.

When I have brought them again from the people, and gathered them out of their enemies' lands, and am sanctified in them in the sight of many nations:

44. Zech. 14:16-19.

Then shall they know that I am the Lord their God, which caused them to be led into captivity among the heathen: but *I have gathered them unto their own land, and have left none of them any more there.*

Neither will I hide my face any more from them: for I have poured out my spirit upon the house of Israel, saith the Lord God.[45]

Missionary Work in the Interval Between The Battle of Armageddon and Christ's Coming in Glory

It appears that there is no real indication as to the length of this important interval. It must be fairly short, because the prince, David, will apparently come to rule just before the battle of Armageddon and will still be alive at the time of Christ's coming in glory.[46] The interval must, however, be of sufficient length to allow for two important missionary efforts to be carried out:

1. The mission to the heathen nations.
2. A final mission to all mankind. This mission will apparently start at this time and continue into the Millennium.

It has been seen from the passages cited above that the miraculous salvation of Israel which Christ will bring to pass during the Battle of Armageddon will occasion the conversion of many of the heathen people. They will come up to Palestine to worship the Lord while he is reigning from Jerusalem. This will probably be a time of great missionary labor among the people of the heathen nations.

Either simultaneously with or following after the mission to the heathen nations will come a final mission to all mankind, in which the righteous will be sought out regardless of race, creed, or nation. These righteous will be gathered out by the people of Israel from among the wicked and brought to Palestine or to the American Zion. The final period of gathering, according to Isaiah, will take place after peace has been extended to Israel "like a river," and Jerusalem has become a "holy mountain," but preparatory to the cleansing of the entire earth by fire:

Hear the word of the Lord, ye that tremble at his word; Your brethren that hated you, that cast you out for my name's

---

45. Ezek. 39:21-29.
46. For references and more details see the preceding chapter.

sake, said, Let the Lord be glorified: but *he shall appear to your joy, and they shall be ashamed.*

A voice of noise from the city, a voice from the temple, a voice of the Lord that rendereth recompence to his enemies.

Before she travailed, she brought forth; before her pain came, she was delivered of a man child.

Who hath heard such a thing who hath seen such things? Shall the earth be made to bring forth in one day or *shall a nation be born at once? for as soon as Zion travailed, she brought forth her children.*

Shall I bring to the birth, and not cause to bring forth? saith the Lord: shall I cause to bring forth, and shut the womb? saith thy God.

Rejoice ye with Jerusalem, and be glad with her, all ye that love her: rejoice for joy with her, all ye that mourn for her:

That ye may suck, and be satisfied with the breasts of her consolations; that ye may milk out, and *be delighted with the abundance of her glory.*

For thus saith the Lord, Behold, *I will extend peace to her like a river, and the glory of the Gentiles like a flowing stream*: then shall ye suck, ye shall be borne upon her sides, and be dandled upon her knees.

As one whom his mother comforteth, so will I comfort you, and *ye shall be comforted in Jerusalem.*

And when ye see this, your heart shall rejoice, and your bones shall flourish like an herb: and the hand of the Lord shall be known toward his servants, and *his indignation toward his enemies.*

For, behold, the Lord will come with fire, and with his chariots like a whirlwind, to render his anger with fury, and his rebuke with flames of fire.

For by fire and by his sword will the Lord plead with all flesh: and the slain of the Lord shall be many.

They that sanctify themselves, and purify themselves in the gardens behind one tree in the midst, eating swine's flesh, and the abomination, and the mouse, shall be consumed together saith the Lord.

For I know their works and their thoughts: it *shall come, that I will gather all nations and tongues; and they shall come, and see my glory.*

And I will set a sign among them, and I will send those that escape of them unto the nations, to Tarshish, Pul, and Lud, that draw the bow, to Tubal, and Javan, to the isles afar off, that have not heard my fame, neither have seen my glory; and they shall declare my glory among the Gentiles.

And they shall bring all your brethren for an offering unto the Lord out of all nations upon horses, and in chariots, and in litters, and upon mules, and upon swift beasts, to my holy mountain 'Jerusalem, saith the Lord, as the children of Israel bring an offering in a clean vessel into the house of the Lord.

And I will also take of them for priests and for Levites, saith the Lord.

For as the new heavens and the new earth, which I will make, shall remain before me, saith the Lord, so shall your seed and your name remain.

And it shall come to pass, that from one new moon to another, and from one sabbath to another, shall all flesh come to worship before me, saith the Lord.

And they shall go forth, and look upon the carcases of the men that have transgressed against me: for their worm shall not die, neither shall their fire be quenched; and they shall be an abhorring unto all flesh.[47]

Apparently the knowledge that God is dwelling with the Israelites will cause many people to be converted, for Zechariah recorded:

Thus saith the Lord of hosts; It shall yet come to pass, that *there shall come people, and the inhabitants of many cities*:

And the inhabitants of one city shall go to another, saying, Let us go speedily to pray before the Lord, and to seek the Lord of hosts: I will go also.

Yea, *many people and strong nations shall come to seek the Lord of hosts in Jerusalem, and to pray before the Lord.*

Thus saith the Lord of hosts; In those days it shall come to pass, that ten men shall take hold out of all languages of the nations, *even shall take hold of the skirt of him that is a Jew, saying, We will go with you: for we have heard that God is with you.*[48]

The Savior, while ministering among the Nephites, repeated a portion of his revelation to Isaiah which may pertain to this period after the battle of Armageddon. He defined it as a time after "the Father hath made bare his holy arm in the eyes of

47. Is. 66:5-24.
48. Zech. 8:20-23.

all the nations," and yet before "all the ends of the earth shall see the salvation of the Father." He spoke of a period when the missionaries shall publish peace upon the mountains, and yet the righteous are to be called out from among the wicked in preparation for their final destruction:

Then will the Father gather them together again, and give unto them Jerusalem for the land of their inheritance.

Then shall they break forth into joy—Sing together, ye waste places of Jerusalem; for the Father hath comforted his people, he hath redeemed Jerusalem.

The Father hath made bare his holy arm in the eyes of all the nations; and all the ends of the earth shall see the salvation of the Father; and the Father and I are one.

And *then* shall be brought to pass that which is written: Awake, awake again, and *put on thy strength, O Zion; put on thy beautiful garments, O Jerusalem*, the holy city, for henceforth there shall be no more come into thee the uncircumcised and the unclean.

Shake thyself from the dust; arise, sit down, O Jerusalem; *loose thyself from the bands of thy neck, O captive daughter of Zion.*

For thus saith the Lord: Ye have sold yourselves for naught and ye shall be redeemed without money.

Verily, verily, I say unto you, that my people shall know my name; yea, in that day they shall know that I am he that doth speak.

And *then* shall they say: *How beautiful upon the mountains are the feet of him that bringeth good tidings unto them, that publisheth peace;* that bringeth good tidings unto them of good, that publisheth salvation; that saith unto Zion: Thy God reigneth!

And then shall a cry go forth: Depart ye, depart ye, go ye out from thence, touch not that which is unclean; go ye out of the midst of her; be ye clean that bear the vessels of the Lord.

For ye shall not go out with haste nor go by flight; for the Lord will go before you, and the God of Israel shall be your rearward.

Behold, my servant shall deal prudently; he shall be exalted and extolled and be very high.[49]

This will apparently be the era in which the Jewish nation will receive the priesthood, for the *Doctrine and Covenants* in-

---

49. III Ne. 20:33-42.

terprets "put on thy strength" as the giving of the priesthood to Israel and "loose thyself from the bands of thy neck" as an exhortation to the scattered remnants of Israel who are yet to be gathered to throw off the curses of God which they are still experiencing because they live among the wicked:

> What is meant by the command in Isaiah, 52nd chapter, 1st verse, which saith: put on thy strength, O Zion — and what people had Isaiah reference to?
>
> He had reference to those whom God shall call in the last days, who should hold the power of the priesthood to bring again Zion, and the redemption of Israel; and *to put on her strength is to put on the authority of the priesthood, which she, Zion has a right to by lineage; also to return to that power which she had lost.*
>
> What are we to understand by Zion loosing herself from the bands of her neck; 2nd verse?
>
> We are to understand that the scattered remnants are exhorted to return to the Lord from whence they have fallen; which if they do, the promise of the Lord is that he will speak to them, or give them revelation. See the 6th, 7th, and 8th verses. *The bands of her neck are the curses of God upon her*, or the remnants of Israel in their scattered condition among the Gentiles.[50]

Summary

Following the return of the Jews and the Ten Tribes to Palestine the Israelite people will rise in wealth and power. Their prosperity will attract the surrounding nations which will wage war against them because of jealousy and greed.

1. It will be the surrounding nations which will attack Palestine. Because their forces are to be so numerous several passages say that all nations will be gathered to battle, yet it has been seen in a preceding chapter that Europe, during this period, will be in devastated condition and the Americas will be under the influence of Zion. Ezekiel's description (the most complete one found in the scriptures) indicates that the war will be local rather than world-wide in character.

2. The war takes its name from the valley of Armageddon which is located about 60 miles northwest of Jerusalem. The war is expected to cover most of the area of Palestine and to continue for at least 3½ years.

50. D & C 113:7-10.

3. During the battle there will be two prophets in Jerusalem who will have power to control the elements. They will be killed and then brought back to life.

4. As the strength of the Israelites is waning and they are about to succumb to their enemies, the Savior will suddenly appear on the Mount of Olives. An earthquake will then split the mount apart and will shake both Palestine and other nations.

5. Many people have understood that Christ's coming on the Mount of Olives was his final coming in glory which would be seen by all men and which would cleanse the earth by fire. This is a mistaken assumption. Numerous events which are prophesied to follow Christ's appearance indicate that his coming on the Mount of Olives is of a local nature with effects which are not typical of his final coming in glory:

   A. The earthquake accompanying his coming destroys part of the city of Jerusalem but does not cause the mountains to melt as will the heat of his coming in glory.

   B. The opposing army continues to fight.
      (1) They are driven back to the North.
      (2) They are smitten with pestilence, hailstones, and a plague which rots their flesh.
      (3) They will turn on one another and fight among themselves.

   C. Most of the opposing army including Gog, their leader, will be slain. Their bodies will lie on the mountains and be eaten by the birds and the beasts.

   D. The weapons of warfare will litter the hills of Israel and provide fuel for fires for seven years.

   E. The victors will rob and spoil the bodies of the vanquished.

   F. The dead bodies will stink.

   G. Burying of the dead will continue for seven months.

   H. Converts are still being called and gathered out from among the wicked.

All of these items are in strong contrast to Christ's coming in glory, during which the corruptible things of the earth, both animate and inanimate which have not abided by terrestrial law, will immediately be destroyed by fire.[51]

51. This will be discussed in the next chapter.

6. Christ's coming on the Mount of Olives will bring about the conversion of the Jews when he shows them the scars of the wounds from his crucifixion.

7. Following the conclusion of the battle there will be an interval before the final coming of Christ in glory in which the gospel will be carried to the heathen nations. There will also be a final mission to all mankind to gather the righteous out from among the wicked in preparation for the cleansing of the earth by fire.

CHAPTER XIV

Christ's Coming in Glory

In preceding chapters three appearances of the Savior have been considered—His coming to the temple in New Jerusalem, His coming to the council at Adam-ondi-Ahman, and His appearance on the Mount of Olives. Following these events, and after the interval in which Palestine will be rebuilt and the righteous gathered in, He will make His most important appearance— His advent in glory.[1] According to the prophecies, the earth will have undergone many changes in preparation for this event. Great earthquakes will have changed the configuration of the land; wars will have raged throughout the world and will have brought political upheaval; famine and pestilence will have swept across the continents, leaving many cities desolate; the earth's population will have been drastically reduced so that there will be but "few men left;" the righteous will have been gathered in to the areas surrounding the new and old Jerusalems; and the wicked who remain will have been bound in sin and will be ready to be swept off the face of the earth. Charles W. Penrose gave this dramatic summary of the final coming of the Savior:

> The tongue of man falters, and the pen drops from the hand of the writer, as the mind is rapt in contemplation of the sublime and awful majesty of his coming to take vengeance on the ungodly and to reign as King of the whole earth.
>
> He comes! The *earth shakes*, and the tall mountains tremble; the *mighty deep rolls back to the north* as in fear, and the *rent skies* glow like molten brass. He comes! The *dead saints burst forth from their tombs*, and *"those who are alive and remain"* are *"caught up"* with them to meet him. The ungodly rush to hide themselves from his presence and call upon the quivering rocks to cover them. He comes! with all the hosts of the righteous glorified. The breath of his lips strikes death

---

1. Other appearances by the Savior in addition to these three are anticipated, e. g.: "For behold, he shall stand upon the Mount of Olives, and upon the mighty ocean, even the great deep, and upon the islands of the sea, and upon the land of Zion." D & C 133:20.

to the wicked. His glory is as a consuming fire. *The proud and rebellious are as stubble; they are burned* and "left neither root nor branch." He sweeps the earth "as with the besom of destruction." He deluges the earth with the fiery floods of his wrath, and the filthiness and abominations of the world are consumed. *Satan and his dark hosts are taken and bound*—and the prince of the power of the air has lost his dominion, for he whose right it is to reign has come, and the "kingdoms of this world have become the kingdoms of our Lord and of his Christ."[2]

Trumps Introduce Christ's Coming

The scriptures describe in detail the coming of the Savior and the dramatic phenomenon which will accompany His advent. Section eighty-eight of the *Doctrine and Covenants* foretells these events:

And there shall be *silence in heaven for the space of half an hour;* and immediately after shall the *curtain of heaven be unfolded,* as a scroll is unfolded after it is rolled up, and the *face of the Lord shall be unveiled;*

And the *saints that are upon the earth, who are alive, shall be quickened and be caught up to meet him.*

And *they who have slept in their graves shall come forth,* for their *graves shall be opened; and they also shall be caught up* to meet him in the midst of the pillar of heaven—

They are Christ's, the first fruits, they who shall descend with him first, and they who are on the earth and in their graves, who are first caught up to meet him; and all this by the voice of the *sounding of the trump* of the angel of God.

And after this another angel shall sound, which is the *second trump;* and then cometh the *redemption of those who are Christ's at his coming;* who have received their part in that prison which is prepared for them, that they might receive the gospel, and be judged according to men in the flesh.

And again, another trump shall sound, which is the *third trump;* and *then come the spirits of men who are to be judged, and are found under condemnation;*

And *these are the rest of the dead;* and they live not again until the thousand years are ended, neither again, until the end of the earth.

And another trump shall sound, which is the *fourth trump,* saying: There are found among *those who are to remain until that great and last day, even the end, who shall remain filthy still.*

2. *Millennial Star,* Vol. XXI, p. 583, September 10, 1859.

And another trump shall sound, which is the *fifth trump,* which is the fifth angel who committeth the everlasting gospel — flying through the midst of heaven, unto all nations, kindreds, tongues, and people;

And this shall be the sound of his trump, saying to all people, both in heaven and in earth, and that are under the earth for every ear shall hear it, and every knee shall bow, and every tongue shall confess, while they hear the sound of the trump, saying: Fear God, and give glory to him who sitteth upon the throne, forever and ever; for the *hour of his judgment is come.*

And again, another angel shall sound his trump, which is the *sixth angel,* saying: *She is fallen who made all nations drink of the wine of the wrath of her fornication;* she is fallen, is fallen!

And again, another angel shall sound his trump, which is the *seventh angel,* saying: *It is finished; it is finished!* The Lamb of God hath overcome and trodden the wine-press alone, even the wine-press of the fierceness of the wrath of Almighty God.

And *then shall the angels be crowned with the glory of his might, and the Saints shall be filled with his glory, and receive their inheritance and be made equal with him.*

And *then shall the first angel again sound his trump in the ears of all living, and reveal the secret acts of men, and the mighty works of God in the first thousand years.*

And then shall the second angel sound his trump, and reveal the secret acts of men, and the thoughts and intents of their hearts, and the mighty works of God in the second thousand years —

And so on, until the seventh angel shall sound his trump; and he shall stand forth upon the land and upon the sea, and swear in the name of him who sitteth upon the throne, that there shall be time no longer; and *Satan shall be bound,* that old serpent, who is called the devil, and shall not be loosed for the space of a thousand years.[3]

Because of the importance and profundity of this scripture, it is repeated here in outline form with comments by Latter-day Saint General Authorities which tend to clarify some of its teachings.

1. There shall be silence in heaven for the space of half an hour. Orson Pratt made this comment about the period of silence:

---

3. D & C 88:95-110.

"Immediately after the sounding of this trump, there will be silence in heaven for the space of half an hour." *Whether the half hour here spoken of is according to our reckoning— thirty minutes, or whether it be according to the reckoning of the Lord* we do not know. We know that the word hour is used in some portions of the Scriptures to represent quite a lengthy period of time. For instance, we, the Latter-day Saints, are living in the eleventh hour, that is the eleventh period of time; and *for aught we know the half hour during which silence is to prevail in heaven may be quite an extensive period of time.* During the period of silence all things are perfectly still; no angels flying during that half hour; no trumpets sounding; no noise in the heavens above; but immediately after this great silence the curtain of heaven shall be unfolded as a scroll is unfolded.[4]

2. The curtain of heaven shall be unfolded as a scroll, and the face of the Lord shall be revealed. It should be noted that the heaven will already have "departed as a scroll when it is rolled together" during an earthquake which is to take place during the sixth thousand years.[5] Because the Lord's coming in glory is to take place later, in the seventh thousand years, it would indicate (1) that there are two different times when the heavens are rolled back, or (2) the text of Revelation has been corrupted, or (3) this interpretation of the *Doctrine and Covenants* is faulty. Note also that this passage speaks of the heavens unfolding, while Isaiah refers to their being *"rolled together as a scroll"*[6] in his description of the Lord's coming in vengeance.

3. The saints who are alive shall be caught up to meet him. Orson Pratt taught that these saints would become translated beings:

> *The mortal Saints will then be transfigured and sanctified, but not immortalized.* They will be prepared for the millennial reign. The tables will then be spread, and the Latter-day and Former-day Saints will be together to partake of the sacrament just as it is this afternoon, only more perfectly prepared.[7]

4. The first of a series of seven trumpets will sound, and those who have been resurrected will be caught up into heaven.

4. JD, 16:328.
5. Rev. 6:14. See D & C 77:6-7.
6. Is. 34:4.
7. JD, 8:52.

Orson Pratt held that these are to be actual trumpet signals and commented on the carrying power of such instruments:

> *We also believe, and so do the inhabitants of the Christian world at large, that there will be an audible sound of a trump*—the trump of the archangel—in the heavens at the time this grand scenery is opened to mankind; that at the sound of that trumpet the dead in Christ will come forth from their silent dusty tombs; that at the sound of that trump the Saints then living will be instantaneously caught up to meet the Lord in the air. This doctrine is believed in by Christians generally who do not spiritualize altogether the sense and meaning of the Scriptures.[8]

This trump was apparently spoken of in another revelation in which the Lord says,

> Hearken ye, for, behold, the great day of the Lord is nigh at hand.
>
> For the day cometh that the Lord shall utter his voice out of heaven; the heavens shall shake and the earth shall tremble, and the trump of God shall sound both long and loud, and shall say to the sleeping nations: Ye saints arise and live; ye sinners stay and sleep until I call again.[9]

The other six trumps sound in order, declaring what the order of the resurrection will be. Note that the events of which the angels speak apparently do not all take place at the time of Christ's coming, but that the angels are predicting and announcing what will take place until the end of the world.[10] Elder Joseph Fielding Smith gives this summary of the order of the resurrections:

> In modern revelation given to the Church, the Lord has made known more in relation to this glorious event. *There shall be at least two classes which shall have the privilege of the resurrection at this time: First those who "shall dwell in the presence of God and his Christ forever and ever"; and second, honorable men, those who belong to the terrestrial kingdom as well as those of the celestial kingdom.*
>
> *At the time of the coming of Christ,* "They who have slept in their graves shall come forth, for their graves shall be

---

8. JD, 18:57-58.
9. D & C 43:17-18.
10. After each of the seven angels has sounded his trump twice, it will only then be time for Satan to be bound for the thousand years of the Millennium. D & C 88:110. See Rev. 20:1-3.

opened; and they also shall be caught up to meet him in the midst of the pillar of heaven — They are Christ's, the first fruits, they who shall descend with him first, and they who are on the earth and in their graves, who are first caught up to meet him; and all this by the voice of the sounding of the trump of the angel of God." These are the just, "whose names are written in heaven, where God and Christ are the judge of all. *These are they who are just men made perfect through Jesus the Mediator of the new covenant, who wrought out this perfect atonement through the shedding of his own blood."*

Following this great event, and *after the Lord and the righteous who are caught up to meet him have descended upon the earth, there will come to pass another resurrection. This may be considered as a part of the first, although it comes later.* In this resurrection will come forth those of the terrestrial order, who were not worthy to be caught up to meet him, but who are worthy to come forth to enjoy the millennial reign.

It is written that the second angel shall sound, which is the second trump, "and then cometh the redemption of those who are Christ's at his coming; who have received their part in the prison which is prepared for them, that they might receive the gospel, and be judged according to men in the flesh."

This other class, which will also have right to the first resurrection, are those who are not members of the Church of the Firstborn, but who have led honorable lives, although they refused to accept the fulness of the gospel.

Also in this class will be numbered those who died without law and hence are not under condemnation for a violation of the commandments of the Lord. The promise is made to them of redemption from death in the following words: "And then shall the heathen nations be redeemed, and they that knew no law shall have part in the first resurrection; and it shall be tolerable for them." These, too, shall partake of the mercies of the Lord and shall receive the reuniting of spirit and body inseparably, thus becoming immortal, but not with the fulness of the glory of God.

All liars, and sorcerers, and adulterers and all who love and make a lie, shall not receive the resurrection at this time, but for a thousand years shall be thrust down into hell where they shall suffer the wrath of God until they pay the price of their sinning, if it is possible, by the things which they shall suffer.

These are the "spirits of men who are to be judged, and are found under condemnation; And these are the rest of the dead; and they live not again until the thousand years are ended, neither again, until the end of the earth."

These are the hosts of the telestial world who are condemned to "suffer the wrath of God on earth"; and who are "cast down to hell and suffer the wrath of Almighty God, until the fulness of times, when Christ shall have subdued all enemies under his feet, and shall have perfected his work."[11]

These seven angels also announce that all upon the earth will bow to the Savior, that the great and abominable church has fallen, and that the Lamb has trodden the winepress alone.

5. Then the angels will be crowned and the Saints will be filled with His glory and be made equal with Him.

6. The seven angels will again sound their trumps in their turn. Each will reveal the secret acts of men during a thousand year period which has passed during the earth's existence. This seems to be the event of which the first section of the *Doctrine and Covenants* speaks:

> For verily the voice of the Lord is unto all men, and there is none to escape; and there is no eye that shall not see, neither ear that shall not hear, neither heart that shall not be penetrated.
>
> And the rebellious shall be pierced with much sorrow; *for their iniquities shall be spoken upon the housetops, and their secret acts shall be revealed.*[12]

Michael (Adam), the seventh angel, will proclaim that there shall be time no longer, and that Satan shall be bound.

Saints Also to Descend

Doctrine and Covenants Section twenty-nine presents the next stage of the story and tells of the Savior's actual coming:

> For the hour is nigh and the day soon at hand when the earth is ripe; and all the proud and they that do wickedly shall be as stubble; and *I will burn them up, saith the Lord of Hosts, that wickedness shall not be upon the earth;*
>
> For the hour is nigh, and that which was spoken by mine apostles must be fulfilled; for as they spoke so shall it come to pass;
>
> *For I will reveal myself from heaven with power and great glory, with all the hosts thereof, and dwell in righteousness*

---

11. Joseph Fielding Smith, *Doctrines of Salvation,* II, 296-98.
12. D & C 1:2-3.

*with men on earth a thousand years, and the wicked shall not
stand.*

And again, verily, verily, I say unto you, and it hath gone
forth in a firm decree, by the will of the Father, that *mine
apostles, the Twelve which were with me in my ministry at
Jerusalem, shall stand at my right hand at the day of my coming in a pillar of fire,* being clothed with robes of righteousness,
with crowns upon their heads, in glory even as I am, to judge
the whole house of Israel, even as many as have loved me and
kept my commandments, and none else.

*For a trump shall sound both long and loud, even as upon
Mount Sinai,*[13] *and all the earth shall quake, and they shall
come forth—yea, even the dead which died in me, to receive a
crown of righteousness,* and to be clothed upon, even as I am, to
be with me, that we may be one.[14]

Orson Pratt gave this impressive list of those who would
accompany the Savior at His coming:

Who will be with Jesus when he appears? The decree has gone
forth, saying, Mine *Apostles* who were with me in Jerusalem
shall be clothed in glory and be with me. The brightness of
their countenance will shine forth with all that efulgence
and fulness of splendour that shall surround the Son of Man
when he appears. There will be all those personages to whom
he alludes. There will be all the *former-day Saints, Enoch and
his city,* with all the greatness and splendour that surround
them: there will be *Abraham, Isaac,* and *Jacob,* as they sit upon
their thrones, together with *all the persons that have been redeemed and brought near unto the presence of God. All* will
be unfolded and unveiled, and all this will be for the wicked to
look upon, as well as the righteous; for *the wicked will not as
yet have been destroyed.* When this takes place, there will be
Latter-day Saints living upon the earth, and they will ascend
and mingle themselves with that vast throng; for they will
be filled with anxiety to go where the Saints of the Church of
the Firstborn are, and the Church of Firstborn will feel an
anxiety to come and meet with the Saints on earth, and this
will bring the general assembly of the redeemed into one; and
thus will be fulfilled the saying of Paul, "that in the dispensation of the fulness of times he might gather together in one all
things in Christ, both which are in heaven and which are on
earth, even in him."[15]

13. See Ex. 19:13-19.
14. D & C 29:9-13.
15. JD, 8:51.

His comment is in some measure an interpretation of *Doctrine and Covenants* 27: 5-14:

> Behold, this is wisdom in me; wherefore, marvel not, for the hour cometh that *I will drink of the fruit of the vine with you on the earth, and with Moroni*, whom I have sent unto you to reveal the Book of Mormon, containing the fulness of my everlasting gospel, to whom I have committed the keys of the record of the stick of Ephraim;
>
> And also with *Elias*, to whom I have committed the keys of bringing to pass the restoration of all things spoken by the mouth of all the holy prophets since the world began, concerning the last days;
>
> And also *John the son of Zacharias*, which Zacharias he (Elias) visited and gave promise that he should have a son, and his name should be John, and he should be filled with the spirit of Elias;
>
> Which John I have sent unto you, my servants, Joseph Smith, Jun., and Oliver Cowdery, to ordain you unto the first priesthood which you have received, that you might be called and ordained even as Aaron;
>
> And also *Elijah*, unto whom I have committed the keys of the power of turning the hearts of the fathers to the children, and the hearts of the children to the fathers, that the whole earth may not be smitten with a curse;
>
> And also with *Joseph* and *Jacob*, and *Isaac*, and *Abraham*, your fathers, by whom the promises remain;
>
> And also with *Michael*, or Adam, the father of all, the prince of all, the ancient of days;
>
> And also with *Peter*, and *James*, and *John*, whom I have sent unto you, by whom I have ordained you and confirmed you to be apostles, and especial witnesses of my name, and bear the keys of your ministry and of the same things which I revealed unto them;
>
> Unto whom I have committed the keys of my kingdom, and a dispensation of the gospel for the last times; and for the fulness of times, in the which I will gather together in one all things, both which are in heaven, and which are on earth;
>
> *And also with all those whom my Father hath given me out of the world.*

Description of The Lord at His Coming

The physical appearance of the Lord at His coming is described in *Doctrine and Covenants* 133: 46-52:

> And it shall be said: Who is this that cometh down from God in heaven with *dyed garments;* yea, from the regions

which are not known, clothed in his *glorious apparel,* traveling in the greatness of his strength?

And he shall say: I am he who spake in righteousness, mighty to save.

And the Lord shall be *red in his apparel,* and his garments like him that treadeth in the wine-vat.

And *so great shall be the glory of his presence that the sun shall hide his face in shame, and the moon shall withhold its light, and the stars shall be hurled from their places.*

And his voice shall be heard: *I have trodden the winepress alone,* and have brought judgment upon all people; and none were with me;

And *I have trampled them in my fury, and I did tread upon them in mine anger,* and their blood have I sprinkled upon my garments, and stained all my raiment; for *this was the day of vengeance which was in my heart.*

And *now the year of my redeemed is come;* and they shall mention the loving kindness of their Lord, and all that he has bestowed upon them according to his goodness, and according to his loving kindness, forever and ever.[16]

A similar description of the Lords coming is given by the Prophet Isaiah:

Who is this that cometh from Edom, with *dyed garments from Bozrah?* this that is glorious in his apparel, traveling in the greatness of his strength? I that speak in righteousness, mighty to save.

Wherefore art thou *red in thine apparel, and thy garments like him that treadeth in the winefat*

I have trodden the winepress alone; and of the people there was none with me: for *I will tread them* in mine anger,

---

16. It is difficult to determine whether this passage refers to Christ's final coming in glory or his appearance on the Mount of Olives. In the preceding chapter Rev. 19:11-16 was interpreted as referring to the earlier event. This passage seems to deal with the latter occasion because:
    1. This appearance is accompanied by great glory, or light, which "shames" the sun because of its brightness.
    2. Rev. 19:15 seems to state that treading the wine press is Christ's appearing during the battle of Armageddon. In that account Jesus treaded the winepress at his coming. In this account of this treading of the winepress is something of the past, as if this is a later appearance. He says that he has done it alone. In the Revelation account he came with the armies of heaven. This isn't necessarily a conflicting item. Christ took the responsibility of smiting the nations alone even though he was accompanied by his hosts.
    3. In this account the Savior announces that the year of his redeemed is come.

and trample them in my fury; and their blood shall be sprinkled upon my garments, and I will stain all my raiment.

For the day of vengeance is in mine heart, and the year of my redeemed is come.

And I looked, and there was none to help; and I wondered that there was none to uphold: therefore mine own arm brought salvation unto me; and my fury, it upheld me.

And I will tread down the people in mine anger, and make them drunk in my fury, and I will bring down their strength to the earth.[17]

Every Eye Shall Witness His Advent

When the Lord comes, everyone will see Him, for a revelation records His commandment to prepare for the time to come "when the veil of the covering of my temple, in my tabernacle, which hideth the earth, shall be taken off, and *all flesh shall see me together.*"[18] The comment was made by Orson Pratt that even the dead would see Him:

> It seems then that the second advent of the Son of God is to be something altogether of a different nature from anything that has hitherto transpired on the face of the earth, accompanied with great power and glory, *something that will not be done in a small portion of the earth like Palestine, and seen only by a few but it will be an event that will be seen by all* — all flesh shall see the glory of the Lord; when he reveals himself the second time, *every eye, not only those living at that time in the flesh, in mortality on the earth, but also the very dead themselves,* they also who pierced him, those who lived eighteen hundred years ago, who were engaged in the cruel act of piercing his hands and his feet and his side, *will also see him at that time.*[19]

This was also the message of John the Revelator, who taught that "he cometh with clouds; and every eye shall see him, and they also which pierced him: and all kindreds of the earth shall wail because of him."[20]

Isaiah also testified that the "glory of the Lord shall be revealed, and all flesh shall see it together."[21]

---

17. Is. 63:1-6. This passage is more difficult to assign to a particular coming than was the preceding one. Here the Savior says he has trodden the winepress alone and that the day of his redeemed has come, yet he says that he will trample them as if it was yet future. No definite assignment of the passage can be made.
18. D & C 101:23.
19. JD, 18:170.
20. Rev. 1:7.
21. Is. 40:5.

Moroni spoke of a time of judgment at Christ's coming, at which time it will be decided who shall dwell with him on the earth:

> Behold, will ye believe in the day of your visitation — behold, when the Lord shall come, yea, even that great day when the earth shall be rolled together as a scroll, and the elements shall melt with fervent heat, yea, in that great day when ye shall be brought to stand before the Lamb of God—then will ye say that there is no God?
>
> Then will ye longer deny the Christ, or can ye behold the Lamb of God? Do ye suppose that ye shall dwell with him under a consciousness of your guilt? Do ye suppose that ye could be happy to dwell with that holy Being, when your souls are racked with a consciousness of guilt that ye have ever abused his laws?
>
> Behold, I say unto you that ye would be more miserable to dwell with a holy and just God, under a consciousness of your filthiness before him, than ye would to dwell with the damned souls in hell.
>
> For behold, when ye shall be brought to see your nakedness before God, and also the glory of God, and the holiness of Jesus Christ, it will kindle a flame of unquenchable fire upon you.[22]

The Lord Himself speaks of this judgment and says that "in mine own due time will I come upon the earth in judgment, and my people shall be redeemed and shall reign with me on earth."[23]

Changes in The Configuration of The Earth

It seems that at the time of Christ's coming the earth will be in commotion and shall reel to and fro:

> The earth is utterly broken down, the earth is clean dissolved, the earth is moved exceedingly.
>
> The earth shall reel to and fro like a drunkard, and shall be removed like a cottage; and the transgression thereof shall be heavy upon it; and it shall fall, and not rise again.[24]

Isaiah explained the great changes which the configuration of the earth will undergo when he prophesied of

22. Mor. 9:2-5.
23. D & C 43:29.
24. Is. 24:19-20.

The voice of him that crieth in the wilderness, Prepare ye the way of the Lord, make straight in the desert a highway for our God.

Every valley shall be exalted, and every mountain and hill shall be made low: and the crooked shall be made straight, and the rough places plain.[25]

It is apparently at Christ's coming in glory that the location of the seas and the continents will be greatly altered, as is described in the *Doctrine and Covenants*:

And he shall utter his voice out of Zion, and he shall speak from Jerusalem, and his voice shall be heard among all people;

And it shall be a voice as the voice of many waters, and as the voice of a great thunder, which shall *break down the mountains, and the valleys shall not be found.*

He shall command the great deep, and it shall be driven back into the north countries, and the islands shall become one land;

And the land of Jerusalem and the land of Zion shall be turned back into their own place, and the earth shall be like as it was in the days before it was divided.

And the Lord, even the Savior, shall stand in the midst of his people, and shall reign over all flesh.[26]

That upheaval, which will combine all the oceans into one area of the earth, will serve to return the earth to the condition it was originally, before it was divided,[27] according to the explanation given by Joseph Fielding Smith:

We are committed to the fact that Adam dwelt on this American continent. But when Adam dwelt here, it was not the American continent, nor was it the Western Hemisphere, *for all the land was in one place, and all the water was in one place. There was no Atlantic Ocean separating the hemispheres.* "And God said, let the waters under the heaven be gathered together unto one place, and let the dry land appear: and it was so. And God called the dry land Earth; and the gathering together of the waters called he Seas: and God saw that it was good."

If all the water was in one place, then naturally all the land was in one place; therefore, the shape of the earth, as to the water and the land surface, was not as we find it today.

---

25. Is. 40:3-4.
26. D & C 133:21-25.
27. See Gen. 10:25, Moses 2:9-10, and Abra. 4:9-10.

Then we read in Genesis that there came a time when the earth was divided. There are some people who believe that this simply means that the land surface was divided among the various tribes, but this is not the meaning; it was an actual dividing of the surface of the earth, *and it was broken up as we find it now.*

The Lord revealed to the Prophet Joseph Smith that when he comes, as a part of the great restoration, this land surface will be brought back to its original form. When that time comes, the land of Zion (Western Hemisphere) and the land of Jerusalem "shall be turned back into their own place, and the earth shall be like as it was in the days before it was divided." John saw this day when "every island fled away, and the mountains were not found."[28]

The Earth Will Be Cleansed by Fire

As Christ comes, every corruptible thing of the earth will be consumed by fire and fervent heat:

And *every corruptible thing, both of man*, or of the *beasts* of the field, or of the *fowls* of the heavens, or of the *fish* of the sea, that dwells upon all the face of the earth, shall be consumed.

And also *that of element shall melt with fervent heat;* and all things shall become new, that my knowledge and glory may dwell upon all the earth.[29]

The *Book of Mormon* states that "the elements should [shall] melt with fervent heat, and the earth should [shall] be wrapt together as a scroll, and the heavens and the earth should [shall] pass away,[30] and also that at God's "command the earth shall be rolled together as a scroll."[31]

Many have wondered what the source of the fire will be at the time of Christ's coming in glory. The angel Moroni explained this matter to the Prophet Joseph, saying that it would be the heavenly hosts (and therefore not atomic or hydrogen bombs) who will burn the wicked:

For behold, the day cometh that shall burn as an oven, and all the proud, yea, all that do wickedly shall burn as stub-

---

28. Joseph Fielding Smith, *Doctrines of Salvation*, III, 74-75.
29. D & C 101:24-25.
30. III Ne. 26:3.
31. Mor. 5:23.

ble; for *they that come shall burn them*, saith the Lord of Hosts, that it shall leave them neither root nor branch.[32]

Again, the Lord said that he himself would burn the earth at this time:

> For the hour is nigh and the day soon at hand when the earth is ripe; and all the proud and they that do wickedly shall be as stubble; and *I will burn them up*, saith the Lord of Hosts, that wickedness shall not be upon the earth;[33]

This will apparently be from the glory which radiates from his person, for revelation records that "the presence of the Lord shall be as the melting fire that burneth, and as the fire which causeth the waters to boil."[34]

It appears that this is what Moses was referring to when he said that if he saw God with his natural eye, he "should have withered and died in his presence."[35]

Isaiah apparently alluded to the Lord's coming in glory when he said that because of gross wickedness, "Therefore hath the curse devoured the earth, and they that dwell therein are desolate: therefore the inhabitants of the earth are burned, and few men left."[36] Such a cleansing by fire is understood to be the baptism of the earth by fire and by the Holy Ghost. Said Orson F. Whitney:

> The earth underwent a *baptism by being immersed in water, for the remission of its sins, the washing away of its iniquities.* "As it was in the days of Noah, so shall it be in the days of the coming of the Son of Man." Is the world to be deluged in water again? No; because God gave a promise to Noah and set his bow in the clouds as a sign that the world should never again be drowned in water; but *in the day of the coming of the Son of Man it will receive the baptism of fire and of the Holy Ghost.* John the Baptist said: "There cometh one mightier than I, after me, the latchet of whose shoes I am not worthy to stoop down and unloose. I indeed have baptized you with water: he shall baptize you with the Holy Ghost and with fire." *Not only man, but the earth itself, which is a living creature, must undergo this ordinance—this dual baptism.*[37]

---

32. JS 2:37.
33. D & C 29:9.
34. D & C 133:41.
35. Moses 1:11.
36. Is. 24:5-6.
37. JD, 26:266.

Orson Pratt added:

> The *second ordinance instituted for the sanctification of the earth, is that of fire and the Holy Ghost.* The day will come when it shall burn as an oven, and all the proud, and all that do wickedly shall be as stubble; after which, the glory of God shall cover the earth, as the waters cover the deep. *Here then is a baptism of fire first, then of the Holy Spirit.* As man receives the baptism of fire and the Holy Spirit through the laying on of the hands of a legal administrator, so the earth receives the same, not through its own agency, but through the agencies ordained of God. As man becomes a new creature by being born again, first of water, then of the spirit, in the same manner the earth becomes a new earth by being born again of these cleansing and purifying elements. *As man becomes a righteous man by the new birth, so the earth becomes a righteous earth through the same process.*[38]

Those who will be consumed by fire will be the more wicked of the people—those who have lived only the telestial law, according to Joseph Fielding Smith:

> When the reign of Jesus Christ comes during the millennium, *only those who have lived the telestial law will be removed.* The earth will be cleansed of all its corruption and wickedness. Those who have lived virtuous lives, who have been honest in their dealings with their fellow man and have endeavored to do good to the best of their understanding, shall remain. . . .
>
> So we learn that all corruptible things, whether men or beasts or element, shall be consumed; but all that does not come under this awful edict shall remain. Therefore, the honest and upright of all nations, kindreds, and beliefs, who have kept the terrestrial or celestial law, will remain. *Under these conditions, people will enter the great reign of Jesus Christ carrying with them their beliefs and religious doctrines. Their agency will not be taken from them.*[39]

This fire will not only cleanse the earth, but it will also renew it, and the earth will be returned to its paradisiacal glory. Isaiah spoke, for example, of a "new heavens and a new earth: and the former shall not be remembered, nor come into mind."[40] In this connection Elder Joseph Fielding Smith commented:

---

38. JD, 1:331.
39. Joseph Fielding Smith, *Doctrines of Salvation,* III, 62-63.
40. Is. 65:17.

Latter-day Saints believe that the day is near, even at the doors, when Christ shall make his appearance as the rightful ruler of the earth. When that time comes, the whole earth and all things which remain upon its face shall be changed, and "the earth will be renewed and receive its paradisiacal glory." *That means that the earth shall be brought back to a similar condition which prevailed when peace and righteousness ruled and before death entered with its awful stain of evil and destruction.*

When that day comes wickedness must cease and every unclean creature shall be swept from the earth for they will not be able to endure the changed conditions.

All "element shall melt with fervent heat; and all things shall become new, that my knowledge and glory may dwell upon all the earth. And in that day the enmity of man, and enmity of the beasts, yea, the enmity of all flesh, shall cease from before my face."[41]

The Marriage of The Lamb

John Taylor, expounding a passage from the *Pearl of Great Price*, taught that the whole latter-day city of Zion will be caught up into heaven, and that there it will be united with the city of Enoch, and they shall descend together:

> By and by when the time came for the accomplishment of the purposes of God, and before the destruction of the wicked, Enoch was caught up to heaven and his Zion with him. And we are told in latter revelation in relation to these matters that a Zion will be built up in our day; that great trouble will overtake the inhabitants of the earth; and that when the time arrives, *the Zion that was caught up will descend, and the Zion that will be organized here will ascend,* both possessed of the same spirit, their peoples having been preserved by the power of God according to His purposes and as His children, to take part in the events of the latter days. We are told that when the people of these two Zions meet, they will fall on each others' necks, and embrace and kiss each other.[42]

In this manner the former Saints will be united with the Latter-day Saints. Christ, the Lamb, will come and be united with the Church, His bride, and their union is termed the "marriage of the Lamb:"

---

41. Joseph Fielding Smith, *Doctrines of Salvation,* III, 56-57.
42. JD, 25:305.

And I heard as it were the voice of a great multitude, and as the voice of many waters, and as the voice of mighty thunderings, saying, Alleluia: for the Lord God omnipotent reigneth.

Let us be glad and rejoice, and give honour to him: for the *marriage of the Lamb is come, and his wife hath made herself ready.*

And to her was granted that she should be arrayed in fine linen, clean and white: for the fine linen is the righteousness of the saints.

And he saith unto me, Write, Blessed are they which are called unto the marriage supper of the Lamb. And he saith unto me, These are the true sayings of God.[43]

In interpreting this passage Elder Joseph Fielding Smith said:

This prophecy of the marriage of the Lamb is a figure of speech, having reference to the second coming of our Savior and the feast, or supper, that the righteous shall receive at his coming. When teaching the Jews, and more especially his disciples, the Savior spoke of the Bridegroom when referring to himself.[44]

Summary

1. Christ's final coming in glory will be preceded by a series of angels' trumpetings. Each angel will predict an important event which is to take place between Christ's coming in glory and the end of the earth. Each angel will also reveal the secret acts of men for one of the thousand years of the earth's existence.

2. When Christ comes he will be accompanied by the hosts of heaven — the Saints of former times. He will be arrayed in red garments.

3. The righteous dead will be resurrected before or at his coming[45] and will be caught up to meet Him in the air. The liv-

---

43. Rev. 19:6-9.
44. Joseph Fielding Smith, *Doctrines of Salvation,* III, 61.
45. See statements in Chapter VI under the section entitled "A Leader Like Unto Moses Is to Be Chosen," which indicate the opinion of the early brethren that many would be resurrected before Christ's final coming in glory. A case can be made for their opinion. Note that D & C 45:45-52 indicates a resurrection will precede the coming of the Savior on the Mount of Olives. The Proclamation issued by the Twelve says the Savior will have resurrected beings with him when he appears in the New Jerusalem temple. The question has previously been raised as to whether some of the 144,000 will be resurrected beings. It is believed that many who participate in the council at Adam-ondi-Ahman will have come forth from the tomb.

ing Saints who are worthy will also be caught up and will descend with the Savior and his angels. Others will be resurrected when Christ arrives on the earth.

4. Every eye will witness his coming. Even the dead will see him.

5. At his coming, the earth will be tossed by mighty earthquakes. The seas will be driven back to the north. The mountains will melt with fervent heat. The entire configuration of the earth will be changed.

6. The earth will be cleansed by fire. Those who have not abided by terrestrial or celestial law will be swept off. Both animate and inanimate objects will be destroyed.

7. The cleansing of the earth by fire is regarded as a baptism by fire to follow the baptism of water which the earth received at the time of Noah.

8. Christ's coming to his Church is known as the "marriage of the Lamb."

CHAPTER XV

The Millennium

Extended Life and Resurrection

The scriptures reveal a detailed picture of the conditions which will exist during the thousand-year period known to Latter-day Saints as the Millennium. Prominent among scriptural teachings is the doctrine that the power of death will be overcome to a degree, and during that era "there shall be no more thence an infant of days, nor an old man that hath not filled his days: for the child shall die an hundred years old; but the sinner being an hundred years old shall be accursed."[1]

Though all mortals shall still have to die during the millennial era, nevertheless a revelation given to Joseph Smith states that they will be changed in the twinkling of an eye to a resurrected state without being buried:

> And he that liveth when the Lord shall come, and hath kept the faith, blessed is he; nevertheless, it is appointed to him to die at the age of man.
>
> Wherefore, children shall grow up until they become old; old men shall die; but *they shall not sleep in the dust, but they shall be changed in the twinkling of an eye.*
>
> Wherefore, for this cause preached the apostles unto the world the resurrection of the dead.[2]

The Prophet also taught that those who "die in the Lord" shall "rise from the dead and shall not die after, and shall receive an inheritance before the Lord, in the holy city."[3] Concerning what thus appears to be a mingling of mortal and immortal beings Orson Pratt commented:

> "Do you think," one may say, "*there will be mortal beings living on the earth, when these heavenly hosts come?*" *Yes, and they will dwell together.* What, people not subject to sickness, or to sorrow, or punishment, people whose bodies are celestial and immortal, who will endure in their bodies to all eternity! Will they mingle with mortal beings? Yes. . . .

---

1. Is. 65:20.
2. D & C 63:50-52.
3. D & C 63:49.

I have no doubt there will be a certain degree of the glory of the immortal beings withheld from the children of mortality, during the whole period of the millennium. Kings and priests will come here to reign, and will mingle freely among their children of whom they are ancestors. And *those who are mortal can receive instruction from those who are immortal,* that will prepare them for the time when the earth is to undergo a still greater change. *The children of mortality will need this preparation in order to live when this earth is burning up, which is to be its final destiny.*[4]

A Period of Peace and Righteousness

According to Isaiah, the Millennium will be a period of peace, when enmities in the animal kingdom which are now regarded as natural will cease and when strife and turmoil will not be permitted to exist:

The wolf also shall dwell with the lamb, and the leopard shall lie down with the kid; and the calf and the young lion and the fatling together; and a little child shall lead them.

And the cow and the bear shall feed; their young ones shall lie down together: and the lion shall eat straw like the ox.

And the suckling child shall play on the hole of the asp, and the weaned child shall put his hand on the cockatrice's den.

They shall not hurt nor destroy in all my holy mountain; for the earth shall be full of the knowledge of the Lord, as the waters cover the sea.[5]

John stated that at the beginning of the Millennium Satan will be bound, and will not be permitted to tempt men:

And I saw an angel come down from heaven, having the key of the bottomless pit and a great chain in his hand.

And he laid hold on the dragon, that old serpent, which is the Devil, and *Satan, and bound him a thousand years,*

And cast him into the bottomless pit, and shut him up, and set a seal upon him, that he should deceive the nations no more,

---

4. JD, 18:320. On this point the Prophet Joseph said "Christ and the resurrected Saints will reign over the earth during the thousand years. They probably will not dwell upon the earth, but will visit it when they please or when it is necessary to govern it." HC 5:212.
5. Is. 11:6-9. See Is. 65:25.

till the thousand years should be fulfilled: and after that he must be loosed a little season.[6]

The *Doctrine and Covenants* adds that "in that day Satan shall not have power to tempt any man."[7] Nephi gave the reason for Satan's lack of power during this period, stating that *"because of the righteousness of his* [Gods] *people, Satan has no power*; wherefore, he cannot be loosed for the space of many years; for he hath no power over the hearts of the people, for they dwell in righteousness, and the Holy One of Israel reigneth."[8]

Erastus Snow commented on the idea of Satan's being bound, and stated that his withdrawal would bring about actual changes in the earth and its atmosphere:

> This promise we have that when the time comes that is written of in the Scripture, that Satan shall be bound, and shall cease to exercise his power and dominion over the hearts of the children of God for the space of a thousand years, the children that shall grow up unto the Lord shall not taste of death; that is they shall not sleep in the earth, but they shall be changed in a moment, in the twinkling of an eye, and they shall be caught up, and their rest shall be glorious.
>
> I thus distinguish between them and us, because at that time they shall grow up with a more complete and perfect understanding of the laws of life and health, and they will observe them. And the temptations and evils that surround us on every hand shall be removed from them. *The elements that are now under the control of the prince and power of the air, and charged with death, which we are constantly brought in contact with, will then be removed; the elements will be sanctified, the curse will be removed from the earth and its surrounding atmosphere, and the powers of darkness that rule in the atmosphere will be confined to their own region,* and the tabernacles of the children of men shall grow up without sin unto salvation.
>
> Hence their tabernacles shall not be subject to pain and sickness like unto ours. *There will be no pain and sickness, because there will be no breach of the laws of life and health.* There will be no intemperance of any kind, because there will be no evil spirit at the elbow continually ready to allure and draw into sin. But the Spirit of the Lord will be with every

6. Rev. 20:1-3.
7. D & C 101:28.
8. I Ne. 22:26.

person to guide him constantly, and the law of the Lord will be written in his heart, so that one will not need to say to another, "This is the way; walk ye in it." There will be no Devil to tempt on the right hand and on the left, saying, "This is the way, walk in it." Thus having this good influence continually around them to keep them in the straight path, they will grow up without sickness, pain, or death.[9]

Nevertheless it appears that there will still be wickedness on the earth. Said Joseph Fielding Smith,

> The Prophet Jospeh Smith has said: *"There will be wicked men on the earth during the thousand years.* The heathen nations who will not come up to worship will be visited with the judgments of God, and must eventually be destroyed from the earth." [*Documentary History of the Church*, V, 212]
>
> The saying that there will be wicked men on the earth during the Millennium has been misunderstood by many, because the Lord declared that the wicked shall not stand, but shall be consumed. In using this term "wicked" it should be interpreted in the language of the Lord as recorded in the *Doctrine and Covenants*, section 84, versus 49-53. Here the Lord speaks of those who have not received the gospel as being wicked as they are still under the bondage of sin, having not been baptized. The inhabitants of the terrestrial order will remain on the earth during the Millennium, and this class is without the gospel ordinances.[10]

Orson Pratt explained this problem even more clearly by stating that men will still have their free agency and will therefore be capable of committing sin:

> The question may arise here—*"will it be possible for men to sin during the Millennium?" Yes. Why? Because they have not lost their agency.* Agency always continues wherever intelligent beings are, whether in heaven, on the earth, or among any of the creations that God has made; wherever you find intelligent beings, there you will find an agency, not to the same extent perhaps, under all circumstances, but yet there is always the exercise of agency where there is intelligence. For instance, when Satan is bound and a seal set upon him in this lowermost pit, his agency is partially destroyed in some things. He will not have power to come out of that pit; now he has that power; then he will not have power to tempt the children of men, now he

---

9. JD, 7:355-56.
10. Joseph Fielding Smith, *Doctrines of Salvation,* III, 63-64.

has that power; consequently his agency then will be measurable destroyed or taken away, but not in full. *The Lord will not destroy the agency of the people during the Millennium, therefore there will be a possibility of their sinning during that time. But if they who live then do sin, it will not be because of the power of the devil to tempt them, for he will have no power over them, and they will sin merely because they choose to do so of their own free will.*[11]

Home Life and Sociality as
The Lord Dwells Among Men

According to Isaiah, home life will continue during the Millennium much as it is now:

> And they shall build houses, and inhabit them; and they shall plant vineyards, and eat the fruit of them.
>
> They shall not build, and another inhabit; they shall not plant, and another eat: for as the days of a tree are the days of my people, and mine elect shall long enjoy the work of their hands.
>
> They shall not labour in vain, nor bring forth for trouble; for they are the seed of the blessed of the Lord, and their offspring with them.[12]

Brigham Young expressed the same idea as he defined the Millennium:

> The Millennium consists in this—every *heart in the Church and Kingdom of God being united in one*; the Kingdom increasing to the *overcoming of everything opposed to the economy of heaven*, and *Satan being bound*, and having a seal set upon him. All things else will be as they are now, we shall eat, drink, and wear clothing. Let the people be holy, and the earth under their feet will be holy.[13]

The Scriptures affirm that men will continue to enjoy the same sociality which is now theirs:

> When the Savior shall appear we shall see him as he is. We shall see that he is a man like ourselves.
>
> And *that same sociality which exists among us here will exist among us there*, only it will be coupled with eternal glory, which glory we do not now enjoy.[14]

---

11. JD, 16:319-20.
12. Is. 65:21-23.
13. JD, 1:203.
14. D & C 130:1-2.

A modern revelation records the Lord's promise that "I will reveal myself from heaven with power and great glory, with all the hosts thereof, and dwell in righteousness with men on earth a thousand years, and the wicked shall not stand."[15] Apparently the Kingdom of God will be turned over to the Savior, and He "shall be in their midst, and his glory shall be upon them, and he will be their king and their lawgiver."[16] Said a revelation to Joseph Smith:

> But, verily I say unto you that in time ye shall have no king nor ruler, for I will be your king and watch over you.
>
> Wherefore, hear my voice and follow me, and you shall be a free people, and *ye shall have no laws but my laws when I come*, for I am your lawgiver, and what can stay my hand?[17]

Government of the Saints

Latter-day Saints believe that there will be two world capitals during the Millennium. Isaiah states "out of Zion [the New Jerusalem] shall go forth the law, and the word of the Lord from Jerusalem."[18] Orson Pratt gave this explanation concerning the law:

> But Zion is also to be built up. Another city, not old Jerusalem, but a new Jerusalem, called Zion, upon the great western hemisphere, preparatory to the coming of the Lord. "Out of Zion shall go forth the law," says the prophet. What law? *A law to regulate the nations, a law teaching them how to be saved, a law informing the kings and emperors and the nobles of the earth how they can save themselves, and how they can save their dead.*[19]

Many will be given inheritances during this period on which to dwell. These will be appointed by "one mighty and strong", according to the *Doctrine and Covenants*:

> And it shall come to pass that I, the Lord God, will send one mighty and strong, holding the scepter of power in his hand, clothed with light for a covering, whose mouth shall utter words, eternal words; while his bowels shall be a fountain of truth, to set in order the house of God, and *to arrange by lot the inheritances of the saints whose names are found, and*

---

15. D & C 29:11.
16. D & C 45:59.
17. D & C 38:21-22.
18. Is. 2:3.
19. JD, 14:350.

*the names of their fathers, and of their children, enrolled in the
book of the law of God;*

While that man, who was called of God and appointed, that
putteth forth his hand to steady the ark of God, shall fall by
the shaft of death, like as a tree that is smitten by the vivid
shaft of lightning.

And *all they who are not found written in the book of remembrance shall find none inheritance in that day,* but they
shall be cut asunder, and their portion shall be appointed them
among unbelievers, where are wailing and gnashing of teeth.[20]

---

20. D & C 85:7-9. This is a highly controversial scripture because it has been
seized upon and exploited by apostate factions which have broken off
from the Church. Several leaders of these groups have claimed to be
the "one mighty and strong." The following statements of clarification
are taken from an official pronouncement of the First Presidency of the
Church published in the *Improvement Era* in 1907. The pronouncement
was written to explain the intent of section 85 of the Doctrine and Covenants which pertains to the functions of Edward Partridge as the Bishop
of Jackson County.

   "Those, however, who have so far proclaimed themselves as being the
"one mighty and strong," have manifested the utmost ignorance of the
things of God and the order of the Church. Indeed their insufferable
ignorance and egotism have been at the bottom of all their pretensions,
and the cause of all the trouble into which they have fallen. They seem
not to have been aware of the fact that the Church of Christ and of the
Saints is completely organized, and that *when the man who shall be
called upon to divide unto the Saints their inheritances comes, he will be
designated by the inspiration of the Lord to the proper authorities of the
Church, appointed and sustained according to the order provided for the
government of the Church.*

   "Certainly in the face of this plain statement of the Lord's that the sins
of Edward Partridge were forgiven him, we do not feel that his sad and
early death was the fulfillment of the threatened judgment of the revelation. But that he was the man so threatened in that revelation, there can
be no question; not only on account of what is here set forth, but also
because Orson Pratt, one familiar with Edward Partridge and an active
participant in all these historical matters, publicly declared from the
pulpit in Salt Lake City, about the time of the death of President Young,
that the man referred to in that passage of the revelation in question,
was Bishop Edward Partridge. Of the fact of his statement, there can be
no doubt; and at the time he was the historian of the Church as well as
a member of the quorum of the Apostles.

   "Now, as to the 'one mighty and strong,' who shall be sent of God,
to 'set in order the house of God, and to arrange by lot the inheritance
of the Saints.' Who is he? What position will he hold in the Church?
In what manner will he come to his calling? We draw attention first of
all to the fact that *this whole letter to William W. Phelps, as well as
the part afterwards accepted as the word of the Lord, related to the affairs
of the Church in Zion, Independence, Jackson County, Missouri.* And
inasmuch as through his repentance and sacrifices and suffering, Bishop
Edward Partridge undoubtedly obtained a mitigation of the threatened

Orson Pratt also taught that the Saints in Zion will have received only a stewardship until after the resurrected Saints have come forth and received their inheritances, and that after the resurrection the living saints will receive their eternal portion:

> You may perhaps ask when this time will come? for the Saints to receive bona fide inheritances. *The time will come for the Saints to receive their stewardships, when they shall return to the lands from whence they have been driven; but the inheritances will not be given, until the Lord shall first appoint to the righteous dead their inheritances, and afterwards the righteous living will receive theirs.* This you will find recorded in the Doctrine and Covenants; and in the same Book it is predicted that there is to be one *"mighty and strong,"* as well as to *be an immortal personage,* — one that is clothed upon with light as with a garment: — one whose bowels are a fountain of truth. His mission will be to divide, by lot, to the Saints their inheritances, according to their faithfulness in their stewardships. *This too agrees with another revelation,* given on the 27th Dec. 1832, which says, in great plainness, that when the Saints are resurrected and caught up into heaven, and the living Saints are also caught up, and that *when the seventh angel shall have sounded his trump, then the Saints shall receive their inheritances.* [Doctrine and Covenants 88:95-110] *The time is there specified, concerning the period that the Lord has in his own mind, when inheritances shall be given. Finally after the Saints have been resurrected and caught up, in connection with all the then living Saints, into heaven; and after the seventh*

judgment against him of falling 'by the shaft of death, like as a tree that is smitten by the vivid shaft of lightning,' so the occasion for sending another to fill his station—'one mighty and strong to set in order the house of God, and to arrange by lot the inheritances of the Saints'—*may also be considered as having passed away and the whole incident of the prophecy closed.*

"If, however, there are those who will still insist that the prophecy concerning the coming of one 'mighty and strong' is still to be regarded as relating to the future, *let the Latter-day Saints know that he will be a future bishop of the Church who will be with the Saints in Zion, Jackson County, Missouri, when the Lord shall establish them in that land;* and he will be so blessed with the spirit and power of his calling that he will be able to set in order the house of God, pertaining to the department of the work under his jurisdiction; and in righteousness and justice will 'arrange by lot the inheritances of the Saints.' *He will hold the same high and exalted station that Edward Partridge held;* for the latter was called to do just this kind of work—that is, to set in order the house of God as pertaining to settling the Saints upon their inheritances. . . ." "One Mighty and Strong," *Improvement Era*, Vol. X, No. 12, October, 1907, pp. 930, 939-41.

angel sounds his trump, the earth will be given to the Saints of the Most High for an inheritance to be divided out to them.[21]

Judgment, during the Millennium, will be given to the Saints. In the words of John the Revelator,

> And I saw thrones, and they sat upon them, and *judgment was given unto them*: and I saw the souls of them that were beheaded for the witness of Jesus, and for the word of God, and which had not worshipped the beast, neither his image, neither had received his mark upon their foreheads, or in their hands; and *they lived and reigned with Christ a thousand years.*[22]

This was further clarified in the *Book of Mormon*, where the role of the Apostles in the judgment program is outlined:

> And he said unto me: Thou rememberest the twelve apostles of the Lamb? Behold *they are they who shall judge the twelve tribes of Israel; wherefore, the twelve ministers of thy seed shall be judged of them;* for ye are of the house of Israel.
>
> And these twelve ministers whom thou beholdest shall judge thy seed. And, behold, they are righteous forever; for because of their faith in the Lamb of God their garments are made white in his blood.[23]

Orson Pratt taught that the two sets of apostles are to each have twelve thrones set up in their particular lands and that judgment process will continue to function in the eternal worlds:

> And Jesus and the Twelve Apostles will be in our midst. And we have an account of their thrones. "And Jesus said unto them, Verily, I say unto you, that ye which have followed me, in the regeneration when the Son of Man shall sit in the throne of his glory, ye also shall sit upon twelve thrones, judging the twelve tribes of Israel." Then the twelve tribes will come back, and *twelve men sitting on twelve thrones, in the land of Palestine*, will reign over them. *The Twelve disciples raised up in this land, 1800 years ago, are to have their thrones;* who, after being judged themselves by the Twelve at Jerusalem, will sit upon their thrones and will judge the remnant of the tribe of Joseph. *And they will have that work to do in the eternal worlds.*[24]

---

21. JD, 21:150-51.
22. Rev. 20:4.
23. I Ne. 12:9-10.
24. JD, 19:176.

He stated also while speaking of the original twelve apostles, that the process of judging will be a continuous process—a process of rule rather than of judgment, and the judges will sit as the judges in Israel did before the time of Saul. Others besides the apostles will hold responsibility:

"And these will be the men that will be with Jesus when he descends upon the Mount of Olives, after the graves of the just have been opened. In the resurrection they will come forth immortal, eternal, clothed upon with the fulness of that glory that pertains to the celestial kingdom. They will also reign as kings and priests here on the earth. *To some of the raised Saints there will be given ten cities to rule over. To others there will be given five cities to rule over, according to their works here in this life. All will not have the same power. All will not have the same rule.* The Twelve shall have twelve thrones—one throne each, to judge the twelve tribes of Israel. *The tribes will need judging, during the whole thousand years they live on the earth; they will need judges in their midst,* to make manifest unto them that which is important for men, and women, and children, to know.

These twelve men who are appointed to judge these twelve tribes of Israel cannot be as it were the judges over all the earth at the same time. *They cannot be everywhere present at the same moment, and hence there will be other judges, other men of God,* those who are accounted worthy in the sight of the Most High.[25]

Brigham Young told of the righteousness of the judgment they will render:

When the judgment is given to the Saints, it will bo [sic] *because of their righteousness,* because they will judge even as the angels and as the Gods, and not as the wicked do at the present time, who care not for God nor for justice, who care not for truth nor mercy, love nor kindness, who judge according to the wickedness of their hearts.[26]

Spirit To Be Poured Out

There will be a great outpouring of the Holy Spirit during the Millennium, according to the Prophet Joel:

And it shall come to pass afterward, that *I will pour out my spirit upon all flesh;* and your sons and your daughters

---

25. JD, 20:155.
26. JD, 19:7.

shall prophesy, your old men shall dream dreams, and your young men shall see visions:

And also upon the servants and upon the handmaids in those days will I pour out my spirit.[27]

During the Millennium the Lord will reveal many things which are at the present hidden from the world. Note the promises He has made:

Yea, verily I say unto you, *in that day when the Lord shall come, he shall reveal all things* —

Things which have passed, and hidden things which no man knew, things of the earth, by which it was made, and the purpose and the end thereof —

Things most precious, things that are above, and things that are beneath, things that are in the earth, and upon the earth, and in heaven.[28]

Joseph Smith commented on the truths which will be revealed to man:

Neither can they nor we be made perfect without those who have died in the gospel also; for it is necessary in the ushering in of the dispensation of the fulness of times, which dispensation is now beginning to usher in, that a whole and complete

---

27. Joel 2:28-29. Although this passage is often quoted by Latter-day Saint writers in reference to the restoration of the Gospel, B. H. Roberts commented on it and applied it directly to the Millennium: "Because Peter, referring to the Spirit that was then resting upon the Twelve Apostles, said, 'this is that which was spoken by the Prophet Joel,' etc., the very general opinion prevails that Joel's prophecy was then fulfilled; and hence the *last days* were come. This is an entire misapprehension of the purpose of Peter in making the quotation as it is also of the quoted passage itself. Beyond all controversy Peter meant only: This Spirit which you now see resting upon these Apostles of Jesus of Nazareth, is that same Spirit which your Prophet Joel says will, in the last days, be poured out upon all flesh. Obviously [sic] he did not mean that this occasion of the Apostles receiving the Holy Ghost was a complete fulfillment of Joel's prediction. To insist upon such an exegesis would be to charge the chief of the Apostles with palpable ignorance of the meaning of Joel's prophecy. On the occasion in question the Holy Ghost was poured out upon the Twelve Apostles, who were given the power to speak in various tongues; *Joel's prophecy for its complete fulfillment requires that the Spirit of the Lord, the Holy Ghost, shall be poured out upon all flesh; and undoubtedly refers to that time which shall come in the blessed millennium* when the enmity shall not only cease between man and man, but even between beast of the forests and of the fields; and between man and beast, as described by Isaiah . . ." HC, 1: XXXii.

28. D & C 101:32-34.

and perfect union, and welding together of dispensations, and keys, and powers, and glories should take place, and *be revealed from the days of Adam even to the present time. And not only this, but those things which never have been revealed from the foundation of the world, but have been kept hid from the wise and prudent, shall be revealed unto babes and sucklings in this, the dispensation of the fulness of times.*[29]

Among the revelations which must come forth is the Book of Enoch, which will contain Adam's prophecy of the future of the world:

And the Lord administered comfort unto Adam, and said unto him: I have set thee to be at the head; a multitude of nations shall come of thee, and thou art a prince over them forever.

And Adam stood up in the midst of the congregation; and, notwithstanding he was bowed down with age, being full of the Holy Ghost, *predicted whatsoever should befall his posterity unto the latest generation.*

These things were all written in the book of Enoch, and are to be testified of in due time.[30]

Truths pertaining to the physical creation of the earth and universe will also be made known:

God shall give unto you knowledge by his Holy Spirit, yea, by the unspeakable gift of the Holy Ghost, that has not been revealed since the world was until now;

Which our forefathers have awaited with anxious expectation to be revealed in the last times, which their minds were pointed to by the angels, as held in reserve for the fullness of their glory;

A time to come in the which nothing shall be withheld, whether there be one God or many gods, they shall be manifest.

All thrones and dominions, principalities and powers, shall be revealed and *set forth upon all who have endured valiantly for the gospel of Jesus Christ.*

And also, if there be bounds set to the heavens or to the seas, or to the dry land, or to the sun, moon, or stars —

All the times of their revolutions, all the appointed days, months, and years, and all the days of their days, months, and

29.   D & C 128:18.
30.   D & C 107:55-57.

years, and all their glories, laws, and set times shall be revealed in the days of the dispensation of the fulness of times—

According to that which was ordained in the midst of the
Council of the Eternal God of all other gods before the world
was, that should be reserved unto the finishing and the end
thereof, when every man shall enter into his eternal presence
and into his immortal rest.

How long can rolling waters remain impure? What power
shall stay the heavens? *As well might man stretch forth
his puny arm to stop the Missouri River in its decreed course,
or to turn it up stream, as to hinder the Almighty from pouring down knowledge from heaven upon the heads of the Latter-
day Saints.*[31]

Apparently the truths will be so wonderful that "since the
beginning of the world have not men heard nor perceived by the
ear, neither hath any eye seen, O God, besides thee, how great
things thou hast prepared for him that waiteth for thee."[32]
It will probably be because of this rich outpouring of the Holy
Spirit that "the earth shall be full of the knowledge of the Lord,
as the waters cover the sea."[33]

During the Millennial era the redeemed will be filled with
the knowledge of the Lord, and will sing a new song, the lyrics
of which have already been given:

The Lord hath brought again Zion;
The Lord hath redeemed his people, Israel,
According to the election of grace,
Which was brought to pass by the faith
And covenant of their fathers.
The Lord hath redeemed his people;
And Satan is bound and time is no longer.
The Lord hath gathered all things in one.
The Lord hath brought down Zion from above.
The Lord hath brought up Zion from beneath.
The earth hath travailed and brought forth her strength;
And truth is established in her bowels;
And the heavens have smiled upon her;

31. D & C 121:26-33.
32. D & C 133:45.
33. Is. 11:9.

And she is clothed with the glory of her God;
For he stands in the midst of his people.
Glory, and honor, and power, and might,
Be ascribed to our God; for he is full of mercy,
Justice, grace and truth, and peace,
Forever and ever, Amen.[34]

Orson Pratt taught that at this time even the animal kingdom shall also be endowed with greater intelligence.

The knowledge of God will cover the whole earth, as the waters cover the great deep. *And then the animal creation will manifest more intelligence and more knowledge than they do now, in their fallen condition.* Indeed, we have a declaration, by John the Revelator, that when this time shall come, they will even know how to praise God. He says, "and every creature which is in heaven, and on the earth, and under the earth and such as are in the sea, and all that are in them, heard I, saying, Blessing, and honor and glory, and power, be unto him that sitteth upon the throne, and unto the Lamb for ever and ever." *What? The animal creation endowed with language? Yes, a language of praise,* saying something concerning the Lamb that was slain, and about his glory and excellency. What a beautiful creation this will be when all these things are fulfilled.[35]

Many Churches During The Millenium

According to George Q. Cannon, during the Millennium, all men will know the Lord, and be acquainted with His rule and law:

If you read the 20th chapter of the Revelations, you will see that the Lord revealed to John that there shall be a thousand year's rest, a millennium or millennial era, when the earth shall rest from wickedness, and when knowledge shall cover it as waters cover the deep, and when one man shall not have to say to another, "Know ye the Lord?" but when, according to the words of the Prophet, *"All shall know him, from the least even unto the greatest;"* when God's will shall be written in the hearts of the children of men, and they will understand his law.[36]

Apparently men will not only know of Christ but they will bow and give allegiance to His law, for Paul states,

34. D & C 84:99-102.
35. JD, 20:18.
36. JD, 14:321.

Wherefore God also hath highly exalted him, and given him a name which is above every name:

That at the name of Jesus every knee should bow, of things in heaven, and things in earth, and things under the earth;

And that every tongue should confess that Jesus Christ is Lord, to the glory of God the Father.[37]

The same idea is contained in latter-day revelation:

Wherefore, I say unto you that I have sent unto you mine everlasting covenant, even that which was from the beginning.

And that which I have promised I have so fulfilled, and *the nations of the earth shall bow to it; and, if not of themselves, they shall come down, for that which is now exalted of itself shall be laid low of power.*[38]

But it appears that the above scriptural references may not be interpreted to mean that everyone will join the Church of Christ. Brigham Young repeatedly taught that there would still be a variety of churches on the earth during the Millennium:

When the nations shall see the glory of God together, the spirit of their feelings may be couched in these words, "I will be damned if I will serve you." In those days the Methodists and Presbyterians, headed by their priests, will not be allowed to form into a mob to drive, kill, and rob the Latter-day Saints; neither will the Latter-day Saints be allowed to rise up and say, "We will kill you Methodists, Presbyterians, &c.," *neither will any of the different sects of Christendom be allowed to persecute each other.*

What will they do? They will hear of the wisdom of Zion, and *the kings and potentates of the nations will come up to Zion to inquire after the ways of the Lord, and to seek out the great knowledge, wisdom, and understanding manifested through the Saints of the Most High. They will inform the people of God that they belong to such and such a Church, and do not wish to change their religion.*

They will be drawn to Zion by the great wisdom displayed there, and will attribute it to the cunning and craftiness of men. It will be asked, "What do you want to do, ye strangers from afar." "We want to live our own religion." "Will you

37. Phil. 2:9-11.
38. D & C 49:9-10.

bow the knee before God with us?" O Yes, we would as soon do it as not;" and *at that time every knee shall bow, and every tongue acknowledge that God who is the framer and maker of all things, the governor and controller of the universe. They will have to bow the knee and confess that He is God, and that Jesus Christ, who suffered for the sins of the world is actually its Redeemer;* that by the shedding of his blood he has redeemed men, women, children, beasts, birds, fish, the earth itself, and everything that John saw and heard praising in heaven.

They will ask "If I bow the knee and confess that he is that Saviour, the Christ, to the glory of the Father, will you let me go home, and *be a Presbyterian?*" "Yes." "And not persecute me?" "Never." "Won't you let me go home and *belong to the Greek Church?*" "Yes." "Will you *allow me to be a Friend Quaker, or a Shaking Quaker?*" "O yes, anything you wish to be, but remember that you must not persecute your neighbors, but must mind your own business, and let your neighbors alone, and *let them worship the sun, moon, a white dog, or anything else they please, being mindful that every knee has got to bow and every tongue confess. When you have paid this tribute to the Most High, who created you and preserves you, you may then go and worship what you please, or do what you please,* if you do not infringe upon your neighbors.[39]

On another occasion he said,

In the millennium men will have the privilege of being Presbyterians, Methodists or Infidels, but they will not have the privilege of treating the name and character of Deity as they have done heretofore. No, but every knee shall bow and every tongue confess to the glory of God the Father that Jesus is the Christ.[40]

He commented that many will remain members of their respective churches because they will not humble themselves sufficiently to accept the Gospel and be taught, even though they will have an adequate witness of the truthfulness of the Church:

I most assuredly expect that the time will come when every tongue shall confess, and every knee shall bow, to the Savior, though the people may believe what they will with regard to religion. The kingdom that Daniel saw will actually

39. JD, 2:316-17. See Mos. 27:31.
40. JD, 12:274.

make laws to protect every man in his rights, as our government does now, whether the religions of the people are true or false. We believe this as sincerely as we believe anything else; and I think that the course of this people has proved it, as far as the acts of the children of men are concerned. *All creation could ask for no more witnesses than they have, that the New Testament is true, that Jesus is the Christ, that the Holy Prophets are true, that the Book of Mormon is true, and that Joseph Smith was a Prophet and Revelator. But the Lord has so ordained that no man shall receive the benefits of the everlasting Priesthood without humbling himself before Him, and giving Him the glory, for teaching him, that he may be able to witness to every man of the truth, and not depend upon the words of any individual on the earth, but know for himself,* live "by every word that proceedeth out of the mouth of God," love the Lord Jesus Christ and the institutions of His kingdom, and finally enter into His glory. Every man and woman may be a Revelator, and have the testimony of Jesus, which is the spirit of prophecy, and foresee the mind and will of God, concerning them, eschew evil, and choose that which is good.[41]

President Young also held that there would be millions during the Millennium who would refuse to accept Christ as their redeemer:

When all nations are so subdued to Jesus that every knee shall bow and every tongue shall confess, *there will still be millions on the earth who will not believe in him*: but they will be obliged to acknowledge his kingly government. You may call that government ecclesiastical, or by whatever term you please; *yet, there is no true government on earth but the government of God, or the holy Priesthood.* Shall I tell you what that is? In short, *it is a perfect system of government—a kingdom of Gods and angels and all beings who will submit themselves to that government.* There is no other true government in heaven or upon the earth. Do not blame me for believing in a pure and holy government.[42]

The efforts of the Church will be directed towards three major objectives during the Millennium: (1) missionary work, (2) temple work, and (3) teaching the Saints and preparing them for exaltation.

41. JD, 2:189.
42. JD, 7:142.

Missionary Work

Concerning missionary work during the Millennium, President Joseph Fielding Smith said:

> *The gospel will be taught far more intensely and with greater power during the millennium, until all the inhabitants of the earth shall embrace it.* Satan shall be bound so that he cannot tempt any man. Should any man refuse to repent and accept the gospel under those conditions then he would be accursed. Through the revelations given to the prophets, we learn that *during the reign of Jesus Christ for a thousand years eventually all people will embrace the truth. . . . If the knowledge of the Lord covers the earth as the waters do the sea, then it must be universally received.* Moreover, the promise of the Lord through Jeremiah is that it will no longer be necessary for anyone to teach his neighbor, "saying, Know the Lord: for they shall all know me, from the least of them unto the greatest of them, saith the Lord."[43]

It is anticipated that the fourth missionary effort of the last days, the final mission to all mankind, will continue during the Millennium. However, the reader will note that President Joseph Fielding Smith's interpretation that everyone will accept the gospel is not supported by the statements of the brethren cited in the previous section.

Temple Work

Many Latter-day Saint leaders have commented on the temple work which will be carried on during this peaceful era. George Q. Cannon, after quoting several passages of scripture pertinent to temple work, declared,

> I quote these passages as they occur to my mind. You are all familiar with them. They will be fulfilled, and there will be a thousand years' rest, during which period Satan will be bound, and when the *seed of the righteous will increase and cover the land.* In that glorious period everything on the face of the earth will be beautiful; disease and crime, and all the evils that attend our present state of existence will be banished; and during that period, as God has revealed, *the occupation of his people will be to lay a foundation for the redemption of the dead,* the unnumbered millions who lived and died on the earth without hearing and obeying the plan of salvation.[44]

---

43. Joseph Fielding Smith, *Doctrines of Salvation,* III, 64-65.
44. JD, 14:321-22.

John Taylor spoke of the thousands of temples which will then exist:

> This is a great work. Well might it be said to Joseph Smith, "You are laying the foundation of a great work" – so vast that very few can begin to comprehend it. We read sometimes about the millennium. But what do we know about it? It is a time when this work will be going on, and *Temples, thousands of them, will be reared* for the accomplishment of the objects designed, in which communications from the heavens will be received in regard to our labors, how we may perform them, and for whom.[45]

Wilford Woodruff stated that Temples would be built throughout the American continents and in Europe:

> When the Savior comes, a thousand years will be devoted to this work of redemption; and Temples will appear all over this land of Joseph, *North and South America and also in Europe and elsewhere*; and all the descendants of Shem, Ham, and Japheth who received not the Gospel in the flesh, must be officiated for in the Temples of God, before the Savior can present the Kingdom to the Father, saying, "It is finished."[46]

It was President Young's teaching that resurrected beings will return to the earth and reveal the necessary data for temple work to be completed for the dead:

> The Gospel is now preached to the spirits in prison, and when the time comes for the servants of God to officiate for them, *the names of those who have received the Gospel in the spirit will be revealed by the angels of God and the spirits of just men made perfect; also the places of their birth, the age in which they lived, and everything regarding them that is necessary to be recorded on* [sic] *earth*, and they will then be saved so as to find admittance into the presence of God, with their relatives who have officiated for them. The wicked will be cleansed and purified as by fire; some of them will be saved as by fire.[47]

In connection with this theme he also said,

> Our bodies are now mortal. In the *resurrection* there will be a reunion of the spirits and bodies, and *they will walk, talk, eat, drink, and enjoy. Those who have passed these ordeals are society for angels – for the Gods, and are the ones who will*

45. JD, 25:185.
46. JD, 19:230.
47. JD, 9:317.

come into the Temple of the Lord that is to be built in the latter days, when saviours shall come up upon Mount Zion, and will say, "Here, my children, I want this and this done. Here are the names of such and such ones, of our fathers, and mothers — our ancestors; we will bring them up. Go forth, you who have not passed the ordeals of death and the resurrection—you who live in the flesh, and attend to the ordinances for those who have died without the law." Those who are resurrected will thus dictate in the Temple. When the Saints pass through death, they cannot officiate in this sinful world, but they will dictate those who are here.[48]

Erastus Snow stated that Joseph Smith will direct the temple work conducted during the Millennium:

The morning of the resurrection dawns upon us. Ere long we will find Joseph and his brethren overseeing and directing the labors of the Elders of Israel in the Temples of our God, laboring for the redemption of the dead, which work will continue during the thousand years' rest when the Savior will bear rule over the whole earth.[49]

Saints Will Be Prepared for Exaltation

A third purpose of the Millennium will be the preparation of the Saints for exaltation. This may be done, in part, by resurrected beings who will have returned from the celestial realms. According to Orson Pratt they will teach the children of men and impart to them many precious truths:

The Lord Jesus Christ will be here, a part of the time, to instruct us, and *those ancient patriarchs, Adam included, will come down out of their ancient celestial world, where they were first made spiritual.* They are coming upon this creation; and they will have their homesteads here; and they will frequently, no doubt, take great joy in gathering together their faithful children, from the day of their own probation to the one hundredth generation. It will be some pleasure for one of our ancestors that was born a hundred generations ago to say, "Come, my children, you that are here in the flesh that have not as yet become immortal, you that dwell upon the face of this earth, partially redeemed — come, I have some glorious tidings to communicate to you. *I have something that you are not in possession of, knowledge you have not gained, because we have been up in*

---

48. JD, 8:225.
49. JD, 23:188.

yonder celestial world; we have been dwelling in the presence of our Father and God. We were restored there in the dispensation in which we died and in which we were translated, and we have learned a great many things that the children of mortality do not know anything about. Come, gather yourselves together, that you may behold your former fathers, your father's fathers and so on, until you extend back for a hundred generations. Hear the instructions that they shall impart to you. *They will tell you about the celestial kingdom, and the higher glory thereof, and the blessings that are to be enjoyed by those that attain to the fulness of that kingdom."* Will not this be encouraging to those that are yet mortal, during the millennium? I think it will. Then will the knowledge of the fathers, the knowledge of the earth, and of the things of God, and the knowledge of that which is celestial, and great, and glorious, and far beyond the comprehension of imperfect beings as we now are in our fallen state—then that knowledge will be opened up to the minds of the children of men, during their respective generations here upon the earth, during the great sabbath of creation. What is all this for? *It is to prepare their children, during the millennium that they may have this earth made celestial, like unto the more ancient one, that they, with this creation, may be crowned with the presence of God the Father, and his Son Jesus Christ. We gain this knowledge and information by degrees.* Our children are educated and taught, until the heavens become familiar with them; the Lord becomes familiar with them; his countenance becomes familiar to all the righteous of the earth.[50]

The Millennium will also constitute a rest for the earth:

And there shall be mine abode, and it shall be Zion, which shall come forth out of all the creations which I have made; and for the space of a thousand years the earth shall rest.[51]

Summary

1. The millennium will be a thousand-year period during which the Lord and his Saints will dwell together upon the earth. Christ will not always be on the earth but will come here when he is needed.

2. The period will be one of peace and righteousness. Satan will be bound, but men will still be capable of committing sin.

---

50. JD, 21:203-04.
51. Moses 7:64. See Moses 7:48.

3. The New and Old Jerusalem will serve as two world capitals. The authority for the two divisions of the Kingdom of God is to be united at some time in a council in old Jerusalem. Christ will be the King. Under him will function the two original sets of Twelve, who will judge the people of the earth. The other Saints will serve under them in various administrative capacities.

4. The Spirit of the Lord will reveal many things during the millennium which men will not have previously known. In this time nothing will be withheld from man. Resurrected beings will be on the earth and will teach men many important things.

5. During the Millennium all men will acknowledge that Jesus is the Christ but many of them will refuse to join His church. There will be many other churches on the earth.

6. The efforts of the Church will be directed towards three major objectives during the millennium:

    A. Missionary work—the final mission to all mankind.

    B. Temple work – Spirit beings and resurrected beings will reveal the information needed to conduct the work in the thousands of temples which will have been constructed.

    C. Teaching the Saints and preparing them for exaltation – this will be done to a great extent by resurrected beings sent from the presence of God.

CHAPTER XVI

Events at the End of the Earth

The Battle of Gog and Magog

It is prophesied that as the millennial epoch draws to a close, some men will depart from the ways of righteousness and Satan will be loosed for a little season. He will gather out the wicked from among the earth, and bring them to battle against the righteous:

> And when the thousand years are expired, Satan shall be loosed out of his prison,
> And shall go out to deceive the nations which are in the four quarters of the earth, Gog and Magog, to gather them together to battle: the number of whom is as the sands of the sea.[1]

This battle will be known as the battle of Gog and Magog. It should not be confused with the battle of Armageddon which, though it involves the figures of Gog and Magog, takes place before the millennium. Said the Prophet Joseph Smith:

> The battle of Gog and Magog will be after the millennium. The remnant of all the nations that fight against Jerusalem were commanded to go up to Jerusalem to worship in the millennium.[2]

Elder George Q. Cannon taught that it will be because men depart from the principles of millennial society that Satan is loosed:

> The devil has set up every means in his power to hamper the children of men, to throw around them barriers to prevent their carrying out the will of God. And when we obey the commandments of God, we will defeat the adversary of our souls. When we carry out the purposes and the revelations which God has given and made known unto us, we gain immensely. We gain power and strength, and in a little while the adversary will be bound in our midst, so that he will not have power to tempt us, and this will be brought about by our obeying the com-

1. Rev. 20:7-8.
2. HC, 5:298.

mandments of God and the revelations of the Lord Jesus Christ. *I also believe that when Satan is loosed again for a little while, when the thousand years shall be ended, it will be through mankind departing from the practice of those principles which God has revealed, and this Order of Enoch probably among the rest.* He can, in no better way, obtain power over the hearts of the children of men, than by appealing to their cupidity, avarice, and low, selfish desires. This is a fruitful cause of difficulty.[3]

It was the teaching of Orson Pratt that Satan will be able to tempt only mortal beings at this time, and will have no power over those who will be resurrected beings. He also stated that those who sin will not do so in ignorance, but theirs will be a wilful rebellion against God:

When the period called the Millennium has passed away, Satan will again be loosed. Now the query arises, *Will Satan have power to deceive those who have lived on the earth, and have fallen asleep for a moment, and have received their immortal bodies? No, he will not. When they have passed through their probation, and have received their immortal bodies, Satan will have no power over them.* Thus generation after generation will pass away, during the Millennium, but by and by, at the close of that period, unnumbered millions of the posterity of those who lived during the Millennium will be scattered in the four quarters of the earth, and Satan will be loosed, and will go forth and tempt them, and overcome some of them, so that they will rebel against God; *not rebel in ignorance or dwindle in unbelief, as the Lamanites did; but they will sin wilfully against the law of heaven,* and so great will the power of Satan be over them, that he will gather them together against the Saints and against the beloved city, and fire will come down out of heaven and consume them.[4]

The battle of Gog and Magog will be arrayed in similar fashion to the battle in the pre-existence when Michael struggled against Satan and his forces.[5] In this final battle the leader of the hosts of the righteous will again be Adam, or Michael, according to the *Doctrine and Covenants*:

And then he [Satan] shall be loosed for a little season, that he may gather together his armies.

---

3. JD, 16:119-20.
4. JD, 16:322.
5. See Rev. 12:4, 7-9.

And Michael, the seventh angel, even the archangel, shall gather together his armies, even the hosts of heaven.

And the devil shall gather together his armies; even the hosts of hell, and shall come up to battle against Michael and his armies.[6]

Orson Pratt told of the existence of government during the millennium and then explained that those who fall to Satan's temptations will apostatize from that government:

This will be the order of things to exist here on the earth, and which will be recognized by all nations that will then exist, and it will continue for a thousand years. *And at the expiration of that time this kind of government will not even then be done away, although as many as can be influenced by Satan to apostatize will do so, at that time, and there will be a great division of the people,* at the end of the thousand years. *The Saints then, will have become very numerous, probably more numerous than ever before;* and they will be obliged to gather together in one place, as we now do from the four quarters of the earth. They will have to pitch their camps round about, for the "beloved city" will not be large enough for them. It is called by John the Revelator, the camp of the Saints, a beloved city, where the Saints gather to, from the nations of the earth. *Satan will gather his army, consisting of all those angels that fell and left the courts of heaven, when he did, besides all those that will apostatize from the truth, at the end of the thousand years:* They too will mingle with the immortal ones of Satan's army, all being of the same spirit and mind. He with his army will come against the Saints, and the beloved city, and encompass them round about. His army will be so great that it will be able to come upon the Saints on all sides: he is to encompass their camp. *Because of the favorable position he is to hold, in that great last battle, and because of the vast number of his army, he doubtless believes that he will get the mastery and subdue the earth and possess it. I do not think he fully understands all about the designs of God. . . .*[7]

Satan and his forces will encompass the Saints in the "beloved city"[8] and will make war upon them. Then fire will come down from heaven and consume the hosts of evil, and Satan will be cast away. Said a revelation to Joseph Smith:

6. D & C 88:111-113.
7. JD, 18:345-46.
8. Whether this is New Jerusalem or the holy Jerusalem is not clear.

And then cometh the battle of the great God; and the devil and his armies shall be cast away into their own place, that they shall not have power over the saints any more at all.

For Michael shall fight their battles, and shall overcome him who seeketh the throne of him who sitteth upon the throne, even the Lamb.

This is the glory of God, and the sanctified; and they shall not any more see death.[9]

John also foretold the fall of Satan and his host:

And they went up on the breadth of the earth, and compassed the camp of the saints about, and the beloved city: and *fire came down from God out of heaven, and devoured them.*

And the devil that deceived them was cast into the lake of fire and brimstone, where the beast and the false prophets are, and *shall be tormented day and night for ever and ever.*[10]

It appears that this destruction by fire will mark the end of the millennium and at that time those who are yet mortal will be changed to resurrected beings for a revelation in the *Doctrine and Covenants* states:

For Satan shall be bound, and when he is loosed again he shall only reign for a little season, and then cometh the end of the earth.

And he that liveth in righteousness shall be changed in the twinkling of an eye, and the earth shall pass away so as by fire.

And the wicked shall go away into unquenchable fire, and *their end no man knoweth on earth, nor ever shall know, until they come before me in judgment.*[11]

As to the final state of Satan and his hosts, only the following has been revealed:

[Jesus] Who glorifies the Father, and saves all the works of his hands, except those *sons of perdition who deny the Son after the Father has revealed him.*

Wherefore, he saves all except them—*they shall go away into everlasting punishment,* which is endless punishment, which is eternal punishment, to reign with the devil and his angels in eternity, where their worm dieth not, and the fire is not quenched, which is their torment—

---

9. D & C 88:114-16.
10. Rev. 20:9-10.
11. D & C 43:31-33.

And the end thereof, neither the place thereof, nor their torment, no man knows;

Neither was it revealed, neither is, neither will be revealed unto man, except to them who are made partakers thereof;

Nevertheless, I, the Lord, show it by vision unto many, but straightway shut it up again;

Wherefore, the end, the width, the height, the depth, and the misery thereof, they understand not, neither any man except those who are ordained unto this condemnation.

And we heard the voice, saying: Write the vision, for lo, this is the end of the vision of the sufferings of the ungodly.[12]

Consideration of Chronological Sequence of Final Events

John the Revelator enumerated three important events which are to take place at the end of this earth's temporal existence:

And I saw a great white throne, and him that sat on it, from whose face the *earth and the heaven fled away;* and there was found no place for them.

And I saw the dead, small and great, stand before God; and the books were opened: and another book was opened, which is the book of life: and the dead were judged out of those things which were written in the books, according to their works.

And the sea gave up the dead which were in it; and death and hell delivered up the dead which were in them: and they were judged, every man, according to their works.

And death and hell were cast into the lake of fire. This is the second death.

And whosoever was not found written in the book of life was cast into the lake of fire.[13]

Thus the order in which John says these events will transpire is (1) the dissolution of the earth and the heaven, (2) the judgment, and (3) the resurrection of the rest of the dead. Note that the latter two seem to take place simultaneously. Orson Pratt described these events in a slightly different order:

The Prophet Isaiah speaks of the earth dying: "And they that dwell therein shall die in like manner." As it shall die, so shall all who dwell upon it. When shall it see death? Not until after the

12. D & C 76:43-49.
13. Rev. 20:11-15.

Millennium, after the reign of righteousness for the space of one thousand years: after, too, "the little season," during which period of time Satan will be loosed out of his prison. It will continue in its temporal state with a portion of the curse upon its face, until the devil shall gather together his armies at the end of the thousand years, when he will marshall them, bringing them up on the breadth of the earth, *and compassing the camp of the Saints and the beloved city. Then the Lord will make the final change; then the last trump will sound, which will bring forth all the sleeping nations;* they will come forth with immortal bodies no more to be subject to temporal death. They will come forth from their sleeping tombs, and the sea will give up the dead which is in it. The graves of the wicked will be opened, and they will come forth; and a *great white throne will appear*, as recorded in the 20th chapter of Revelations, and the personage who sits on it is described. *Jesus comes then in his glory and power, in a manner far greater than has ever been manifested on this earth before;* so great will be the glory of him who sits upon the throne, that *from before his face the earth and the heaven will flee away,* and no place shall be found for them.[14]

And on another occasion he said,

Then after Satan's army is devoured, and after Satan is cast into hell, and all over whom he has power—then all the inhabitants of the earth will be judged; this great white throne that I have been reading about, will appear; the great and final judgment will come; and *when this white throne appears, the earth itself and the literal, temporal heavens that are overhead will flee away,* and there will be found no place for them.[15]

It would seem, then, that these three important events are closely connected, but that John's order is not chronological. *Doctrine and Covenants* 29:26 indicates that the final resurrection will take place before the earth passes away:

But, behold, verily I say unto you, *before the earth shall pass away,* Michael, mine archangel, shall sound his trump, and then shall all the dead awake, for their graves shall be opened, and they shall come forth—yea, even all.

Thus the order of final events is (1) the resurrection of the rest of the dead (the second resurrection) (2) the appearance of Christ on the white throne and the pronouncement of the final

---

14. JD, 18:321.
15. JD, 21:326.

judgment and (3) the passing away of the heaven and earth. These events will be discussed separately so that they may be considered with greater clarity.

Second Resurrection

It has been seen that the first resurrection which takes place at the beginning of the Millennium will be a resurrection of the righteous who will inherit the celestial and terrestrial kingdoms. The second resurrection will transpire after the Millennium is completed, and will include those who will inherit the telestial kingdom and also the Sons of Perdition. Said a revelation to Joseph Smith,

> And again, we saw the *glory of the telestial,* which glory is that of the lesser, even as the glory of the stars differs from that of the glory of the moon in the firmament.
>
> These are they who received not the gospel of Christ, neither the testimony of Jesus.
>
> These are they who deny not the Holy Spirit.
>
> These are they who are thrust down to hell.
>
> *These are they who shall not be redeemed from the devil until the last resurrection, until the Lord, even Christ the Lamb, shall have finished his work.*[16]

Apparently these are they who will be judged and found under condemnation when Christ comes in glory at the beginning of the Millennium. The prophetic trumps which will sound at Christ's coming will foretell their fate:

> And again, another trump shall sound, which is the third trump; and then *come the spirits of men who are to be judged, and are found under condemnation;*
>
> *And these are the rest of the dead; and they live not again until the thousand years are ended, neither again, until the end of the earth.*
>
> And another trump shall sound, which is the fourth trump, saying: There are found among those who are to remain until that great and last day, even the end, *who shall remain filthy still.*[17]

---

16. D & C 76:81-85.
17. D & C 88:100-102. Note that these trumps are predictive, and they are not recording the actual event in their present context. The doctrine of the resurrection is involved and further comment on the doctrines that all men will resurrect, the complete restoration of the body, the resurrection of little children, and so forth, will not be made here. The reader is referred to the large variety of commentaries by Latter-day Saint authors which treat this doctrine in great detail.

A revelation recorded in the *Doctrine and Covenants* states that the second resurrection will be introduced by Michael (Adam), who will give the signal by a trumpet blast:

> But, behold, verily I say unto you, *before the earth shall pass away, Michael, mine archangel, shall sound his trump, and then shall all the dead awake,* for their graves shall be opened, and they shall come forth — yea, even all.
>
> And the righteous shall be *gathered on my right hand unto eternal life;* and the wicked on my left hand will I be ashamed to own before the Father;
>
> Wherefore I will say unto them—*Depart from me, ye cursed, into everlasting fire, prepared for the devil and his angels.*
>
> And now, behold, I say unto you, never at any time have I declared from mine own mouth that they should return, for where I am they cannot come, for they have no power.
>
> But remember that all my judgments are not given unto men; and as the words have gone forth out of my mouth even so shall they be fulfilled, that the first shall be last, and the last shall be first in all things whatsoever I have created by the word of my power, which is the power of my Spirit.[18]

Final Judgment

It appears that the Savior has reserved the right to pass upon all the inhabitants of the world in the last day, when they stand before Him to be judged, for a revelation records His statement that

> I am Alpha and Omega, Christ the Lord; yea, even I am he, the beginning and the end, the Redeemer of the world.
>
> I, having accomplished and finished the will of him whose I am, even the Father, concerning me — having done this that I might subdue all things unto myself —
>
> *Retaining all power, even to the destroying of Satan and his works at the end of the world, and the last great day of judgment, which I shall pass upon the inhabitants thereof, judging every man according to his works and the deeds which he hath done.*[19]

A revelation to the Prophet also indicates that the wicked are being held back until this day of judgment, for it records the Lord's declaration that "the residue of the wicked have I kept in chains of darkness until the judgment of the great day, which shall come at the end of the earth."[20]

---

18. D & C 29:26-30.
19. D & C 19:1-3.
20. D & C 38:5.

John the Revelator, in his vision of the day of judgment saw that "the books were opened: and another book was opened, which is the book of life: and the dead were judged out of those things which were written in the books, according to their works.[21] The Prophet's reiteration of the importance of these records is incorporated in the *Doctrine and Covenants*:

> You will discover in this quotation [Rev. 20:12] that the books were opened; and another book was opened, which was the book of life; but the dead were judged out of those things which were written in the books, according to their works; consequently, *the books spoken of must be the books which contained the record of their works, and refer to the records which are kept on the earth. And the book which was the book of life is the record which is kept in heaven;* The principle agreeing precisely with the doctrine which is commanded you in the revelation contained in the letter which I wrote to you previous to my leaving my place—that *in all your recordings it may be recorded in heaven.*[22]

Alma the Younger, in the *Book of Mormon* records that the final judgment will be the time when every knee shall bow and acknowledge that the Redeemer is a God, and all mankind will confess their guilt to Him:

> Yea, every knee shall bow, and every tongue confess before him. Yea, even at the last day, when all men shall stand to be judged of him, then shall they confess that he is God; then shall they confess, who live without God in the world, that the judgment of an everlasting punishment is just upon them; and they shall quake, and tremble, and shrink beneath the glance of his all-searching eye.[23]

It was Jacob's teaching that the judgment will take place after the resurrection of all men, and that all men will have a perfect knowledge of their righteousness or of their wickedness:

> O how great the plan of our God? For on the other hand, the paradise of God must deliver up the spirits of the righteous, and the grave deliver up the body of the righteous; and the spirit and body is restored to itself again, and *all men become incorruptible, and immortal, and they are living souls, having a perfect knowledge like unto us in the flesh, save it be that our knowledge shall be perfect.*

21. Rev. 20:12.
22. D & C 128:7.
23. Mos. 27:31.

Wherefore, we shall have a perfect knowledge of all
our guilt, and our uncleanness, and our nakedness; and the
righteous shall have a perfect *knowledge of their enjoyment,*
and their righteousness, being clothed with purity, yea, even
with the robe of righteousness.

*And it shall come to pass that when all men shall have
passed from this first death unto life, insomuch as they have
become immortal, they must appear before the judgment-seat
of the Holy One of Israel; and then cometh the judgment,*
and then must they be judged according to the holy judgment
of God.[24]

Like Jacob, Moroni also emphasized that the judgment will
come after the resurrection and explained that men, after the
judgment, will remain happy or unhappy as they had previously
been:

And because of the redemption of man, which came by
Jesus Christ, they are brought back into the presence of the
Lord; yea, this is wherein all men are redeemed, because the
*death of Christ bringeth to pass the resurrection, which bring-
eth to pass a redemption from an endless sleep, from which sleep
all men shall be awakened by the power of God when the trump
shall sound; and they shall come forth, both small and great,
and all shall stand before his bar,* being redeemed and loosed
from this eternal band of death, which death is a temporal
death.

And then cometh the judgment of the Holy One upon them;
and then cometh the time that he that is filthy shall be filthy
still; and he that is righteous shall be righteous still; *he that
is happy shall be happy still; and he that is unhappy shall be
unhappy still.*[25]

Latter-day Saints believe that men will be judged for their
works, as is set forth in the *Doctrine and Covenants*:

But behold, and lo, we saw the glory and the inhabitants
of the telestial world, that they were as unnumerable as the
stars in the firmament of heaven, or as the sand upon the sea-
shore;

And heard the voice of the Lord saying: *These all shall
bow the knee, and every tongue shall confess to him who sits
upon the throne forever and ever;*

24. II Ne. 9:13-16.
25. Mor. 9:13-14.

*For they shall be judged according to their works, and
every man shall receive according to his own works,* his own
dominion, in the mansions which are prepared;

And they shall be servants of the Most High; but where
God and Christ dwell they cannot come, worlds without end.[26]

The Prophet Alma taught that words and thoughts will also
be considered in addition to their works:

*For our words will condemn us, yea, all our works will
condemn us; we shall not be found spotless, and our thoughts
will also condemn us; and in this awful state we shall not dare
to look up to our God;* and we would fain be glad if we could
command the rocks and the mountains to fall upon us to hide
us from his presence.

But this cannot be; we must come forth and stand before
him in his glory, and in his power, and in his might, majesty,
and dominion, *and acknowledge to our everlasting shame that
all his judgments are just;* that he is just in all his works, and
that he is merciful unto the children of men, and that he has
all power to save every man that believeth on his name and
bringeth forth fruit meet for repentance.[27]

Orson Pratt commented on the possible length of the day of
judgment, and, though its length has not been revealed, he con-
cluded that it must either continue over a long period of time
or else the judgment will be performed by God's agents:

Taking all these passages of Scripture together, we may look for
a general reckoning with all the inhabitants of this earth, both
the righteous and the wicked. How long this day, called the
day of judgment, will be, is not revealed. It may be vastly longer
than what many suppose. *It seems to me that unless there were
a great number engaged in judging the dead, it would require
a very long period of time;* for, for one being to personally in-
vestigate all the idle thoughts and words of the children of men
from the days of Adam down until that time, it would require a
great many millions of years, and therefore *I come to another
conclusion, namely, that God has his agents, and that through
those agents the dead will be judged.*[28]

26. D & C 76:109-12.
27. Alma 12:14-15.
28. JD, 17:182.

Christ and The Saints To Be
Crowned and Exalted

At the end of the judgment, when all enemies have been overcome by the Savior and all have been resurrected and will have acknowledged Him, Christ will present the kingdom to the Father and will in turn be crowned with power. The *Doctrine and Covenants* speaks of a time when

> . . . Christ shall have subdued all enemies under his feet, and shall have perfected his work;
>
> *When he shall deliver up the kingdom, and present it unto the Father,* spotless, saying: I have overcome and have trodden the wine-press alone, even the wine-press of the fierceness of the wrath of Almighty God.
>
> *Then shall he be crowned with the crown of his glory, to sit on the throne of his power to reign forever and ever.*[29]

The Apostle Paul tells of this event, and reveals that Christ and His dominion will eventually be subjected to the Father:

> For as in Adam all die, even so in Christ shall all be made alive.
>
> But every man in his own order: Christ the first-fruits; afterward they that are Christ's at his coming.
>
> *Then cometh the end, when he shall have delivered up the kingdom of God, even the Father; when he shall have put down all rule and all authority and power.*
>
> For he must reign, till he hath put all enemies under his feet.
>
> *The last enemy that shall be destroyed is death. . . .*
>
> *And when all things shall be subdued unto him, then shall the Son also himself be subject unto him that put all things under him, that God may be all in all.*[30]

Though Christ shall turn over this kingdom to His Father, it will be delegated back to the Savior, and "this earth will be Christ's."[31]

---

29. D & C 76:106-08.
30. I Cor. 15:22-26, 28.
31. D & C 130:9. That the Saints are actually to reign was stressed in a

Those who are faithful and who have attained exaltation will also be crowned and given power over all things, and shall be privileged to dwell in the presence of God and Christ forever, according to the *Doctrine and Covenants*:

They are they who are the *church of the Firstborn.*

They are they *into whose hands the Father has given all things —*

They are they who are *priests and kings*, who have received of his *fulness*, and of his *glory;*

And are *priests of the Most High*, after the order of Melchizedek, which was after the order of Enoch, which was after the order of the Only Begotten Son.

Wherefore, as it is written, *they are gods*, even the sons of God —

Wherefore, *all things are theirs*, whether life or death, or things present, or things to come, all are theirs and they are Christ's and Christ is God's.

And *they shall overcome all things.*

Wherefore, let no man glory in man, but rather let him glory in God, who shall subdue all enemies under his feet.

These shall dwell in the presence of God and his Christ forever and ever.[32]

It is the belief of Latter-day Saints that those who inherit the celestial kingdom will be made equal by God to Himself in power, might, and in dominion.[33] It is through the power of

letter from the Presidency of the High Priesthood to the general membership of the Church: "Reflect for a moment, brethren, and enquire, whether you would consider yourselves worthy a seat at the marriage feast with Paul and others like him, if you had been unfaithful? Had you not fought the good fight, and kept the faith could you expect to receive? Have you a promise of receiving a crown of righteousness from the hand of the Lord, with the Church of the First Born? Here then, we understand that Paul rested his hope in Christ, because he had kept the faith, and loved his appearing and from His hand he had a promise of receiving a crown of righteousness. *If the Saints are not to reign, for what purpose are they crowned?* In an exhortation of the Lord to a certain Church in Asia, which was built up in the days of the Apostles, unto whom He communicated His word on that occasion by His servant John, He says, 'Behold, I come quickly: hold that fast which thou hast, that no man take thy crown.' And again, 'To him that overcometh will I grant to sit with me in my throne, even as I also overcame, and am set down with my Father in His throne' (see Rev. iii)." HC, 2:20.

32. D & C 76:54-62.
33. D & C 76:95.

the Priesthood that they will share the kingdom of the Father, according to the *Doctrine and Covenants*:

> For whoso is faithful unto the obtaining these two priesthoods of which I have spoken, and the magnifying their calling, are sanctified by the Spirit unto the renewing of their bodies.
>
> They become the sons of Moses and of Aaron and the seed of Abraham, and the church and kingdom, and the elect of God.
>
> And also all they who receive this priesthood receive me, saith the Lord;
>
> For he that receiveth my servants receiveth me;
>
> And he that receiveth me receiveth my Father;
>
> *And he that receiveth my Father receiveth my Father's kingdom; therefore all that my Father hath shall be given unto him.*
>
> And this is according to the oath and covenant which belongeth to the priesthood.[34]

In the "Mormon" concept of the afterlife, those who gain exaltation shall have all power, and the angels are subject to them:

> And *they shall pass by the angels, and the gods, which are set there, to their exaltation and glory in all things,* as hath been sealed upon their heads, which glory shall be a fulness and a continuation of the seeds forever and ever.
>
> *Then shall they be gods, because they have no end;* therefore shall they be from everlasting to everlasting, because they continue; then shall they be above all, because all things are subject unto them. *Then shall they be gods, because they have all power, and the angels are subject unto them.*[35]

Brigham Young taught that no man from this dispensation will be able to enter the courts of heaven without the approbation of Joseph Smith:

> As I have frequently told them, *no man in this dispensation will enter the courts of heaven, without the approbation of the Prophet Joseph Smith, jun.* Who has made this so? Have I? Have this people? Have the world? No; but the *Lord Jehovah has decreed it.* If I ever pass into the heavenly courts, it will be by the consent of the Prophet Joseph. *If you ever pass through the gates into the Holy City, you will do so upon his certificate that you are worthy to pass.* Can you pass without his inspec-

34. D & C 84:33-39.
35. D & C 132:19b-20.

tion? No; neither can any person in this dispensation, which is the dispensation of the fulness of times. *In this generation, and in all the generations that are to come, every one will have to undergo the scrutiny of this Prophet.*[36]

Heber C. Kimball referred to a vision that Joseph Smith received, in which he saw that Adam would conduct men to the throne one by one to be crowned:

> This brings to my mind the vision that Joseph Smith had, when he saw *Adam open the gate of the Celestial City and admit the people one by one.* He then saw Father Adam conduct them to the throne one by one, when they were crowned Kings and Priests of God. I merely bring this up to impress upon your minds the principles of order, but it will nevertheless apply to every member of the Church.[37]

According to a revelation given to Joseph Smith, after this earth is renewed (transfigured), the exalted will receive their inheritance upon it:

> Nevertheless, he that endureth in faith and doeth my will, the same shall overcome, and *shall receive an inheritance upon the earth when the day of transfiguration shall come;*
> *When the earth shall be transfigured,* even according to the pattern which was shown unto mine apostles upon the mount: of which account the fulness ye have not yet received.[38]

It was the assertion of Brigham Young that the Saints would not receive their inheritances until all else had been completed and until this earth is "placed in the cluster of the celestial kingdoms:"

> When shall we receive our inheritances so that we can say they are our own? When the Savior has completed the work, when the faithful Saints have preached the Gospel to the last of the spirits who have lived here and who are designed to come to this earth; when the thousand years of rest shall come and thousands and thousands of Temples shall be built, and the servants and handmaids of the Lord shall have entered therein and officiated for themselves, and for their dead friends back to the days of Adam; when the last of the spirits in prison who will receive the Gospel has received it; when the Savior comes and receives his ready bride, and all who can be are saved in

36. JD, 8:224.
37. JD, 9:41.
38. D & C 63:20-21.

the various kingdoms of God—celestial, terrestrial, telestial, according to their several capacities and opportunities; when sin and iniquity are driven from the earth, and the spirits that now float in this atmosphere are driven into the place prepared for them; and when the earth is sanctified from the effects of the fall, and baptized, cleansed, and purified by fire, and returns to its paradisiacal state, and has become like a sea of glass, a urim and thummim; *when all this is done, and the Savior has presented the earth to his Father, and it is placed in the cluster of the celestial kingdoms, and the Son and all his faithful brethren and sisters have received the welcome plaudit — "Enter ye into the joy of the Lord," and the Savior is crowned, then and not till then, will the Saints receive their everlasting inheritances.*[39]

That those who do not merit exaltation will be sent to dwell on a "lesser creation" was taught by Orson Pratt:

If we are not thus prepared, where shall we go? God is the author of many creatures besides those that are celestial. He will prepare a creation just adapted to the condition of such people—those who are not sanctified by the Gospel in all its fullness, and who do not endure faithful to the end, will find themselves located upon one of the lower creations, where the glory of God will not be made manifest to the same extent. There they will be governed by laws adapted to their inferior capacity and to the condition which they will have plunged themselves in. *They will not only suffer after this life, but will fail to receive glory and power and exaltation in the presence of God the Eternal Father; they will fail to receive an everlasting inheritance upon this earth, in its glorified and immortal state.*[40]

Dissolution and Re-establishment of The Earth

The Latter-day Scriptures teach that in a sense the earth is a living being, and that it must undergo many of the same processes entered into by mortal beings in the Lords plan. The earth's longing to be sanctified is described in the book of Moses:

And it came to pass that Enoch looked upon the earth; and he heard a voice from the bowels thereof, saying: Wo, wo is me, the mother of men; I am pained, I am weary, because of

39. JD, 17:117.
40. JD, 18:323.

the wickedness of my children. When shall I rest, and be cleansed from the filthiness which is gone forth out of me? *When will my Creator sanctify me, that I may rest, and righteousness for a season abide upon my face?*[41]

One of the sources for the concept that the earth is also undergoing the redemption processes is the *Doctrine and Covenants'* teaching that the earth must die and then be quickened (resurrected) again:

> And again, verily I say unto you, the earth abideth the law of a celestial kingdom, for it filleth the measure of its creation, and transgresseth not the law —
>
> Wherefore, it shall be sanctified; yea, *notwithstanding it shall die, it shall be quickened again*, and shall abide the power by which it is quickened, and the righteous shall inherit it.[42]

Orson Pratt explained that the earth, like all mankind, must die because of the transgression of Adam:

> Righteousness will abide upon its face, during a thousand years, and the Saviour will bless it with his personal presence: after which the end soon comes, and *the earth itself will die, and its elements be dissolved through the agency of a fire. This death, or dissolution of the earth is a penalty of the original sin.* Infants and righteous men die, not as a penalty of their own sins, but because Adam sinned; so the earth dies, or undergoes a similar change, not because of the transgressions of the children of Adam, but because of the original transgression. *But all mankind are made alive from the first death through the resurrection, so the earth will again be renewed, its elements will again be collected, they will be recombined and reorganized as when it first issued from the womb of chaos.*[43]

But Elder Pratt added that the earth has also been corrupted by the sins which men have committed, and for this reason it also stands in need of redemption:

> Though all mankind are to be fully redeemed from the effects of the original sin, *yet we have great reason to fear that but few will be redeemed from their own sins. Those few who are redeemed will receive the earth for an eternal inheritance;* for the earth, as we have already observed, will be uncondition-

---

41. Moses 7:48.
42. D & C 88:25-26.
43. JD, 1:331.

ally redeemed from the curse of the original sin, and so far as
that sin is concerned, it will be no obstacle to the earth's entering into the presence of God. But as the earth has been corrupted by other sins than the original, it must partake of the
curses of the second death, after it is redeemed from the curses
of the first, unless God has provided a way for its sanctification
and redemption therefrom. *It has seemed good unto the great
Redeemer to institute ordinances for the cleansing, sanctification, and eternal redemption of the earth, not from the original sin, but from the sins of the posterity of Adam.*[44]

Orson Pratt explained that as it dies, this earth will return to its
elemental state and will pass away into space. It then will be
called back and resurrected just as the bodies of mankind will be:

> *Then, after the holy city and the New Jerusalem are taken np*
> [sic] *to heaven, the earth will flee away from before the pres-
> ence of him who sits upon the throne.* The earth itself is to pass
> through a similar change to that which we have to pass through.
> As our bodies return again to mother dust, forming constitu-
> ent portions thereof, and no place is found for them as organ-
> ized bodies, so it will be with this earth. *Not only will the ele-
> ments melt with fervent heat, but the great globe itself will
> pass away. It will cease to exist as an organized world.* It will
> cease to exist as one of the worlds that are capable of being in-
> habited. *Fire devours all things, converting the earth into its
> original elements; it passes away into space.*
>
> *But not one particle of the elements which compose the
> earth will be destroyed or annihilated. They will all exist
> and be brought together again by a greater organizing power
> than is known to man. The earth must be resurrected again,*
> as well as our bodies; its elements will be reunited, and they will
> be brought together by the power of God's word. He will then
> so organize these elements now constituted upon this earth,
> that there will be no curse attached to any of its compound
> thus made. Now death is connected with them, but then every-
> thing will be organized in the most perfect order, just the same
> as it was when the Lord first formed it.[45]

The explanation is made by Elder Pratt that the cities of Jerusalem and New Jerusalem will be preserved at this time by being caught up into heaven:

> As the earth passes through its great last change, two
> of its principal cities — the *Old Jerusalem of the eastern con-*

44. JD, 1:331.
45. JD, 18:346-47.

tinent, and the new Jerusalem of the western continent, will be preserved from the general conflagration, being caught up into heaven. These two cities, with all their glorified throng, will descend upon the redeemed earth, being the grand capitals of the new creation. "Without" or exterior to these holy cities, and upon other creations of an inferior order, far separated from the glorified earth) "will be dogs, and sorcerers, and whoremongers, and murderers, and idolaters, and whosoever loveth and maketh a lie. (Rev. xxii. 15) These are they who are banished from the presence of God, and from the glory of a celestial earth.

Summary

1. At the end of the Millennium many will become wicked. Satan will be loosed and will surround the Saints in the beloved city. The Saints will be led by Michael, or Adam. Fire will come down from heaven and devour the hosts of Satan and they will be banished from the face of the earth. This will be known as the battle of Gog and Magog.

2. The next event to take place will be the second resurrection, in which all who have not previously been resurrected will take up their bodies. Those who are to inherit the telestial kingdom will come forth first and then those who are to be sons of perdition. They will be called forth at the sounds of a trumpet blown by the archangel Michael.

3. All men will then come for final judgment before Christ who will appear seated on a white throne. They will witness for or against themselves and also be judged from the books. Every man will acknowledge that the judgment of Christ is just.

4. Christ will then turn the kingdom over to the Father and will be crowned with glory. The Saints will also be crowned and exalted. Responsibility for governing this earth will be delegated back to Jesus.

5. The cities of New and Old Jerusalem will be caught up into the heavens and the earth will disintegrate or go back to its original elemental form. The earth will then be resurrected, or recreated into a celestial sphere. The two cities and their inhabitants will descend to the earth, which will then be placed "in the cluster of the celestial kingdoms."[46] The Saints will then receive their eternal inheritances.

---

46. JD, 1:332.

CHAPTER XVII

The Earth's Final State

After the earth has passed beyond its temporal existence into a chaotic state, it will apparently be called back together, and will be formed into a celestial sphere. John said that he envisioned "a new heaven and a new earth:[1] for the first heaven and the first earth were passed away; and there was no more sea."[2] A description of the earth in its final state is given in section 130 of the Doctrine and Covenants, which states that:

> This earth, in its *sanctified and immortal state, will be made like unto crystal and will be a Urim and Thummim* to the inhabitants who dwell thereon, whereby all things pertaining to an inferior kingdom, or all kingdoms of a lower order, will be manifest to those who dwell on it; and *this earth will be Christ's.*[3]

Orson Pratt taught that this sanctified earth will become a "heaven" like many others which God has created:

> *This earth, this creation, will become a heaven. The heavens that exist now are innumerable to man. God has from all eternity been organizing, redeeming and perfecting creations in the immensity of space; all of which, when they are sanctified by celestial law, and made new and eternal, become the abode of faithful former inhabitants, who also become immortal, through and by celestial law.* They are the mansions referred to by the Savior—"In my Father's house are many mansions." In other words, we may say, In our Father's dominions are many mansions. *They are not like mansions built by men, they are worlds of greater and lesser magnitude.* The first grade are

---

1. Care should be taken not to confuse the "new heaven and a new earth" described here with the earth as described by Isaiah in his 65th chapter. Isaiah is referring to the earth as it will exist during the Millennium, it seems, while evidently John seems to be referring to the earth in its final, celestialized state.
2. Rev. 21:1. The fact that there will be "no sea" may not necessarily mean that water in some form will not exist. John speaks of the "river of water of life" and also of a tree which bears fruit in the celestial world. Rev. 22:1-2.
3. D & C 130:9.

exalted, celestial bodies, from which celestial light will radiate through the immensity of space.[4]

Descent of New and Old Jerusalem

John the Revelator envisioned the descent of both the New Jerusalem and the holy Jerusalem, which will have been caught up before the disintegration of the earth, to the new celestial world. He described the descent of the New Jerusalem as "coming down from God out of heaven, prepared as a bride adorned for her husband."[5] His description of the Jerusalem which was in Palestine, or the holy Jerusalem, is much more complete. It should be recognized that according to John's prophetic description, the city is to be in the shape of a cube, and that it will be gigantic in its size, for the measurement John gives for its length, width, and height is twelve thousand furlongs, or about 1,377 miles in each of its three dimensions:[6]

> And the city lieth foursquare, and the length is as large as the breadth; and he measured the city with the reed, twelve thousand furlongs. *The length and breadth and the height of it are equal.*
>
> And he measured the wall thereof, an hundred and forty and four cubits, according to the measure of a man, that is, of the angel.[7]

He saw that there would be no temple there, for the Lord God Almighty and the Lamb are to be the temple, and that "the city had no need of the sun, neither of the moon, to shine in it: for the glory of God did lighten it, and the Lamb is the light thereof."[8]

---

4. JD, 18:322.
5. Rev. 21:2.
6. Such a city, of course, would be huge and radically different than any city in existence today. Many commentators make the dimensions and even the city itself figurative. Says Dummelow, for instance, "The city is measured, but as the city is figurative, so are the measurements. All the dimensions are compounded of 12, the number of the OT. and the NT., the number which signifies that God is in the midst of His people. . . . The city is a cube, which taken literally would be monstrous, but in its symbolical meaning [of the number twelve] says that the whole city is a sanctuary like the Holy of Holies of the Tabernacle." (*The One Volume Bible Commentary,* pp. 1090-91) When it is recognized that these two cities are to be the means of transferring all the Saints onto the celestialized earth, the possibility of the city actually having these dimensions becomes more plausible.
7. Rev. 21:16-17.
8. Rev. 21:23.

John indicated that even in its exalted state, the earth will be populated by various nations which will have kings ruling them:

> And the *nations of them which are saved* shall walk in the light of it: and the *kings of the earth do bring their glory and honour into it.*
>
> And the gates of it shall not be shut at all by day: for there shall be no night there.
>
> And *they shall bring the glory and honour of the nations* into it.
>
> And there shall in no wise enter into it any thing that defileth, neither whatsoever worketh abomination, or maketh a lie: but they which are written in the Lamb's book of life.[9]

John spoke also of the tree of life which would be found within the city, and saw that there would be "a pure river of water of life, clear as crystal, proceeding out of the throne of God and of the Lamb."[10]

Meaning of Living in The Presence of God

John revealed that when the earth achieves its celestialized state, "there shall be no more curse: but the throne of God and of the Lamb shall be in it; and his servants shall serve him: and they shall see his face; and his name shall be in their foreheads."[11] This is also taught in the *Doctrine and Covenants*:

> And the redemption of the soul is through him that quickeneth all things, in whose bosom it is decreed that the poor and the meek of the earth shall inherit it.
>
> Therefore, it must needs be sanctified from all unrighteousness, that it may be prepared for the celestial glory;
>
> For after it hath filled the measure of its creation, *it shall be crowned with glory, even with the presence of God the Father;*
>
> That bodies who are of the celestial kingdom may possess it forever and ever; for, for this intent was it made and created, and for this intent are they sanctified.[12]

Orson Pratt commented repeatedly on the nearness of God and of Christ after the earth assumes its celestial state. He ex-

---

9. Rev. 21:24-27.
10. Rev. 22:1.
11. Rev. 22:3-4.
12. D & C 88:17-20.

plained that Christ, after the Millennium would have to withdraw from this earth to visit other creations which are His:

> Says the interrogator—"I do not comprehend this idea of the
> Lord's withdrawing from one [earth] and going to another." In
> order to comprehend this let us come back to our own globe.
> *Do we not expect that the Lord will, by and by, come and visit
> us and stay a little while, about a thousand years.* Yes, and then
> we shall be made glad with the joy of the countenance of our
> Lord. He will be among us, and will be our King, and he will
> reign as a King of kings, and Lord of lords. *He will have a
> throne in Zion, and another in the Temple at Jerusalem,*
> and he will have with him the twelve disciples who were
> with him during his ministry at Jerusalem; and they will eat and
> drink with him at his table; and all the people of this globe
> who are counted worthy to be called Zion, and pure in heart,
> will be made glad by the countenance of their Lord for a thous-
> and years, during which the earth will rest. *Then what?* He
> *withdraws. What for? To fulfill other purposes; for he has other
> worlds or creations and other sons and daughters, perhaps just
> as good as those dwelling on this planet, and they, as well as
> we, will be visited, and they will be made glad ·with the count-
> enance of their Lord.* Thus he will go, in the time and in the
> season thereof, from kingdom to kingdom or from world to
> world, causing the pure in heart, the Zion that is taken from
> these creations, to rejoice in his presence.
>
> But there is another thing I want you to understand. This
> will not be kept up to all eternity, it is merely a preparation
> for something still greater. And what is that? *By and by, when
> each of these creations has fulfilled the measure and bounds
> set and the times given for its continuance in a temporal state,
> it and its inhabitants who are worthy will be made celestial and
> glorified together. Then, from that time henceforth and for-
> ever, there will be no intervening veil between God and his
> people who are sanctified and glorified,* and he will not be under
> the necessity of withdrawing from one to go and visit another,
> because they will all be in his presence.[13]

Elder Pratt explained that God will not have to be here on this
earth for the men of this earth to be in His presence:

> *It matters not how far in space these creations may be lo-
> cated from any special celestial kingdom where the Lord our
> God shall dwell, they will be able to see him at all times.* Why?

---

13. JD, 17:331-32.

Because it is only the fall, and the vail [sic] that has been shut down over this creation, that keep us from the presence of God. . . .

Says one *"Do you mean to say, then, that there is a faculty in man, that he can behold the Lord and be in his presence, though millions on millions of miles distant, on another creation?"* Yes, just as easy as we can behold one another here in this room. We shall then see as we are seen, and know as we are known, and there will be perfect redemption. *In this way all the creations that are redeemed can enjoy the continued and eternal presence of the Lord their God.* I mean those who are made celestial, not those who are in the lower orders, who are governed by telestial laws, but those who are exalted to the highest degree of glory, those who will be made kings and priests, those who have kept celestial law, obeyed celestial ordinances, and received the Priesthood which God has ordained, and to which he has given power and authority to administer and to seal on earth that it may be sealed in heaven. The people who are thus glorified are said to be taken into the bosom of the Almighty; as Enoch says "thou hast taken Zion from all these creations which thou hast made, and thy bosom is there," &c. *He does not mean that the Lord God is right within a few rods of every individual; this would be an impossibility, so far as the person is concerned; but he means that there is a channel of communication, the privilege of beholding Zion, however great the distance;* and the privilege of enjoying faculties and powers like this is confined to those high and exalted beings who occupy the celestial world. *All who are made like him will, in due time, be able to see, to understand and to converse with each other though millions and millions of miles apart.*[14]

Life on The Celestial Earth

According to John, God will dwell among men, and He "shall wipe away all tears from their eyes; and there shall be no more death, neither sorrow, nor crying, neither shall there be any more pain: for the former things are passed away."[15]

An interpretation of a section of *Revelation* which Joseph Smith recorded seems to indicate that not only men, but animals will dwell there as resurrected beings. In speaking of the four beasts of *Revelation* 4:6 the passage states:

They are figurative expressions, used by the Revelator, John, in describing heaven, the paradise of God, *the happiness*

14. JD, 17:332-33.
15. Rev. 21:4.

of man, and of beasts, and of creeping things, and of the fowls of the air; that which is spiritual being in the likeness of that which is temporal; and that which is temporal in the likeness of that which is spiritual; the spirit of man in the likeness of his person, as also the spirit of the beast, and every other creature which God has created.[16]

The *Doctrine and Covenants* teaches that animals will be resurrected and made a part of the new heaven and the celestialized earth:

And the end shall come, and the heaven and the earth shall be consumed and pass away, and there shall be a new heaven and a new earth.

For all old things shall pass away, and all things shall become new, even the heaven and the earth, and all the fulness thereof, both men and beasts, the fowls of the air, and the fishes of the sea;

And not one hair, neither mote, shall be lost, for it is the workmanship of mine hand.[17]

Those who live upon the earth will have spirit children, and they will dwell upon the earth until they are numerous enough to need another creation, according to Orson Pratt:

But that same being who organized the earth will again speak, and eternity will again hear his voice, and the materials of our earth will come together again, and when it unites them in one, and forms them into a world, *it will be a glorious world, a habitation for immortal beings; for kings and for priests, and for those that have been faithful to the end. They will dwell upon it, and the generations of their children will dwell upon it, till they become sufficiently numerous to need another creation. What generation? Generations do you say, Mr.* Pratt? Do you mean to say that these immortal beings are going to have posterity? I do. I mean just what I say. Those who are accounted worthy to inherit this earth, when it shall be made heavenly, celestial beings will *people the earth with their own offspring, their own sons and their own daughters;* and these sons and these daughters which will be born to these immortal beings, will be the same as you and I were before we took these mortal tabernacles.[18]

He also taught that celestialized beings will be able to travel from one planet to another:

---

16. D & C 77:2.
17. D & C 29:23-25.
18. JD, 20:155-56.

He that receiveth my Father, says the Savior, receiveth my Father's kingdom, wherefore all that my Father hath shall be given to him. It is a kind of joint stock inheritance, *we are to become joint heirs with Jesus Christ to all the inheritances and to all the worlds that are made. We shall have the power of locomotion; and like Jesus, after his resurrection, we shall be able to mount up and pass from one world to another.* We shall not be confined to our native earth. There are many worlds inhabited by people who are glorified, for heaven is not one place, but many; *heaven is not one world but many.* "In my Father's house are many mansions." In other words—In my Father's house there are many worlds, which in their turn will be made glorified heavens, the inheritances of the redeemed from all the worlds who, having been prepared through similar experience to our own, will inhabit them; and each one in its turn will be exalted through the revelations and laws of the Most High God, and they will continue to multiply their offspring through all eternity, and *new worlds will be made for their progeny.*[19]

Summary

1. The final state of the earth will be an immortal one in which it will have the appearance of crystal. It is to serve as a Urim and Thummim to its inhabitants, thereby enabling them to look into the earth to receive revelation concerning those on other creations.
2. According to John the Revelator, in the earth's celestialized state there will be separate nations ruled by kings. These kings will seemingly be beings who will have attained exaltation and godhood and their nations will be made up of those who will have attained the celestial kingdom but who did not merit exaltation, and also the progeny of the gods. According to Orson Pratt, the offspring of exalted beings will dwell on the celestialized earth until there is no longer room for them and then their parents will create a new world for them to occupy.
3. It appears that celestialized beings will have a capacity for communication with God which will allow them to speak with him and see him even though he may be millions of miles away. God will not always dwell on this earth. They will also have the ability to travel rapidly from planet to planet.
4. There will be resurrected animal life on the earth in its celestial state.

---

19. JD, 18:297.

APPENDIX I

THE UNITED STATES CONSTITUTION WILL HANG BY A THREAD

This work contains prophecies concerning two times when the United States' Constitution will be in danger of failing. Chapter one tells of prophecies of the Third World War in which the United States and its Constitution will be in danger of collapse. In that chapter prophecies are recorded that the Elders of Israel will provide the balance of power which will preserve the liberty of this nation and the integrity of its guiding document. Chapters four and five tell of a second period of great stress in which the United States' government and its Constitution will again be challenged. In the internal wars the national and state governments of the nation will collapse and dissolve. Law and order will be preserved only by the Saints in the tops of the mountains. They will maintain the Constitution and continue to follow its principles. In both of the periods of war it is anticipated that the Constitution will be in jeopardy and will "hang by a thread."

In addition to the comments by general authorities pertaining to the saving of the Constitution which were cited in chapter five, the following statements are also recorded.

Brigham Young attributed the "hang by a thread" statement to the Prophet:

> Will the Constitution be destroyed? No, it will be held inviolate by this people; and, as Joseph Smith said, *"The time will come when the destiny of the nation will hang upon a single thread.* At that critical juncture, this people will step forth and save it from the threatened destruction." It will be so.[1]

He also referred to it on another occasion,

> Brethren and sisters, our friends wish to know our feelings towards the Government. I answer, they are first rate, and we will prove it too, as you will see if you only live long enough, for that we shall live to prove it is certain; and *when the Constitution of the United States hangs, as it were, upon a single*

---

1. JD, 7:15.

thread, they will have to call for the "Mormon" Elders to save it from utter destruction; and they will step forth and do it.[2]

It was President Young who asserted that the United States' flag will fly when the Kingdom of God bears rule:

When the day comes in which the Kingdom of God will bear rule, the flag of the United States will proudly flutter unsullied on the flag staff of liberty and equal rights, without a spot to sully its fair surface; the glorious flag our fathers have bequeathed to us will then be unfurled to the breeze by those who have power to hoist it aloft and defend its sanctity.[3]

Elder Orson Hyde taught that the Church will never want to be free of the Constitution of this nation:

You may afflict, you may pass laws, you may call upon distant nations to help you, you may shut down the emigration against the Latter-day Saints, you may drive them, you may burn their houses — you may do all this, but they will continue to live and to stretch forth in spite of all the powers beneath the heavens, and become a great people under the Constitution of this great land. *We never want to be freed from the Constitution of our Country. It is built upon heavenly principles.* It is established as firm as the rock of ages, and when those that abuse it shall moulder in corruption under the surface of the earth, the American Constitution will stand and no people can destroy it, because *God raised it by our ancient fathers, and inspired them to frame that sacred instrument.* The Constitution is one thing; corrupt politicians are another thing. One may be bright as the sun at noonday, the other as corrupt as hell itself; that is the difference.[4]

George Q. Cannon taught that the Saints will be the ones who will sustain the Constitution when liberty cannot be found elsewhere:

We came here to stay, here we expect to stay, and here we shall stay as long as we do right. And we shall not only stay here, but we shall spread abroad, and the day will come — and *this is another prediction of Joseph Smith's* — I want to remind you of it, my brethren and sisters, *when good government, constitutional government liberty will be found among the Latter-day Saints, and it will be sought for in vain elsewhere;* when the Constitution of this land and republican government

2. JD, 2:182.
3. JD, 2:317.
4. JD, 24:31. See D & C 101:77-80.

and institutions will be upheld by this people who are now so oppressed and whose destruction is now sought so diligently. *The day will come when the Constitution, and free government under it, will be sustained and preserved by this people.* This is saying a great deal, but it is not saying any more than is said concerning the growth of this work, and that which is already accomplished.[5]

He also said,

> It seems like a strange thing to say, but on all proper occasions I say it with a great deal of pleasure, at home and from home, that I have been taught from early life that the day would come when republican institutions would be in danger in this nation and upon this continent, when, in fact, *the republic would be so rent asunder by factions that there would be no stable government outside of the Latter-day Saints*: and that it is their destiny as a people, to uphold constitutional government upon this land. Now, a great many people think this is a chimera of the brain; they think it folly to indulge in such an idea; but the day will come nevertheless. There are those in this congregation who will witness the time that the maintenance of true constitutional government upon this continent will be dependent upon this people, when it will have to be upheld by us.[6]

Elder Moses Thatcher said that although the Constitution may have been torn to shreds the Saints will "tie it together again:"

> I will say when this nation, having sown to the wind, reaps the whirlwind; when brother takes up sword against brother; when father contends against son, and son against father; when he who will not take up his sword against his neighbor must needs flee to Zion for safety—then I would say to my friends *come to Utah; for the judgments of God, commencing at the house of the Lord, will have passed away, and Utah, undisturbed, will be the most delightful place in all the Union.* When war and desolation and bloodshed, and the ripping up of society come upon the nation, I have said to such, "Come to Utah and *we will divide our morsel of food with you, we will divide our clothing with you,* and we will offer you protection.
>
> I will tell you, my brethren and sisters, the day will come, and it is not far distant, when he who will not take up his sword against his neighbor, will have to flee to Zion for safety;

5. JD, 23:104.
6. JD, 23:122-23.

and it is presupposed in this prediction that Zion will have power to give them protection. We are not going to do it outside of the government either; we are going to do it inside the government. There is no power in this land to turn this people against the government of the United States. *They will maintain the Constitution of this country inviolate, and although it may have been torn to shreds they will tie it together again, and maintain every principle of it,* holding it up to the downtrodden of every nation, kindred, tongue and people, and they will do it, too, under the Stars and Stripes.[7]

7. JD, 26:334.

APPENDIX II

AN ANALYSIS OF THE PROPHECY RECORDED BY EDWIN RUSHTON AND THEODORE TURLEY WHICH IS COMMONLY KNOWN AS THE "WHITE HORSE PROPHECY"

For many years there has been circulated among the membership of the Church copies of a prophecy attributed to Joseph Smith called the "White Horse Prophecy." Various general authorities, on several occasions, have held that there is no foundation to the claim that the Prophet made the prophecy and have stated that it is spurious. In spite of this, many have continued to circulate the prophecy and maintain its validity. This appendix article is written to present the facts in order that the reader may make his own decision on the matter.

The Men Who Recorded The Prophecy

The prophecy was supposedly made by Joseph Smith in the presence of two men: Edwin Rushton and Theodore Turley. It was not, apparently, written down at that time but was written out from memory afterwards. The character of the two men who recorded the prophecy should first be examined.

Edwin Rushton was an English convert who came to the United States a few months before the time when the "White Horse Prophecy" was given in 1843. Little is known of his life until after his coming to Utah in 1851. There he worked as a millman, a farmer and a stock raiser until his death in Salt Lake City in 1904. His membership in the 22nd Quorum of Seventies and his later position as a High Priest and first counselor in the Bishopric of Sixth Ward, Salt Lake City, indicate his standing in the Church.[8] It was he who recorded the prophecy and gave a copy of it to Patriarch John Smith (son of the Prophet's brother Hyrum).

Theodore Turley was a devoted follower of the Prophet and Joseph Smith's history of the Church makes frequent mention of

---

8. Frank Esshom, *Pioneers and Prominent Men of Utah,* (Salt Lake City, Utah: Utah Pioneers Book Publishing Company, 1913), p. 1145.

him. He was chosen to superintend the removing of the poor Saints from Far West in 1839.[9] He was appointed to go with Heber C. Kimball to Jefferson City to see Governor Boggs to secure the release of Joseph and his companions who were in the Liberty and Richmond jails.[10] At the risk of his life he defended the prophetic statement made by Joseph that the Twelve would leave on missions from Far West when he was confronted by the Missouri mobocrats,[11] and accompanied the Twelve to their secret rendezvous there. His was the first home built by the Saints in Commerce, Illinois.[12] He filled a mission to England with Wilford Woodruff and John Taylor.[13] As he returned to the United States hepresided over the shipload of Saints who accompanied him.[14] Elder Turley was one of the close group of friends who went to protect Joseph on his trip to Carthage in May of 1844.[15] Just ten days before the Prophet was martyred he was appointed by Joseph as the Armorer-General of the Nauvoo Legion.[16] It was Turley that the Prophet sent as a trusted messenger to Governor Ford with a letter just five days before his death.[17] After the Prophet's death Theodore Turley came to Utah in 1849 where he lived until he died in Beaver, Utah, in 1872.[18] Theodore Turley was a trusted assistant to Joseph Smith and always supported the Prophet. If Edwin Rushton's recording of the "White Horse Prophecy" was false, wouldn't he have let it be known that such was the case?

The Prophecy

The "White Horse Prophecy" is recorded below in the left-column. The dividing of the prophecy into sections has been done by the present author for convenience of analysis. In the right-hand column are recorded

1. Facts which indicate that the prophecy has been fulfilled.
2. Similar statements from General Authorities which indicate that they either

9. HC, 3:261.
10. HC, 3:285-88.
11. HC, 3:306-08. See HC, 3:336-40.
12. HC, 3:375.
13. HC, 4:76.
14. HC, 4:187.
15. HC, 6:412.
16. HC, 6:502.
17. HC, 6:552.
18. Esshom, *op cit.*, p. 1218.

A. knew of the "White Horse Prophecy" and were giving teachings based on it,

B. knew that the item was an accepted teaching of the Church, or

C. were inspired by the Lord to teach similar teachings.

Any of these reasons would, of course, be grounds for accepting that portion of the "White Horse Prophecy" as being inspired of God and a valid prophecy.

1. On or about the sixth day of May, 1843, a grand review of the Nauvoo Legion was held in Nauvoo. The Prophet Joseph complimented them for their good discipline and evolutions performed.

1. The prophecy's recording of the activities held on this date is historically correct. A portion of the Prophet's history for Saturday, May 6, 1843, reads,

> At half-past nine a.m., I mounted with my staff, and with the band, and about a dozen ladies, led by Emma, and proceeded to the general parade-ground of the Nauvoo Legion, east of my farm on the prairie. *The Legion looked well—better than on any former occasion, and they performed their evolutions in admirable style.*
>
> The officers did honor to the Legion. Many of them were equipped and armed *cap-a-pie.* The men were in good spirits. They had made great improvements both in uniform and discipline, and we felt proud to be associated with a body of men, which, in point of discipline, uniform, appearance, and a knowledge of military tactics, are the pride of Illinois, one of its strongest defenses, and a great bulwark of the western country.[19]

2. The weather being hot, he called for a glass of water. With the glass of water in his hand he said, "I drink to you a toast to the overthrow of the mobocrats."

2. There is a conflict concerning the weather conditions between the Prophet's history for May 6, 1843, and the "White Horse Prophecy." The latter asserts that the weather was hot while the former says the day was windy and cold. While his record does not indicate that he was giving a toast the Prophet did record comments which could have been given in such a manner and which were of a similar nature:

> In the course of my remarks on the prairie, I told the Legion that when we have petitioned those in power for assistance, *they have always told us they had no power to help us. Damn such traitors!* When they give me the power to protect the innocent, I will never say I can do nothing for their good: I will exercise that power, so help me God. At the close of the address, the Legion marched to the city and disbanded in Main Street, about two p. m., *the day being windy and very cold.*[20]

---

19. HC, 5:383-84.
20. HC, 5:384.

3. The next morning a man who had heard the Prophet give the toast returned to visit the mansion of the P r o p h e t , and so abused him with bad language, that the man was ordered out by the Prophet. It was while the two were out that my attention was attracted to them and hearing the man speaking in a loud tone of voice, I went toward them; the man finally leaving. There were present the P r o p h e t Joseph Smith, Theodore Turley and myself. The Prophet began talking to us of the mobbings and drivings and persecutions we as a people had endured.

4. but, said he, "We will have worse things to see; our persecutors will have all the mobbings they want. Don't wish them any harm, for when you see their sufferings you will shed bitter tears for them."

3. The Prophet's history records several visitors for the following morning but gives only a meager clue as to the topic of discussion. The stranger's visit recorded by the "White Horse Prophecy" could easily have been the visit of one of the men who came to call concerning the Kinderhook plates (a set of metal plates uncovered in an excavation in Kinderhook, Illinois) since these men would most probably be non-Mormons and strangers to Nauvoo:

Sunday, 7.—In the forenoon I was visited by several gentlemen, concerning the plates that were dug out near Kinderhook.[21]

4. The Civil War occasioned the fulfillment of this prophecy. When that war began, Missouri was the only slave state above the Mason-Dixon line and was surrounded on three sides by free states. Continual skirmishes were fought between communities in Kansas and Missouri over the question of slavery. Although it had been a slave state, Missouri entered the war as a free state to protect itself from the conquest it knew would be forthcoming. A large group of Southern guerrilla fighters, however, established themselves in western Missouri and especially in the Jackson county area. Aided by the pro-South citizens they continually harassed the Union army from their hideouts. A state of continual warfare existed in western Missouri. Finally, the Union army issued the famous "Order Number 11," which ordered the residents of Cass, Jackson, and Bates counties to evacuate their homes so the guerillas could be wiped out. The Union soldiers then swept down upon the area killing the animals, burning homes and fields, and molesting the inhabitants. This brutality often was in the form of pilaging mobs rather than organized military companies. The order was ruthlessly carried out, and became but a re-enactment on a larger scale, of what had happened to the Saints there thirty years before.

21. HC, 5:384.

5. While this conversation was going on we stood by his south wicket gate in a triangle. Turning to me he said: "I want to tell you something. I will speak in a parable like unto John the Revelator.

5. About a month before the "White Horse Prophecy" was supposedly made the Prophet Joseph suddenly became interested in the book of *Revelation.* This may well have been the result of his association with Orson Hyde. On Sunday, April 2, 1843, Joseph recorded Orson Hyde's talk based on the 19th chapter of *Revelation,* in which reference is made to Christ's coming on a white horse:

> Heard Elder Orson Hyde preach, comparing the sectarian preachers to crows living on carrion, as they were more fond of lies about the Saints than the truth. Alluding to the coming of the Savior, he said, "When He shall appear, we shall be like Him, &c. *He will appear on a white horse as a warrior,* and maybe we shall have some of the same spirit.[22]

That afternoon the Prophet spoke from a text in *Revelation,* and commented that it was the first time he had ever done so:

> At one p.m., attended meeting, I read the 5th chapter of Revelation, referring particularly to the 6th verse, showing from that the actual existence of beasts in heaven. Probably those were beasts which had lived on another planet, and not ours. God never made use of the figure of a beast to represent the kingdom of heaven. When it is made use of, it is to represent an apostate church. *This is the first time I have ever taken a text in Revelation.*[23]

Later that afternoon he continued to study *Revelation,* and he again used it as his text in the evening meeting:

> *Between meetings I read in Revelation with Elder Hyde,* and expounded the same, during which time several persons came in and expressed their fears that I had come in contact with the old scriptures.
> At seven o'clock meeting, I resumed the subject of the beast, and showed very plainly that John's vision was very different from Daniel's prophecy—one referring to things actually existing in heaven; the other being a figure of things which are on earth.[24]

The following day Joseph again recorded that he was "*reading the Book of Revelation with Elder Hyde.*"[25] Again, a week later, during the morning session of conference, he gave an extended dis-

22. HC, 5:323.
23. HC, 5:324.
24. HC, 5:325.
25. HC, 5:326.

course based on the book of *Revelation* and the book of *Daniel*.[26]

In the light of his sudden but extended interest in the writings of St. John it is not difficult to see how he could have given the "White Horse Prophecy" in an allegorical form based on figures found in *Revelation*.

6. You will go to the Rocky Mountains, and you will be a great and mighty p e o p l e established there, which I will call the White Horse of Peace and Safety." When the Prophet said you will see it, I asked him, "Where will you be at that time?" He said, "I shall never go there."

6. *Brigham Young* always held that the westward movement of the Saints had long been the plan which Joseph Smith had advocated. In 1856 he said,

I did not devise the great scheme of the Lord's opening the way to send this people to these mountains. *Joseph contemplated the move for years before it took place,* but he could not get here.[27]

On another occasion Erastus Snow stated that

When the pioneers left the confines of civilization, we were not seeking a country on the Pacific Coast, neither a country to the north or south; *we were seeking a country which had been pointed out by the Prophet Joseph Smith in the midst of the Rocky Mountains,* in the interior of the great North American continent.[28]

7. Your enemies will continue to follow you with persecutions and will make obnoxious laws against you in Congress to destroy the White Horse,

7. The Congress of the United States passed a number of laws during the period from 1862 to 1890 outlawing the practice of plural marriage. These bills were expressly the work of enemies of the Church. Among these laws was an "Anti-bigamy Law" signed by President Lincoln in 1862, punishing the polygamist with a fine of $500 or five years imprisonment or both. The law also had a provision forbidding any religious body to hold real estate valued at more than $50,000. This provision enabled the government later to confiscate all church properties and require the Church to pay a high rent for the use of them.

In March, 1882, Congress passed the "Edmunds" bill which amended the previous law in that it prohibited those living in plural marriage the right to vote or hold public office. It also made vacant all registration and election offices which deprived Utah of the rights of self-government.

The persecution continued and hundreds of men were tried and sent to the penitentiary. In 1884, a "segregation ruling" was developed that enabled the courts to find a separate indictment for every day a man was found guilty of living

26. HC, 5:339-45.
27. JD, 4:41.
28. JD, 16:207.

with a plural wife. Through the accumulation of the separate charges a man could be sent to prison for life. This ruling caused the leaders of the church, President Lorenzo Snow included, to go into exile. However, the United States Supreme Court did not uphold this ruling in a case against President Snow in 1887.

In March, 1887, Congress passed the strongest law, the "Edmunds-Tucker" law. This disincorporated the Church of Jesus Christ of Latter-day Saints and the Perpetual Emigration Fund Company. The Church was placed under very heavy financial stress.

After the death of John Taylor while he was in exile in July, 1887, the crusade against polygamy continued but with more Federal tolerance. The Idaho and Arizona governments did continue to pass laws against the church members. With the writing of the "Manifesto" by Wilford Woodruff in 1890, the attitude of most officials became changed and most men had their prison sentences pardoned. When Utah received statehood in 1896 all the properties of the Church were restored to their rightful owner.

8. but you will have a friend or two to defend you to throw out the worst part of the laws, so they will not hurt much.

8. Several non-Mormons provided valuable assistance to the Saints and proved to be true friends to them in the period shortly after their exodus to the West. Col. Thomas L. Kane gave valuable advice to the brethren concerning the inadvisability of Utah seeking to become a territory rather than a state. He had previously been instrumental in obtaining governmental permission for the Saints to winter at Council Bluffs. In 1858 he came to Utah to intercede during the Utah War and gave counsel and assistance at that time.

Several federal appointees who were sent to Utah when it became a territory proved to be good friends to the Saints. These were Lazarus H. Reed, of New York, who became the territory's Chief Justice, and Benjamin G. Ferris, the Territorial Secretary. President Abraham Lincoln signed Congress' "Anti-bigamy law" in 1862 which made the contracting of a plural marriage punishable by a $500 fine or by imprisonment for a term of five years or both. But out of friendship for the Mormons, with whom he had become acquainted in Illinois, he did not appoint officers to enforce the law.

9. You must continue to petition Congress all the time, but they will treat you like strangers and aliens and

9. Congress established Utah as a territory and named Brigham Young as the first territorial governor. A large number of the other territorial offices were filled by federal appointees from the East. Many of these men were prejudiced against

they will not give you your rights but will govern you with strangers and commissioners;

the Church and sought to bring it into difficulties. Chief Justice Brandebury, Associate Justice Brocchus and Territorial Secretary Broughton D. Harris, three of the earliest appointees, resigned their posts and returned to the East. There they spread rumors that Governor Young was acting in a lawless and seditious manner and that he was wasting the federal funds allocated to the Territory.

In 1855, two unprincipled men were given federal appointments in Utah and their actions brought about the Utah War. Judge William W. Drummond appeared in Utah accompanied by a harlot, who he introduced as his wife. His drunkenness and immorality caused the Saints to dislike him almost from his arrival. George P. Stiles, a Mormon apostate, also received an appointment as a judge. These men circulated a number of false reports about the Church and its leaders and submitted affadavits to Washington which were false and misleading. They made it appear that the Mormons were in rebellion against the United States.

10. you will see the constitution of the United States almost destroyed; it will hang by a thread, as it were, as fine as the finest silk fiber."

10. **Brigham Young:**
Brethren and sisters, our friends wish to know our feelings toward the Government. I answer, they are first rate, and we will prove it too, as you will see if you only live long enough, for that we shall live to prove it is certain; and *when the Constitution of the United States hangs, as it were, upon a single thread, they will have to call for the "Mormon" Elders to save it from utter destruction;* and they will step forth and do it.[29]

For other quotations pertinent to this topic see Chapter five and Appendix one.

11. At this point the Prophet's countenance became sad; he said, "I love the constitution. It was made by the inspiration of God, and it will be preserved and saved by the efforts of the White Horse and the Red Horse, who will combine in its defense.

11. **Brigham Young:**
Will the Constitution be destroyed? No: it will be held inviolate by this people; and, as Joseph Smith said, "The time will come when the destiny of the nation will hang upon a single thread. At that critical juncture, *this people will step forth and save it from the threatened destruction.*" It will be so.[30]

This prophecy speaks in allegorical terms of four "horses." Three of them can be readily identified from clues within the prophecy itself. The "White Horse of Peace and Safety" is obviously the Church in the Rocky Mountains (see No. 6), the "Pale Horse" is defined as the "people of the United States" (see No. 34), and the

29. JD, 2:182.
30. JD, 7:15.

reference to the "Black Horse" says that "they will have fear of becoming slaves again" (see No. 33), which would identify them as the American Negroes. The "Red Horse" is not so clearly identified. Some have interpreted it as being England because of the Prophet's reference to the red coats of the English soldiers (see No. 28) and because of his statement that it will appear as if England had taken possession of this country (see No. 32).

In the author's opinion, the "Red Horse" of the prophecy is the Indian people of America. These are his reasons:

1. The other three horses are all references to groups in the United States. This would lead one to expect the fourth group to be similarly located.

2. The Prophet apparently used skin color as a guide for determining the coloring for his horses. If the black horse refers to the negro, it would be expected that the red horse would be the "redskin," or Indian. The term "Pale Horse" could easily relate to the term "paleface," and the "White Horse" could easily be a term symbolizing the purity of the Saints.

3. The "Red Horse," according to the prophecy, is to combine with the Church. What would be a more logical combination than the Church and the Indian people? The missionary effort of the Church has been largely directed toward that people since its inception, and Mormondom regards the Book of Mormon as having been written to convert the Lamanites to the history of their fathers. The Church today is making a major effort to cultivate its relationship with the Indian people, as is witnessed by its Indian missions and Indian program in the Seminaries. By way of contrast, there is nothing at all which would lead one to expect any special relationship between the Church and England.

4. A large-scale conversion of the Lamanites is expected shortly after the period in which the "Red Horse" and the "White Horse" are to unite—in the early days of the New Jerusalem period. People often ask why they would suddenly start to join the Church in large numbers after resisting, to a large degree, its missionary efforts for so many years. What would be a more logical preparation for this conversion than an alliance during the internal wars?

5. It is prophesied that the Lamanite will rise up against the gentiles in the Americas. If the White Horse prophecy is valid it provides an important clue to the manner in which this uprising will take place. Mormon 5:24 is an example of the prophecies dealing with the

Lamanite uprising, in which the gentiles receive the warning: "Therefore, repent ye, and humble yourselves before him, lest he shall come out in justice against you—*lest a remnant of the seed of Jacob shall go forth among you as a lion, and tear you in pieces, and there is none to deliver.*"

For other quotations pertinent to this topic see Chapters four and five.

12. The White Horse will raise an ensign on the tops of the mountains of peace and safety.

12. **Brigham Young:**
An inland Empire will be established in these valleys of the mountains, which will be a place of refuge for millions of people to gather to, when the great day of the judgments of God comes upon the earth, and *the righteous come here for safety.* Our people will go East, West, North, and South, but the day will come, when they will be glad to come back. We will be shut out from the rest of the world.[31]

For other quotations pertinent to this topic see Chapters four and five.

13. The White Horse will find the mountains full of minerals

13. **Brigham Young:**
When we first came into this valley we had no knowledge that our brethren could find gold in California, or perhaps we might have been digging gold over there at this time; but our thoughts were occupied with how we should get our wives and children here; we were thinking about wheat, potatoes, water melons, peaches, apples, plums, &c. *But allow me to tell you that gold and silver, plantina, zinc, copper, lead, and every element that there is in any part of the earth, can be found here;* and all that is required, when we need them, is a philosophical application to make them subservient to our wants.

Here we pause, and think—"What! is there gold here, silver here? Are the finest and most beautiful silks that were ever made, to be found here? Yes. Is there fine linen here? Yes, and the finest broad-cloths, and shawls and dresses of every description. We are walking over them, drinking them, and breathing them every day we live. They are here with us, and we can make ourselves rich, for all these things are within our reach.[32]

---

31. Statement by Brigham Young to Benjamin Kimball Bullock as recorded by the latter's son, Ben H. Bullock. The author has a copy of notarized statements pertaining to the validity of this and other prophecies recorded by Bullock on file.
32. JD, 1:268-69.

14. and they will become very rich. You will see silver piled up in the streets.
"You will see gold shoveled up like sand.

14. Orson Pratt:
Now, when the time comes for purchasing this land, we will have means. How this means will be brought about it is not for me to say. Perhaps the Lord will open up mines containing gold and silver, or in some other way as seemeth to him best, *wealth will be poured into the laps of the Latter-day Saints till they will scarcely know what to do with it.* I will here again prophesy on the strength of former revelation that there are no people on the face of the whole globe, not even excepting London, Paris, New York, or any of the great mercantile cities of the globe—*there are no people now upon the face of the earth, so rich as the Latter-day Saints will be in a few years to come.* Having their millions; therefore they will purchase the land, build up cities, towns, and villages, build a great capital city, at headquarters, in Jackson County, Missouri.[33]

15. Gold will be of little value even in a mercantile capacity, for the people of the world will have something else to do in seeking for salvation.

15. Heber C. Kimball:
I will tell you a dream which Brother Kesler had lately. He dreamed that there was a sack of gold and a cat placed before him, and that he had the privilege of taking which he pleased, whereupon he took the cat, and walked off with her. Why did he take the cat in preference to the gold? Because *he could eat the cat, but could not eat the gold.* You may see about such times before you die.[34]

For another statement pertaining to this topic see JD, 1:250.

16. "The time will come when the banks in every nation will fail and only two places will be safe where people can deposit their gold and treasures. These places will be the White Horse and England's vaults."

16. The author is unaware of any statement or prophecy referring to England's vaults. *Orson Pratt,* however, asserted that the rich will bring their wealth to the West:
A flowing stream is one that runs continually; and the Gentiles will, in that day, come to us as a flowing stream, and we shall have to set our gates open continually, they will come as clouds and as doves in large flocks. Do you suppose that the Gentiles are going to be ignorant of what is taking place? "Now this will not be the case, they will perfectly understand what is taking place. The people will see that the hand of God is over this people; they will see that He is in our midst, and that He is our Watchtower, that He is our shield and our defence, and therefore, they will say, *"Let us go up and put our riches in Zion, for there is no safety in our own nations."*[35]

---

33. JD, 21:136.
34. JD, 3:262.
35. JD, 3:16.

17. "A terrible revolution will take place in the land of America, such as has never been seen before; for the land will be literally left without a supreme government, and every species of wickedness will run rampant.

17. Orson Pratt:

God has sent forth his warning message in the midst of this nation, but they have rejected it and treated his servants with contempt; the Lord has gathered out His people from their midst, and has planted them here in these mountains; and he will speedily fulfill the prophecy in relation to the overthrow of this nation, and their destruction. *We shall be obliged to have a government to preserve ourselves in unity and peace; for they, through being wasted away, will not have power to govern;* for state will be divided against state, city against city, town against town, and the whole country will be in terror and confusion; mobocracy will prevail and their [sic] will be no security, through this great Republic, for the lives and property of the people.[36]

18. Father will be against son, and son against father, mother against daughter and daughter against mother. The most terrible scenes of murder and bloodshed and rapine that have ever been looked upon will take place.

18. Jedediah M. Grant:

Three days before the Prophet Joseph started for Carthage, I well remember his telling us we should see the fulfillment of the words of Jesus upon the earth, where he says *the father shall be against the son, and the son against the father; the mother against the daughter, and the daughter against the mother; the mother-in-law against the daughter-in-law, and the daughter-in-law against the mother-in-law; and when a man's enemies shall be those of his own household.*

The Prophet stood in his own house when he told several of us of the night the visions of heaven were opened to him, in which he saw the American continent drenched in blood, and he saw nation rising up against nation. He also saw the father shed the blood of the son, and the son the blood of the father, the mother put to death the daughter, and the daughter the mother; and natural affection forsook the hearts of the wicked; for he saw that the Spirit of God should be withdrawn from the inhabitants of the earth, in consequence of which there should be blood upon the face of the whole earth, except among the people of the Most High. The Prophet gazed upon the scene his vision presented, until his heart sickened, and he besought the Lord to close it up again.[37]

For other quotations pertinent to this topic see Chapter four.

---

36. DEN, 8:265, October 2, 1875.
37. JD, 2:147.

19. Peace will be taken from the earth and there will be no peace only in the Rocky Mountains.

19. **Brigham Young:**

We are blessed in these mountains; this is the best place on earth for the Latter-day Saints. Search for the history of all nations and every geographical position on the face of the earth, and you cannot find another situation so well adapted for the Saints as are these mountains. Here is the place in which the Lord designed to hide His people . . . *It has been designed, for many generations, to hide up the Saints in the last days, until the indignation of the Almighty be over. His wrath will be poured out upon the nations of the earth.*[38]

For other quotations pertinent to this topic see Chapter four.

20. This will cause many hundreds and thousands of the honest in heart to gather there;

20. **Brigham Young:**

An inland Empire will be established in these valleys of the mountains, *which will be a place of refuge for millions of people to gather to,* when the great day of the judgments of God comes upon the earth, and the righteous come here for safety.[39]

For other quotations pertinent to this topic see Chapter four.

21. not because they would be saints but for safety and because they would not take up the sword against their neighbor.

21. **George Q. Cannon:**

I expect to see the day when the Latter-day Saints will be the people to maintain constitutional government on this land. Men everywhere should know that we believe in constitutional principles, and that we expect that it will be our destiny to maintain them. That the prediction will be fulfilled that was made forty-four years ago the seventh of last March, wherein God said to Joseph Smith—"Ye hear of wars in foreign lands; but behold I say unto you, they are nigh, even at your doors, and not many years hence ye shall hear of wars in your own lands;" but *the revelation goes on to say that the day will come among the wicked, that every man that will not take his sword against his neighbor, must needs flee unto Zion for safety. A portion of that revelation has been fulfilled, the remainder will be.* The causes are in operation to bring it about. We are not alone in the thought that the republic is drifting steadily in that direction; that we are leaving the old constitutional

---

38. DN, Vol. 11, No. 9, May 1, 1861.
39. Statement made by Brigham Young to Benjamin Kimball Bullock as recorded by the latter's son, Ben. H. Bullock. The author has a copy of notarized statements pertaining to the validity of this and other prophecies recorded by Bullock on file.

landmarks, and that the time is not far distant when there will be trouble in consequence of it, when there will be civil broils and strife; *and to escape them, we believe, men will be compelled to flee to the "Mormons,"* despised as they are now.[4]

For other quotations pertinent to this topic see Chapter four.

22. "You will be so numerous that you will be in danger of famine, but not for the want of seed time and harvest, but because of so many to be fed.

22. **Wilford Woodruff:**

Lay up your wheat and other provisions against a day of need, for the day will come when they will be wanted, and no mistake about it. *We shall want bread, and the Gentiles will want bread, and if we are wise we shall have something to feed them and ourselves when famine comes.*[41]

For other quotations pertinent to this topic see Chapter four.

23. Many will come with bundles under their arms to escape the calamities, and there will be no escape except by fleeing to Zion.

23. **Heber C. Kimball:**

I am very thankful that so many of the brethren have come in with handcarts; my soul rejoiced, my heart was filled and grew as big as a two-bushel basket. Two companies have come through safe and sound. Is this the end of it? No; *there will be millions on millions that will come much in the same way,* only they will not have handcarts, for *they will take their bundles under their arms,* and their children on their backs, and under their arms and *flee.*[42]

For other quotations pertinent to this topic see Chapter four.

24. "Those that come to you will try to keep the laws and be one with you, for they will see your unity and the greatness of your organization.

24. **Orson Pratt:**

The Gentiles will, in that day, come to us as a flowing stream, and we shall have to set our gates open continually, they will come as clouds and as doves in large flocks. . . . many of them will come that have never heard the servants of God; but *they will hear that peace and health dwell among us, and that our officers are all peace officers, and our tax-gatherers men of righteousness.*[43]

25. The Turkish Empire or the Crescent will be one of the first powers that will be disrupted, for freedom must be given for the Gospel to be preached in the Holy Land.

25. In 1917 British forces, under the direction of General Allenby, conquered Palestine and wrested it from the grasp of the Turkish empire, which had controlled it for four centuries. This opened the way for the return of the Jews to Palestine in greatly increased numbers.

For further information on this topic see Chapter eight.

40. JD, 18:10.
41. JD, 18:121.
42. JD, 4:106.
43. JD, 3:16.

26. "The Lord took of the best blood of the nations and planted them on the small islands now called England and Great Britain, and gave them great power in the nations for a thousand years and their power will continue with them, that they may keep the balance of power and keep Russia from usurping her power over all the world.

26. Many members of the Church who are of English descent have patriarchal blessings indicating that they are of the House of Israel. England has, since the time of this prophecy, maintained a position of world power in spite of the damage she has incurred during the two World Wars. England today serves as a balance of power between the United States and Russia.

27. England and France are now bitter enemies, but they well [sic] be allied together and be united to keep Russia from conquering the world.

27. England and France are now united, both politically and economically, to oppose the Russian goal of world conquest.

28. "The two Popes, Greek and Catholic, will come together and be united. The Protestant religions do not know how much they are indebted to Henry the VIII for throwing off the Pope's Bull and establishing the Protestant faith. He was the only monarch who could do so at the time, and he did it because this nation, England, was at his back to sustain him. One of the peculiar features in England is the established red coat, a uniform making so remarkable a mark to shoot at, and yet they have conquered wherever they have gone. The reason for this will be known by them some day. The Lion and the Unicorn of Israel

28. It should be noted that, in the light of the current trend towards the merging of many of the churches, fulfillment of this prophecy would be in keeping with the spirit of the times. The present Roman Catholic Pope has stressed the idea of other churches merging with the Roman church on several occasions.

is their ensign, the wisdom and statesmanship of England comes from having so much of the blood of Israel in the nation.

29. "While the terrible revolution of which I have spoken has been going on, England will be neutral until it becomes so inhuman that she will interfere to stop the shedding of blood.

29. No evidence has been found to substantiate this portion of the prophecy.

30. England and France will unite together to make peace, not to subdue the nations;

30. This is clearly the spirit which has characterized the alliance between France and England during the twentieth century.

31. they will find the nations so broken up and so many claiming government, till there will be no responsible government.

31. This condition is expected to exist on a worldwide scale later, during the period of universal conflict. The prophecy would definitely apply to this period if this portion was dealing with the United States in particular.
For quotations pertinent to this topic see Chapter four.

32. Then it will appear to the other nations or powers as though England had taken possession of the country.

32. No evidence has been found to substantiate this portion of the prophecy.

33. The Black Horse will flee to the invaders and will join with hem, [sic] for they will have fear of becoming slaves again, knowing England did not believe in slavery, fleeing to them they believe would make them safe; armed with British bayonets the doings of the Black Horse will be terrible."
(Here the Prophet said he could not bear to look longer upon the scene as shown him in vision and asked the Lord to close the scene.)

33. No evidence has been found to substantiate this portion of the prophecy.

34. Continuing, he said, "During this time the great White Horse will have gathered strength sending out Elders to gather the honest in heart among the Pale Horse, or people of the United States, to stand by the Constitution of the United States, as it was given by inspiration of God.

34. Orson Pratt:
The hand of the Lord will be over us to sustain us, and we will spread forth. He will multiply us in the land; He will make us a great people, and strengthen our borders, and *send forth the missionaries of this people to the four quarters of the earth to publish peace and glad tidings of great joy* and proclaim that there is still a place left in the heart of the American continent where there are peace and safety and refuge from the storms, desolations and tribulations coming upon the wicked.[44]

For other quotations pertinent to this topic see Chapter four.

35. "In these days God will set up a kingdom, never to be thrown down, for other kingdoms to come unto.

35. John Taylor:
The Almighty has established this kingdom with order and laws and everything pertaining thereto, that we might understand his will and operate in his kingdom, that we might be taught of God and understand correct principles, that *when the nations shall be convulsed, we may stand forth as saviours,* and do that which will be best calculated to produce the well-being of the human family and finally *redeem a ruined world, not only in a religious but in a political point of view.*[45]

For other quotations pertinent to this topic see Chapter five.

36. An [sic] these kingdoms that will not let the Gospel be preached will be humbled until they will.

36. Orson Pratt:
At the present time there are some nations who will not permit any religion to be proclaimed within their borders except that which is established by law. *When God shall cast down thrones, which he will soon do; when He shall overturn kingdoms and empires, which time is very near at hand, then other governments will be formed more favorable to religious liberty, and the missionaries of this Church will visit those nations. . . .* And so we might enumerate what God is doing among these despotic powers, overturning and changing long-established usages and institutions, that His servants may go by His own command; to deliver the great and last message of the Gospel to the inhabitants of the earth, preparatory to the coming of his Son.[46]

For other quotations pertinent to this topic see Chapter one.

44. JD, 12:345.
45. JD, 9:342.
46. JD, 18:63-64.

37. "England, Germany, Norway, Denmark, Sweden, Switzerland, Holland, and Belgium have a considerable amount of blood of Israel among their people which must be gathered. These nations will submit to the kingdom of God. England will be the last of these kingdoms to s u r r e n d e r , but when she does she will do it as a whole in comparison as she threw off the Catholic power. The nobility know that the Gosepl [sic] is true but it has not enough pomp and grandeur and influence for them to embrace it. They are proud and will not acknowledge the kingdom of God, or come unto it, until they see the power which it will have.

37. **Orson Pratt:**
    The law for the government of all nations will go forth from Zion as the laws for the government of the United States now go forth from Washington. Zion will be the seat of government and her officers will be far more respected, and have far more influence, than those of any government on earth; *all nations will yield perfect obedience to their command and counsels.*[47]

For other quotations pertinent to this topic see Chapter five.

38. Peace and safety in the Rocky Mountains will be protected by a cordon band of the White Horse and the Red Horse.

38. Only the idea of the Church being separated from the rest of the United States can be substantiated. Said *Heber C. Kimball,* for instance:
    Lay up your stores, and take your silks and fine things, and exchange them for grain and such things as you need, and the time will come when we will be obliged to depend upon our own resources; for *the time is not far distant when the curtain will be dropped between us and the United States.* When that time comes, brethren and sisters, you will wish you had commenced sooner to make your own clothing. I tell you, God requires us to go into home manufacture; and, prolong it as much as you like, you have got to do it.[48]

For other quotations pertinent to this topic see Chapter four.

39. "The coming of the Messiah among this people will be so

39. **Charles W. Penrose:**
    Among the first-mentioned of these three classes of men, the Lord will make his ap-

47. Orson Pratt, *The Seer,* Vol. II, Oct. 1853, pp. 266-67.
48. JD, 5:10.

n a t u r a l, that only those who see Him will know that He has come, but He will come and give His laws unto Zion, and minister u n t o His people. This will not be His coming in the clouds of heaven to take vengeance on the wicked of the world.

40. The Temple in Jackson County will be built in this generation.

pearance first; and that appearance will be unknown to the rest of mankind. He will come to the Temple prepared for him and his faithful people will behold his face, hear his voice, and gaze upon his glory. *From his own lips they will receive further instructions for the development and beautifying of Zion and for the extension and sure stability of his kingdom.*[49]

40. This is a restatement of D & C 84:4-5:

Verily this is the word of the Lord, that the city New Jerusalem shall be built by the gathering of the saints, beginning at this place, even the place of the temple, which temple shall be reared in this generation.

For verily this generation shall not all pass away until an house shall be built unto the Lord, and a cloud shall rest upon it, which cloud shall be even the glory of the Lord, which shall fill the house.

Concerning this passage *Orson Pratt* said,

As regards the number of years by which a generation shall be measured, we have no specific definite period given to us by revelation; the Lord speaks in terms that are general in relation to generations. Among the Nephites, immediately after Christ's appearance to them, a generation was a *hundred years,* and in the fourth generation they were destroyed, as a nation; except some few who went over to the Lamanites. We find generations numbering from father to son, and from son to grandson, etc., and when we come to average generations, according to the statistics of nations, we find them to be about *thirty years* to a generation; but when the Lord speaks in general terms, and says, This generation shall not pass away, until a House shall be built to his name, as is given in this "Book of Covenants," and a cloud should rest upon it; *in that case I do not think he is limited to any definite period, but suffice it to say that the people living in 1832, when the revelation was given, will not all pass away; there will be some living when the House spoken of will be reared,* on which the glory of God will rest. Already forty-five years have passed away since that revelation was given, concerning the building of that House.[50]

49. *Millennial Star,* September 10, 1859.
50. JD, 19:215.

41. The saints will think there will not be time to build it, but with all the help you will receive you can put up a great temple quickly. They will have all the gold, silver, and precious s t o n e s ; for these things only will be used for the beautifying of the temple;

41. The *Proclamation issued by the Quorum of the Twelve* called upon the kings of the earth to supply their wealth to help build up the kingdom:

And now, O ye kings, rulers, and peoples of the Gentiles, hear ye the word of the Lord, for this commandment is for you. You are not only required to repent and obey the Gospel in its fulness, and thus become members or citizens of the kingdom of God; but *you are also hereby commanded, in the name of Jesus Christ, to put your silver and your gold,* your ships and steam-vessels, your railroad trains and your horses, chariots, camels, mules, and litters, into active use for the fulfillment of these purposes. For be it known unto you, that the only salvation which remains for the Gentiles, is for them to be identified in the same covenant, and to worship at the same altar with Israel. In short, they must come to the same standard; for there shall be one Lord, and His name one, and He shall be king over all the earth.[51]

42. all the skilled mechanics you want, and the Ten Tribes of Israel will help you build it.

42. Chapter six explains that three groups will participate in the building of the New Jerusalem. While no other prophecy is known which says that the Ten Tribes will help build the temple, it is known that the Gentiles who will be gathered in to the New Jerusalem after the coming of the Ten Tribes will still have to help construct the city. It is logical that the Ten Tribes would also have to participate in the construction work since they will come before the majority of the Gentiles.

43. When you see this land bound with iron you may look toward Jackson County."

43. Brigham Young:
By and by there will be a *gulf between the righteous and the wicked* so that they can not trade with each other, and national intercourse will cease.[52]
As Chapters four and six indicate, the cutting off of the mountains from the rest of the country will immediately precede the return of the Saints to Jackson county.

44. At this point he made a pause, and looking up as though the vision was still in view, he said, "There is a land b e y o n d the R o c k y Mountains that will be invaded by the heathen Chi-

44. Ezra Taft Benson:
There is little doubt that the leaders of Red China view war as inevitable and await only the propitious moment in which to strike.[53]
For other quotations pertinent to this topic see Chapter one.

51. "Proclamation of the Twelve Apostles of the Church of Jesus Christ of Latter-day Saints," *Millennial Star,* October 22, 1845.
52. JD, 12:284.
53. IE, December 1960, p. 944.

nese unless great care and protection are given." Speaking of the heathen nations he said, "Where there is no law there is no condemnation, a n d this will apply to them.

45. Power will be given the White Horse to rebuke nations afar off, and they will be one with the White Horse, but when the law goes forth they will obey; for the law will go forth from Zion.

45. Brigham Young:
We have a nation here in the mountains that will be a kingdom by-and-by, and be governed by pure laws and principles. What do you call yourselves? some may ask. Here are the people that constitute the kingdom of God. It may be some time before that kingdom is fully developed, but the time will come when the kingdom of God will reign free and independent.

There will be a kingdom on the earth, that will be controlled upon the same basis, in part, as that of the Government of the United States; and it will govern and protect in their rights the various classes of men, irrespective of their different modes of worship; for *the law must go forth from Zion, and the word of the Lord from Jerusalem, and the Lord Jesus will govern every nation and kingdom upon the earth.*[54]

46. The last great struggle Zion will have to contend with will be when the whole of the Americas will be made the Zion of our God.

46. Brigham Young:
You may build up Zion, and learn to be men, and not children. *It was a perfect sweepstakes when the Prophet called North and South America Zion.* Let us go to and build the Temple with all our might, that we may build up the kingdom when established and her cords lengthened.[55]

47. Those opposing will be called Gog and Magog (some of the world led by the Russian Czar) and their power will be great, but all opposition will be overcome and then this land will be the Zion of our God."

47. There is nothing which supports this portion of the prophecy, and it of all the parts analyzed is most likely to be in error since it is a conflicting statement both doctrinally and chronologically. It is not known whether the parenthetic statement was made by the Prophet or whether it was inserted by the recorders or later interpreters.

Observations Concerning the Prophecy

The reader will note, after examining the prophecy and the evidence given to substantiate it that:

1. The historical events the prophecy records pertaining to the

54. JD, 5:329-30.
55. HC, 6:321.

manner it was given are generally in harmony with the history recorded by the Prophet.

2. Every portion of the prophecy pertaining to the past era of the Saints' exodus to the West, territorial problems, the fall of the Turkish Empire, etc., has been literally fulfilled.

3. In general, the prophecy conforms to the pattern for the future which is established by the entire series of prophecies quoted in this work.

4. Almost all of the prophecy which is pertaining to the future has been substantiated by similar prophecies or teachings by other General Authorities.

5. There are, however, several areas of conflict. The most serious of these is Rushton's report on the weather conditions for May 6, 1843. This conflict would seem to indicate that he had waited a considerable time before recording the prophecy, which would raise question as to the overall accuracy of his recording.

6. The portions of the prophecy pertaining to foreign nations and their relationship to the Church during the period of internal conflict in the United States are generally unsubstantiated. This is the area which refers to the "Horses." If there was error in recording the prophecy this would most likely be the area in which the errors occurred. This is the portion which has occasioned criticism of the prophecy.

7. If the prophecy is fictitious and is not inspired, then it is *extremely remarkable* in its conformacy to the pattern of prophecy found in the scriptures and in statements by General Authorities. Whoever wrote it (and it would apparently be Edwin Rushton) would have to have had a familiarity with the prophecies far superior to that of the average Latter-day Saint.

8. While it is impossible to say with certainty that the prophecy is valid and that it *was* made by Joseph Smith, the overwhelming weight of the evidence at hand causes the author to be of that opinion. Consequently portions of the prophecy have been used in this work in areas where they form part of an established pattern. Until positive proof can be obtained, however, the author feels that the "White Horse Prophecy" should be used with care and discretion.

APPENDIX III

NOTES ON JACKSON COUNTY AND THE PLAT OF THE CITY OF ZION

Jackson County, Missouri is a choice land which will make a fit home for the people of Zion. Beautiful descriptions have been written of the area, two of which are quoted here. The first was written by the Prophet Joseph on the day the land of Zion was consecrated for the gathering of the Saints, August 2, 1831:

> The country is unlike the timbered states of the East. As far as the eye can reach the beautiful rolling prairies lie spread out like a sea of meadows; and are decorated with a growth of flowers so gorgeous and grand as to exceed description; and nothing is more fruitful, or a richer stockholder in the blooming prairie than the honey bee. Only on the water courses is timber to be found. There in strips from one to three miles in width, and following faithfully the meanderings of the streams, it grows in luxuriant forests. The forests are a mixture of oak, hickory, black walnut, elm, ash, cherry, honey locust, mulberry, coffee bean, hackberry, boxelder and bass wood; with the addition of cottonwood, butterwood, pecan, and soft and hard maple upon the bottoms. The shrubbery is beautiful, and consists in part of plums, grapes, crab apple, and persimmons.

> The soil is rich and fertile; from three to ten feet deep, and generally composed of a rich black mould, intermingled with clay and sand. It yields in abundance, wheat, corn, sweet potatoes, cotton and many other common agricultural products. Horses, cattle and hogs, though of an inferior breed, are tolerably plentiful and seem nearly to raise themselves by grazing in the vast prairie range in summer, and feeding upon the bottoms in winter. The wild game is less plentiful of course where man has commenced the cultivation of the soil, than in the wild prairies. Buffalo, elk, deer, bear, wolves, beaver and many smaller animals here roam at pleasure. Turkeys, geese, swans, ducks, yea a variety of the feathered tribe, are among the rich abundance that grace the delightful regions of this goodly land — the heritage of the children of God.

The season is mild and delightful nearly three quarters of the year, and as the land of Zion, situated at about equal distances from the Atlantic and Pacific oceans, as well as from the Alleghany and Rocky mountains, in the thirty-ninth degree of north latitude, and between the sixteenth and seventeenth degrees of west longitude, it bids fair — when the curse is taken from the land — to become one of the most blessed places on the globe. The winters are milder than the Atlantic states of the same parallel of latitude, and the weather is more agreeable; so that were the virtues of the inhabitants only equal to the blessings of the Lord, which He permits to crown the industry of those inhabitants, there would be a measure of the good things of life for the benefit of the Saints, full, pressed down, and running over, even an hundred-fold. The disadvantages here as in all new countries, are self-evident, lack of mills and schools; together with the natural privations and inconveniences which the hand of industry, the refinement of society, and the polish of science, overcome.

But all these impediments vanish when it is recollected what the Prophets have said concerning Zion in the last days; how the glory of Lebanon is to come upon her; the fir tree, the pine tree, and the box tree together, to beautify the place of His sanctuary, that He may make the place of His feet glorious. Where for brass, He will bring gold; and for iron, He will bring silver; and for wood, brass; and for stones, iron; and where the feast of fat things will be given to the just; yea, when the splendor of the Lord is brought to our consideration for the good of His people, the calculations of men and the vain glory of the world vanish, and we exclaim, "Out of Zion the perfection of beauty, God hath shined."[56]

In 1937, Elias S. Woodruff, President of the Central States Mission, wrote an article for the Improvement Era in which he described Jackson County in that day:

The Land of Zion today is beautiful even more so, possibly, than when the first group of Latter-day Saints viewed it as they came with the Prophet Joseph Smith to see this region which had been designated of the Lord by revelation as the central gathering place of His people.

Its rolling hills are covered with green pastures, some timber, and with productive farms which are dotted by well-kept homes, housing a contented and happy people. Progressive little cities and towns have grown where once there was a wil-

---

56. HC, 1:197-98.

derness, giving to Jackson County, in addition to its placid agricultural aspect, a decidedly urban appearance. Jackson is likewise a county made beautiful, not only by its natural endowments, but by a well-developed community planning project, the results of which have given this region a pleasing distinctiveness.

Jackson County is keeping well abreast of the times, and is growing commercially, industrially, educationally, and religiously. Fine paved highways form a network over the entire area, passing by farms, through cities and over bridges. . . .

Following the departure of the Saints, Jackson County returned to the hands of non-Mormons, and for years remained so. Only comparatively recently has the Church re-entered this area, but it has been with great success. Friends have been raised up to the Latter-day Saints where once there were none to defend them, and today Mormons and non-Mormons live peacefully side by side.

The Church has a beautiful chapel in this "center place," this former central gathering place. It has a progressive printing establishment, and the headquarters of the Central States Mission are located there.

The word of the Lord is going forth from Independence in the form of millions of tracts and pamphlets, as well as copies of the Book of Mormon. This literature is sent to the far corners of the earth, and from the office in Independence the missionary activities in four states are directed.

The Church owns much of the original temple lot of sixty-three acres, the mission headquarters being located but a short distance from this lot. The presidents of the mission have been accepted on an honored basis among the business men of the city of Independence; have been accorded membership in civic organizations, such as the Chamber of Commerce and the Kiwanis Club, and have wide circles of friends and acquaintances.

A notable feature of Independence today is the high type of citizenry who reside there. They seem a group apart from the inhabitants of many surrounding sections, and seem to represent in their lives the best attributes of dependable, loyal citizens.

Because of progressive and constructive tactics, the county has become one of the leading sections of this entire region. It has an area of 600 square miles, or 294,939 acres. Forty-eight per cent of the land area is crop land, while 45½ is in pasture. On this acreage are 3,494 farms, divided as follows: 615 dairy farms, 592 general farms, 550 livestock farms, 159 grain farms, 120 truck farms.

Of the total 3,494 farms in the country, 2,410 are operated by their owners. In 1934, there were 15,108 acres in wheat, which yielded a total crop of 278,090 bushels. In the same year, 7,285 farmers raised 124,997 bushels of oats and in the production of corn the ten year average is shown to be 30 bushels per acre. In 1934 there were 48,620 acres in this crop. In the same year there were 10,897 acres in alfalfa, 3,464 acres in lespedeza; 2,019 acres in potatoes, raised for commercial distribution; and there were 212,657 fruit trees and 185,138 grape vines. Eighteen thousand cows in the county produced eleven million gallons of milk.

Figures for 1930 show that the county produced $1,032,000 farm produce, $1,460,000 livestock, and $2,993,000 meat and livestock products.

The assessed valuation of Jackson County is $461,396,210. There are 1300 miles of hard-surfaced highways, not including 742 miles of paved streets in Kansas City. With the exception of Westchester County, New York, Jackson County has more paved roads than any other county in America. There is no single point in Jackson County that is not within two miles of a hard surfaced highway.

Among other interesting information regarding Jackson County, is the following: Twelve trunk line railroads and four electric railroads run into Kansas City. In 1931 more than 125 million bushels of wheat were harvested; which with 1,665,-445 head of cattle and other animals made a total value of $139,500,000. There are 6,274 retail stores with a total net annual sales of $375,000,000.

Kansas City, compared with other American cities, has established itself in a commendable manner. It has one of the largest livestock exchanges in the world; boasts a great winter wheat and hay market and flour milling production; and possesses a great horse and mule market; excells in meat packing and grain elevator capacity.

The annual mean temperature of Jackson County is 55 degrees and the annual mean precipitation is 37.31 inches.

No one traveling through the county and observing its many advantages, can help feeling that it is indeed a land of promise.[57]

57. IE, September 1937, pp. 556-59, 587.

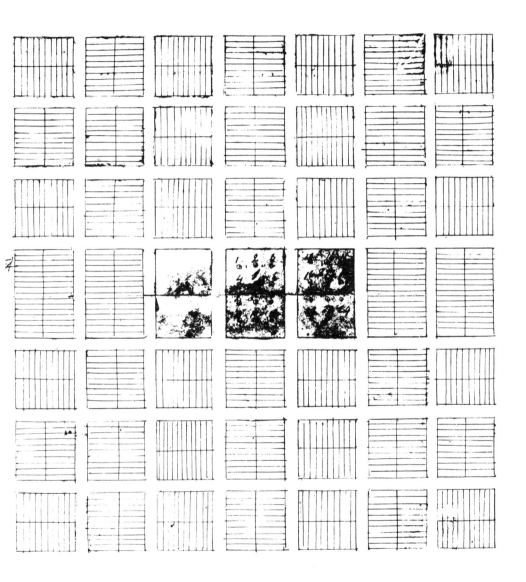

Joseph Smith's Plat of The City of Zion.

This photo, showing the actual drawing made by the Prophet, is used through the courtesy of the Church Historian's Office.

BIBLIOGRAPHY

Latter-day Saint Scriptures

The Book of Mormon. (trans.) Joseph Smith, Salt Lake City, Utah: The Church of Jesus Chirst of Latter-day Saints, 1949.

The Doctrine and Covenants of the Church of Jesus Christ of Latter-day Saints. Salt Lake City, Utah: The Church of Jesus Christ of Latter-day Saints, 1948.

The Holy Bible. King James Version; Salt Lake City, Utah: The Church of Jesus Christ of Latter-day Saints, 1950.

The Pearl of Great Price. Salt Lake City, Utah: The Church of Jesus Christ of Latter-day Saints, 1950.

Latter-day Saint Historical Sources

Berrett, William Edwin. *The Restored Church: A Brief History of The Growth and Doctrines of the Church of Jesus Christ of Latter-day Saints.* 8th ed.; Salt Lake City, Utah: The Department of Education of the Church of Jesus Christ of Latter-day Saints, 1949.

Billeter, Julius C. *The Temple of Promise: Jackson County, Missouri.* Independence, Missouri: Zion's Printing and Publishing Company, 1946.

Church News. (May 28, 1960) Salt Lake City, Utah.

Conference Reports. Salt Lake City, Utah: Deseret News Printing and Publishing Establishment, 1880-1901, 1923-26, 1930-61.

Cowley, Matthais F. *Wilford Woodruff.* Salt Lake City, Utah: Deseret News, 1916.

Deseret Evening News. VIII (October 2, 1875). Salt Lake City, Utah.

Deseret News. XI, XXXIII, CCCLIII, Salt Lake City, Utah.

Franklin Ward Historical Record. Franklin, Idaho: June 16, 1882.

Hancock, Mosiah Lyman. *Life Story of Mosiah Lyman Hancock.* (Typewritten copy is available in the Brigham Young University Library).

Improvement Era. I-LXIV. Salt Lake City, Utah: The Improvement Era, 1897-1961.

Johnson, Benjamin F. *My Life's Review.* Independence, Missouri: Zion's Printing and Publishing Company, 1947.

Journal of Discourses. I-XXVI. Liverpool: F.D. and S.W. Richards, 1854-1886.

Juvenile Instructor. XXV (March 15, 1890).

Latter-day Saint Messenger and Advocate. II, No. 1 (October, 1835).

Little, James Amasa. "Biography of Lorenzo Dow Young." *Utah Historical Quarterly,* XIV (1946).

Ludlow, Daniel H. *Latter-day Prophets Speak.* 2nd ed.; Salt Lake City, Utah: Bookcraft, 1948.

Lundwall, N. B. (comp.) *Assorted Gems of Priceless Value.* Salt Lake City, Utah: Bookcraft, 1947.

Lundwall, N. B. (comp.) *Inspired Prophetic Warnings to all Inhabitants of the Earth.* 6th ed. enlarged; n.p.; n.d.

Lundwall, N. B. (comp.) *Temples of the Most High.* 10th ed. enlarged; Salt Lake City, Utah: Bookcraft, n.d.

McGavin, Cecil. *Nauvoo the Beautiful.* Salt Lake City, Utah: Stevens and Wallis, 1946.

Millenial Star. VI (October, 1845), XIX (October, 1857), XXI (September, 1859).

The Seer. Orson Pratt, ed. Washington, D.C.: 1853-54.

Smith, Joseph. *History of the Church of Jesus Christ of Latter-day Saints.* 7 Vol.; 2nd ed. rev.; Salt Lake City, Utah: The Deseret Book Company, 1959.

Smith, Joseph Fielding. *Essentials in Church History.* 13th Ed.; Salt Lake City, Utah: Deseret News Press, 1950.

Wilcox, Amanda H. *Prophetic Sayings of Heber C. Kimball to Amanda H. Wilcox.* n.p., n.d. (pamphlet on file in the Brigham Young University Library).

Young Woman's Journal. V, No. 11 (August, 1894).

Latter-day Saint Doctrinal Sources

Andrus, Hyrum L. *Joseph Smith and World Government.* Salt Lake City, Utah: Deseret Book Company, 1958.

Berrett, William E. *Teachings of the Book of Mormon.* Salt Lake City, Utah: Deseret Book Company, 1952.

Doxey, Roy W. *The Doctrine and Covenants and the Future.* Salt Lake City, Utah: Mutual Improvement Associations of the Church of Jesus Christ of Latter-day Saints, 1953-54.

Jacob, Carl H. *Superbombs, Saints and Scriptures.* Rexburg, Idaho: Monitor Publishing Co., 1959.

McConkie, Bruce R. *Mormon Doctrine.* Salt Lake City, Utah: Bookcraft, 1958.

Pratt, Parley P. *A Voice of Warning and Instruction to All People Or an Introduction to the Faith and Doctrine of the Church of Jesus Christ of Latter-day Saints.* New Edition; Salt Lake City, Utah: Deseret News Press, n.d.

Pratt, Parley P. *Key to the Science of Theology: Designed as an Introduction to the First Principles of Spiritual Philosophy, Religion, Law and Government, as delivered by the Ancients, and as Restored in this Age, for the Final Development of Universal Peace, Truth and Knowledge.* 5th ed.; Salt Lake City, Utah: George Q. Cannon and Sons Publishers, 1891.

Richards, Le Grand. *A Marvelous Work and a Wonder.* Salt Lake City, Utah: Deseret Book Company, 1953.

Richards, Le Grand. *Israel! Do You Know?* Salt Lake City, Utah: Deseret Book Company, 1954.

Roberts, B. H. *Rasha—the Jew: A Message to All Jews.* Salt Lake City, Utah: Deseret News Press, 1932.

Rolapp, Henry H. (comp.) *Gospel Quotations from the Bible, Book of Mormon, Doctrine and Covenants and Pearl of Great Price.* 4th ed. rev.; Salt Lake City, Utah: The Deseret Book Company, 1956.

Sjodahl, J. M. *The Reign of Antichrist or the Great "Falling Away"* Salt Lake City, Utah: The Deseret News, 1913.

Skousen, W. Cleon. *Prophecy and Modern Times.* Salt Lake City, Utah: Deseret News Press, 1952.

Smith, Joseph Fielding. *Answers to Gospel Questions.* 2 Vols., Salt Lake City, Utah: Deseret Book Company, 1957-58.

Smith, Joseph Fielding. *Doctrines of Salvation.* 3 Vols., Salt Lake City, Utah: Bookcraft, 1954-56.

Smith, Joseph Fielding. *The Signs of the Times*. Salt Lake City, Utah: Deseret News Press, 1952.

Smith, Joseph Fielding. *The Way to Perfection: Short Discourses on Gospel Themes*. 5th ed.; Salt Lake City, Utah: Genealogical Society of Utah, 1943.

Smith, Robert W., and Smith, Elizabeth A. *Scriptural and Secular Prophecies Pertaining to the Last Days*. 10th ed. rev. and enlarged; Salt Lake City, Utah: Pyramid Press, 1948.

Sperry, Sidney B. *The Voice of Israel's Prophets: A Latter-day Saint Interpretation of the Major and Minor Prophets of the Old Testament*. Salt Lake City, Utah: Deseret Book Company, 1952.

Swensen, Russell Brown. *The Influence of the New Testament on Latter-day Saint Eschatology from 1830-1846*. Chicago, Illinois: University of Chicago, 1931. (microfilm).

Talmage, James E. *A Study of the Articles of Faith: Being a Consideration of the Principal Doctrines of the Church of Jesus Christ of Latter-day Saints*. 31st ed. in English; Salt Lake City, Utah: The Church of Jesus Christ of Latter-day Saints, 1952.

Warner, Ross W. *The Fulfillment of Book of Mormon Prophecies*. Provo, Utah: Brigham Young University, 1961. (Unpublished Master's Thesis).

Whitehead, Earnest L. *The House of Israel: A Treatise on the Destiny, History and Identification of Israel in All The Five Branches*. Independence, Missouri: Zion's Printing and Publishing Co., 1947.

Whitney, Orson F. *Saturday Night Thoughts: A Series of Dissertations on Spiritual, Historical and Philosophic Themes*. rev. ed.; Salt Lake City, Utah: Deseret Book Company, 1927.

Widstoe, John A. *Evidence and Reconciliations*. 3 Vols. Salt Lake City, Utah: Bookcraft Inc., 1960.

Other Reference Books

"Antichrist." *Encyclopedia Britannica*, 1957, Vol. II, pp. 59-61.

Atlas of the Bible Lands. Maplewood, New Jersey: C. S. Hammond & Co., n.d.

Butterick, George Arthur (ed.) *The Interpreter's Bible*, Vols. II, V, VI, XII; New York: Abingdon Press, 1957.

Dummelow, J. R. (ed.) *A Commentary on the Holy Bible by Various Writers*. New York: The Macmillian Company, 1958.

"Eschatology." *Encyclopedia Britannica*, 1957, Vol. VIII, pp. 702-04.

Esshom, Frank. *Pioneers and Prominent Men of Utah*. Salt Lake City, Utah: Utah Pioneers Book Publishing Company, 1913.

Funk and Wagnalls New Standard Bible Dictionary: Designed as a Comprehensive Help to the Study of the Scriptures, their Languages, Literary Problems, History, Biography, Manners and Customs, and their Religious Teachings. 3rd ed. rev.; Garden City, New York: Garden City Books, 1936.

"Millennium." *Encyclopedia Britannica*, 1957, Vol. XV, pp. 495-97.

"Miller, William." *Encyclopedia Britannica*, 1957, Vol. XV, p. 497.

Pfeiffer, Robert H. *Introduction to the Old Testament*. New York: Harper and Brothers Publishers, 1948.

Steinmueller, John E. *A Companion to Scripture Studies: Volume III. Special Introduction to the New Testament*. New York City: Joseph F. Wagner, Inc., 1943.

Tenney, Merril C. *The New Testament: An Historical and Analytic Survey*. Grand Rapids, Michigan: Wm. B. Eerdman's Publishing Company, 1953.

Wright, George Ernest and Filson, Floyd Vivian. (eds.) *The Westminister Historical Atlas to the Bible*. Philadelpia: The Westminister Press, 1946.

Other Doctrinal Sources

Dowling, John. *Reply to Miller: A Review of Mr. Miller's Theory.* New York: J. R. Bigelow, 1842.

Emeric de St. Dalmas, H. G. *The Time of the End and the "Weeks" of Daniel: A Discovery and Restatement.* London: Chas. J. Thynne, 1917.

Hurewitz, J. C. *The Struggle for Palestine.* New York: W. W. Norton and Company Inc., 1950.

Klausner, Joseph. *The Messianic Idea in Israel: From Its Beginning to the Completion of the Mishnah.* New York: The Macmillan Company, 1955.

Maxwell, Arthur S. *Great Prophecies for Our Time.* Mountain View, California: Pacific Press Publishing Association, 1943.

Portune, Albert J. *The Truth About Earthquakes.* Pasadena, California: Radio Church of God, 1961.

Ritchie, John. *?Debe El Cristiano Guardar El Sabado?* Los Angeles: Casa Biblica de Los Angeles, n.d.

Rutherford, J. F. *Vindication: The name and word of the Eternal God proven and justifies by Ezekiel's Prophecy and revealing what must speedily come to pass upon the nations of the world.* Brooklyn, New York: Watch Tower Bible and Tract Society, 1931.

Spicer, W. A. *Our Day in the Light of Prophecy.* Mountain View, California: Pacific Press Publishing Association, 1917.

Urguhart, John. *The Wonders of Prophecy or What are We to Believe?* 4th ed. rev.; New York: Gospel Publishing House, n.d.

Miscellaneous

"*An Interesting Letter.*" Letter of Benjamin F. Johnson to George S. Gibbs, 1903. (Unpublished copy on file in the Brigham Young University Library.

"Exultant Birthday for Israel," *Life,* XLIV (May 5, 1958).

"Israel Hurdles Its First 10 Years," *Business Week,* (May 3, 1958).

Peretz, Don: "Israel's First Decade, 1948-1958," *Foreign Political Bulletins,* XXXVII (April 1, 1958).

LIST OF QUOTATIONS FROM MAJOR SOURCES

OLD TESTAMENT

Genesis

10:1-3	199
10:25	239

Exodus

19:13-19	143-44
19:13-19	234

Leviticus

1:5,11	190

Judges

5:19	202

II Kings

9:27	202
23:29	202

Isaiah

2:3	252
4:5-6	87
4:5-6	114
5:26-30	137-38
11:1-5	180
11:1-5	181
11:6-9	180
11:6-9	248
11:6-10	181
11:9	259
11:10	180
11:10	181
11:11	135
11:12	135
11:13	192
11:13-16	185
11:14-15	193
11:16	194
18:5-6	38
18:7	39
19:23	137
24:5-6	241
24:19-20	238
27:12-13	194
34:4	230
35:8-10	137
40:3	137
40:3-4	239
40:5	237
49:20	192
51:19-20	205
55:3-5	180
59:19-21	216-18
60:1-22	216-18

Isaiah (Cont.)

63:1-6	236-37
65	289
65:17	242
65:20	247
65:21-23	251
65:25	248
66:5-24	220-22
66:18-21	137
66:23-24	212

Jeremiah

23:5-6	179
30:9	179
31:20-21	137
31:38-40	189
33:7-16	185

Ezekiel

34:23-24	179
37:15-27	184-85
37:15-28	185
38:2-6	198-99
38:9-12	198
38:16	185
38:16	193
38:18-20	209
38:21	212
38:22	211
39:1-5	213
39:6	211-12
39:9-16	214
39:17-20	213
39:21-23	201
39:21-29	219-20
40:28-37	190
40-42	190
42:20	190
43:18-27	191
44,45	125
44:1-3	181
44:1-3	215
44:2-4	184
44:11	190
45:1-8	187
45:7.13-16	182
45:17	181
46:2	190
46:2,12	181
46:3,9	190
46:24	190
47-48	187
47:1-8	190
47:15-21	187

Ezekiel (Cont.)

48:1-5	182
48:1-7	187
48:8-22	187
48:23-29	187

Daniel

7:9-10	167
7:9-10	175
7:9,11-12	163
7:13-14	175
7:14	175
7:21-22	175

Hosea

3:4-5	179

Joel

2:2-10	204
2:10,31	146
2:20	212-13
2:28-29	256-57
3:1-4	201
3:9-14	197
3:12-14	202
3:12-15	146
3:15	211
3:19	193

Zechariah

3:8-9	179
4:14	205
6:11-13	179
6:12-13	184
8:20-23	222
10:3-10	185
10:3-11	193-94
10:10	192
12:8	211
12:10-14	215
12:11	202
13:6	215
13:7-9	204-05
14:2	201
14:2	206
14:4-5	206-08
14:10	211
14:12,15	212
14:13	212
14:16-19	218-19

Malachi

3:1-4	123

NEW TESTAMENT

BOOK OF MORMON

DOCTRINE AND COVENANTS

1:2-3	233	76:81-85	275	90:9-10	31
1:4	17	76:95	281		
1:17-18	17	76:106-08	280	97:15-16	115
1:23	17	76:109-12	278-79	97:23-26	39
		77:2	293-94		
5:19	38	77:6	141	101:11	31
		77:6-7	118	101:23	237
19:1-3	276	77:6-7	230	101:24-25	240
		77:7-11	122	101:28	249
27:5-14	235	77:12	142-43	101:32-34	257
		77:12	143	101:77-80	298
29:9	241	77:13	143		
29:9-13	233-34	77:14	185	103:15-17	83
29:11	252				
29:13	143	84:2	114	105:5	93
29:14-20	147	84:4-5	319		
29:16	40	84:33-39	282	107:55-57	258
29:18-19	212	84:49-53	250		
29:23-25	294	84:55-59	39	109:30	40
29:26	274	84:96-97	38		
29:26-30	276	84:99-102	259-60	110:11	129
		84:114-15	44		
36:8	114			112:24-26	46
		85:	253		
38:5	276	85:7-9	252-53	113:4	180
38:21-22	252			113:4	181
		87:1	1	113:4,6	181
42:36	114	87:2	2	113:6	181
		87:3	1	113:7-10	224
43:17-18	231	87:3	1		
43:21-23	144	87:3	2	115:6	58
43:29	238	87:4	3		
43:31-33	272	87:4-5	56	116	169
		87:6	2		
45:25	31	87:6	37	121:12	40-41
45:25	127			121:26-33	258-59
45:28	19	88:17-20	291		
45:28-30	22	88:25-26	285	124:2,3,6,9	102
45:30-33	37-38	88:84	35		
45:45-52	244	88:84-92	58	128:7	277
45:47-50	209-11	88:88	36	128:18	257-58
45:51-52	139	88:89-91	36	128:24	123
45:51-52	215	88:89-91	144		
45:59	252	88:95	155	130:1-2	251
45:66-70	114	88:95	156	130:9	280
45:69	8	88:95	156	130:9	289
45:69	160	88:95	156	130:12-13	1
		88:95-99	154		
49:9-10	261	88:95-110	153	132:19b-20	282
49:24	111	88:95-110	155	132:38-39	179
		88:95-110	254		
63:20-21	283	88:95-110	228-29	133:8-12	58
63:32	24	88:96	156	133:12	58
63:33-34	46	88:97	156	133:20	227
63:49	247	88:99	156	133:21-25	239
63:50-52	247	88:100-02	275	133:26-34	119
		88:100-06	156	133:27	118
65:2,5-6	69-70	88:108-10	156	133:41	241
		88:110	231	133:45	259
76:43-49	272-73	88:111-13	270-71	133:46-52	235-36
76:54-62	281	88:114-16	272	133:58	205
				133:68-70	41

PEARL OF GREAT PRICE

Moses		*Joseph Smith I*		*Joseph Smith II*	
1:1-11	241	1:23	8	2:37	240-41
2:9-10	239	1:27	9	2:40	181
7:48	267	1:29	9	2:41	20
7:48	284-85	1:29	35		
7:64	267	1:30	9	2:45	31
Abraham		1:31	17-18	2:45	35
4:9-10	239				

JOURNAL OF DISCOURSES

(The letters are the initials of the speaker.)

Vol. I (1851-54)

180-82 (PPP)	75
182 (PPP)	78
203 (BY)	251
250 (HCK)	311
268-69 (BY)	310
331 (OP)	242
331 (OP)	285
331 (OP)	285-86
332 (OP)	286-87

Vol. II (1843, 1852-55)

57 (OP)	94
146-47 (JMG)	50
147 (JMG)	312
182 (BY)	297-98
182 (BY)	308
189 (BY)	262-63
295 (OP)	39
316-17 (BY)	261-62
317 (BY)	298

Vol. III (1852-56)

16 (OP)	61
16 (OP)	311
16 (OP)	314
18 (OP)	107-08
135 (PPP)	77
262 (HCK)	64-65
262 (HCK	311

Vol. IV (1856-57)

41 (BY)	306
106 (HCK)	62
106 (HCK)	314
231-32 (WW)	120

Vol. V (1856-57)

9 (HCK)	64
10 (HCK)	63
10 (HCK)	64
10 (HCK)	318
329-30 (BY)	79
329-30 (BY)	321

Vol. VI (1839, 1844, 1852-59)

152 (OH)	68-69
342 (BY)	73
342 (BY)	73-74
346-47 (BY)	73

Vol. VII (1854-60)

15 (BY)	68
15 (BY)	297
15 (BY)	308
142 (BY)	263
185-86 (OP)	14
186 (OP)	4
186 (OP)	6
186 (OP)	6
186 (OP)	7
186 (OP)	18
187 (OP)	5-6
188 (OP)	7-8
188 (OP)	161
188-89 (OP)	201-02
215 (OP)	69
355-56 (ES)	249-50

Vol. VIII (1860-61)

51 (OP)	234
52 (OP)	230
123 (BY)	37
143 (BY)	54
224 (BY)	282-83
225 (BY)	265-66

Vol. IX (1860-62)

27 (HCK)	91
27 (HCK)	99
41 (HCK)	283
270 (BY)	45
317 (BY)	265
342 (JT)	76
342 (JT)	317
343 (JT)	77

Vol. X (1859-64) ....

146-47 (JT)	104
147 (JT)	98-99
335-36 (BY)	47

Vol. XI (1859-67)

279 (BY)	113

Vol. XII (1867-69)

241 (BY)	65
274 (BY)	262
284 (BY)	62
284 (BY)	320
344 (OP)	44-45
344 (OP)	51-52
345 (OP)	59
345 (OP)	317

Vol. XIII (1868-70)

313 (BY)	99

Vol. XIV (1869-70)

64 (OP)	24
65-66 (OP)	160
321 (GQC)	260
321-22 (GQC)	264
349-50 (OP)	183
350 (OP)	252
352 (OP)	198

Vol. XV (1870-73)

72-73 (OP)	165
332-33 (OP)	145
362-63 (OP)	84
362-63 (OP)	84-85
364 (OP)	86-87
365 (OP)	98
365-66 (OP)	122-23

Vol. XVI (1873-74)

119-20 (GQC)	269-70
207 (ES)	306
276 (LS)	94
319-20 (OP)	250-51
322 (OP)	270
325-26 (OP)	123-24
328 (OP)	230
329 (OP)	154-55

Vol. XVII (1874-75)

117 (BY)	283-84
156 (BY)	74-75

JOURNAL OF DISCOURSES—(Continued)

Vol. XVII (1874-75)
(Cont.)

156-57 (BY)	70
182 (OP)	279
185-56 (OP)	172-73
187-88 (OP)	173-74
299 (OP)	32
301 (OP)	100-01
301-02 (OP)	108
302 (OP)	109
304 (OP)	87
319 (OP)	39
331-32 (OP)	292
332-33 (OP)	292-93

Vol. XVIII (1875-77)

10 (GQC)	62
10 (GQC)	313-14
25 (OP)	119
25 (OP)	119
25 (OP)	125
25 (OP)	182
38 (WW)	31
57-58 (OP)	231
63-64 (OP)	4
63-64 (OP)	317
64 (OP)	23
64 (OP)	32
64 (OP)	138
121 (WW)	65
121 (WW)	314
122 (WW)	46
128 (WW)	25
137 (JT)	73
170 (OP)	137
176-77 (OP)	20
177 (OP)	23
227 (OP)	144
297 (OP)	295
320 (OP)	247-48
321 (OP)	273-74
322 (OP)	289-90
323 (OP)	284

Vol. XVIII (1875-77)
(Cont.)

338-39 (OP)	169-72
339-40 (OP)	19
339-40 (OP)	163-64
341 (OP)	55
342 (OP)	174-75
345-46 (OP)	271
346 (OP)	118
346-47 (OP)	286
355-56 (BY)	90

Vol. XIX (1867, 1877-78)

7 (BY)	256
38 (BY)	121
176 (OP)	255
215 (OP)	319
230 (WW)	265

Vol. XX (1878-79)

18 (OP)	260
146 (OP)	22
150-51 (OP)	50
150-51 (OP)	161
151 (OP)	50-51
152 (OP)	44
153 (OP)	183
155 (OP)	256
155-56 (OP)	294
318 (JT)	51

Vol. XXI (1878-81)

8 (JT)	69
31 (JT)	69
135 (OP)	103
136 (OP)	93
136 (OP)	311
149 (OP)	90-91
149-50 (OP)	92
150-51 (OP)	254-55
150-53 (OP)	92
152-53 (OP)	94-95

Vol. XXI (1878-81)
(Cont.)

153 (OP)	83-84
154 (OP)	97-98
154 (OP)	98
203-04 (OP)	266-67
299 (WW)	44
301 (WW)	55
326 (OP)	274
330 (OP)	117

Vol. XXII (1879-82)

36 (OP)	177-78

Vol. XXIII (1880-83)

104 (GQC)	298-99
122-23 (GQC)	299
188 (ES)	266
305 (DHW)	76

Vol. XXIV (1879, 1882-83)

23 (OP)	90
23 (OP)	91
23 (OP)	103
24-25 (OP)	97
25-26 (OP)	116
29 (OP)	115-16
31 (OP)	298
31-32 (OP)	178
156-57 (JFS)	87-89
215 (CWP)	189

Vol. XXV (1878-84)

33-34 (ES)	85
34 (ES)	86
185 (JT)	265
222 (CWP)	79-80
305 (JT)	243

Vol. XXVI (1881-86)

266 (OFW)	241
334 (MT)	299-300

HISTORY OF THE CHURCH

Vol. I (1805-34)

xxxii (BHR)	257
176 (JS)	119
197-98 (JS)	323-24
294 (JS)	303
315 (JS)	33
315 (JS)	49
358 (JS)	95
359 (JS)	96
359-62 (JS)	96

Vol. II (1834-37)

20	281
260 (JS)	125
381 (JS)	87

Vol. III (1837-39)

35 (JS)	169
35 (BHR)	175
261 (JS)	302
285-88 (JS)	302
306-08 (JS)	302
336-40	302
375 (JS)	302
386-87 (JS)	167-68
389 (JS)	176
390-91 (JS)	49-50
390-91 (JS)	60-61
391 (JS)	174

Vol. IV (1839-42)

xxxi (BHR)	129
11 (JS)	40
76 (JS)	302
89 (JS)	52-53
187 (JS)	302
207-09 (JS)	168-69
211-12 (JS)	192

Vol. V (1842-43)

212 (JS)	248
212 (JS)	248
298 (JS)	269
323 (JS)	305

HISTORY OF THE CHURCH — (Continued)

Vol. V (1842-43) (Cont.)		*Vol. VI (1843-44)*		*Vol. VII (1842-48)*	
324 (JS)	305				
325 (JS)	305	58 (JS)	25	213 (BY)	71
326 (JS)	125	116 (JS)	52	379 (BY)	71
326 (JS)	305	196 (JS)	124	381 (BY)	71
337 (JS)	190	253 (JS)	179	381 (BY)	71-72
339-45 (JS)	305-06	260-61 (JS)	70		
383-84 (JS)	303	321 (BY)	321	381-82 (BY)	72
384 (JS)	303	365 (JS)	124	382 (GQC)	68
384 (JS)	304	412 (JS)	302	382 (GQC)	72
394 (JS)	52	502 (JS)	302	382 (GQC)	74
530 (JS)	123	552 (JS)	302	439 (BY)	71
552-53 (BHR)	21				

CHRONOLOGICAL INDEX OF EVENTS

This index is designed to summarize the quotations upon which the chronology of this study is based.

Times of the Gentiles
The fulness of the gospel shall break forth when the times of the Gentiles is come in. 19

Fulness of the Gentiles
The fulness of the Gentiles was soon to come in 1823. 20

World wars began in the last days
When England calls on other nations for assistance, war shall be poured out upon all nations. 2

Preparatory wars cause governments to be formed which will accept the Missionaries
God shall soon cast down thrones and form other governments more favorable to religious liberty and the missionaries of this Church will visit those nations. 4

The Elders of the Church will traverse all the nations of Europe after the despotic governments are torn down. 4

God will bring his gospel unto those who are of the House of Israel. 9

The Missionaries are to preach in Russia during the coming century after Communism is overruled. 12, 13-14

Christ contrasts the two periods of wars. 8-9

Nephi, while expounding Isaiah's prophecies, contrasts the two periods of wars. 9-10

Mission to the Gentile Nations (First Period of Missionary labor)
After they have been fully warned by God's servants, the Spirit of God will withdraw from the Gentile nations. 7-8

The Missionaries will preach in Russia during the coming century after Communism is overruled. 13-14

The Gospel is to be preached unto all nations and then comes the destruction of the wicked. 17-18

God will send the Gospel to every Gentile nation before he will permit his servants to go to the scattered remnants of Israel. 20

The Last warning will be taken first to the Gentiles and then to the House of Israel after the Gentile nations reject the Gospel. 22

Slaves to rise up against their masters
The slaves will rise up at a time many days after Great Britain calls on other nations for assistance (W.W. I). 3

The slaves will rise in a time when their masters shall be marshalled and disciplined for war. 3

Third World War

Saints to remain in foreign lands and suffer persecution during the preparatory wars

Fulfilling of the times of the Gentiles

Saints and friends in foreign lands to gather to America

Judgments to be poured out

Wars of complete destruction

Internal wars in the United States

When the Lord shall waste away this nation he will command this people to return to Missouri. 87

When you see this land bound with iron you may look toward Jackson county. 87

The Saints will return to Jackson county defending themselves on the right and the left as when they came to the West. 87-89

When this nation reaps the whirlwind, when he who will not take up the sword against his brother must flee to Zion, when the judgments which commence at the house of the Lord will have passed away, Utah will be undisturbed and be the most delightful place in all the Union. We will offer protection there. 299-300

World-Wide warfare during the U.S. internal wars

When the Lord tells the elders to "come home," nation will rise against nation and states will rise against states in our own land. 37

People will be fleeing from state to state during the internal wars. It will mean the complete overthrow of this nation and the nations of Europe. 56

Peace will be taken from the earth and there will be no peace except in the Rocky Mountains. 55

When the nations shall be convulsed the Saints will stand forth as Saviours and redeem a ruined world in both a religious and political manner. 76

I expect one nation after another to rise against us until they will all be broken to pieces. 77

When the times of the Gentiles are fulfilled there will be an uprooting of their governments and institutions. 77

Saints to gather to the mountains

Cache valley will be filled with tens of thousands of Saints during or after the time when New York, Boston, and Albany are destroyed. 44

Those who will not take up the sword against their neighbors during the internal wars must flee to Zion. 51

Peace will be taken from the earth and there will be peace only in the Rocky Mountains. This will cause many to gather there. 55

Let them who are among the Gentiles flee to Zion. 58

There will be a gathering together on the land of Zion when the wrath of God shall be poured out upon the whole earth. 58

An inland empire for millions will be established when the great day of the judgments of God comes upon the earth. 58

The Rocky Mountains have been designed to hide up the Saints in the last days, until the indignation of the Almighty is over. 313

An inland empire will be established in the mountains to which millions will gather when the judgment of God come upon the earth. 313

Famine during the internal wars

The pursuit of farming and agriculture will be neglected and people will think themselves well off if they can flee from city to city. 52

You will be so numerous that you will be in danger of famine when many come to escape the calamities. 64

Gathering of the tribes of Israel to Palestine

Rule of David the prince

ALPHABETICAL INDEX

ALPHABETICAL INDEX—(*Continued*)

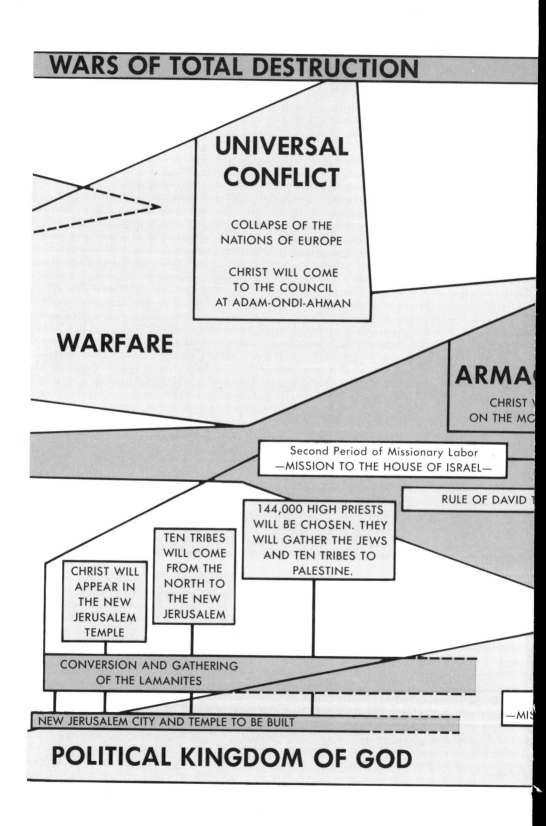

WARS OF TOTAL DESTRUCTION

UNIVERSAL CONFLICT

COLLAPSE OF THE
NATIONS OF EUROPE

CHRIST WILL COME
TO THE COUNCIL
AT ADAM-ONDI-AHMAN

WARFARE

ARMA

CHRIST
ON THE MO

Second Period of Missionary Labor
—MISSION TO THE HOUSE OF ISRAEL—

RULE OF DAVID

144,000 HIGH PRIESTS
WILL BE CHOSEN. THEY
WILL GATHER THE JEWS
AND TEN TRIBES TO
PALESTINE.

TEN TRIBES
WILL COME
FROM THE
NORTH TO
THE NEW
JERUSALEM

CHRIST WILL
APPEAR IN
THE NEW
JERUSALEM
TEMPLE

CONVERSION AND GATHERING
OF THE LAMANITES

NEW JERUSALEM CITY AND TEMPLE TO BE BUILT

—MIS

POLITICAL KINGDOM OF GOD